EXCAVATIONS AT CILL DONNAIN
A Bronze Age Settlement and Iron Age Wheelhouse in South Uist

By

Mike Parker Pearson and Marek Zvelebil[†]

With contributions by

Sean Bell, Andrew Chamberlain, Gordon Cook,
Chris Cumberpatch, Martin Dearne, Irene Deluis,
Karen Godden, Pam Grinter, John Hamshaw-Thomas,
Kate MacDonald, Peter Marshall, Eddie Moth,
Jean-Luc Schwenninger, Helen Smith, Saleem ul Haq,
Soultana-Maria Valamoti and Kim Vickers

Sheffield Environmental and Archaeological
Research Campaign in the Hebrides
VOLUME 9

OXBOW BOOKS
Oxford and Philadelphia

Published in the United Kingdom in 2014 by
OXBOW BOOKS
10 Hythe Bridge Street, Oxford OX1 2EW

and in the United States by
OXBOW BOOKS
908 Darny Road, Havertown, PA 19083

Hardcover Edition ISBN 978-1-78297-627-1
Digital Edition ISBN 978-1-78297-628-8

A CIP record for this book is available from the British Library

Library of Congress Cataloging-in-Publication Data

Parker Pearson, Michael, 1957-
  Excavations at Cill Donnain : a Bronze Age settlement and Iron Age wheelhouse in South Uist / by Mike Parker Pearson and Marek Zvelebil ; with contributions by Sean Bell, Gordon Cook, Chris Cumberpatch, Martin Dearne, Irene Deluis, Karen Godden, Pam Grinter, John Hamshaw Thomas, Kate MacDonald, Peter Marshall, Eddie Moth, Jean Luc Schwenninger, Helen Smith, Saleem ul Haq, Soultana Maria Valamoti and Kim Vickers. -- Hardcover edition.
      pages cm. -- (Sheffield Environmental and Archaeological Research Campaign in the Hebrides ; volume 9)
    Includes bibliographical references and index.
  ISBN 978-1-78297-627-1 (hardcover)
  1. South Uist (Scotland)--Antiquities. 2. Excavations (Archaeology)--Scotland--South Uist. 3. Bronze age--Scotland--South Uist. 4. Iron age--Scotland--South Uist. 5. Human settlements--Scotland--South Uist. 6. Dwellings--Scotland--South Uist. 7. Material culture--Scotland--South Uist. 8. Human ecology--Scotland--South Uist. 9. Social archaeology--Scotland--South Uist. 10. Economics, Prehistoric--Scotland--South Uist. I. Zvelebil, Marek. II. Title.
  DA880.S75P36 2014
  936.1'14--dc23
                          2014027123

Typeset by M.C. Bishop at The Armatura Press
Printed in the United Kingdom by Short Run Press, Exeter

For a complete list of Oxbow titles, please contact:

UNITED KINGDOM
Oxbow Books
Telephone (01865) 241249, Fax (01865) 794449
Email: oxbow@oxbowbooks.com
www.oxbowbooks.com

UNITED STATES OF AMERICA
Oxbow Books
Telephone (800) 7919354,
Fax (610) 8539146
Email: queries@casemateacademic.com
www.casemateacademic.com/oxbow

Oxbow Books is part of the Casemate Group

Front Cover: Stages in constructing the Cill Donnain wheelhouse (drawn by Irene Deluis)
Back Cover: (left) Reconstructions of Middle Iron Age pottery (drawn by Irene Deluis); (right) The Cill Donnain wheelhouse during excavation

Contents

List of Figures..vi
List of Tables...xi
Acknowledgements...xii
Contributors...xiii
Preface...xiv

1   Introduction..1
    Mike Parker Pearson and Helen Smith
    Introduction...1
    The geology and soils..1
    The SEARCH project...4
    The site setting...5
    Conclusion...9

2   The excavations 10
    Marek Zvelebil and Mike Parker Pearson
    Introduction...10
    The 1989 excavations..10
    The 1990 excavations..14
    The 1991 excavations..16
    The stratigraphic sequence..17
    The 1992 reconstruction project..19
    The 2003 evaluation of the Cordoned Urn settlement...19
    Post-excavation analysis of records and finds from the 1989–1991 excavations..21
    Student reminiscences..24

3   Early–Middle Bronze Age (phase 1): a Cordoned Urn settlement...27
    Mike Parker Pearson with Kate MacDonald
    Introduction...27
    The extent of the settlement mound – coring in 2003...27
    The 1991 excavations: the northwest trench...29
    Recording of the sand quarry in 2003..31
    Optically stimulated luminescence (OSL) dating *Jean-Luc Schwenninger*..33
    Pottery *Chris Cumberpatch and Mike Parker Pearson*...35
    Bone and stone tools *Mike Parker Pearson*..35
    The faunal remains *John Hamshaw-Thomas, Kim Vickers and Mike Parker Pearson*..37
    Discussion...37

4   Late Bronze Age/Early Iron Age occupation (phase 2): eighth–early sixth centuries BC.......................................40
    Mike Parker Pearson
    Introduction...40
    Windblown sand..40
    Ploughing 40
    Pit 142...40
    Other deposits..41
    Conclusion...43

5   Before construction of the wheelhouse (phase 3)..45
    Mike Parker Pearson
    Introduction...45
    The sand layer..45
    Gully 191..46
    Possible hearths..48

Other deposits...49
The human skull fragment *Andrew Chamberlain*...51
Conclusion..54

6   Construction and initial use of the wheelhouse (phases 4 and 5)................................57
     Mike Parker Pearson and Marek Zvelebil
     Introduction...57
     The construction of the wheelhouse (phase 4)..57
     The hearth..66
     Cut features within the house...67
     The house floor (phase 5)...68
     Accumulation of deposits outside the wall of the wheelhouse (phase 5)..................70
     The stone structure in the southern trench...72

7   Modification and abandonment of the wheelhouse (phases 6–8)................................77
     Mike Parker Pearson and Marek Zvelebil
     Introduction...77
     Modifications to the wheelhouse interior (phase 6)...77
     Accumulation of deposits outside the wall of the wheelhouse (phase 6)..................78
     Abandonment of the wheelhouse (phase 7)...78
     The small, stone-walled structure and re-use of the wheelhouse (phase 8)..............80

8   The midden overlying the wheelhouse (phase 9)...88
     Mike Parker Pearson
     Introduction...88
     The earliest midden layers..88
     Upper layers of the midden...94
     The southern excavation trench...101
     The top of the stratigraphic sequence (phase 10)...101

9   The pottery...106
     Chris Cumberpatch
     Introduction...106
     The manufacture of the Cill Donnain III pottery..106
     Chronology of and parallels for the Cill Donnain III assemblage............................113
     The stratigraphic phases and their ceramic associations..117
     The fragmentation of the pottery assemblage...119
     Conclusion...119
     Ceramic artefacts *Mike Parker Pearson*..128

10   The metal finds and industrial debris..129
     Martin Dearne and Mike Parker Pearson
     The copper-alloy artefacts *Martin Dearne*..129
     The lead object *Mike Parker Pearson*...131
     The iron objects *Martin Dearne*...132
     Bronze-casting clay refractories *Mike Parker Pearson*..133
     The crucible *Mike Parker Pearson*...134
     The metalworking slag *Martin Dearne and Mike Parker Pearson*........................135
     Fuel ash slag *Mike Parker Pearson*...135

11   The stone tools...139
     Mike Parker Pearson
     Introduction...139
     The coarse stone tools..139
     The flint tools...141
     The pumice...143
     The slate...144

12   Bone, ivory and antler tools and ornaments..145
     Mike Parker Pearson with species identification by John Hamshaw-Thomas and Kim Vickers
     Discussion..145

Catalogue of the worked bone, ivory and antler...147

13 The faunal remains...155
Kim Vickers with Saleem ul Haq and John Hamshaw-Thomas
Introduction..155
Excavation methods and fish bone...155
Laboratory methods..155
Overview...156
Preservation..157
Species representation...157
Element representation..161
Ageing...162
Sex..165
Pathology..165
Butchery and bone-working..167
Biometry...167
Discussion...168
Conclusion 173

14 The carbonized plant remains...174
Pam Grinter and Soultana-Maria Valamoti
Introduction..174
Methodology...174
Quantification and identification..174
Results from the 1989 material...175
Results from the 1991 material...175
Plant husbandry, land use and subsistence...176
Conclusion..177

15 Marine mollusca...178
Sean Bell and Karen Godden
Introduction..178
Methodology...178
Results from the 1989 excavations...178
Results from the 1990 and 1991 excavations...178
Discussion...183

16 Radiocarbon dating...186
Peter Marshall and Gordon T. Cook
Introduction..186
Methods..186
Results..186
Stable isotopes..186
Methodological approach..187
The samples..187
The sequence..187
The chronology of Cill Donnain III...189

17 Conclusion: Cill Donnain's prehistoric landscape...190
The evolution of settlement on Cill Donnain's machair *Mike Parker Pearson*.........190
Occupation and activity at Cill Donnain in the Iron Age *Mike Parker Pearson with Marek Zvelebil*.................199
The Cill Donnain III wheelhouse in the context of the Hebridean Iron Age *Mike Parker Pearson*......................208
Conclusion *Mike Parker Pearson*..214

Appendix Context list and phasing for the 1989, 1990 and 1991 excavations at Cill Donnain III..................................216

Bibliography...220

Index 229

List of Figures

Preface Marek Zvelebil making the best of South Uist's inclement weather

1.1. Map of South Uist, showing Cill Donnain III and other archaeological sites investigated by the SEARCH project and its successors

1.2. Map of the Uists, showing the areas of west-coast machair, with the position of Figure 1.5 also marked

1.3. The machair and other landscape zones of South Uist

1.4. Map of archaeological sites in the Cill Donnain area; site 85 is the Cill Donnain III wheelhouse

1.5. Archaeological remains mapped in 1989 on Cill Donnain machair. CDI is the Early Bronze Age site of Cill Donnain I; 1 is the Cill Donnain III wheelhouse; 2, 4, 7 and 10 are field walls; 5, 6 and 11 are stone structures; 8 is an eroding structure; 9 was (erroneously) identified as a stone 'cist'; 12 is structure/walls (?)

1.6. Cill Donnain III at the start of excavations in 1989 in the sand blow-out on the west side of the dune, seen from the north

1.7. Plan of the area of the sand blow-out around site 85 (Cill Donnain III)

1.8. Locations of survey squares and auger holes in the sand blow-out around the site (Cill Donnain III) prior to excavation

1.9. The flat-topped sand dune immediately east of the excavation site in 2003, viewed from the west; the post-1991 sand quarry (centre left) was trial-trenched in 2003

2.1. Plan of the trenches excavated in 1989, 1990 and 1991

2.2. The excavation trenches in 1989, viewed as a composite photograph from the west

2.3. The one-metre grid, initially laid out with string prior to excavation in 1989, viewed from the east

2.4. The exposed sand face within the quarry prior to excavation, with string grid in place, viewed from the west

2.5. Marek Zvelebil at Cill Donnain III in 1989; the midden layer is behind his head

2.6. The student team in 1989: Mark Plucenniek sits left front next to Gill Holloway, and those at the back (left to right) include Eddie Moth, Adrian Chadwick, Alwen Pearson, Barbara Brayshay, Karen Miller, Jacqui Mulville, Sylvia Ross, Jo Hambly and Saleem ul Haq

2.7. Plan of the Iron Age wheelhouse at the end of the 1989 season. The curving dashed line is the vertical edge of the eroding sand quarry (see Figure 2.3)

2.8. Plan of the Iron Age wheelhouse at the end of the 1990 season

2.9. Digging the wheelhouse in 1990, viewed from the southeast; in the photo (from left to right, back to front) are Paul Rainbird, Mark Plucenniek, Crispin Flower, Liz Elford, Alyson Evans, Alan Parry, Clare Davidson, Cheryl Gansecki, Beth McMartin and Naomi Korn

2.10. Backfilling of the excavations in 1990 at Cill Donnain, viewed from the north

2.11. The student team in 1991: Marek stands on the left, seated behind him are (from left to right) Jacqui Mulville, Helen Smith and Mark Collard. From the left at the back are Howard Benge, Steve Webster, Claire Cunnington (née Coleman), Anna Badcock, Tim Insoll, Dave Giles, Guy Holman and Paul Gething

2.12. Plan of the Iron Age wheelhouse at the end of the 1991 season

2.13. Re-siting the stones of the wheelhouse in the grounds of Taigh-tasgaidh Chill Donnain in 1992, viewed from the south, with the stones of the doorway at the front right of the picture

2.14. The post-1991 sand quarry at Cill Donnain in 2003, viewed from the southwest; Quarry Trenches 1, 2 and 3 can be seen within it from right to left

2.15. The numbered metre squares of the main trench and the southern trench of the 1989–1991 excavations; the co-ordinates are those of the 1990–91 seasons

2.16. The long section of the exposed face of the sand quarry in 1989. Note: all context numbers on this section belong to the 1989 sequence: 1/1989–17/1989

2.17. Location of the 1989 long section in relation to the position of the wheelhouse. The curving dashed line shows the section line along the quarry face. It cut the southwest sector of the wheelhouse

2.18. Interpretation of the long section, showing the pre-wheelhouse levelling layer, the wheelhouse's wall core, robbed inner wall face and internal floor, all covered by windblown sand and midden. Note: all context numbers on this section belong to the 1989 sequence: 1/1989–17/1989

3.1. Plan of the 1991 northwest trench (showing its stepping-in) in relation to the later sand quarry and the 2003 quarry trenches

3.2.   Contour plot of the Early–Middle Bronze Age Cordoned Urn-period settlement mound at Cill Donnain
3.3.   Location of the excavation trenches overlaid on the contour plot of the settlement mound
3.4.   Stratigraphic matrix of Early–Middle Bronze Age contexts in the northwest trench and the three quarry trenches
3.5.   Section drawing of part of the north side of the northwest trench
3.6.   Section drawing of the entire north side of the northwest trench
3.7.   Section drawing of the east end of the northwest trench
3.8.   Plan of the sterile sand (156) at the base of the northwest trench, cut by layer 157
3.9.   Plan of the surface of layer 153, showing the position of pot SF129
3.10.   Plan of the surface of layer 140=149, showing patches of layer 141, context 147 and pit 142
3.11.   Section drawings of Quarry Trenches 1–3
3.12.   Quarry Trench 1, viewed from the north
3.13.   Quarry Trench 2, viewed from the west
3.14.   Quarry Trench 3, viewed from the south
3.15.   Positions of OSL samples within a schematic section through the Cill Donnain III site. Layer 1 is sterile wind-blown sand at the base of the sequence; layer 2 is the EBA–MBA layer; layer 3 is the windblown sand layer 131=162; and layer 4 is the wheelhouse and midden layer
3.16.   Spatial distributions of pottery in: (a) layer 157, (b) layer 153=155, and (c) layer 140=149
4.1.   Stratigraphic matrix for Late Bronze Age contexts
4.2.   The surface of sand layer 135, showing ploughmarks: full plan (top) and initial plan of the east half of the trench (bottom)
4.3.   Ploughmarks within layer 135, viewed from the southwest
4.4.   Layer 135 with a row of stones, overlaid on its east side by windblown sand layer 131
4.5.   Section through layer 135 showing pit 142
4.6.   Plan of pit 142
4.7.   Pit 142 after excavation, viewed from the south
5.1.   The numbered metre squares of the main trench of the 1989–1991 excavations, overlaid on the plan of the wheelhouse; the co-ordinates are those of the 1990–91 seasons
5.2.   Stratigraphic matrix for the Iron Age contexts pre-dating construction of the wheelhouse
5.3.   The human skull fragment (SF145) with its right eye socket visible, within layer 162
5.4.   Plans of gully 191, linear feature 215 and pit 223
5.5.   Section drawings of gully 191, linear feature 215 and pit 223
5.6.   Plan of layer 130, lying on top of layer 131=162, in the northwest trench (see Figures 3.1 and 5.1 for location)
5.7.   Plan of layer 132, a possible hearth, in the northwest trench (see Figures 3.1 and 5.1 for location)
5.8.   Plan of a humic soil (187), a shell layer (173) and a domed patch of peat ash (189), both cut by pit 186 (phase 4)
5.9.   Section drawing, south–north, through the organic layer 104
5.10.   Layer 104, to the southwest of the doorway jambs, with layers 105 and 173
5.11.   The student has her back to layer 104 (still *in situ*) while midden layer 103 (phase 9) is visible as a dark strip within the baulk to the right
5.12.   The basal part of layer 163 in plan
5.13.   The middle part of layer 163 in plan
5.14.   The upper part of layer 163 in plan
5.15.   The human skull fragment (SF145) showing evidence of a depressed lesion on top of the head
6.1.   Stone structural elements of the wheelhouse in its constructional phase. The dashed line in the bottom left marks the line of part of the 1989 section
6.2.   Stone structural elements of the wheelhouse superimposed over cut features beneath
6.3.   Plan of cut features beneath the eastern half of the wheelhouse
6.4.   Stratigraphic matrix for the Iron Age layers associated with construction and initial use of the wheelhouse
6.5.   Cut features, including stone holes for the inner wall face, viewed from the northeast; gully 191 is visible to the right
6.6.   The northwest sector of the inner wall face, viewed from the northeast (NB to preserve future readers from puzzlement, the possibly mysterious 'object' at the top right is Dave Giles's dreadlocks)
6.7.   The revetted side of the inner wall face in its north sector, viewed from the north
6.8.   The doorway of the wheelhouse, viewed from the east; on the left are stones associated with the building's collapse and dismantling
6.9.   The robbed-out inner wall face in the southwest sector, viewed from the southwest; the wheelhouse interior is to the right of the feature, and the layers above are the midden 5=1/1989 (top) and the windblown sand layer 21=36=2/1989 (middle)

6.10.   The outer wall face in the southwest sector, viewed from the north; the sand wall core is to its left

6.11.   The eroded wall core of sand (layer 24) on the north and east sides of the wheelhouse interior and inner wall face, viewed from the east

6.12.   The eroded wall core of sand (layer 24) on the north and east sides of the wheelhouse interior and inner wall face, viewed from the south

6.13.   The base of the northeast pier, viewed from the southwest

6.14.   The base of the north pier, viewed from the south

6.15.   The base of the northwest pier, viewed from the southeast

6.16.   Plan of floor layers 166 amd 170 with hearth 178 (and pit 184 beneath it)

6.17.   The modified hearth (phase 6) above hearth (178), viewed from the north

6.18.   Plan of the pit (184) beneath the hearth

6.19.   Section drawing of the relationship between the hearth (178) and the pit (184) beneath

6.20.   The modified hearth (phase 6) above hearth (178), viewed from the northwest

6.21.   Plan of floor layers 166 amd 170 with hearth 178, showing that floor 166 covered pit 184

6.22.   Floor 166, viewed from the east

6.23.   Floor 170, viewed from the east

6.24.   Distribution of pottery sherds within floors 166 and 170

6.25.   The stone structure and other stones at the base of the south trench

6.26.   Section drawing of the stone structure and layers above it

6.27.   Section drawing of layers to the north of the south trench

7.1.   The wheelhouse early in the 1991 excavation season, viewed from the east; Marek Zvelebil is in the foreground

7.2.   Modifications within the wheelhouse (phase 6), consisting of the remodelled hearth and wall (174)

7.3.   Stratigraphic matrix for the Iron Age layers associated with the wheelhouse's modification and abandonment. Several contexts from the 1989 season have had to be omitted, either because their stratigraphic position is unclear or because the same context number was used for multiple contexts

7.4.   Wall 174 with the modified hearth behind it, viewed from the northwest

7.5.   Plan of the modified hearth and wall 174 with surrounding rubble

7.6.   The modified hearth, viewed from the south; the 'zigzag' stone is in the centre of the picture

7.7.   Close-up of the modified hearth, viewed from the south-southeast

7.8.   Outline plan of the modified hearth, wall 174 and layer 16/1989 as recorded during the 1989 season

7.9.   Stones from the modified hearth and from the original hearth (178) below, viewed from the southeast

7.10.   Distribution of rubble in the wheelhouse interior and to its south (phase 7); the wheelhouse walls, wall 174 and the modified hearth are shaded

7.11.   Plan of structure 167 (phase 8) within the abandoned wheelhouse

7.12.   Structure 167, viewed from the south

7.13.   The interior of the wheelhouse, viewed from the east, showing the rubble-free areas within

7.14.   Structure 167, viewed from the southeast; the gaps in the wheelhouse wall are visible in the foreground

8.1.   Stratigraphic matrix for the Iron Age layers associated with the midden

8.2.   Stratigraphic matrix for the Iron Age layers associated with the midden, as depicted in MZ's original matrix

8.3.   Section showing the midden layer (5=1/1989) on top of windblown sand (layer 21=36=2/1989), viewed from the south

8.4.   Ploughmarks in the tops of layers 102 and 103 in the southeast corner of the main trench, viewed from the east

8.5.   Plan of the base of the midden after removal of layer 5=1/1989 in the eastern part of the main trench

8.6.   Section drawings A and B through the midden layers

8.7.   Section drawings C and D through the midden layers

8.8.   Section drawing E through the midden layers

8.9.   Positions of section drawings A–E within the main trench

8.10.   Section drawing of both sides of a temporary baulk through the midden and abandonment layers on top of the north side of the wheelhouse

8.11.   Plan of layers within the midden, generally its lower levels; layer 15/1989 inside the abandoned wheelhouse is different from 15/1989 outside it, and those contexts recorded in 1989 (left half of plan) are not necessarily at the same stratigraphic level as those in the right half

8.12.   Section drawing of layers 53 and 54 in the northeast part of the main trench; the precise position of this drawn section is not known with certainty

8.13.   The spread of stones, with pottery, animal bones and hammerstones, in the northeast corner of the main trench within layer 5=1/1989, viewed from the south

8.14.   Plan of the spread of stones in the northeast corner of the main trench within layer 5=1/1989

8.15. The spread of stones in the northeast corner of the main trench within layer 5=1/1989, viewed from the east
8.16. Section drawing of midden layers in the western part of the main trench
8.17. Layers 1/1989, 2/1989, 12/1989, 16/1989 and 17/1989 in the central part of the main trench within the ruins of the wheelhouse
8.18. Section drawing of layers 2/1989 (=21=36) and 12/1989 in the central part of the main trench
8.19. Layer of burnt peat ash (23) on top of the sand wall core (24; phase 4) of the wheelhouse
8.20. Plan of upper layers within the midden deposits; those recorded in 1989 (left half of plan) are not necessarily at the same stratigraphic level as those in the right half
8.21. Layers 101, 102 and 103 as recorded at different levels in the southeast corner of the main trench; the plough-marks shown in Figure 8.4 were visible at the level of the lower plan
8.22. Section drawings of contexts 55–59 within the south-central part of the main trench
8.23. Layers 1/1989, 1's'/1989 and 2/1989 within the south trench
8.24. Heap of disturbed stones in the south area of the main excavation trench (context 10/1989), viewed from the east
8.25. Four large boulders (right) and a setting of probably disturbed stones (left) within the west half of the main trench, viewed from the south
9.1. Impressed, applied and incised motifs on ceramics
9.2. Incised decorative motifs represented at Cill Donnain III; this is the key to Table 9.4
9.3. Average ceramic sherd weights
9.4. Collared Urn ceramics from phase 1
9.5. Late Bronze Age ceramics from phase 2
9.6. Middle Iron Age ceramics from phase 3, contexts 104–162
9.7. Middle Iron Age ceramics from phase 3, contexts 163–191
9.8. Late Iron Age ceramics from the floor (166) of the wheelhouse
9.9. Late Iron Age ceramics from the abandonment phase of the wheelhouse
9.10. Ceramics from phase 9, context 5
9.11. Ceramics from phase 9, contexts 31 and 103
9.12. Reconstructions of Middle Iron Age pottery (*c.* 100 BC–AD 300) from South Uist
9.13. Reconstructions of Late Iron Age pottery (*c.* AD 300–600) from South Uist
9.14. Reconstructions of Late Iron Age pottery (*c.* AD 600–900) from South Uist
9.15. Ceramic artefacts SF30 and context 59
10.1. Copper-alloy artefacts from Cill Donnain III
10.2. Iron artefacts from Cill Donnain III
10.3. Clay refractory fragments from contexts 160 and 163
10.4. Crucible fragment from context 187
11.1. Coarse stone artefacts from Cill Donnain III
11.2. Flint artefacts from Cill Donnain III
11.3. Pumice artefacts from Cill Donnain III
12.1. Bone and ivory artefacts from Cill Donnain III
12.2. Whale bone artefacts from Cill Donnain III
12.3. Antler artefacts from Cill Donnain III
15.1. Summary of marine shell fragments recovered from Bronze Age deposits (phases 1–2) at Cill Donnain III, based on 10,764 identified fragments
15.2. Summary of marine shell fragments recovered from phases 3 and 4 at Cill Donnain III, based on 18,304 identified fragments
15.3. Summary of marine shell fragments from phases 5 to 8 at Cill Donnain III, based on 7,691 identified fragments
15.4. Summary of marine shell fragments from phase 9 at Cill Donnain III, based on 86,082 identified fragments
15.5. Summary of marine shell fragments excluding common periwinkle and limpet from phases 1 and 2 at Cill Donnain III, based on 350 identified fragments
15.6. Summary of marine shell fragments excluding common periwinkle and limpet, from phases 3 and 4 at Cill Donnain III, based on 137 identified fragments
15.7. Summary of marine shell fragments excluding common periwinkle and limpet from phases 5 to 8 at Cill Donnain III, based on 89 identified fragments
15.8. Summary of marine shell fragments excluding common periwinkle and limpet from phase 9 at Cill Donnain III, based on 326 identified fragments
16.1. Probability distributions of dates from Cill Donnain III. Each distribution represents the relative probability that an event occurred at a particular time. These distributions are the result of simple radiocarbon calibration (Stuiver and Reimer 1993)

16.2.   Probability distributions of dates from Cill Donnain III: each distribution represents the relative probability that an event occurs at a particular time. For each of the radiocarbon dates two distributions have been plotted, one in outline, which is the result of simple calibration, and a solid one, which is based on the chronological model used. Figures in brackets after the laboratory numbers are the individual indices of agreement which provide an indication of the consistency of the radiocarbon dates with the prior information included in the model (Bronk Ramsey 1995). The large square brackets down the left-hand side along with the OxCal keywords define the model exactly

17.1.   Distribution of Beaker-period settlements (*c*.2400–1800 BC) in the Cill Donnain area

17.2.   Barbed-and-tanged arrowhead, scrapers, bone point and pottery from Cill Donnain I (site 87), a Beaker-period and Early Bronze Age settlement

17.3.   Schematic section drawing of the location of Cill Donnain I (site 87) within machair dunes

17.4.   The site of Cill Donnain I (site 87; from Hamilton and Sharples 2012)

17.5.   Distribution of Early Bronze Age Food Vessel (*c*.2200–1800 BC) and Cordoned Urn settlements (*c*.1900–1500 BC) in the Cill Donnain area

17.6.   Distribution of Late Bronze Age settlements (*c*.1300–750 BC) in the Cill Donnain area

17.7.   Distribution of Early Iron Age settlements (*c*.750–200 BC) in the Cill Donnain area

17.8.   Distribution of Middle Iron Age settlements (*c*.200 BC–AD 300) in the Cill Donnain area

17.9.   Distribution of Late Iron Age settlements (*c*.AD 300–800) in the Cill Donnain area

17.10. Distribution of Norse-period settlements (*c*.AD 800–1300) in the Cill Donnain area

17.11. Distribution of Later Medieval and Post-Medieval settlements (*c*.1300–1700) in the Cill Donnain area

17.12. Excavated wheelhouses of South Uist: a) Kilpheder (after Lethbridge 1952), b) A' Cheardach Bheag (after Young and Richardson 1960), c) A' Cheardach Mhor (after Fairhurst 1971), d) Hornish Point (after Barber 2003), e) Cill Donnain III (this volume), f) Bornais mound 1 (after Sharples 2012b), g) Gleann Uisinis (after Thomas 1866–1868)

17.13. Excavated wheelhouses of Barra: a) Allt Chrisal (T17) first phase (after Foster and Pouncett 2000), b) Allt Chrisal (T17) second phase (after Foster and Pouncett 2000), c) Allasdale dunes (after Wessex Archaeology 2008), d) Allasdale (after Young 1953)

17.14. Excavated wheelhouses of North Uist and Lewis: a) Cnip phase 1, Lewis (after Armit 2006), b) Cnip phase 2, Lewis (after Armit 2006), c) Sollas, North Uist (after Campbell 1991), d) Clettraval, North Uist (after Scott 1948), e) the Udal, North Uist (after Crawford in Selkirk 1996), f) the Udal, North Uist (after Crawford in Selkirk 1996), g) Baile Sear, North Uist (after Barber 2003), h) Eilean Maleit, North Uist (after Armit 1998), i) Bac Mhic Connain, North Uist (after Beveridge 1911), j) Bagh nam Feadag, Grimsay (after McKenzie 2005), k) Gearraidh Iochdrach, North Uist (after Beveridge 1911), l) Cnoc a Comhdhalach, North Uist (after Beveridge 1911)

17.15. Unexcavated probable wheelhouses of Barra and South Uist: a) T166, Barra (from Branigan and Foster 1995: fig. 3.9), b) T132, Barra (from Branigan and Foster 1995: fig. 3.9), c) T160, Barra (from Branigan and Foster 1995: fig. 3.9), d) USS 013, South Uist (from Raven 2012: fig. 7.12), e) T164, Barra (from Branigan and Foster 1995: fig. 3.9), f) K34, Barra (from Branigan 2000: fig. 11.1)

17.16. A reconstruction of the Cill Donnain III wheelhouse, showing the stone frame of the building

17.17. A reconstruction of the Cill Donnain III wheelhouse, showing the walls in place

17.18. A reconstruction of the Cill Donnain III wheelhouse, showing the roof partly completed

17.19. A reconstruction of the completed Cill Donnain III wheelhouse

List of Tables

3.1   Optically stimulated luminescence (OSL) dates from Cill Donnain III

9.1.   Total numbers and weights of sherds by phase

9.2.   Ceramic fabric groups by context and phase

9.3.   Sherd numbers, weights, rims and decorated sherds by context and phase

9.4.   Incised decoration by context and phase. For the key, see Figure 9.2

9.5.   Impressed decoration by context and phase

9.6.   Applied decoration by context and phase

9.7.   Rim types by context and phase

10.1   Clay refractory debris from Cill Donnain III

10.2   Metalworking slag from Cill Donnain III

10.3   Quantities of different types of metalworking slag

10.4   Weight (g) of types of iron-working slag, by phase

10.5   Contextual distribution of metalworking slag from phase 7

10.6   Contextual distribution of metalworking slag from phase 9

10.7   Contextual distribution of fuel ash slag from Cill Donnain III

10.8   Spatial distribution of fuel ash slag in phase 9

11.1   Coarse stone tools from Cill Donnain III

11.2   Worked flint from Cill Donnain III

11.3   Unworked pumice from Cill Donnain III

12.1   Bone, ivory and antler artefacts by phase

12.2   Bone, ivory and antler artefact types by phase

13.1   Summary of contexts and number of specimens by excavation year, and phase

13.2   Distribution of fragments making up less than 10% of a complete element in the 1990 assemblage by phase and taxa

13.3   Occurrence of gnawed bone in the 1989 and 1990 assemblages (information for the 1991 assemblage unavailable)

13.4   Frequency of burning by phase and taxa.

13.5.   NISP and MNI quantification of the species present at Cill Donnain III

13.6i.   Element representation by phase for the 1991 assemblage (based on NISP)

13.6ii.   Element representation by phase for the 1990 assemblage (based on NISP)

13.6iii.   Element representation for the 1989 assemblage (based on NISP, phasing information not available)

13.7.   Frequency of element fragments not recordable under the 1990 recording scheme (NISP)

13.8.   Fusion data from the 1989 and 1990 assemblages at Cill Donnain III

13.9.   Recorded pathologies in the 1990 and 1991 assemblages

13.10.   Occurrence of butchery in the 1990 assemblage

13.11.   Occurrence of butchery in the 1989 assemblage (percentages are calculated on the basis of identified fragments)

13.12.   Measurements taken on the 1990 postcranial assemblage

13.13.   Measurements taken on the 1990 tooth assemblage

14.1.   Samples of carbonized plant remains from Cill Donnain III (1989)

14.2.   Percentage of wild species per total number of seeds and chaff from Cill Donnain III (1989)

14.3.   Samples of carbonized plant remains from Cill Donnain III (1991)

15.1.   Total numbers of marine shell fragments recovered from Cill Donnain III, by species

15.2.   Sea snails recovered from Cill Donnain III, by context

15.3.   Marine bi-valves and land snails recovered from Cill Donnain III, by context

15.4.   Marine shell recovered in 1989, by context

15.5.   Marine shell recovered in 1990 and 1991 from the Late Iron Age midden (phase 9), by context

15.6.   Marine shell recovered in 1990 and 1991 from deposits associated with the occupation and abandonment of the wheelhouse (phases 5–8), by context

15.7.   Marine shell recovered in 1990 and 1991 from pre-wheelhouse Middle Iron Age layers (phases 3–4), by context

15.8.   Marine shell recovered in 1990 and 1991 from Bronze Age deposits (phases 1–2), by context

16.1.   Cill Donnain III radiocarbon results

16.2.   Cill Donnain III chi-square test results

Acknowledgements

Illustrations were drawn by:
Marcus Abbott (3.2)
Chris Cumberpatch (9.1-9.3)
Irene Deluis (1.3, 2.15, 2.16, 2.18, 3.1, 3.5–3.11, 3.16, 4.2, 4.4–4.6, 5.4–5.10, 6.18–6.19, 6.25, 6.27–6.28, 7.8, 8.10, 8.16, 9.4–9.15, 10.2–10.4, 11.1–11.3, 12.1–12.3, 17.2, 17.16–17.19)
Ian Dennis (1.1, 1.4, 17.1, 17.5–17.11)
Karen Godden (15.1–15.8)
Anne Leaver (17.4)
Peter Marshall (16.1–16.2)
Colin Merrony and John Raven (17.15)
Eddie Moth (or other unknown illustrators in Sheffield) (1.2, 1.5, 1.7, 1.8, 2.1, 2.7, 2.8, 2.12, 5.12–5.14, 6.1, 6.3, 6.26, 7.2, 7.5, 7.10-7.11, 8.5–8.8, 8.11–8.12, 8.14, 8.17–8.23, 10.1; all updated to publication standard by M Parker Pearson)
Mike Parker Pearson (2.17, 3.3–3.4, 4.1, 5.1–5.2, 6.2, 6.4, 6.16, 6.21, 7.3, 8.1–8.2, 8.9, 17.12–17.15)
Jean-Luc Schwenninger (3.15, 17.3)

Photographs were taken by:
Marek Zvelebil (1.6)
Mike Parker Pearson (1.9, 2.13–2.14, 3.12–3.14, 5.15)
Jean-Luc Schwenninger (Preface, 2.2–2.5, 2.10–2.11, 4.3, 4.7, 5.3, 5.11, 6.5–6.10, 6.13–6.15, 6.17, 6.20, 6.22–6.24, 7.1, 7.4, 7.6–7.7, 7.9, 7.12–7.14, 8.3, 8.13, 8.24–8.25)
Unknown (2.6, 2.9, 6.11, 6.12, 8.15)

Contributors

Sean Bell, Manor Oaks Farm, 389 Manor Lane, Sheffield

Andrew Chamberlain, Faculty of Life Sciences, University of Manchester, Manchester

Gordon Cook, SUERC, Rankine Avenue, Scottish Enterprise Technology Park, East Kilbride, G75 0QF

Chris Cumberpatch, independent consultant, Sheffield <Cgc@ccumberpatch.freeserve.co.uk>

Martin Dearne, c/o Department of History, Classics and Archaeology, Birkbeck, University of London, London WC1

Irene Deluis, archaeological illustrator, Sheffield <irene@irenedeluis.plus.com>

Karen Godden, c/o Institute of Archaeology, UCL, Gordon Square, London WC1

Pam Grinter, c/o Birmingham Archaeo-Environmental, University of Birmingham, Edgbaston, Birmingham

John Hamshaw-Thomas, c/o Silverdale School, Bents Crescent, Sheffield

Kate MacDonald, Uist Archaeology, Clarkston, Lochboisdale, South Uist

Peter Marshall, Chronologies, 25 Onslow Road, Sheffield

Mike Parker Pearson, Institute of Archaeology, UCL, Gordon Square, London WC1

Jean-Luc Schwenninger, Research Laboratory for Archaeology and History of Art, University of Oxford, Oxford

Helen Smith, c/o School of Conservation Sciences, Bournemouth University

Saleem ul Haq, Archaeology department, Government of Punjab, Lahore, Pakistan

Soultana-Maria Valamoti, School of History and Archaeology, Aristotle University of Thessaloniki, Greece

Kim Vickers, c/o Department of Archaeology, University of Sheffield, Northgate House, West Street, Sheffield

Preface

Marek Zvelebil died aged 59 on 7th July 2011, just days before we planned to start finally bringing this project to publication. He directed the excavations at Cill Donnain over three field seasons in 1989–1991 and many of the specialist reports were written within the next few years, but Marek did not find easy the post-excavation stage of the project. By 2005 he had given up on the manuscript and handed responsibility to me. This was Marek's first and only experience of being sole director of an archaeological excavation; whilst he enjoyed field survey, running a major excavation project turned out not to be his *forte*. As a leading authority on the Mesolithic–Neolithic transition, he was also straying far from his area of expertise in taking on this Iron Age site. The story goes that his Sheffield colleagues drew him into the department's SEARCH project in the Western Isles by telling him that the site at Cill Donnain could be Mesolithic since it was clearly a shell midden, a type of site often dating to the Mesolithic in northern Europe.

In 1991 I joined Sheffield University's South Uist arm of the SEARCH project and, together with Niall Sharples, began excavations at the broch of Dun Vulan. We visited the Cill Donnain excavation frequently during that three-week season and were able to follow its progress fairly closely. The weather that year was extremely wet, and vir-

Marek Zvelebil making the best of South Uist's inclement weather

tually no work was possible in the first week because of torrential rain. Marek's team then worked through two weeks of bad weather to complete the excavation, reaching the bottom of the wheelhouse deposits and exploring a small part of the underlying Bronze Age remains. Marek's heart, though, was not in the work and he was often to be found during working hours in the lounge bar of the Lochboisdale Hotel or taking an early bath in our staff lodgings at South Lochboisdale House. After working hours, Marek enjoyed the finer things in life. The availability of produce in the local shops in South Uist was strictly limited twenty years ago but we all looked forward to Marek's turn on the cooking rota – a haunch of venison would be mysteriously obtained, high-quality wines purchased, and rich French sauces conjured out of multiple packs of butter.

Marek made many friends on the island during his stay and was keen to come back in later years, initially to supervise the re-locating of the wheelhouse, stone by stone, to the grounds of the rebuilt Taigh-tasgaidh Chill Donnain (Cill Donnain Museum), where it can still be seen in the grass on the south side of the driveway. He then came back to South Uist for the last time during our excavation season in 1998, using our rented accommodation in Polochar House as an office where he could wrestle with writing up his excavation.

Historic Scotland had contributed funds to the Cill Donnain excavation and were keen that Marek should bring the results to full publication. As the years passed and there was little evidence of progress, it became apparent that Marek would need help. Various colleagues and students provided input: Jenny Moore carried out an initial edit of some specialist reports, and Rob Dinnis typed up the list of context descriptions. Rod McCullagh, Historic Scotland's officer in charge of excavation grants, discussed with me how we could 'rescue' the publication of this important site. In 2009 and 2010, we came up with a programme of future work to see the project to completion. Marek was happy with the proposal and with contributing any further information that I could not obtain from the project's records during the course of writing-up. Sadly, he died just as I was about to start.

Mike Parker Pearson
August 2013

Chapter 1 Introduction

Mike Parker Pearson and Helen Smith

Introduction

The SEARCH project (Sheffield Environmental and Archaeological Research Campaign in the Hebrides) commenced in 1987 and covered the southern islands of Scotland's Western Isles, also known as the Outer Hebrides. One team, led by Keith Branigan, Pat Foster and Colin Merrony, concentrated their research on Barra and the small isles at the southernmost end of the island chain (Branigan 2005; Branigan and Foster 1995; 2000; 2002) and another team was based on South Uist (Figure 1.1; Parker Pearson *et al.* 2004). A third team carried out an integrated series of environmental projects investigating palynology, vegetation, palaeoentomology, dune geomorphology, climate change, phytoliths, animal husbandry, crop processing and related fields across South Uist and Barra (Gilbertson *et al.* 1996).

The first major excavation carried out by the SEARCH project on South Uist was the rescue excavation of what was thought to be a shell midden at Cill Donnain, directed by Marek Zvelebil in 1989–1991 (Zvelebil 1989; 1990; 1991).[1] Lasting three summer seasons, the excavation revealed the remains of a circular, stone-walled house dating to the Iron Age and known as a wheelhouse. This term refers to the plan of these distinctive Hebridean roundhouses – the interior is sub-divided by stone piers forming a radial plan so that, from above, they resemble the spokes of a wheel. Wheelhouses are known only in the Outer Hebrides and Shetland (Crawford 2002); many have been excavated in the last century or so by archaeologists. Wheelhouses were used as dwellings and provide evidence of daily life in the period *c.*300 BC – AD 500 (the end of the Early Iron Age, the Middle Iron Age and the beginning of the Late Iron Age). Buried beneath the Cill Donnain wheelhouse lay the remains of a

Bronze Age settlement, partly investigated by Zvelebil in 1991 and further explored by Mike Parker Pearson and Kate MacDonald in 2003.

The geology and soils

The Outer Hebrides are situated 60–80km off the northwest coast of Scotland, separated from the mainland by The Minch in the north and the Sea of the Hebrides in the south. Forming a breakwater against the Atlantic, the Outer Hebrides provide some shelter to the Inner Hebrides, situated to the east, and to the Scottish mainland, from Cape Wrath in the north to Ardnamurchan in the south. The archipelago of the Western Isles stretches 213km from the Butt of Lewis to Barra Head, and consists of 119 named islands, of which only 16 are now permanently inhabited (Boyd 1979). The island chain, once known as 'The Long Island' (Carmichael 1884), divides geographically into two main groups, the Sound of Harris separating Lewis and Harris (total area *c.*214,000 ha) from the southern islands, namely North Uist, Benbecula, South Uist and Barra (total area *c.*76,000 ha).

South Uist (Uibhist a Deas) is an island 30km north–south and 12km east–west. To the north of it lies Benbecula and, beyond, North Uist. To the south, beyond the island of Eriskay (Eirisgeigh) and a number of small, uninhabited islands, are Barra and the southern isles.

The Outer Hebrides were formed over 3,000 million years ago from an eroded platform of Precambrian Lewisian gneiss whose primary components are quartz and mica. This forms a mountainous band on the islands' eastern seaboard. On the west coast the sea bed is shallow, owing to a submerged platform forming an extensive area of continental shelf. In the Uists, the glacial deposits

---

[1] In its Anglicized form Cill Donnain is Kildonan. In recent years it has become the norm to use the Gaelic form for place-names in the Western Isles, although the older literature uses English forms (e.g. Bornish for Bornais, Kilpheder for Cille Pheadair). For an English–Gaelic glossary of place-names relevant to the archaeology of South Uist and adjacent islands, refer to Sharples (2012b: xvii–xviii) or Parker Pearson (2012b: 426–8).

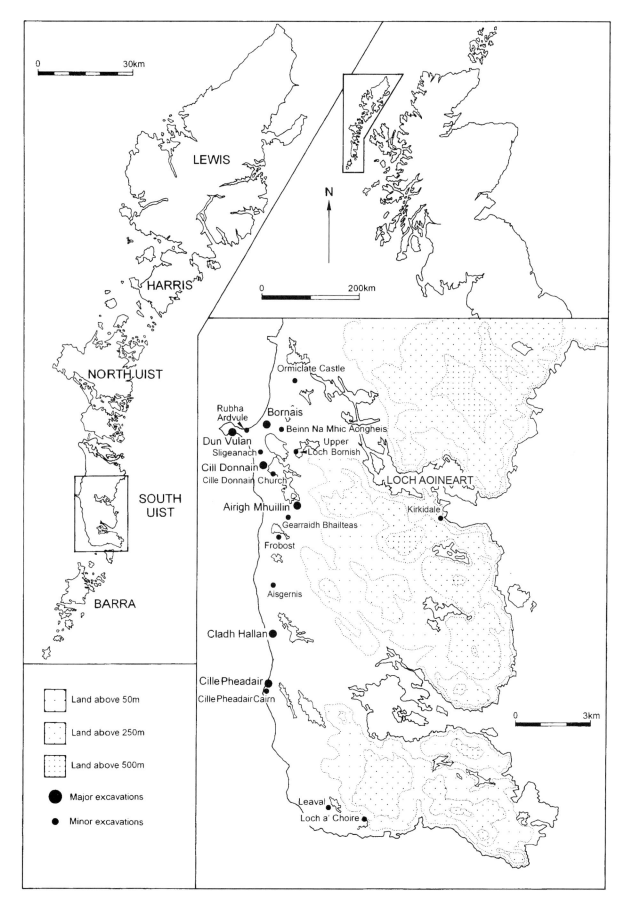

Figure 1.1 Map of South Uist, showing Cill Donnain III and other archaeological sites investigated by the SEARCH project and its successors

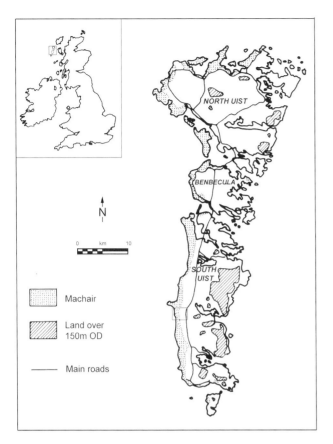

Figure 1.2 Map of the Uists, showing the areas of west-coast machair, with the position of Figure 1.5 also marked

Figure 1.3 The machair and other landscape zones of South Uist

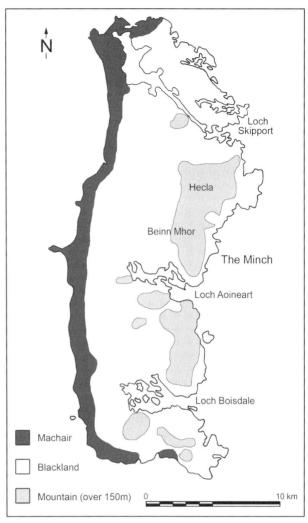

are now eroded in places or overlain by peat, particularly in the upland regions in the east, and divided by oligotrophic freshwater lochs. On the western seaboard, the glacial deposits and peat are overlain by highly calcareous windblown sand, forming dune systems and sandy plains with eutrophic lochs (Boyd and Boyd 1990).

The southern Outer Hebrides can be divided into three broad zones of soil types. On South Uist (Figure 1.2), the eastern third is the hilly and mountainous area that comes down to the sea in a series of three fjord-like sea lochs separated by a rugged coastline of low cliffs. The middle zone is an area of shallow peat soils, known as 'blackland', interspersed with myriad small freshwater lochs. To the west, the sea covers the shallow shelf that stretches out for about 20km from the coastline. This was formerly dry land in the Mesolithic and Early Neolithic but has since become inundated. The most distinct landform of South Uist and the Western Isles is the zone of calcareous sand that covers the island's west coast and is known as *machair*. With the associated dune systems, the machair covers approximately 120 square kilometres along the west coast of North Uist, Benbecula and South Uist. The machair forms an almost continuous fertile strip along this exposed Atlantic coast. It supports grass vegetation and extends inland for about a kilometre along the west coast

of South Uist; small pockets of machair can also be found on Barra and on the north and south coasts of the Uists and Benbecula (Figures 1.2–1.3).

The machair, therefore, comprises grassland formed on gently sloping shell-sand deposits. The nature and evolution of machair formation is discussed in detail by Ritchie and colleagues (1976; 1979; 1985; Ritchie and Whittington 1994; Ritchie *et al.* 2001; Edwards *et al.* 2005). Large quantities of shell sand were swept landwards, aided by rising sea level, to form an extensive pre-machair dune system. High-energy waves and strong Atlantic winds caused the deflation of beach dunes and swept sand inland. Where the sand stabilized, calcophile grassland established to form long stretches of sandy machair plain. Ritchie (1979: 115–17) suggested that sand deposition might have begun as early as 3750 BC, with primary deposition from 3000 cal BC to 2500 cal BC, followed by stabilization in the Beaker period (2400–1800 cal BC). More recently, Edwards *et al.* (2005) have discovered that machair sand began to form from at least the mid-eighth millennium BP (*c.*5500 BC; see also Ritchie 1985; Ritchie and Whittington 1994). However, the complete absence of Mesolithic and Neolithic settlement sites on the machair shows that it had not stabilized until the end of the third millennium BC.

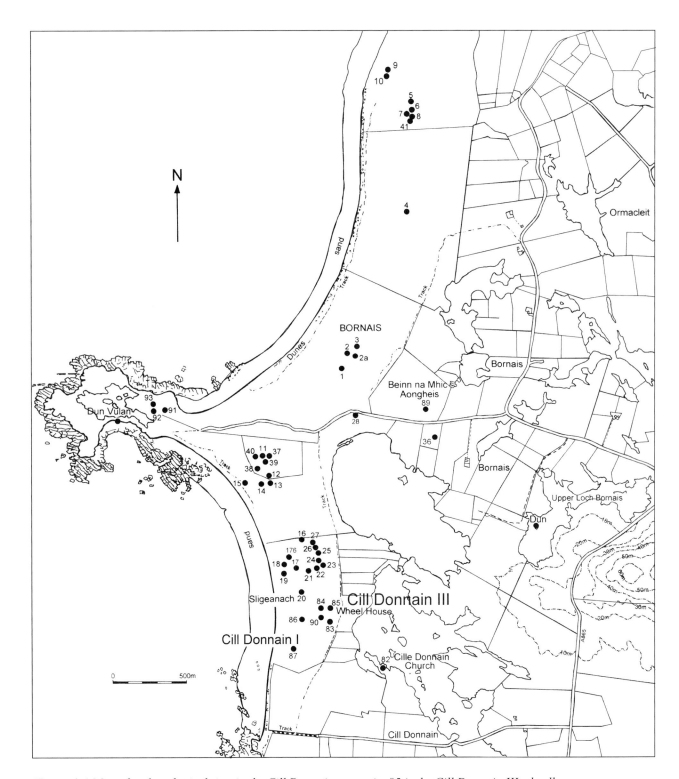

Figure 1.4 Map of archaeological sites in the Cill Donnain area; site 85 is the Cill Donnain III wheelhouse

The calcareous soils of the machair have high pH values, 6.5 to 7.5 in top soils and 7.5 to 8.0 in subsoils. The dune-machair soils range from calcareous regosols and brown calcareous soils to poorly drained calcareous gleys and peaty calcareous gleys, depending on the drainage conditions and level of the water table (Glentworth 1979; Hudson 1991). Water percolating from the freely draining sands has contributed to the formation of lochs and fens in the slack behind the machair. Areas of machair are prone to seasonal flooding (see Sharples 2012b: figs 139–140).

The SEARCH project

The main aim of the SEARCH project was to investigate the long-term adaptation of human societies to the marginal environment of the Outer Hebrides. Sheffield

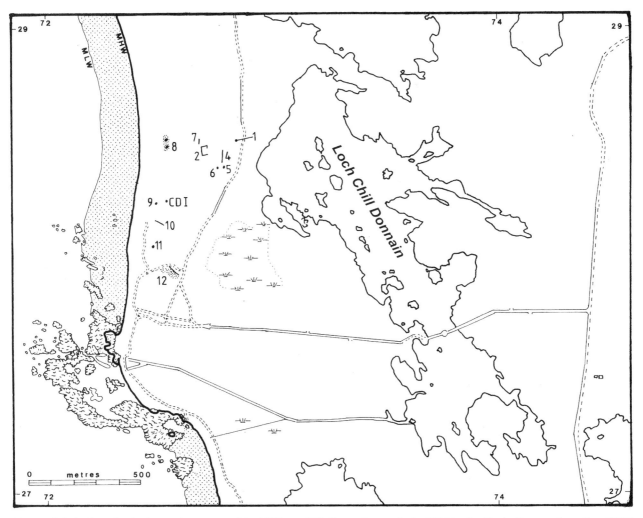

Figure 1.5 Archaeological remains mapped in 1989 on Cill Donnain machair. CDI is the Early Bronze Age site of Cill Donnain I; 1 is the Cill Donnain III wheelhouse; 2, 4, 7 and 10 are field walls; 5, 6 and 11 are stone structures; 8 is an eroding structure; 9 was (erroneously) identified as a stone 'cist'; 12 is structure/walls (?)

University's Department of Archaeology and Prehistory[2] was at the forefront of environmental and processual archaeology in the 1970s and 1980s and this was an opportunity to ground models of human–environment interaction, cultural adaptation to natural constraints, and long-term processes of culture change in a field project in which most of the staff and students of the department collaborated as a joint venture.

Initial survey work was carried out in 1987 by Martin Wildgoose, Richard Hodges and David Gilbertson. Wildgoose identified a number of midden sites on the South Uist machair, three of which were eroding and were thus targeted for excavation. One of these was Cill Donnain III, the subject of this report. After excavation in 1989–1991, the surviving walls of the Cill Donnain wheelhouse were moved in 1992 to the grounds of Taightasgaidh Chill Donnain (Cill Donnain Museum) where they were re-erected under Marek Zvelebil's supervision.

The site setting

The Cill Donnain wheelhouse site (known as Cill Donnain III or site 85 of the machair survey; Parker Pearson 2012c) is located on South Uist's machair at NF 7284 2857 (Figure 1.4). The site lies on the eastern edge of a large sand valley or 'blow-out' among the dunes, within 100m of the western shore of Loch Chill Donnain (Figures 1.5–1.8). It lies on the gentle eastern slope of the blow-out, at the foot of a high, steep-sided dune whose flat summit provides excellent views of the surrounding machair (Figure 1.9). This dune probably formed within the last thousand years because there is compelling evidence that it sits on top of a large archaeological site, the northern edge of which has been detected at the base of the dune's north side. The remains of Norse-period settlement emerging beneath the southeast side of this dune indicate that the windblown sand accumulated at some time after about AD 1200. Coring with a soil auger in 2003 revealed that the Iron Age deposits, of which the wheelhouse formed a part, continue eastwards beneath the large dune.

---

[2] Now the Department of Archaeology.

Figure 1.6 Cill Donnain III at the start of excavations in 1989 in the sand blow-out on the west side of the dune, seen from the north

Archaeological finds have been made on the machair of Cill Donnain for many years. In the 1960s, Coinneach Maclean (later to become a friend and colleague of Marek Zvelebil as post-graduate students together at Cambridge) found a small group of bronze items on Cill Donnain machair around NF 727 283 (NF72NW 15). A bronze mushroom-headed pin found by Maclean (NF72NW 14) probably came from the Cill Donnain wheelhouse site. Other archaeological remains in the vicinity of the wheelhouse include a nearby standing stone on Cill Donnain machair at NF 7273 2860 (now buried under a dune), and two nearby sites (sites 86 and 87[3], also known as Cill Donnain I and II; see Parker Pearson 2012c; Hamilton and Sharples 2012).

Human remains were found in the vicinity (NF72NW 3) of Cill Donnain wheelhouse though the precise location has not been recorded: the left parietal of a human skull fragment (recorded as site 213), found in 1989 by Dave Gilbertson in a dune to the north of Cill Donnain wheelhouse (NF 728 287), has been radiocarbon-dated to cal AD 420–640 at 95.4% probability (GU-9835; 1530±55 BP). Other burials of this period from South Uist's machair include an inhumation under a cairn at Cille Pheadair dating to cal AD 640–780 (Parker Pearson *et al.* 2004) and an eroded burial at Aird a'Mhachair, dated to *c.*AD 605–655 (SCAPE Trust 2006). A stone cist

cemetery at Smercleit (site 237; Parker Pearson 2012c), at the south end of the island, may also date to the Pictish period (the Late Iron Age).

There are now some 54 known settlement sites located on the machair of Cill Donnain and Bornais (the township that lies to the north of Cill Donnain). These range in date from the Early Bronze Age to the Norse period. Some, particularly those of earlier date, are low and small. Others are extremely large mounds, reaching over 6m in height and over 50m in diameter. The full inventory of these machair sites can be found in Parker Pearson 2012c. We can divide these archaeological sites into eight chronological groups on the basis of their ceramics (see also Campbell 2002):

- Copper Age/Early Bronze Age (*c.*2500–1500 BC);
- Middle Bronze Age (*c.*1500–1300 BC);
- Late Bronze Age / Early Iron Age (*c.*1300–200 BC);
- Middle Iron Age (*c.*200 BC – AD 300);
- earlier Late Iron Age (*c.*AD 300–800);
- Viking Age or Norse period (AD 800–1250);
- Late Medieval (AD 1250–1500);
- Post-Medieval (AD 1500–1700).

Earlier Bronze Age

With no Neolithic sites yet discovered on the machair, its

---

[3]　All site numbers refer to the catalogue of machair sites published in Parker Pearson 2012b.

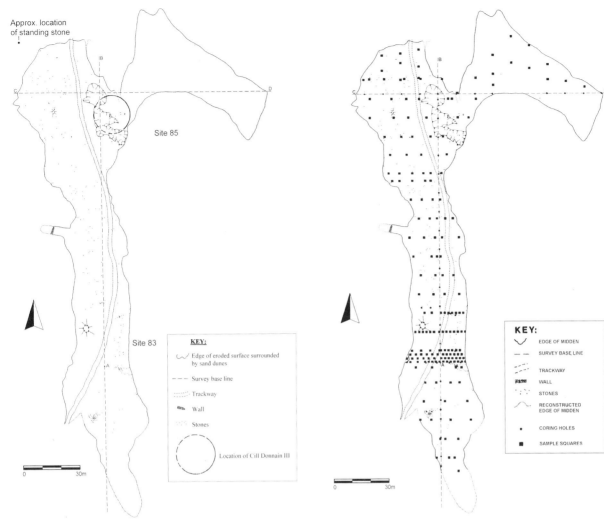

Figure 1.7 Plan of the area of the sand blow-out around site 85 (Cill Donnain III)

Figure 1.8 Locations of survey squares and auger holes in the sand blow-out around the site (Cill Donnain III) prior to excavation

archaeological sequence begins with the Beaker period. Early Bronze Age settlement remains on Cill Donnain machair consist of seven scatters in the area known as Sligeanach ('shelly'; Sharples 2012a). Certainly four of these (sites 17, 18, 87, 176) and probably all seven sites (also sites 19–21) on Cill Donnain machair can be dated to the Early Bronze Age (these sites are shown on Figure 1.4; see Figures 17.1 and 17.5 for detail):

- Cill Donnain I (site 87) was trial-trenched in 1988 by Linda Kennedy Allen (1988) and is associated with radiocarbon dates on carbonized seeds of 2350–1890 cal BC at 95% probability (OxA-3353; 3710±80 BP) and 2140–1690 cal BC at 95% probability (OxA-3354; 3560±80 BP; Gilbertson *et al.* 1996), along with surface finds of a barbed-and-tanged flint arrowhead, a leaf-shaped arrowhead, four thumbnail scrapers, a fragment of battle-axe, four bone pins/points, and Beaker and other Early Bronze Age pottery (Hamilton and Sharples 2012). The curved stone walls of one, and probably two other, small Early Bronze Age houses are

currently visible on the surface of site 87.

- Sherds of Beaker ware and EBA decorated coarse wares have been found on sites 17 and 18.
- Other sites likely to be of the same date or earlier are two small, shallow spreads (sites 21 and 176); site 21 has produced a flake from an igneous rock.
- Other sites possibly within this date range are sites 19 and 20.
- Beneath the Cill Donnain III wheelhouse (site 85) there is a partially excavated deposit of cordoned vessels of earlier Bronze Age type (see Chapter 3).

Later Bronze Age and Early Iron Age
Excavations by Niall Sharples on Cill Donnain machair in the Sligeanach area (west of the Cill Donnain wheelhouse) have identified two settlement mounds of Early Iron Age date (Sharples 2012a; see Figures 17.6–17.7). There is also Early Iron Age activity beneath the broch of Dun Vulan on the Ardvule promontory (Parker Pearson

Figure 1.9 The flat-topped sand dune immediately east of the excavation site in 2003, viewed from the west; the post-1991 sand quarry (centre left) was trial-trenched in 2003

and Sharples 1999) and on an islet within Upper Loch Bornais (Marshall and Parker Pearson 2012). Settlements of the Later Bronze Age, such as have been found at Cladh Hallan five miles to the south and Machair Mheadhanach at the north end of South Uist, have not been identified in the Cill Donnain area except at Cill Donnain III itself.

Middle Iron Age
Aside from the Cill Donnain III wheelhouse (site 85), settlements of the Middle Iron Age have been identified at Dun Vulan broch (Parker Pearson and Sharples 1999), Bornais site 1 (with occupation dating to the Middle Iron Age, Late Iron Age and Norse period; Sharples 2012b), Bornais site 15, Ormacleit site 9, and, further north, at Staoinebrig sites 30 and 32 (see Figure 17.8 for the Cill Donnain area). Cill Donnain site 85 is almost certainly part of a larger multi-period settlement including sites 83 and 84. Pottery of this date has been found on a site off the machair on the artificial island in Upper Loch Bornais (Marshall and Parker Pearson 2012). This islet might originally have been the site of an Early Iron Age dun or broch.

Late Iron Age
Sherds with the characteristic flaring rims and brushed surfaces of pottery from the Late Iron Age or Pictish period have been found on the machair on over a dozen sites, five of them excavated (see Figure 17.9). The most secure contexts are the excavated sites of Cill Donnain wheelhouse (site 85), Dun Vulan (Parker Pearson and Sharples 1999), Bornais site 1 (Sharples 2012) and, further north,

the wheelhouses of A' Cheardach Mhor (site 117; Young and Richardson 1960) and A' Cheardach Bheag (site 110; Fairhurst 1971). At Dun Vulan this pottery was found inside and outside the broch; in the latter setting it is associated with three radiocarbon dates. At Bornais it was associated with a stone-walled building and associated layers (Sharples 1997; 2012b). At Cill Donnain it is associated with the later phases of the wheelhouse (Zvelebil 1989; 1990; see Chapters 6–8).

The Norse period
Settlement mounds with Viking Age pottery or other finds have been identified in the Cill Donnain environs at Bornais (sites 1, 2, 3, 14, 28 and 40) and Cill Donnain (sites 83 and 84; see Figure 17.10). Sites 83 and 84 are adjacent to the Cill Donnain wheelhouse; site 83 is a collection of building stone and midden material just 50m south of the wheelhouse. It includes the surviving long wall of a longhouse and is probably a later phase of the same large settlement (now buried under the large dune) of which the excavated wheelhouse was an outlier. A single sherd of grass-tempered pottery found on Cill Donnain site 27 is now thought to date to the Late Bronze Age or Early Iron Age rather than being a fragment of Norse-period platter ware (Sharples 2012a).

The Late Medieval period
Medieval settlement occupation has been identified on the promontory in Loch Chill Donnain where the ancient church of Cille Donnain is located (site 82; Fleming 2012; Fleming and Woolf 1992; Parker Pearson 2012a; see Figure 17.11). Excavated finds from the Cille Donnain church

site include local and imported pottery indicative of domestic activity. However, it is not clear whether that material was transported from an otherwise unknown settlement to increase the soil depth of the church 'platform' or was deposited from adjacent dwellings on the peninsula. It is likely that the Cill Donnain settlement shifted from the machair to the peaty 'blacklands' on the other side of the loch around the fourteenth century.

The post-Medieval period
Pont's map of *c.*1595 records the location of Cill Donnain as 'Kildonn[ien]', north of Gearraidh Bhailteas and south of Bornais. On his map it is located on the southeast shore of Chill Donnain loch and thus off the machair. This may reference the site of Cille Donnain church and its immediate environs. On Blaue's map of 1654, Cill Donnain is recorded as 'Kildonnen' and is marked as being further to the east of the loch (see Parker Pearson 2012c; Raven 2012).

Conclusion

In summary, the Cill Donnain landscape is rich in archaeological sites of all periods from the Beaker period to the post-Medieval period, spanning some 4000 years. Not only that but the two periods represented by the excavated remains at Cill Donnain III – the Earlier–Middle Bronze Age and the Middle–Late Iron Age – are well-represented by known sites in its close vicinity, recorded not only by recent survey but also by excavation of many of them in recent years. Thus Zvelebil's Cill Donnain III excavation can be placed in a local archaeological and landscape context that is exceptional for Scotland as well as for the Outer Hebrides; comparisons can be made with nearby settlements occupied at the same time to understand material, social and economic patterns and differences among the local Iron Age population. These aspects are considered further in Chapter 17.

Chapter 2 The excavations

Marek Zvelebil and Mike Parker Pearson

Introduction

The Cill Donnain (Kildonan) III site appeared as a small discrete midden, sited within a much narrower, but fairly continuous cultural 'surface'. Both the midden and the surface were subsequently buried by sand in the process of dune formation. By 1987 the site was exposed to wind erosion and the dunes were deflating rapidly. The site was also used as a quarry for midden soil to spread on the local fields and as a dump for abandoned vehicles, dead sheep and cattle, and other refuse. As a result of these activities, the continued existence of the midden was under threat and rescue excavations of the site began in 1989, followed by two more field seasons in 1990 and 1991: the total area excavated was about 50m × 40m, but the immediate threat was to an area 20m × 20m.

The 1989 excavations

In June 1989, a three-week rescue excavation took place at the exposed midden as part of fieldwork carried out by SEARCH (Sheffield Environmental and Archaeological Research Campaign in the Hebrides) in the area. The objectives of the excavation were:

1. to clarify the existence or absence of structural remains embedded within the midden;
2. to retrieve evidence of the food resources used by those who created the midden, in order to understand the local economy and intensity of use of the environment;
3. to assess the evidence for contact/exchange/social interaction with other communities;
4. to collect and analyse samples of dog-whelks in order to monitor changes in the nature of the coastal environment, particularly wave action and the degree of storminess.

The excavation trenches and the one-metre grid

During the three weeks of excavation (11th–30th June 1989) an area of approximately 150 sq m was opened around the eroding edge of the midden. This was divided into:

- the main area of excavation, of 100 sq m, located in the central part of the midden, and
- the southern trench, of about 50 sq m, which opened southwards from the southern edge of the eroded area (Figures 2.1–2.2).

In both the central and southern excavation areas, a one-metre grid was laid out (Figures 2.3–2.4), which served as the basic reference system for the recording of finds, features and deposits (see Figure 2.15 for the grid square numbers covering the area excavated during the 1989 season: the numbering for that year runs from 0 to 99 in the main trench and 50 to 144 in the southern trench).

Context numbering and stratigraphy

Even though the excavation was carried out on a rescue basis, and was originally designed to be completed during the three weeks of the 1989 excavation season, every effort was made to separate each class of data by context and by square. However, Cill Donnain III had suffered considerable erosion, both natural and anthropogenic. In the end, some locations were so disturbed that only very proximate spatial assignations were possible; other contexts contained very few finds and were so similar in nature one to another that assignation of finds to a context group rather than to individual contexts seemed more practical. A decision was made in 1989 to assign context numbers by *type* of deposit and not by unique stratigraphic position; thus context 7/1989, for example, was used to describe many small deposits of windblown sand, regardless of where such deposits occurred spatially or stratigraphically. This must be borne in mind by

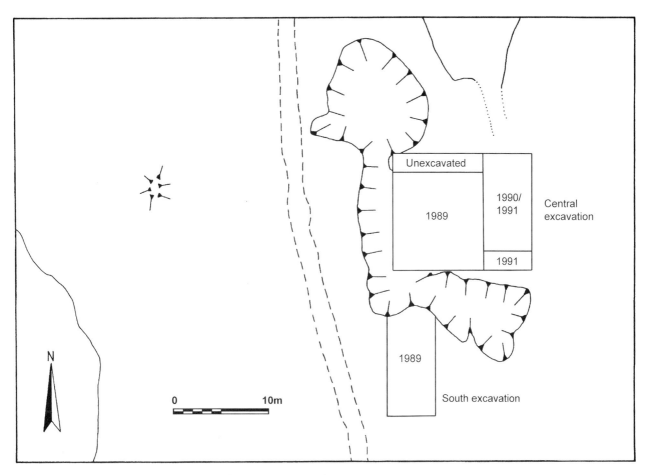

Figure 2.1 Plan of the trenches excavated in 1989, 1990 and 1991

Figure 2.2 The excavation trenches in 1989, viewed as a composite photograph from the west

the reader throughout this monograph: contexts excavated in 1989 do not have unique numbers and the reader should also be aware that some context numbers re-occur in several different phases (see Appendix for the full list of context numbers, with phasing).

Additionally, the reader should note that context numbers used in the 1990 excavations do not match those of 1989; the simple numbering system of 1989 (1, 2, 3, n…) was re-used at the start of the second season of excavation, creating duplicate context numbers, with no concordance to allow identification of, or comparison between, contexts excavated in different years. The site archive is sufficiently detailed to have permitted adequate unravelling of the problem thus created. The user

of this report must, however, work with context numbers that apply to more than one context: MPP has throughout made every attempt to clarify which context is being referred to.

Methods and results

In the central excavation area, the grid was laid out over an area of 10m × 10m, encompassing a quarried area in the west of the grid, where the uppermost deposit consisted of sand and eroding sandy soil containing shell and bone; the steep, almost vertical profile of the sinuous quarry edge revealed a deep stratigraphic sequence. Work began with the cleaning of the profile to reveal:

Figure 2.3 The one-metre grid, initially laid out with string prior to excavation in 1989, viewed from the east

Figure 2.4 The exposed sand face within the quarry prior to excavation, with string grid in place, viewed from the west

Figure 2.5 Marek Zvelebil at Cill Donnain III in 1989; the midden layer is behind his head

1. The top layer of soil (context 1/1989), developing on a layer of windblown sand (context 0/1989) only a few centimetres deep and very poor in organic content.
2. A rich organic layer below the topsoil, containing large numbers of animal bones, carbonized grain, pottery and some artefacts. Episodes of burning and a large circular stone feature were associated with this upper cultural layer, which during excavation was typologically dated to the Iron Age (context 1/1989=5/1990). This is the main midden layer (Figure 2.5).
3. The stone uprights of a circular structure (context 10/1989=168/1991 and 169/1991) and a hearth buried under the main midden layer.
4. A layer of windblown sand under the upper cultural layer, reaching a depth of 0.40m–0.50m and containing few finds (context 2/1989=30/1990).
5. A second organic layer underlying the windblown sand and reaching a depth of 0.60m–0.80m. Large boulders and a small circular feature, probably a hearth, were sited on the top of this layer, at the juncture of the windblown sand and the organic deposit (context 3/1989=31/1990 and 59/1990).

Subsequently, deposits were excavated in 1m-square units away from the steep quarry edge to its north, south and east. In all, 15 types of deposit (broadly equating to 15 different contexts) were recognized in the course of the 1989 excavation.

In the southern trench, the general stratigraphy was similar to that of the central trench, although its sequence was complicated by episodes of slope-wash, slippage or other forms of downslope transport of cultural materials and mixing of cultural deposits; such movement had also occurred in the southern portion of the central trench and in the eroded area between the two trenches. By excavating southwards, the boundary of the midden was established, extending roughly parallel with the southern edge of the eroded area, about 5m from its eroding sand face.

Finds consisted mainly of bones of domesticated and wild animals, some of which were worked, shells of marine molluscs, carbonized grains of cereals, coarse Iron Age pottery fragments and a few metal items, of which the best preserved was a bronze clover-headed pin. Both shells and artefacts were collected and recorded, in the main, by context and by square location (see above and Figure 2.15 for more information on the grid squares). In three instances, artefacts collected from strategically placed one-metre squares were point-provenanced as a form of stratigraphic and contextual control.

In addition to artefacts, bulk samples were taken from each context for the purposes of soil analyses, shell content analyses, pollen analyses, phytolith analysis, beetle analyses and carbonized plant analyses. Flotation of these environmental samples and the analysis of samples for marine mollusca took place while the excavation was in progress. Although it was soon evident that pollen and beetle remains had not survived in the dry, calcareous machair sand, analyses of carbonized plant remains (see Chapter 14) and marine mollusca (see Chapter 15) were successful. Sediments were analysed by means of geomorphology, soil micromorphology and optically stimulated luminescence dating (Schwenninger 1996) and for plant phytoliths (not reported on in this monograph).

It was clear from the first excavation season that the Cill Donnain midden contained more extensive archaeological deposits than had been anticipated from the limited surface survey results. The top cultural layer was extremely rich in finds and dietary remains. Beneath it, the circular structure, identified as an Iron Age roundhouse, was only partially excavated in 1989, and most of the structure remained buried until 1990 under unexcavated deposits to the east of the main 1989 excavation area. The lower cultural layers, under the windblown sand on which the circular house sat, also required investigation.

Given the richness and the complexity of the site, three weeks of rescue excavation with a team of students for whom this was a training excavation (Figure 2.6) was too short a period of time to gain full understanding of the site. Accordingly the site was backfilled at the end of the 1989 season and further excavation took place in 1990.

Figure 2.6 The student team in 1989: Mark Plucenniek sits left front next to Gill Holloway, and those at the back (left to right) include Eddie Moth, Adrian Chadwick, Alwen Pearson, Barbara Brayshay, Karen Miller, Jacqui Mulville, Sylvia Ross, Jo Hambly and Saleem ul Haq

The 1990 excavations

The second excavation season ran from 12th–30th June 1990. A trench measuring 10m × 5m metres was opened adjacent to the eastern limit of the 1989 excavation (Figure 2.1). The sparse grass vegetation was de-turfed with shovels, exposing context 0, a thin layer of windblown dune sand up to 150mm thick below the vegetation mat, which was disturbed by roots and modern surface activity: surface finds from the whole area were bagged prior to excavation. These included modern finds such as water-work glass, plastic, *etc.*, mixed with unstratified prehistoric finds of shell, animal bone and pot fragments.

In and around the stone structure whose western area had been uncovered in 1989 (Figure 2.7), cultural layers were removed down to the underlying sterile deposit of windblown sand, exposing in full the remains of the wheelhouse (Figure 2.8).

The 1990 excavation area, therefore, covered the eastern portion of the circular structure of stone uprights, first seen in 1989 and then identified tentatively as an Iron Age roundhouse. The 1990 excavation area could be roughly divided into three zones:

• the areas outside the structure (the southwest, southeast, northwest and northeast sections of the excavated area);
• the structure itself;
• the area inside the structure.

In addition to the wheelhouse itself, about 40 different types of deposit, forming a part of the upper cultural layer, were recorded. Unfortunately, as described above, a new sequence of context numbers was used in 1990, with no reference to the list of numbers used in 1989; as a result, some contexts were re-numbered and some context numbers were duplicated, resulting in major difficulties when unravelling the site stratigraphy and the site archive during post-excavation.

Spatially, these deposits can be grouped into three types: those within the structure, those outside it, and those covering homogeneously the entire area. In general, depositional contexts inside and outside the structure were described separately, with the exception of the broad continuous deposits that covered the entire area: *e.g.* context 0, context 1, context 5, and context 30. Chronologically, the deposits either pre-dated the wheelhouse, or were contemporary with it, or were deposited after its abandonment.

In addition to the circular wall of the wheelhouse, the base of a wall cutting across its interior from the west was also exposed, suggesting that the house had at least one internal division. No such dividing wall was found in the eastern section of the house. A large number of stones, particularly in the western part of the structure, no doubt resulted from debris deposited during the house's abandonment; these made it difficult

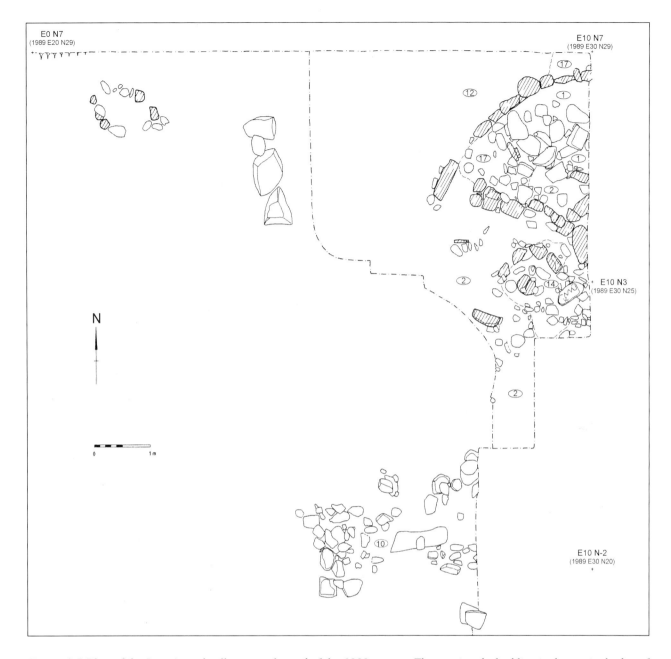

Figure 2.7 Plan of the Iron Age wheelhouse at the end of the 1989 season. The curving dashed line is the vertical edge of the eroding sand quarry (see Figure 2.3)

to reconstruct the original structure and its later additions.

Most of the midden, and the wheelhouse layers beneath it, were excavated in 1989, leading to the conclusion that a cultural surface, earlier than the structure and containing domestic debris, existed on the site (see point 5, above). In 1990, therefore, a 1m × 1m test pit was opened in the northwest part of the site, to sample the depth and content of this cultural layer beneath the sterile windblown sand deposit. This lower cultural layer lay about 0.50m beneath the floor of the wheelhouse, and it contained animal bones and Bronze Age pottery. This lower organic layer was also associated with several large boulders and a hearth; it extended over most of the site, raising the possibility of the existence of other buried structural remains.

Even with a large team of students (Figure 2.9), it was not possible to complete the excavation. The trench was backfilled for a second time (Figure 2.10), with the intention of returning in 1991.

Recording methods and the one-metre grid: linking the 1989 and 1990 excavation records

In 1990, the main excavation area extended east of the 1989 excavation into the dune face. The east-to-west-running, southern edge of the 1989 excavation was located and adopted as the east–west baseline of the 1990 excavation. A 10m × 5m grid was laid two metres *north* of this line: the excavated area in 1990 therefore extended 2m north of the limit of the 1989 excavation. Grid

Figure 2.8 Plan of the Iron Age wheelhouse at the end of the 1990 season

squares were numbered by their southwest co-ordinates, with numbering starting at 100; *i.e.* square 100 was located in the southwest corner of the 1990 gridded area, but note that it is *not* immediately adjacent to the first grid row of 1989 (see Figure 2.15).

The 1990 gridded area's co-ordinates, relative to the new baseline (*i.e.* two metres north of the southern edge of the 1989 trench), were: southwest: E10/N0, southeast: E15/N0, northwest: E10/N10; northeast: E15/N10. During the writing of this report the 1989 excavation records have been adapted to this grid established in 1990. Some square numbers are duplicated, since they occur in both the 1989 southern trench and in the 1990 trench. A large boulder to the south of the 1989 excavation area was chosen as the TBM in 1990 and marked with spray paint.

The 1991 excavations

When the excavation finished in 1990 it was clear that MZ was dealing with a wheelhouse structure that had undergone several phases of reconstruction. During the final excavation season in 1991 (Figure 2.11), the overlying debris and displaced stone rubble were removed and successive phases of occupation were examined (Figure 2.12).

The aims of the 1991 season were:

1. to investigate the deposit underlying the stone foundations of the wheelhouse, in order to elucidate the relationship of this earlier occupational episode to the wheelhouse itself;
2. to complete the excavation of the lower cultural layers that were now known to represent an earlier

Figure 2.9 Digging the wheelhouse in 1990, viewed from the southeast; in the photo (from left to right, back to front) are Paul Rainbird, Mark Plucenniek, Crispin Flower, Liz Elford, Alyson Evans, Alan Parry, Clare Davidson, Cheryl Gansecki, Beth McMartin and Naomi Korn

2.10   Backfilling of the excavations in 1990 at Cill Donnain, viewed from the north

occupational episode that might also contain remains of structures.

The excavations lasted from 9th–30th June 1991. The 1990 excavation trench, measuring 10m × 5m, was re-opened and an additional 2m × 5m trench was added to the 1990 eastern excavation area along its southern edge (see Figure 2.1).

In order to reach the lower cultural layer, a further trench 3m × 5m was opened in the northwest part of the site (the northwest trench, which lay within the area of the old 1989 trench; see Figure 3.1). After the removal of the wheelhouse structure, this trench was expanded eastwards by an additional three metres. In all, therefore, the northwest trench, reaching the lower cultural layer, covered 24 sq m.

The stratigraphic sequence

The excavations in and around the wheelhouse enable us to identify nine broad phases of activity at Cill Donnain III:

Figure 2.11 The student team in 1991: Marek stands on the left, seated behind him are (from left to right) Jacqui Mulville, Helen Smith and Mark Collard. From the left at the back are Howard Benge, Steve Webster, Claire Cunnington (née Coleman), Anna Badcock, Tim Insoll, Dave Giles, Guy Holman and Paul Gething

1. Features and deposits associated with the lower cultural layer and containing earlier Bronze Age pottery. The excavation of this layer revealed three layers of dark brown, organic cultural deposits, without any discrete features except a large circular pit (see Chapters 3 and 4). These deposits contained pottery fragments, animal bone and a few artefacts. Artefacts include flint flakes, thumbnail scrapers and a bipolar flint core. Pottery fragments include Cordoned Urn sherds of Early–Middle Bronze Age date (*c.*1600–1500 cal BC, based on the Cladh Hallan pottery sequence and the Irish dates for such pottery in settlement contexts; see Chapter 3).
2. Deposits associated with Late Bronze Age artefacts including weathered fragments of ceramic moulds for casting metalwork (*c.*800–750 cal BC; see Chapter 4).
3. Iron Age features and deposits underlying the main circular structure of the wheelhouse; the stone uprights of the circular house wall in the western section of the house are set into these Middle Iron Age deposits dating to cal AD 70–240 (see Chapter 5).
4. Construction of the aisled wheelhouse itself, consisting of upright stones forming its inner wall face and doorway, together with pier bases and internal cut features (see Chapter 6). This can be modelled as cal AD 205–310 (at 68% probability).
5. Occupation of the wheelhouse, consisting of a hearth

and a floor (see Chapter 6). In 1992, a radiocarbon date on carbonized grain from the hearth (177) produced a determination of cal AD 210–560 at 95.4% probability (OxA-3356; 1670±75 BP; Hedges *et al.* 1992: 338). More dates have since been obtained from this phase of the house and its end can now be modelled more precisely to *c.*cal AD 495–540 (at 68% probability).
6. Later changes made to the wheelhouse included modification of the hearth and construction of a wall extending from one of the pier bases towards the centre of the house (after *c.*AD cal 495–540; see Chapter 7).
7. Abandonment of the wheelhouse (see Chapter 7).
8. After abandonment of the wheelhouse, a smaller round structure was built within the circular house foundations. The structure consisted of stones set on their edge over the pier bases, making use of the original outside wall of the house and of the sub-dividing wall built during the previous modification (see Chapter 7).
9. Finally, a Late Iron Age midden layer covered the whole structure and this part of the settlement area (see Chapter 8). Ploughmarks were found on part of this surface. Among the metal artefacts, a plate-headed knee brooch, dated to *c.*AD 250–400, and a penannular brooch were found in this layer. In 1992, carbonized grain from layer 103 (broadly contemporary with the midden) provided a radiocarbon date for this phase of activity of cal AD 720–1030 at

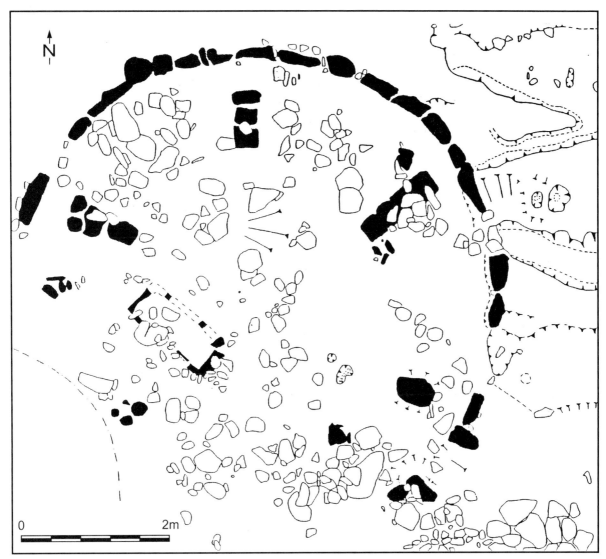

Figure 2.12 Plan of the Iron Age wheelhouse at the end of the 1991 season

95.4% probability (OxA-3353; 1115±70 BP). However, this grain may be intrusive; further dates from the midden have been obtained in recent years and these place the end of activity around cal AD 580–665 (at 68% probability).

The 1992 reconstruction project

With the close of the 1991 season, the original objective of investigating the eroding cultural remains at Cill Donnain by rescue excavation had been met. The site was backfilled and its surface stabilized by removing eroding edges and restoring uniformity to the surface of the slope. Further stabilization, in the form of natural re-seeding of the dune surface with vegetation, has taken place in subsequent years.

During two weeks in June 1992 MZ supervised the removal of the wheelhouse's wall stones from the site; with the help of the late Neil Macmillan of Milton House (Gearraidh Bhailteas), the stones were taken to Taigh-tasgaidh Chill Donnain. Here, within the grounds

of the museum, the wall stones were set within a concrete base by Robert Tye, where they can be seen today (Figure 2.13). Care was taken to replicate the correct positions of the stones and the axis of the building.

The 2003 evaluation of the Cordoned Urn settlement

In July 2003, Mike Parker Pearson and Kate MacDonald recorded damage to archaeological deposits at Cill Donnain, caused by a small sand quarry located immediately northwest of the former site of the wheelhouse (Figure 2.14). The quarry had cut through Early Bronze Age layers to the sterile sand below and revealed the site's stratigraphic sequence in its exposed sides.

Three small excavation trenches (Quarry Trenches 1–3) were cut against the quarry sides by MPP and KM, who also carried out a small programming of coring on the Cill Donnain site, within and beyond the footprint of the 1989–1991 excavations. This employed a 2½" hand-operated soil auger on a 5m grid across the surface of the

Figure 2.13 Re-siting the stones of the wheelhouse in the grounds of Taigh-tasgaidh Chill Donnain in 1992, viewed from the south, with the stones of the doorway at the front right of the picture

Figure 2.14 The post-1991 sand quarry at Cill Donnain in 2003, viewed from the southwest; Quarry Trenches 1, 2 and 3 can be seen within it from right to left

site and the results revealed the brown soil layers of a buried Cordoned Urn-period settlement mound (Parker Pearson 2003; Parker Pearson and Seddon 2004). This mound is only visible on the surface on its east side, where it has been damaged by recent quarrying. Otherwise, it is buried beneath a thin layer of clean sand that separates it from Middle Iron Age levels that were recorded by MZ's team in 1989–91 (this clean sand layer was recorded as context 135 in 1991).

Post-excavation analysis of records and finds from the 1989–1991 excavations

During the five to ten years after the excavations, a number of specialist analyses and reports were carried out on the mammal bones from the 1989 and 1991 seasons, the carbonized plant remains from the 1989 and 1991 seasons, the marine mollusca, the metal artefacts and iron slag, and the pottery. No phasing information on the site's excavated contexts was available, so these preliminary reports could not be finalized. Nor was there any detailed report prepared on the excavations themselves, other than the outline given above in this chapter, although a good number of illustrations were prepared by Eddie Moth.

Between 1991 and 2001 MZ made several attempts at writing a full account of the excavations, but could not bring it to completion. Although he had help from Rob Dinnis, then a student in Sheffield, who transcribed descriptions of each context, and from Jenny Moore, who organized all the specialist contributions so far into an edited whole, it became clear to MZ and others that he would not be able to complete the writing-up of the site into a publishable monograph.

As described above, certain problems within the excavation records needed to be unravelled. Context numbers used in 1989 were re-used in 1990 for entirely different contexts; there is no relationship whatsoever between, for example, context 12 of 1989 and context 12 of 1990. With no concordance to allow comparison and identification of contexts excavated in the two seasons of work (to show, for example, that context 10 in 1989 was the same as context 169 in 1991), it has been a time-consuming task to make sense of the site archive. Furthermore, as noted above, context numbers were assigned in 1989 by *type* of deposit and not by unique stratigraphic position; thus context 12/1989 was burnt peat ash, regardless of where such deposits occurred spatially or stratigraphically. Even when 12/1989 was sub-divided into 12a–12e, for example, *four* separate locations in the stratigraphic levels and in the plans are all identified as 12e/1989.

Additionally, certain contexts (3/1989 and 4/1989) consisted of composite layers that spanned two or more stratigraphic phases; for example, layer 3/1989 was both part of the floor layer of the wheelhouse *and* the layer beneath the wheelhouse, while layer 4/1989 was the wall core of the wheelhouse, *and* the later accumulation of deposits outside the wheelhouse, *and* the deposits forming after the wheelhouse had been abandoned. The incompatible numbering systems of the 1989 and 1990–1991 seasons have been resolved through careful study of sections and plans, to find concordances. No renumbering of the duplicate context numbers has been attempted, for fear of creating future confusion in the site archive. Instead, contexts excavated and recorded in 1989 are identified as 1/1989, 2/1989, 3/1989 onwards, whereas those from 1990–1991 are contexts 1, 2, 3 onwards (see Appendix for the full context list and phasing).

A second problem was caused by changing the co-ordinates of the site grid between the 1989 and 1990 seasons:

- In 1989, the central trench's southeast corner co-ordinates were E30/N20; this became E10/N-2 in 1990.
- The trench's northeast corner changed from E30/N30 in 1989 to E10/N8 in 1990.
- During work in 2011 to prepare this monograph, the decision was taken to convert these two sets of grid numbers to a single system.
- Because positions of finds were recorded by co-ordinates in 1990 and 1991, but by numbered one-metre squares (numbered 1–99) in 1989, it has proved easiest to adopt the 1990–1991 co-ordinates universally for all seasons.
- This has meant employing some minus numbers for the northings of the south trench and for the southernmost two metres of the central trench (see Figure 2.15 for co-ordinates and square numbers).

Other problems discovered in the site archive include incomplete coverage of the site by plans and sections. In some instances, for example, solitary one-metre squares were planned with no reference to anything outside that particular square. One of the more important sections across the site, along the north edge of the excavation west of the wheelhouse, seems not to have been drawn. Nor was every context marked on a plan and/or section. A small number of features were not given context numbers; these remain unnumbered in this report, being referred to with written descriptions. These last problems are far from unusual in any excavation archive, particularly in records deriving from a student training project, and are fairly easily managed.

A Harris matrix was produced by MZ before his death; although it was incomplete, it has provided the framework from which a site report, divided into different phases, could be produced. Post-excavation work on the archive has also revealed information about the stratigraphy that had not been noticed during excavation; again, such post-excavation discoveries are not unusual. For example:

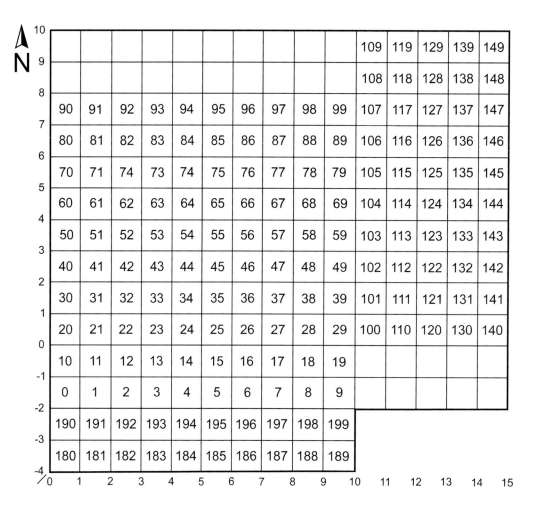

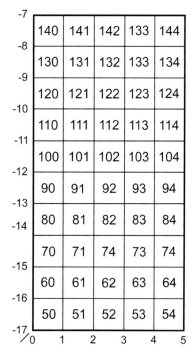

Figure 2.15 The numbered metre squares of the main trench and the southern trench of the 1989–1991 excavations; the co-ordinates are those of the 1990–91 seasons

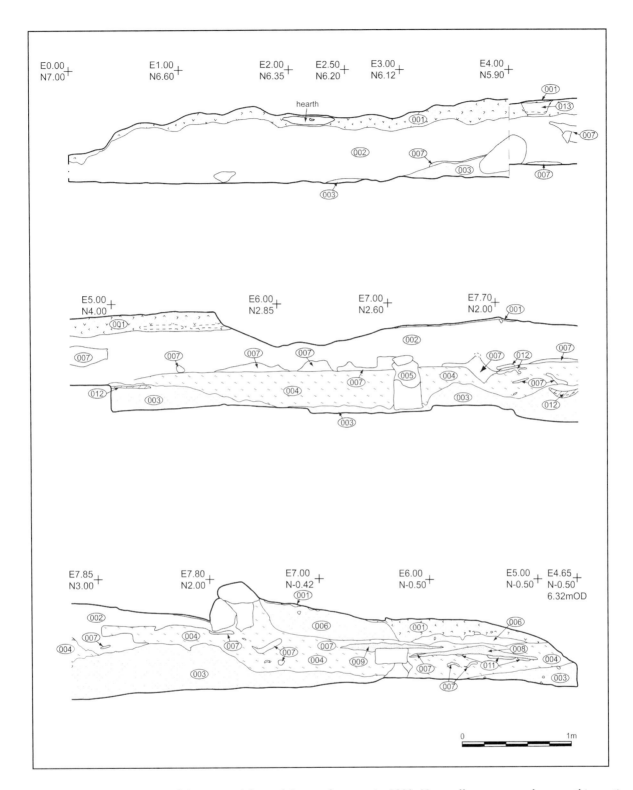

Figure 2.16 The long section of the exposed face of the sand quarry in 1989. Note: all context numbers on this section belong to the 1989 sequence: 1/1989–17/1989

- What were thought to be 'floor' layers extending beyond the interior of the wheelhouse, under its wall and beyond, were not recognized during excavation as being earlier than true floor layers within the house.
- The wheelhouse wall consisted not simply of an inner stone wall face (as identified during excavation) but also of a 2m-thick wall core of sand and an outer stone

wall face. Although this is evident in the long section of the exposed dune face, drawn in 1989 (Figures 2.16–2.18), it was not recognized until 2011 when MPP's writing of the structure report began. Twenty years ago, no-one in the SEARCH team had the knowledge to identify such features but identification on the drawn section of this ancient method of building was

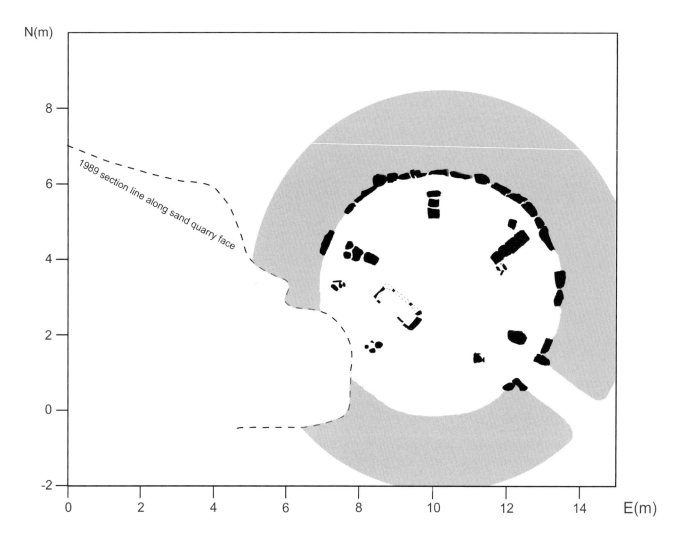

Figure 2.17 Location of the 1989 long section in relation to the position of the wheelhouse. The curving dashed line shows the section line along the quarry face. It cut the southwest sector of the wheelhouse

made easy by the many subsequent years of experience on the adjacent sites of Cladh Hallan, Bornais and Cille Pheadair.

Writing-up excavations from long ago is always difficult, especially after the excavator's death; there are always small details that might have been refined or reinterpreted were he or she still alive. Nonetheless, it is also a process of 'excavation' in which discoveries are made and unforeseen sequences revealed. It is a credit to MZ that he left his records and archive in good order, so that they could be interrogated with relative ease. It has, however, been a rather time-consuming task to make sense of the somewhat ill-judged recording system used on site, especially given that the site itself is relatively small. To be frank, I have some regrets about having taken on this task of bringing Cill Donnain to publication, as the time it has taken to unravel the stratigraphy, and edit the older specialist reports to match the new phasing, has delayed post-excavation work on other, better-excavated and more important South Uist sites. A small grant from Historic Scotland paid for some of my

time, for additional illustrations, and for the essential final report on the animal bone; I am, as always, very grateful to Rod McCullagh for his support at all times, and to Karen Godden for her months of unpaid labour revising the various manuscripts.

Student reminiscences

Around 45 archaeology students from Sheffield University took part in the Cill Donnain III excavations as part of their summer fieldwork. A good proportion became professional archaeologists in later life. MZ would have been the first to acknowledge that the excavation was not perfect – this was the first of Sheffield's forays into excavation on the machair, beyond his (or any other staff member's) previous field experience – and yet the opportunity to work in the Western Isles proved to be a formative experience for many of the students.

In 1989 and 1990 MZ's supervisor was Mark Pluciennick; postgraduate students Barbara Brayshay, Jacqui Mulville, Jean-Luc Schwenninger and Helen Smith provided environmental archaeological expertise

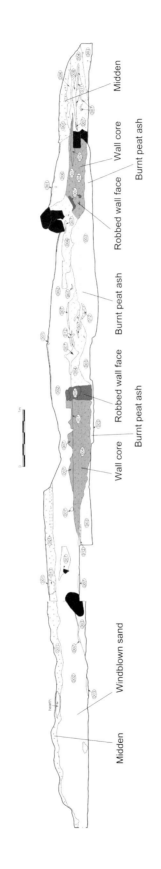

Figure 2.18 Interpretation of the long section, showing the pre-wheelhouse levelling layer; the wheelhouse's wall core, robbed inner wall face and internal floor; all covered by windblown sand and midden. Note: all context numbers on this section belong to the 1989 sequence: 1/1989–17/1989

throughout. I have not been able to find a full list of the Sheffield undergraduates who went to South Uist in 1989. For the 1990 season, the Sheffield University undergraduate students who dug at Cill Donnain were drawn from Jon Bedford, Claire Davidson, Liz Elford, Alyson Evans, Crispin Flower, Danja Foss, Kathryn Fradkin, Cheryl Gansecki, Liz Harwood, Dan Johnson, Naomi Korn, Joan Lightning, Guy Liversidge, Liz MacKay, Beth McMartin, Jane Morris, Alan Parry, Neal Price, Paul Rainbird, Miranda Richardson, Alistair Tait and Cynthia van Gilder. The 1991 team included Jacqui Mulville, Jean-Luc Schwenninger and Helen Smith again, with volunteer Dave Giles and undergraduates Tim Insoll, Steve Webster, Mark Collard, Howard Benge, Steve Webster, Claire Coleman, Anna Badcock, Guy Holman and Paul Gething.

While working on the site archive, I contacted several archaeologists who dug at Cill Donnain as students, nearly 25 years ago now, to pick their brains for any useful information they remember about the site. To complete the picture of what happened at Cill Donnain, I include here two brief accounts of the excavation, and the SEARCH project in general:

Mark Pluciennik, then a postgraduate student at Sheffield and later a lecturer in archaeology at Leicester University, remembers working as a site supervisor at Cill Donnain:

'Marek chose me because he knew me as a (rather theoretical!) PhD student rather than for any knowledge or experience of excavating Iron Age structures, and I didn't know enough then to say 'no'! Marek insisted that the methodology should be a combination of American-style and Danish-style techniques of excavating shell middens; as a result it was dug in spits and squares.[1] He also wanted to three-dimensionally plot and record slope angles for every single find (including shells). We managed to persuade him that this wasn't practical; but Chad had to excavate 1m squares like that which took him three weeks or so... Some of the other diggers resisted digging in spits (or even recording in squares). Marek also insisted on pedestalling any stones[2] (and I remember you [MPP and Niall Sharples] helpfully 'accidentally' destroying a large pedestal on a

visit ...)... Meanwhile I was having huge rows with Marek not only over method but also because he insisted on taking the van to go drinking at the Lochboisdale Hotel every day, leaving me with no transport (or communication) at all should there be an emergency. I was not a happy bunny. But the students were all pretty good and highly responsible, and they could see some of the problems and generally rallied around. And some of them were a lot more experienced than me, which helped!'

Tim Insoll, then an undergraduate and now a professor of archaeology at Manchester University, recalls:

'For me the abiding memory of the excavations in South Uist in 1991 is that I came up there on the sleeper train from London, having buried my father, and joined the dig late, so it was all rather a surreal experience.

The archaeology was not particularly exciting, from an Africanist perspective, but the survey led by Andrew Fleming was memorable, striding out across the landscape with an amazing density of monuments that Andrew seemed to find everywhere. Marek's site was not very well run, if I seem to remember correctly; Marek did not seem happy directing the excavation ... I think that some of the comments were harsh though, and he had been given a training excavation he had little interest in.

The camaraderie of the group was particularly good, as a year we got on well, fortunately as we (males and females separately) were sharing dormitory-style accommodation in a village school and village hall. We were allowed extensive use of the project minibuses which meant that for the summer solstice we drove to a high cliff and sat there smoking, most people did then, and drinking. Also we bought immense numbers of crabs and one of the students, who was from the year below but had come along, his name escapes me, had chef experience from the army, he was a mature student, so we cooked these in the school kitchens in their cauldrons.

It was in hindsight a very enjoyable season and, before mobile phones and internet, peaceful. I think now an unrepeatable experience.'

---

[1] In contrast to the large-scale, open-area style of excavation favoured in later SEARCH excavations on South Uist's machair.

[2] A problematic choice, because such pedestalled stones end up isolated from their contexts, and their pedestals interfere with investigation of layers beneath.

Chapter 3 Early–Middle Bronze Age (phase 1): a Cordoned Urn settlement

Mike Parker Pearson with Kate MacDonald

Introduction

Beneath a layer of windblown sand (135) under the Iron Age wheelhouse, there lies a well-preserved sequence of deposits containing Early–Middle Bronze Age pottery. This was initially investigated in 1991 within a trench 5m east–west × 3m north–south, known as the northwest trench (dug within the northern part of the 1989 excavation area). Below layer 153, this trench narrowed to 3m east–west × 2m north–south, leaving 1m-wide steps along its east, west and north sides (Figure 3.1).

In July 2003, MPP and Kate MacDonald recorded the damage to Bronze Age layers caused by a small sand quarry north of the 1991 trench; this quarry had been dug between 1991 and 2003 (see Figure 2.14). We also carried out a soil augering programme, coring at 5m intervals within the footprint of the 1989–1991 excavation as well as to its south, north and west, to establish the extent and character of these Early–Middle Bronze Age deposits.

The extent of the settlement mound – coring in 2003

Twenty-five cores were made on a 5m grid, covering an area of up to 20m east–west by 30m north–south. Four cores from along the southern part of the western edge of the 1989 trench indicated that any Bronze Age layers here had been destroyed by erosion that took place before the 1989–91 excavation. Elsewhere the Early–Middle Bronze Age (EBA–MBA) deposits could be identified beneath the Iron Age levels because they were separated from them by a thick layer of clean, windblown sand (equating to layer 135 in the 1991 excavation). Depths of deposit were measured with a dumpy level as distances below the height of instrument.[1]

The bottom of the EBA–MBA deposits was at 3.95–4.00m OD across most of the site, with the land surface on which they lie falling to 3.68–3.72m OD in the northeast and to 3.65m OD in the southwest. This suggests that the EBA–MBA settlement occupied a low ridge of sand 20m wide, running northwest–southeast (Figure 3.2). Alternatively or additionally, the lowered contours on the northwest end of the mound (where the mound has a stepped appearance) may be due to a sunken-floored area in that part of the site.

The EBA–MBA deposits were deepest within the centre of the mound, at around 4.75m OD, reaching a maximum depth of 4.96m OD some 5m east of the quarry's edge. Most of the cores produced samples of mid-brown to dark brown sand from the upper layers of the EBA–MBA deposits (perhaps equivalent to layer 140=149 in the 1991 trench and layers 4, 13 and 18 in Quarry Trenches 1–3 respectively; see below).

At the base of the sequence, four cores produced thin layers of red or orange peat ash, one of them in the centre of the mound, north of Quarry Trench 1, and the other three on the northeast edge of the mound. Such deposits indicate the presence either of house floors and hearths or of the midden layers produced from such deposits. The former is more likely given the thinness of these red/orange layers and their positions at the base of the sequence.

A sequence of deposits to 3.35m OD was detected by coring 5m north of Quarry Trench 1; beneath a red-brown sand containing a Bronze Age sherd, there was a mid-brown sand that might have been the fill of a pit or similar feature cut into the sterile sand layer beneath. The fortuitous recovery of a sherd from the peat-ash-derived layer above suggests that this lower deposit was sealed by EBA–MBA deposits rather than being the fill of an intrusive pit dating to the Iron Age.

In summary, this Early–Middle Bronze Age settlement mound (Figures 3.2–3.3) contains stratified deposits, surviving to a depth of almost a metre and now known to

---

[1] Designated arbitrarily as 5.00m while we were on the site, but actually at 7.25m OD; the field record has been amended accordingly for publication here.

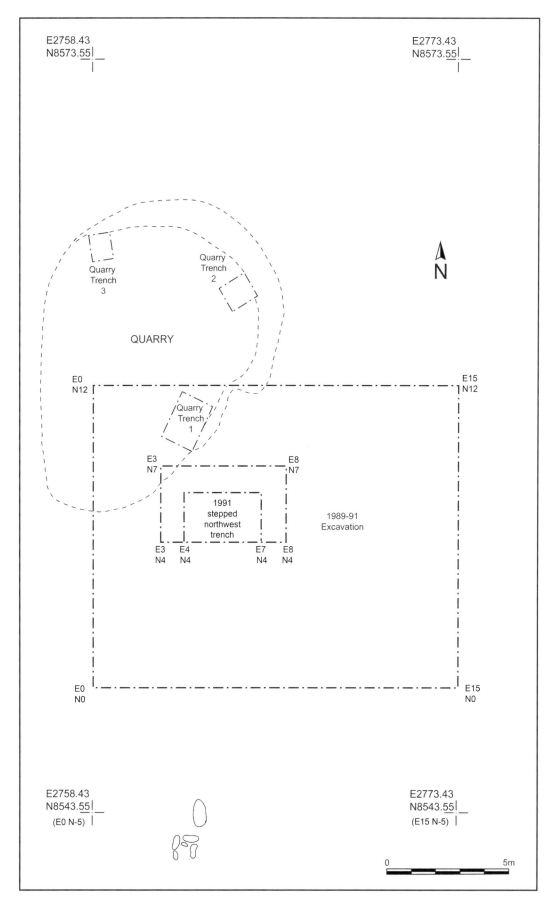

Figure 3.1 Plan of the 1991 northwest trench (showing its stepping-in) in relation to the later sand quarry and the 2003 quarry trenches

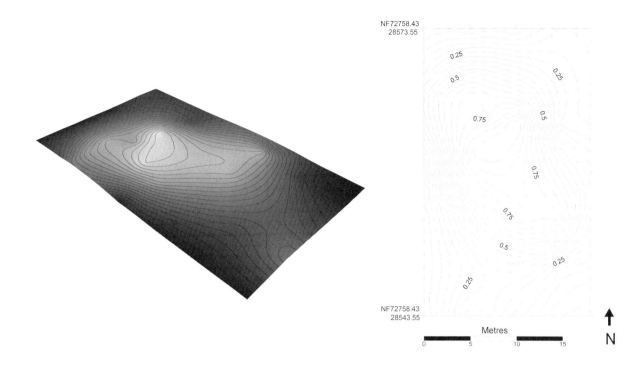

Figure 3.2 Contour plot of the Early–Middle Bronze Age Cordoned Urn-period settlement mound at Cill Donnain

cover an area at least 23m northwest–southeast by 15m northeast–southwest. The deepest layers were encountered within the central spine of this buried mound and the deepest one of these is likely to have been the fill of a cut feature contemporary with the Early–Middle Bronze Age deposits.

As much as 150 cu m of stratified settlement deposits may remain *in situ* within this mound, making it an unusually well-preserved example of a settlement from a period for which such remains are archaeologically under-represented throughout Britain and Europe. The settlement was located on a dune ridge, dropping away 0.40–0.70m on all sides.

The 1991 excavations: the northwest trench

At the base of this trench (see Chapter 2 for location in relation to other trenches), a homogeneous, deep layer of sterile grey/white sand (156) with a depth of at least 1m was encountered (Figures 3.4–3.7). The present water table is in this layer, at 2.93m OD. This sterile sand is likely to have been the top of the aeolian deposit of machair sand that formed in the third millennium BC, before Beaker-period and Early Bronze Age settlements were established on top of it (Hamilton and Sharples 2012; Parker Pearson 2012c; Sharples 2012a).

The first deposit with evidence of human activity was context 157 (Figure 3.8). This thin layer lay on top of the sterile sand (156) and beneath layer 155. It curved westwards from one long side of the trench to the other and was between 0.50m–1m wide. It is reported in the excavation record as being visible in the north section (although

is not shown) as a very thin and irregular/discontinuous band of orange sandy silt that covered the top of 156. In excavating the three squares E4/N5, E5/N5, E6/N5 within the northwest trench, it was identified as an irregular patch containing some flecks of carbonized wood.

Context 153 was a dark grey/brown layer, initially identified in square E5/N6, widening to the east. As digging progressed, contexts 153 and 155 were identified as the same deposit (0.15m thick) but grading in colour from dark grey/brown (153) to dark brown silty sand with flecks of carbonized wood and evidence of burning but no finds (155). Layer 153 is the upper component of 153=155, lying on top of a discontinuous deposit of distinct patches of sterile, grey/white windblown sand (154) interleaved within context 153=155 (Figure 3.5). The finds from context 153=155 (all recorded as coming from context 153) include the body sherds of a pot in many pieces (SF129), found resting on top of layer 157 (Figures 3.8–3.9). Layer 153=155 was broadly level and horizontal, with its surface varying in height from 3.77m OD to 3.90m OD.

Layer 153=155 was covered by grey shell sand (152), around 0.05m thick, the lower boundary of which blended into the underlying layer (153=155). Layer 152 was also discontinuous, disappearing in places (in square E5/N6). Above layer 152 in square E5/N6 lay an organic dark brown silty sand layer (151), containing shell and carbonized wood fragments, that graded to its darkest at the bottom of the deposit. It was covered by a discontinuous layer or lens of sterile, light grey/white sand (150). All finds from contexts 150–152 were recorded as 140, the context that lay above (Figure 3.5).

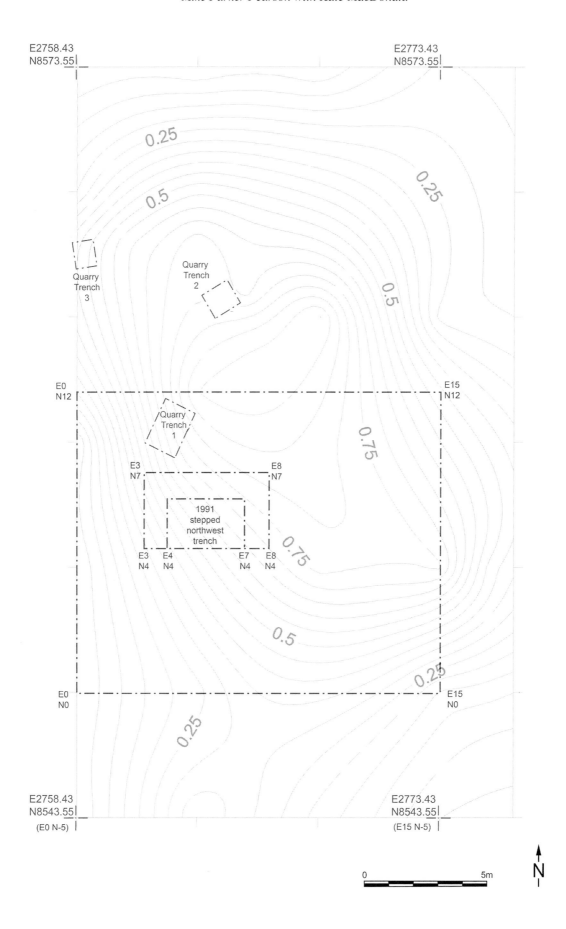

Figure 3.3 Location of the excavation trenches overlaid on the contour plot of the settlement mound

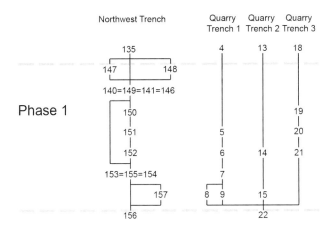

Figure 3.4 Stratigraphic matrix of Early–Middle Bronze Age contexts in the northwest trench and the three quarry trenches

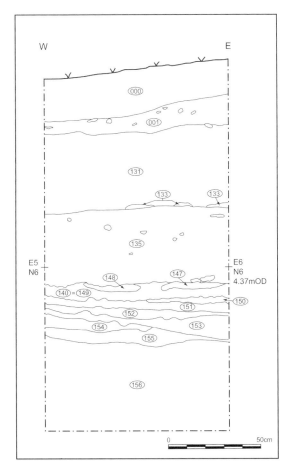

Figure 3.5 Section drawing of part of the north side of the northwest trench

Context 140=149 was a layer of red-brown sandy silt lying beneath layer 135 in square E6/N6, its uneven surface sloping to the west and south (from 4.30m OD to 4.09m OD). Few coarse inclusions were noted but it contained pottery, animal bone, marine shell and quantities of carbonized wood. The layer was far from homogeneous, with patches and variations in colour. It contained dark, burnt areas of little depth (<20–30mm). It had evidence of many bald patches and heavy burning. The deposit

contained very large quantities of black, greasy organic silt, particularly within the upper part of the context. This may have been decayed organic material and peat.

Layer 140=149 appeared to cover and fill in the irregular surface of layer 141, a white windblown shell sand with very few inclusions (no pot or bone), lying under 140 in square E6/N6 but also in patches in the top part of layer 140 (Figure 3.10). These patches appeared identical and varied in depth from 10mm to 100mm but were generally thin (20–50mm). A deposit of grey/white shell sand (146) lay within square E5/N6 at the base of layer 140. Although it appeared to be similar to layer 141 (and may be part of the patchwork of sand layers found in this trench) it is stratigraphically a distinct and separate unit.

Within the top of layer 140=149, there were two discrete patches (147 and 148) interleaved within that larger deposit (Figures 3.5, 3.10). Context 147 was a patch of black silty soil with carbonized wood fragments in square E5/N6 and context 148 was a second black patch that appeared to be no more than a stain.

These layers (from 153=155 to 140=149) contained large sherds of Cordoned Urn pottery, indicating that the basal deposits in the Cill Donnain III cultural sequence are likely to date to *c.* 1600–1500 BC (see below). They form a 0.30m-deep sequence starting at 3.95m OD, and are sealed beneath a 0.40m-deep layer of windblown sand (135; phase 2). Within the northwest trench, this deep sequence (153=155 to 135; Figures 3.4–3.6) was cut through by only one feature, a pit (142; phase 2) dug from the surface of layer 135 and penetrating the top of layer 156 in the east end of the northwest trench (Figure 3.10).

Recording of the sand quarry in 2003

In summer 2003 a borrow-pit for sand extraction (12m north–south by 10m east–west) was noted just 2m north of the northern edge of the 1991 northwest trench. All archaeological deposits within this small quarry had been destroyed but EBA–MBA layers were visible in its sides. Further cleaning and cutting back of its exposed face was carried out at three locations (Quarry Trenches 1–3; Figures 2.14, 3.1, 3.3).

Quarry Trench 1

Quarry Trench 1 measured 2m northeast–southwest × 1.3m northwest–southeast, and was positioned against the southeast face of the quarry, just 1m from the edge of the 1991 northwest trench. Above clean windblown sand (22, equivalent to layer 156 in the 1991 excavation; Figure 3.4) was a 0.10m-thick layer of light brown sand (9). On the surface of layer 9, a stone in the section marked the northern edge of a darker brown sand layer (7), only 0.03m thick, that was covered by equally thin layers of white sand (6) and black sand (5). At 0.12m north of the stone, another thin, dark layer (8) terminated (Figures 3.11–3.12).

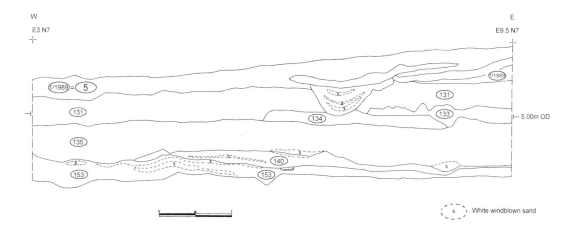

Figure 3.6 Section drawing of the entire north side of the northwest trench

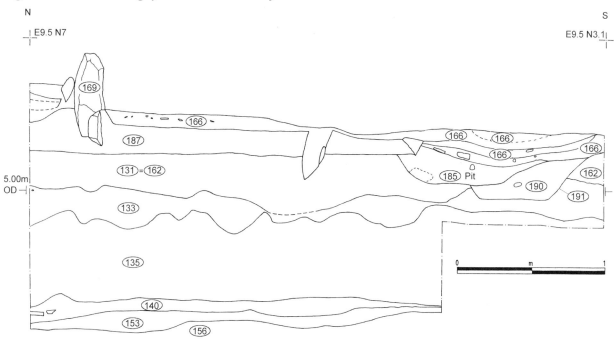

Figure 3.7 Section drawing of the east end of the northwest trench

All these layers were covered by dark brown sand (4), up to 0.30m deep. This was, in turn, covered by a 0.28m-deep layer of clean windblown sand (3). Ploughmarks were visible in the top of this layer. Above layer 3 there was a dark grey layer (2) containing Iron Age pottery, immediately beneath the topsoil (1). Layers 1, 2 and the upper component of 3 were truncated by the 1989–1991 excavation trenches.

Layers 7, 6 and 5 in this small 2003 trench can be tentatively equated with contexts 155, 154 and 153 respectively. It is possible that the stone abutting layer 7 formed the north wall of a building for which layers 5–7 were its floor layers. Layer 4 probably equates with layer 135, and layer 3 with layer 131 (see Figure 4.1). Ploughmarks were recorded in the top of layer 3; similar ploughmarks were also noted in the 1991 trench in the top of 135 (see Chapter 4).

Quarry Trench 2
Quarry Trench 2 was located 4m northeast of Quarry Trench 1 and was 1m square (Figure 3.13). Its 1m-deep east section (Figure 3.11) revealed a sequence similar to that of Quarry Trench 1. The first layer above sterile sand (22) was grey/brown sand (15), covered by mottled white and brown sand (14). This was covered by a layer of dark brown sand (13) up to 0.25m thick. Above it was the layer of windblown sand (12) with ploughmarks in its surface. The uppermost layers were a sequence of four black, light brown, brown and grey Iron Age deposits (all layer 11), covered by topsoil (10). Layer 13 equates with layer 4 in Quarry Trench 1, and layer 12 with layer 3.

Quarry Trench 3
Quarry Trench 3 was located 6m northwest of Quarry Trench 1 and was 1m square (Figure 3.14). Its north section

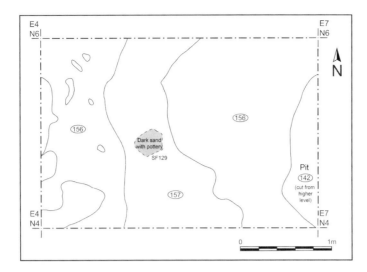

Figure 3.8 Plan of the sterile sand (156) at the base of the northwest trench, cut by layer 157

revealed a sequence 0.60m deep (Figure 3.11). The sterile sand (22) at its base was covered by a mixed layer of white and brown sand (21). Above this was a light brown sand (20) below a cream-coloured sand (19) below dark brown sand (18). Above layer 18 was the windblown layer (17), equivalent to layers 3, 12 and 131 (see above; Figure 4.1) but its brown/yellow colour was not as clean as these. Above it lay the topsoil (16). Layer 18 equates with layers 4 (Quarry Trench 1) and 13 (Quarry Trench 2). Layer 21 appeared to equate with layer 14.

Optically stimulated luminescence (OSL) dating

Jean-Luc Schwenninger

A group of eight samples were taken in 1991 for optically stimulated luminescence (OSL) dating and were analysed at Royal Holloway College, London, in 1995 (Table 3.1; Figure 3.15). Two of the samples came from different depths within the sterile windblown sand (156) beneath the Cordoned Urn occupation layers, one was taken from within these layers (157–140), and one was taken from the windblown sand layer (131=162; see Chapter 5) between them and the Iron Age cultural layers above. In addition, another four samples were taken from different levels within the Iron Age layers.

The dates of the samples from the lowest layers are consistent with estimations of machair formation (Ritchie 1979; Edwards *et al.* 2005).

- The deepest of the samples (numbered as OSL 84, from layer 156) dated to 5940±1840 BP, providing a date of 5785–2105 BC.
- Slightly higher up within the same layer, sample OSL 87 dated to 3145–1385 BC (4260±880 BP).
- The sample (OSL 96) from within the layers of Cordoned Urn occupation (contexts 157–140) provided a

date of 2535–1175 BC (3850±680 BP), consistent with radiocarbon dates elsewhere for Cordoned Urns dating to *c.*1900–1500 cal BC (Sheridan 2003) or *c.*1600–1500 based on the Cladh Hallan sequence (Parker Pearson and Parsons in prep.) and dates for Irish Cordoned Urn settlement pottery (Grogan and Roche 2009; 2010).
- One other early determination from the Cill Donnain III sequence, from the base of the Iron Age layers (OSL 606), provided a date of 2375–1535 BC (3950±420 BP), consistent with this Early–Middle Bronze Age occupation; it may derive from earlier material incorporated into Iron Age levels.

The OSL dates from the Iron Age layers, including the wheelhouse and its covering midden, can be mentioned here.

- A date of AD 25–625 (1670±300 BP) from sample OSL 602 in sand layer 131=162 (phase 3; see Chapter 5) is consistent with finds of Middle Iron Age pottery within it.
- Sample OSL 81 dated to 125 BC–AD 635 (1740±380 BP) – the Middle to Late Iron Age – and OSL 607 to AD 655–1015 (1160±180 BP) – the Late Iron Age or Norse period.
- Sample OSL 98 dated to AD 1195–1475 (660±140 BP) and thus falls outside the sequence, being later than any archaeological evidence for use or habitation at the Cill Donnain site.

Sample no.	Context	Date before 1995	±	Date range
OSL 84	156 lower	5940	1840	5785-2105 BC
OSL 87	156 upper	4260	880	3145-1385 BC
OSL 96	157-140	3850	680	2535-1175 BC
OSL 602	131=162	1670	300	AD 25-625
OSL 606	Iron Age	3950	420	2375-1535 BC
OSL 98	Iron Age	660	140	AD 1195-1475
OSL 81	Iron Age	1740	380	125 BC-AD 635
OSL 607	Iron Age	1160	180	AD 655-1015

Table 3.1 Optically stimulated luminescence (OSL) dates from Cill Donnain III

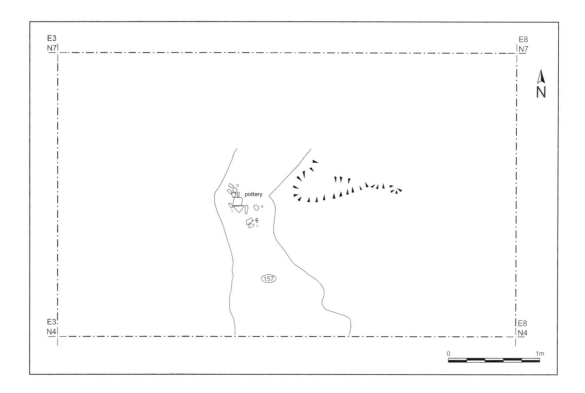

Figure 3.9 Plan of the surface of layer 153, showing the position of pot SF129

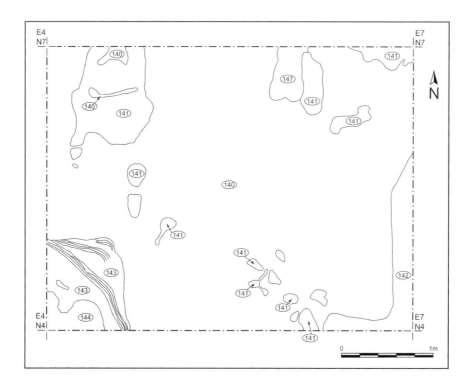

Figure 3.10 Plan of the surface of layer 140=149, showing patches of layer 141, context 147 and pit 142

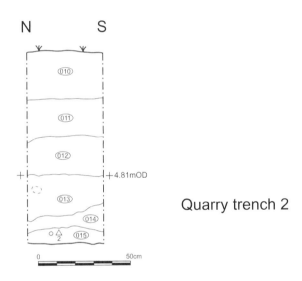

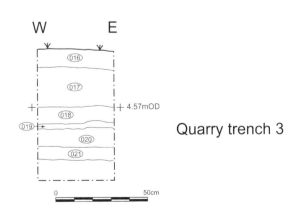

Figure 3.11 Section drawings of Quarry Trenches 1–3

Pottery

Chris Cumberpatch and Mike Parker Pearson

The northwest trench (1991)

A total of 473 sherds (3.9kg) were recovered from the Early–Middle Bronze Age layers within the northwest trench (see tables in Chapter 9). They derive from three fabric groups (groups 1–2: coarse and gritty with abundant quartz; group 4: large angular rock inclusions; and 'other'). Most are of fabric groups 1–2. Of the 12 rim sherds, six are flat-topped, five are unidentifiable and one has been classified as 'sharply everted'. Only two sherds are decorated, one from context 157 with a plain horizontal cordon and one from context 153 with a tool-impressed horizontal cordon.

The fragmentation of sherds was less than for the Iron Age layers above, with an average weight per sherd of 8.3g in contrast to the average sherd weight of 4.4g for sherds from the site overall. This was partly due to the recovery of four sherds from a single vessel (SF129) within context 153 but also reflects the generally lower level of attrition of sherds in these early layers. Within layers 157 and 153, sherds were mostly distributed across the northwest half of the trench (Figures 3.16a–3.16b). Layer 157 appears to have formed a curving boundary, to the southeast of which no sherds were recovered within layer 153. In contrast, sherds from layer 140=149 were distributed throughout the trench, particularly within its centre (Figure 3.16c).

The quarry trenches (2003)

A small quantity of pottery was recovered from Quarry Trenches 2 and 3. The fragments from Quarry Trench 2 were unstratified and consist of four sherds (total weight 19g); one of these is an everted rim of Middle Iron Age date. The unstratified material from Quarry Trench 3 may also be a mixture of Iron Age and Bronze Age sherds (nine sherds; 22g).

Stratified pottery from Quarry Trench 3 consists of a cordon-decorated sherd (13g) from context 19 and a complete base (267g) from context 21. The base's diameter is 85mm.

Bone and stone tools

Mike Parker Pearson

The northwest trench

The only non-ceramic artefacts from the Bronze Age phase were of stone, consisting of a hammerstone from context 140 and two worked stones from context 149 (see Chapter 11).

Figure 3.12 Quarry Trench 1, viewed from the north

Figure 3.13 Quarry Trench 2, viewed from the west   *Figure 3.14 Quarry Trench 3, viewed from the south*

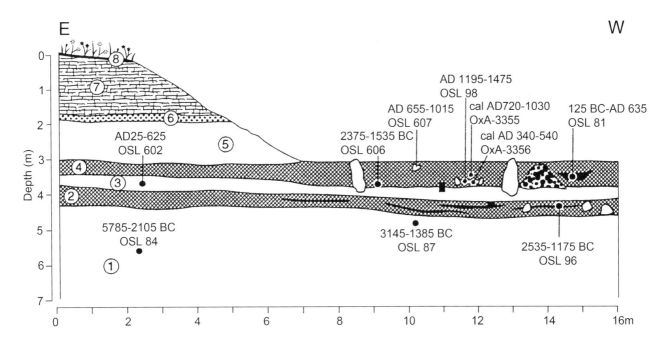

Figure 3.15 Positions of OSL samples within a schematic section through the Cill Donnain III site. Layer 1 is sterile windblown sand at the base of the sequence; layer 2 is the EBA–MBA layer; layer 3 is the windblown sand layer 131=162; and layer 4 is the wheelhouse and midden layer

The quarry trenches

Finds from the quarry trenches were few. The only non-ceramic find from Quarry Trench 2 was a bone point (SF2) from layer 15 (see Chapter 12). Quarry Trench 1 produced a small fragment (SF1) of fine-grained ceramic mould from layer 4, likely to date to the Late Bronze Age (see Chapter 10).

The faunal remains

John Hamshaw-Thomas, Kim Vickers and Mike Parker Pearson

The northwest trench

Only 57 mammal bones were identifiable to species from the Bronze Age layers (see Table 13.5). These included cattle bones and sheep/goat bones from layers 153 and 157 (Early–Middle Bronze Age), and cattle bones, sheep and pig from layer 140, with a single sheep/goat bone from layer 146 (Late Bronze Age). These numbers are too low to record anything other than the presence of the three species.

The quarry trenches

Two fragments of unidentifiable mammal bone were found in context 21 in Quarry Trench 3.

Discussion

A certain amount of information can be gleaned from the investigations of this phase at Cill Donnain III, even though interpretation of the deposits excavated in the northwest trench in 1991 is difficult. Not only were they excavated within a small *sondage*-sized area but there has been a gap of 20 years between excavation and writing-up. In that time, however, excavations of similarly early sequences within the nearby machair sites of Cladh Hallan (Parker Pearson *et al.* 2004; in prep.) and Sligeanach (Sharples 2012a) have provided valuable insights not possible in 1991. The 2003 auger programme at Cill Donnain has also provided a better understanding of the context of the 1991 trench within the Cordoned Urn settlement mound.

The deposits excavated in 1991 lay on the southwest side of a low settlement mound measuring 23m northwest–southeast by 15m northeast–southwest, its contours revealed by coring in 2003. The coring results show that, although these layers were only *c.*0.35m thick within the trench, they were adjacent to organic-rich layers around 0.50m deep on their east and northeast sides, 0.35m deep on their north side, and 0.23m thick on their south side. Thin layers of black and reddened sand at the base of the sequence, similar to contexts 150–157, were detected to the northeast of the 1991 stepped trench (red-brown sand with pottery) and in Quarry Trench 1 (layers 5 and 7).

By comparison with layers at the Late Bronze Age to Early Iron Age settlement of Cladh Hallan, these thin layers of black and reddened soil are best interpreted as the floor of a house, the northern wall of which was detected in

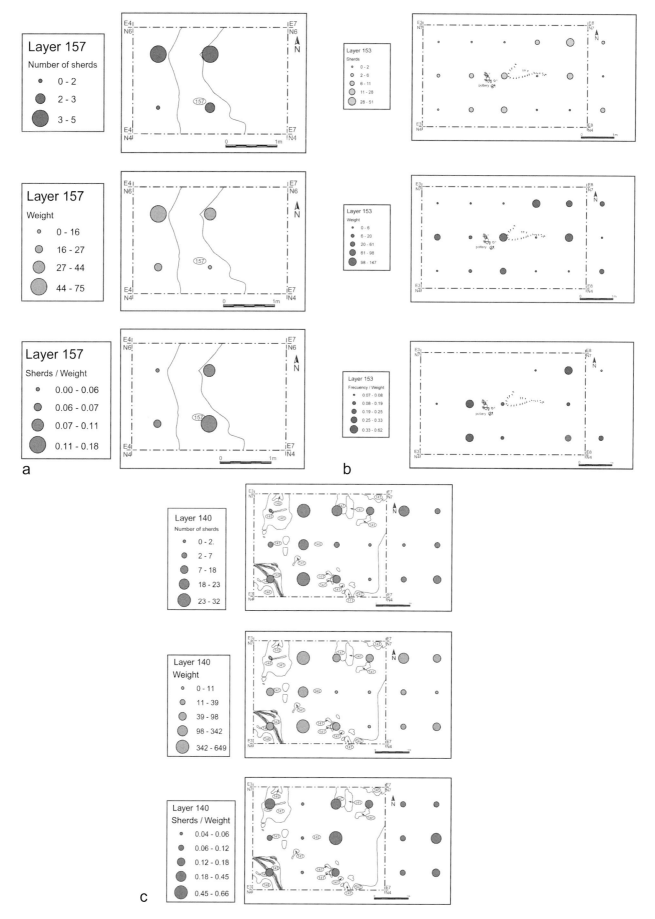

Figure 3.16 Spatial distributions of pottery in: (a) layer 157, (b) layer 153=155, and (c) layer 140=149

Quarry Trench 1 (at the northern limit of layer 7). The large slabs of pottery from the contexts excavated in 1991 also support this interpretation of these layers being part of a house floor. The overall distribution of pottery from layers 153 and 157 also indicates that all sherds were confined to within the curving outer edge of layer 157, whose outer edge was about 0.10m higher than its inner edge. Equally, the surface of the sterile sand below (156) was lower to the east of layer 157, suggesting that this area had been more subject to erosion. This strengthens the possibility that these layers were the remnants of an oval or circular house floor within the east end of the excavation trench. There was, however, no trace of a wall in the 1991 trench.

We may tentatively propose that a structure, presumably a dwelling, stood in this part of the site, in dimension around 4m across. Similar layers were revealed during the 2003 coring along the northeastern edge of the settlement mound and may derive from another building – possibly sunken-floored – in that part of the site.

The mound's northwest–southeast axis is on the same alignment as a Middle Bronze Age U-shaped house (6.20m × 3m; *c.*1670–1320 BC) excavated at Cladh Hallan (Parker Pearson *et al.* 2004: 63-4). This same axis is also shared with a 4.40m-wide oval-shaped structure within Midden 1 at Northton, Harris, thought to date to the same period (Simpson *et al.* 2006: 157-8). However, the Cordoned Urn ceramics indicate that the Cill Donnain mound is likely to contain a sequence of buildings dating to *c.*1900–1500 BC (or possibly *c.*1600–1500 BC on the basis of Irish dates; see below), earlier than the occupation at Cladh Hallan or Northton. As such, it is unique in Britain.

At the time of writing, there are no excavated Cordoned Urn settlements anywhere in Britain, although over 40 are known in Ireland (Grogan and Roche 2009: 129–39; 2010: 41–2). Cordoned Urns are normally recovered from cremation burials and were used as containers for human remains in southern and eastern Scotland, the Isle of Man, Wales and the Peak District, and Ireland (Waddell 1995). Radiocarbon dates for Cordoned Urns range from *c.*1900 to 1400/1300 BC at 1σ values (Sheridan 2003: 207). They were broadly contemporary with Collared Urns (found throughout Britain *c.*2000–1500 BC, but not in western

Scotland) and with the later stages of British Beakers (*c.*2400–1800 BC) and Food Vessels or Vase Urns (*c.*2100–1750 BC, possibly extending to 1750–1500 BC; Sheridan 2003: 203). Grogan and Roche consider that the less formally decorated styles found on domestic sites date to the later part of the Early Bronze Age and throughout the Middle Bronze Age (*c.*1600–1100 BC).

The Cill Donnain settlement mound falls in a chronological gap between the Hebridean Beaker and Food Vessel settlements of Sligeanach (Sharples 2012a), Cill Donnain I (Hamilton and Sharples 2012), Northton (Harris; Simpson *et al.* 2006), Rosinish (Benbecula; Shepherd and Tuckwell 1977) and Ardnave (Islay; Ritchie and Welfare 1983) on the one hand and, on the other, the Middle Bronze Age structures at Cladh Hallan (Parker Pearson *et al.* 2004: 63-4) and Northton (Simpson *et al.* 2006: 157-8). Whilst Cordoned Urn pottery was found at Cladh Hallan, it was associated largely with a settlement destroyed by quarrying (Parker Pearson *et al.* in prep.).

The prehistoric landscape context of this Early–Middle Bronze Age settlement at Cill Donnain is particularly striking: it lies within 50m of a prehistoric standing stone, recently buried under windblown sand, and within a few hundred metres of well-preserved Beaker-period and other Early Bronze Age settlements at Cill Donnain I (Hamilton and Sharples 2012) and Sligeanach (Sharples 2012a). An airborne heat-sensing survey has identified a circular anomaly beneath dunes about 500m to the west, potentially a buried stone circle (Richard Tipping pers. comm.). Further afield, the only other settlement remains with Cordoned Urn pottery are found at Cladh Hallan, almost five miles to the south.

The coring programme also revealed that the depths of Middle Iron Age deposits at Cill Donnain III increase from west to east, indicating that the small wheelhouse excavated in 1988–91 was a peripheral building constructed on the western edge of a much larger Middle Iron Age mound, whose full dimensions are hidden under a large dune. The juxtaposition of the Middle Iron Age wheelhouse directly on top of the Early Bronze Age mound is notable and raises the possibility that the relationship was more than simply fortuitous.

Chapter 4 Late Bronze Age/Early Iron Age occupation (phase 2): eighth–early sixth centuries BC

Mike Parker Pearson

Introduction

The stratigraphic sequence above the Early–Middle Bronze Age layers and beneath the Middle Iron Age wheelhouse can be divided into two parts. The lower contexts, observed only within the northwest trench (measuring 5m northwest–southeast × 3m northeast–southwest), consisted of a deep layer of windblown sand whose surface was cultivated and dug into by a single pit. Above these features lay a sequence of sand layers and discrete organic deposits sealed beneath a largely sterile layer (131=162) of possibly windblown sand (Figure 4.1). Within Quarry Trenches 1–3, layers 4, 13 and 18 probably equate to layer 135 whilst layers 3, 12 and 17 are probably the same as layer 131=162.

Windblown sand

The Early–Middle Bronze Age layers were sealed beneath a thick layer (0.40m deep) of discoloured sand (135; Figures 3.5–3.7), identified as brown sand in 2003 (layers 4, 13 and 18) in Quarry Trenches 1, 2 and 3. It was described in the 1991 excavation records as a compact, fine-grained, red-brown sandy soil made up of general organic material and sand, generally uniform but with isolated spots and patches of more orange sand, containing some shells, pot and bone. It may be that

these finds derived from the disturbed surface of this layer. Flotation of a sample from this deposit yielded no carbonized plant remains (see Chapter 14).

Ploughing

Ploughmarks (and evidence of recent rabbit burrowing disturbance) were noted on top of the sand layer (135) as well as layers 3, 12 and 17 in Quarry Trenches 1 and 2. The ploughmarks mostly ran north-northeast–south-southwest and were unevenly spaced between 0.05m and 0.50m apart (Figures 4.2–4.3). In square E6/N7, the ploughmarks also ran east-northeast–west-southwest, providing evidence of cross-ploughing. A plan of layer 135, before the windblown sand layer (131; see Chapter 5) was removed to reveal the ploughmarks, shows three stones that possibly form part of a curving wall line (Figure 4.4). There is no other record in the site archive of this linear feature which might conceivably have formed the eastern wall of a building.

Pit 142

Layer 135 was also cut by a pit (142), 2m north–south × 2.25m east–west and at least 1m deep, circular in plan towards its base, stepped and then sub-rectangular in plan higher up (Figures 3.8, 3.10, 4.5–4.7). It was filled with grey/green-brown sand (also 142) and was cut from beneath or within layer 134 (a layer of sand above 135; see Figure 3.6). Suggestions that the pit had been re-cut cannot be verified from the site records. Finds from this pit include a ceramic mould fragment, an ivory pin (SF158), pottery, animal bone and marine shell with a little carbonized wood, together with grains of barley, dock/sorrel (*Rumex* spp) and sedge (Cyperaceae). The pit cut through the underlying Bronze Age layers so some or all of these materials may be residual.

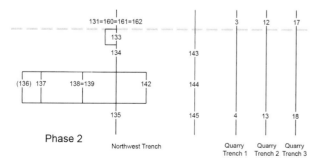

Figure 4.1 Stratigraphic matrix for Late Bronze Age contexts

Figure 4.2 The surface of sand layer 135, showing ploughmarks: full plan (top) and initial plan of the east half of the trench (bottom)

Other deposits

Two discrete deposits sat on top of layer 135: an irregular spread of black, burnt sand with flecks of carbonized wood (137), and a circular area of black burnt sand with carbonized wood, pottery and bone (138=139). Pottery from layer 138 appears to be of Late Bronze Age type. Another suspected deposit (136) turned out to be modern, the result of machine damage by the JCB at the beginning of excavation. In the east of the trench, a layer of fine, light brown/white shell-rich sand (133) overlay layer 134 (see Figures 3.5–3.7). It spread across the trench from E5/E6, extending and thickening to the west.

In the southern end of the trench (in E3/N4), there was a sequence of three layers that cannot be related to the overall sequence within this northwest trench . The lowest of these was sterile white/grey shell sand (145), thought to be windblown (presumably the same as 135). Above this was dark brown/black organic sand with pottery and bone (144), beneath a series of fine lenses of apparently water-borne deposits (143; see Figure 3.10) under 130 (possibly re-deposited modern sediment ponding within the trench).

These deposits were covered by a deep layer of sand (131=160=161=162) containing Middle Iron Age pottery (see Chapter 5).

Figure 4.3 Ploughmarks within layer 135, viewed from the southwest

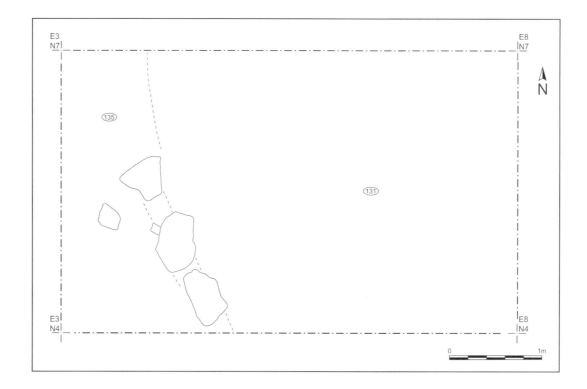

Figure 4.4 Layer 135 with a row of stones, overlaid on its east side by windblown sand layer 131

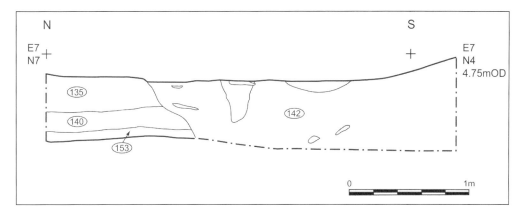

Figure 4.5 Section through layer 135 showing pit 142

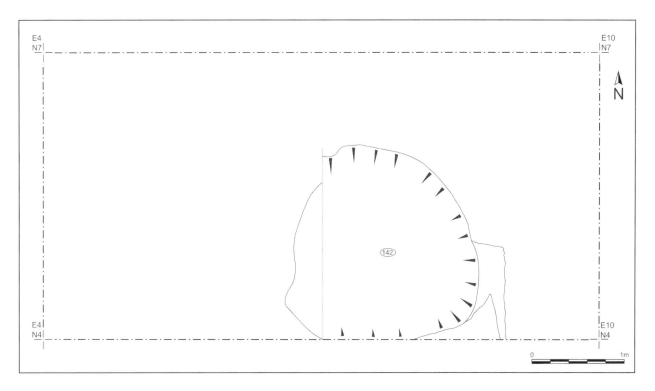

Figure 4.6 Plan of pit 142

Conclusion

Dating of this part of the sequence relies on radiocarbon dates of carbonized grain as well as on ceramics. The clay refractory material for bronze-casting (described in Chapter 10) can be dated on typological grounds to the Late Bronze Age. Rim styles and vessel shapes (as far as they can be reconstructed) of pottery from these layers are closely comparable with those from the final Late Bronze Age and earliest Iron Age (phases 12–13) at Cladh Hallan, although a grass-marked sherd from layer 135 at Cill Donnain III is of a form dating to the Late Bronze Age (Parker Pearson and Parsons in prep.). Radiocarbon-dating of two carbonized barley grains (SUERC-37615 and SUERC-37616) from layer 134 at Cill Donnain produced a combined date within the eighth–early sixth centuries BC, straddling the bronze–iron transition (see Table 16.1).

Pit 142, dug through Early–Middle Bronze Age layers,

is likely to contain residual pottery from that earlier phase and this is borne out by the presence of 55 sherds in the fill of pit 142 from very thick-walled EBA–MBA vessels with angular rock inclusions. Other finds in this pit include the ivory pin and a fragment of clay refractory material; another fragment came from layer 4 within Quarry Trench 1.

The pottery from the lower sequence within this LBA/EIA stratigraphic block is much more fragmented than in the Early–Middle Bronze Age layers beneath, with average sherd weights mostly between 2g and 5g (in contrast to an average of 8.3g in the phase 1 contexts). This greater degree of fragmentation could reflect the deposition of midden material upon a ploughed field, rather than discard within a settlement. However, such fragmentation is common in the layers above associated with the Iron Age wheelhouse.

Figure 4.7 Pit 142 after excavation, viewed from the south

Chapter 5 Before construction of the wheelhouse (phase 3)

Mike Parker Pearson

Introduction

The sequence beneath the wheelhouse, across the entire 1990–1991 trench, consisted of a series of features and deposits on top of a deep sand layer (131=162) and included a gully and two possible hearths. Diagnostic sherds indicate a date range of *c.*AD 100–300 for these deposits, *i.e.* the later part of the Middle Iron Age. There appears to have been a gap of several centuries in occupation between the Late Bronze Age/Bronze Age–Iron Age transition (see previous chapter) and the Middle Iron Age.

The position of the wheelhouse is overlaid on the site grid with co-ordinates and square numbers in Figure 5.1.

The sand layer

The windblown sand layer (135 in phase 2; see Chapters 3 and 4) was covered by 131 (phase 3; Figure 5.2) in the west end of the northwest trench and by 134 (phase 2) in the east end. Context 134 (see Figure 3.6) was a layer of fine orange/brown sand (with much rabbit disturbance), deepening westwards and not extending east of the E5 co-ordinate. It contained very little bone or shell; radiocarbon-dating of two carbonized barley grains from layer 134 straddles the bronze–iron transition, giving a combined date within the eighth–early sixth centuries BC for phase 2.

Context 131=162 (see Figures 3.5–3.7) was a layer of light brown or fawn shell sand underlying layer 132 and, at the east end of the trench, layer 130. It extended across the whole trench but was heavily disturbed by rabbit burrowing and contained only a few fragments of pottery, bone and carbonized wood. It was equated with layer 162, a more-or-less sterile, light grey/light yellow windblown sand. Layer 131=162 was dated by optically stimulated luminescence (OSL), dating to AD 25–625 (OSL 602; 1670±300 BP; see Schwenninger in Chapter 3 and Figure 3.15).

Layer 162 (E9/N1) contained the right frontal bone of a human skull broken at the sutures (SF145), exhibiting healed blunt-force trauma (in an oval area 14mm × 9mm) on top of the head 50mm from the right brow (Figure 5.3). It dates to 710–390 cal BC at 95.4% probability or 540–393 cal BC at 91.1% probability (SUERC-37629; 2385±30 BP), much earlier than its apparently Middle Iron Age context.

Layer 160, below layer 21, was also part of this deposit 131=162, as was layer 161. Context 160 consisted of a featureless, heterogeneous medium-dark brown organic sand, with darker patches of soil rich in fragments of carbonized wood and stains of the same material. One of these darker patches forming a circular spread (in E12/N6) was defined as layer 161 but can be treated as part of 160 (see Figure 5.14). Context 165 (in squares E12/N6–E12/N9, E10/N5–E10/N6 and elsewhere) was treated as layer 160.[1] Layer 160 contained sherds of decorated Middle Iron Age pottery together with pottery of Late Bronze Age/Early Iron Age type, indicating that this was a mixed deposit; it also produced a fragment of copper-alloy sheet and 10 fragments of clay refractories for bronze-casting, one of which is part of a sword-handle mould (see Chapter 10). Other Late Bronze Age/Early Iron Age sherds came from layers 163 (together with four fragments of clay refractories), 164 and 171, also presumably containing residual material.

Layer 131=162 was not a sterile layer of windblown sand, even though finds of bone, shell and pottery were rare within it. It contained within it a small, discrete deposit (164) of burnt red clay, looking like brick and associated with dark sand (see Figure 5.14). Layer 131=162 could have been a levelling layer, brought in to form a surface on which the wheelhouse was to be constructed, or even a windblown sand layer later ploughed so as to distribute cultural material within it.

The presence of a human skull fragment within layer 131=162 – beneath the wheelhouse's south side – hints at

---

[1] The site records hint at there having been some confusion between layer 165 and layer 5, a context that is described in Chapter 8.

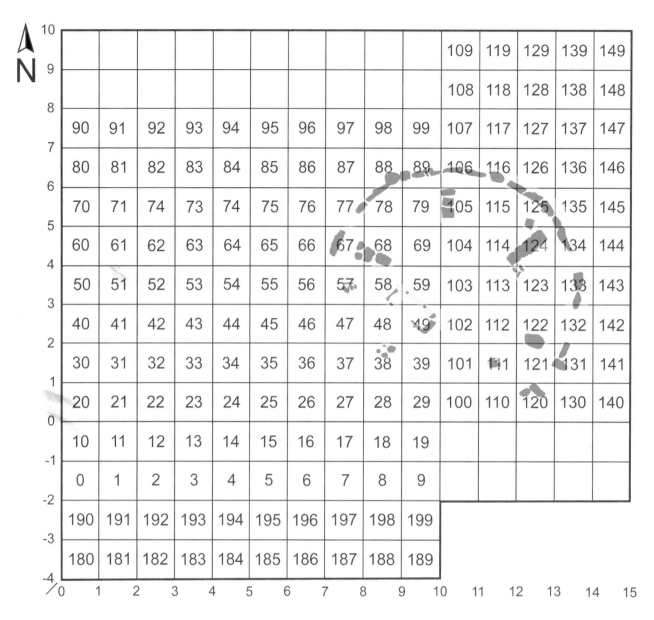

Figure 5.1 The numbered metre squares of the main trench of the 1989–1991 excavations, overlaid on the plan of the wheelhouse; the co-ordinates are those of the 1990–91 seasons

this deposit's purpose as a foundation layer, since human remains have frequently been found in the foundation deposits of earlier roundhouses at Cladh Hallan (Parker Pearson *et al.* in prep.) and broadly contemporary structures at Dun Vulan (Parker Pearson and Sharples 1999: 169, 353), Cnip (Lewis; Armit 2006: 36, 66, 74, 244–7) and elsewhere in the Hebrides (Mulville *et al.* 2003). It is also worth noting that, in several cases, including Cill Donnain III, the human remains appear to be appreciably older than the foundational contexts in which they were deposited. Unfortunately there is no other means of deciding on the character of layer 131=162, whether as a laid foundation layer for the wheelhouse or as a pre-existing sand layer. It does, however, mark a chronological break with the Late Bronze Age layers below.

A variety of layers were found on top of the sand layer 131=162 but beneath the stones of the wheelhouse (169;

phase 4; see Chapter 6). A gully (191), pre-dating the building, was also cut into layer 131=162.

Gully 191

The gully ran northeast–southwest, widening from 0.43m across and 0.20m deep in the northeast to 0.85m across and 0.44m deep in the southwest where its form became less distinct (Figures 5.4–5.5; see also Figures 6.2–6.3, 6.5). The gully was recorded on the context sheet as being beneath the floor of the wheelhouse (166) but the site matrix and section shows its fill (190) beneath layer 130=187 (see below and Figure 3.7), deposited prior to the construction of the wheelhouse's walls. The gully (191) was filled with light brown sand (190), with lenses of white and orange sand, containing pottery sherds, a fragment of clay refractory for bronze-casting, animal bone and shell.

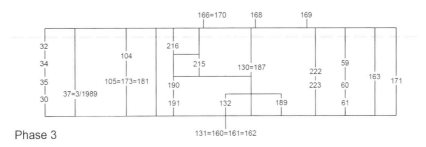

Figure 5.2 Stratigraphic matrix for the Iron Age contexts pre-dating construction of the wheelhouse

Figure 5.3 The human skull fragment (SF145) with its right eye socket visible, within layer 162

To the southwest the gully was cut by a feature (215). This is described in the site records as a pit or a posthole, 0.50m × at least 0.26m (truncated by section) and 0.44m deep, located at E9.30/N3.45 (square 93), with almost vertical sides sloping gently to a circular concave base (Figures 5.4–5.5); its fill of grey/brown sand contained pottery, bone and shell. However, amongst the site drawings, a plan shows feature 215 to have been in fact a linear feature almost 3m long east–west, with its west end unidentifiable within an area of disturbance. Whether a pit or a gully, this second cut feature was partly covered by a lens of sterile sand (216), and both 215 and 216 were covered by the wheelhouse floor (166=170; phase 5; see Chapter 6).

Both features (215 and 191) appear to meet under the hearth of the wheelhouse (phase 5; see Chapter 6). It is possible that one or both were constructed as drains leading from the hearth towards the west and/or north walls. Examples of such 'drains' are known from the North Uist

moorland wheelhouse of Clettraval (Scott 1948) and from Bagh nam Feadag wheelhouse, Grimsay (McKenzie 2005), as well as from the South Uist machair sites of Dun Vulan (Building B; Parker Pearson and Sharples 1999: 137–9) and Cladh Hallan (Parker Pearson *et al.* 2004: plate 9), though the latter two examples are not associated with hearths. However, neither of these features at Cill Donnain III provided any evidence of having been lined or capped by stones as is usual elsewhere for such structures.

Another feature that probably belongs to this phase of construction is an oval pit (223), 1.40m east–west × 0.90m north–south × 0.28m deep, with sides sloping at 70°–90° to a fairly flat and level base (Figures 5.4–5.5). It was filled with dark organic sand (222) with pottery, bone and shell inclusions and a stone 0.12m across. The pit was cut into sand layer 131=162.

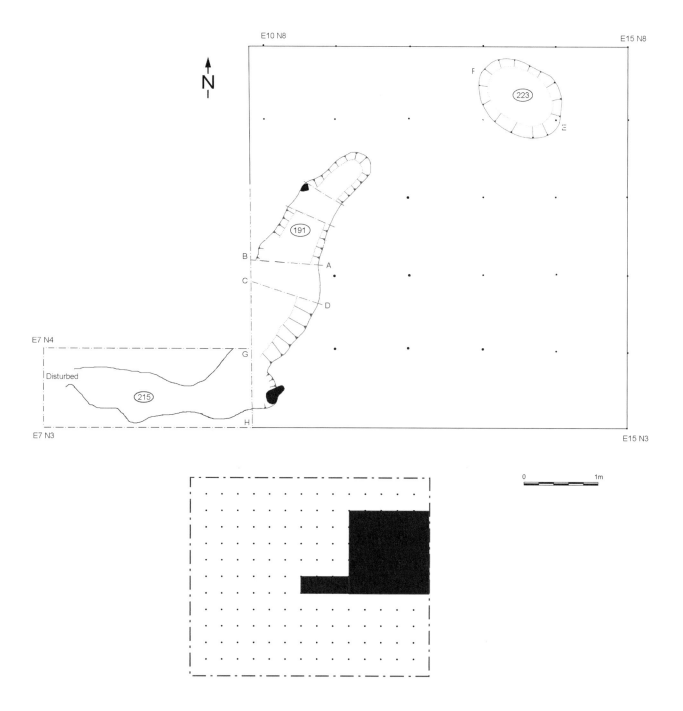

Figure 5.4 Plans of gully 191, linear feature 215 and pit 223

Possible hearths

Two discrete deposits lay on top of layer 131=162 and beneath 130=187 (described below; Figure 5.6). One deposit (in square E6/N4, to the west of the wheelhouse) was a small irregular patch of dark red/brown organic sand (132), lying within a small circular hollow up to 0.07m deep (Figure 5.7). The other was a domed patch of red and orange peat ash (189), measuring 2m northeast–southwest × 1m southeast–northwest and up to 0.10m thick, filling a slight hollow with its surface sloping to the west (Figure 5.8). Both are possibly small hearths.

Layers 130 and 187 are equated on the site matrix (Figure 5.2). Context 130 was an area of fine, dark brown

organic sand located in the east of the northwest trench (Figure 5.6). Context 187 was a heterogeneous mixture of humic brown soil, carbonized wood inclusions and smears of red peat ash found directly beneath the northwest quadrant of the wheelhouse and extending underneath the structure to around the E7 co-ordinate (Figures 3.7, 5.8). It might have been a platform laid to facilitate construction of the wheelhouse. Layer 187 is shown on a site plan with the peat-ash deposit 189 apparently within it, as if 189 were later than it; however, deposit 189 is certainly earlier than layer 187, so the drawing must show context 189 as revealed when the upper part of 187 was removed to expose the deposit's domed surface.

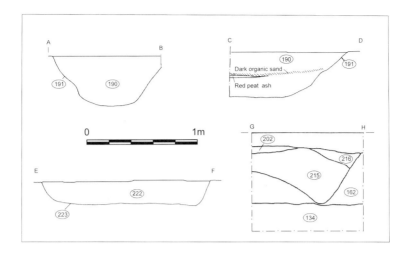

Figure 5.5 Section drawings of gully 191, linear feature 215 and pit 223

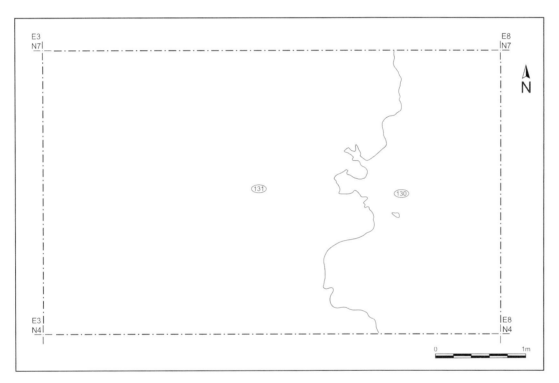

Figure 5.6 Plan of layer 130, lying on top of layer 131=162, in the northwest trench (see Figures 3.1 and 5.1 for location)

Other deposits

Southeast of the inner wall line of the wheelhouse built in phase 4, there lay a banked deposit of dark organic sand (104), extending at least 1.50m southwest–northeast and at least 0.35m wide and up to 0.20m high (Figures 5.9–5.11). During the initial stages of post-excavation, this was thought to be a surviving but eroded hump of wall core material still *in situ*, on the basis of parallels with the sand cores of the roundhouse walls at Cladh Hallan. Two barley grains from layer 104 date to the late first–early third centuries AD (cal AD 70–240 at 95.4% probability, SUERC-37625, 1865±30BP; cal AD 70–240 at 95.4% probability, SUERC-37624, 1865±25BP), potentially slightly earlier than the wheelhouse itself. This slight dis-

crepancy could be due to layer 104 being a midden layer long pre-dating the building of the wheelhouse's wall that was protected from later erosion beneath the since-vanished sand core of this wall. Alternatively, layer 104 is indeed filling of the wall core, possibly with material that was relatively ancient when re-deposited during the wheelhouse's construction (*cf* Armit 2006: 220). Layer 104 is covered by rubble and midden deposits of phase 9 (103; see Chapter 8).

Other layers deposited prior to wheelhouse construction were 173, 181 and 105, all equated together as the same context. Layer 173 was a medium-brown, shell layer with carbonized wood inclusions, in squares E9/N0–E12/N2 (Figures 5.8, 5.10); it produced an iron object (SF54) and

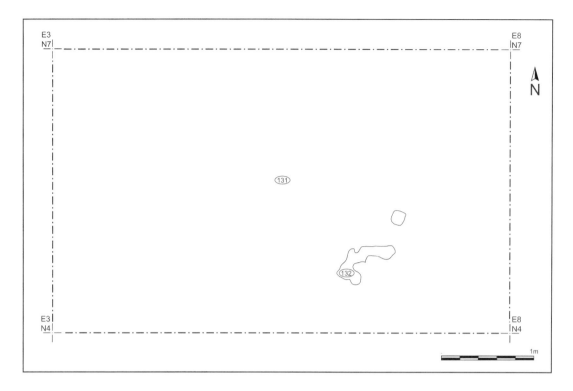

Figure 5.7 Plan of layer 132, a possible hearth, in the northwest trench (see Figures 3.1 and 5.1 for location)

an antler peg (SF41). A radiocarbon date on carbonized grain from layer 173 produced a date of cal AD 20–220 (95% probability; SUERC-37614, 1900±30 BP).[2]

Layer 181 was a grey/brown organic sand underlying layer 59 (described below) and southwest of the wheel-house's doorway; layer 181 produced a fragment of copper-alloy strip (SF63). Another pre-wheelhouse de-posit was a consolidated layer of reddish peat ash (37), dark brown to black with carbonized wood inclusions and shell, below the wall stones in the northwest part of the wheelhouse. There is no indication in the site records as to whether it was the same as layer 187 (also found in this area; see above). Most of this layer was excavated in 1989, presumably as context 3/1989 (see below). Outside the house to its east (in E14/N3) thin lenses of red peat ash (171) may pre-date the wheelhouse's construction.

In the northeastern part of the 1991 excavation, a mottled brown/black sandy layer (163), of unspecified thickness with dense carbonized wood fragments, ap-pears to pre-date the wheelhouse, its top running southwestwards as a low ridge outside the inner wall face of the house. Layer 163 was recorded as being of various shapes and sizes during its excavation. In the lowest and earliest plan, it is shown as one of several soil discolorations, an oval spread *c.*1.20m east–west × 1m north–south, centred on E14/N7 (Figure 5.12). High-er up it is represented as a continuous linear spread, southwest to northeast, possibly composed of two differ-ent components (Figure 5.13). Finally, the uppermost plan depicts it as a linear spread over a metre wide (just

the northernmost of the two components seen in Figure 5.13; Figure 5.14).

In the northeast corner of the 1990 trench, a series of layers (30, 35, 34 and 32; see sections in Figures 8.7–8.10) were found beneath layer 24, the sand core of the wheelhouse's wall (phase 4) on its north side. Context 32 was a silty layer rich with flecks and fragments of car-bonized wood (in squares 107, 108, 109, 117, 118 and 119) below context 24 and above contexts 34, 35 and 30. This layer produced a small bone point (SF150) and a piece of worked antler (SF133).

In a higher stratigraphic position than layer 32, context 34 was a light sand lens below context 24 in the northeast section of the 1990 excavation (squares 117 and 118), containing very few finds. Context 35 was a mottled layer between contexts 34 and 30 in squares 117 and 118.

Two contexts (layer 59 and the lower component of 3/1989 [see layer 37, above]) are described in the site re-cords as 'floor layers' outside the wheelhouse but contemporary with it. This initial interpretation cannot stand: these layers would have been buried beneath the wheelhouse's wall core and must thus pre-date the build-ing: they are not floors. Contexts 59 and 3/1989, and the layers below them, are therefore considered in this chapter, since they belong to phase 3.

Context 59 (see Figure 8.6) was a dark layer of burn-ing, lying level with the base of the wheelhouse's stone wall and extending above the wall base, up to half the height of the stone uprights in the southwest part of the roundhouse. Layer 59 formed an oval stain around the

---

[2] See Figure 16.2 for the place of these phase 3 dates in the model of the wheelhouse chronology.

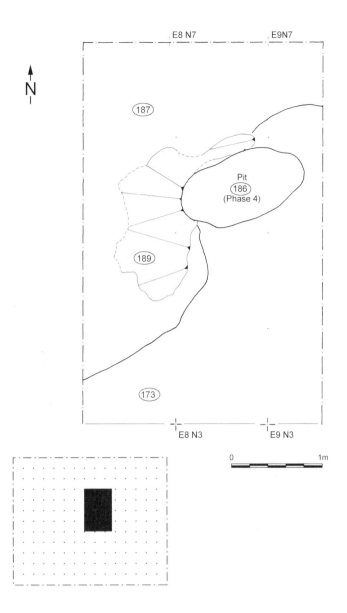

Figure 5.8 Plan of a humic soil (187), a shell layer (173) and a domed patch of peat ash (189), both cut by pit 186 (phase 4)

stones, about 0.05m–0.10m deep. It produced large quantities of charred grain and carbonized wood; amongst the pottery from this context is a sherd modified into a disc, one of two ceramic artefacts from the site (see Chapter 9). A possible interpretation of layers 59 and 3/1989 is that they formed parts of a building surface laid down to facilitate construction of the wheelhouse on otherwise unconsolidated soft sand.

Below layer 59 was layer 60 and, below that, 61. Context 60 was a rich, dark brown deposit of organic sand located under the wheelhouse wall and layer 59 (in squares 90 and 91). Context 61 was a medium/dark brown layer containing burnt material and a piece of worked antler (SF114), surrounded by stones (in squares 111 and 112).

The human skull fragment

Andrew Chamberlain

The specimen (SF145) is the right half of a human frontal bone (Figure 5.15). The bone is complete and almost intact, with some minor damage at places along the coronal suture and to the posterior margin of the orbital plate.

The specimen is probably of a late adolescent or adult, as shown by the well-developed frontal sinus (which extends laterally for about half of the width of the orbit) together with the prominence of the superciliary arch – both are features that achieve full expression around the age of puberty. However the specimen is very small – the

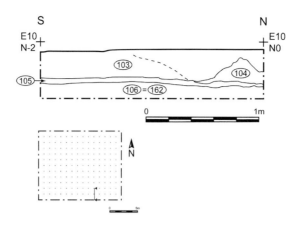

Figure 5.9 Section drawing, south–north, through the organic layer 104

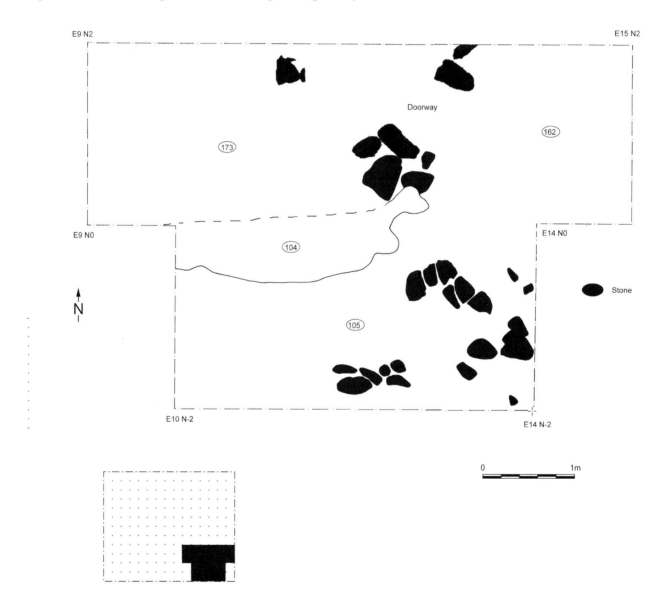

Figure 5.10 Layer 104, to the southwest of the doorway jambs, with layers 105 and 173

Figure 5.11 The student has her back to layer 104 (still in situ) while midden layer 103 (phase 9) is visible as a dark strip within the baulk to the right

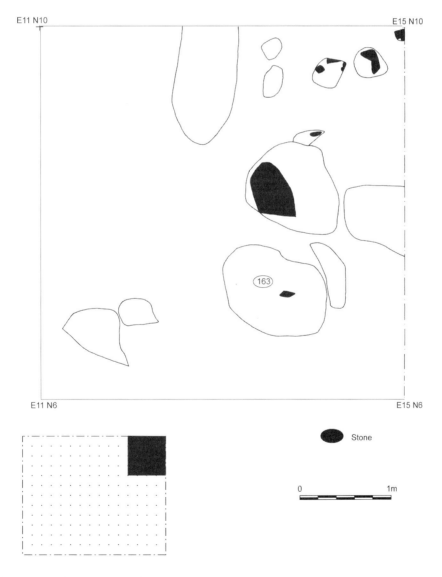

Figure 5.12 The basal part of layer 163 in plan

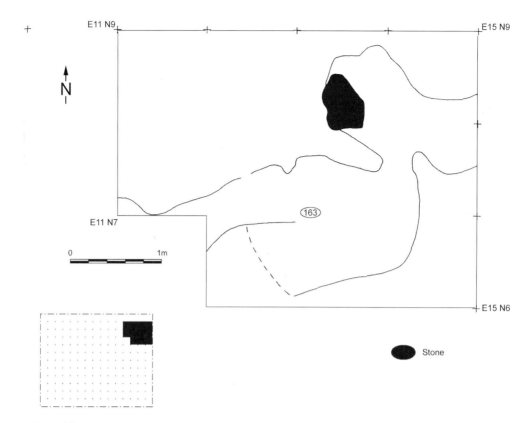

Figure 5.13 The middle part of layer 163 in plan

frontal chord is 102mm, a value that falls two standard deviations below the average for British prehistoric female crania (Brodie 1994). On the basis of its size the specimen is therefore likely to be from a female.

The metopic suture is unfused, a condition that occurs in up to 10% of adults in British populations (Brothwell 1981). There is minor development of cribra orbitalia in the posterior part of the roof of the right orbit. On the external surface of the bone there is a distinct depressed and roughened oval area of bone cortex located 28mm lateral to the metopic suture and 44mm anterior to bregma. This lesion has antero-posterior and medio-lateral dimensions of 10mm and 18mm respectively, and both the margin and the interior of the lesion show evidence of bone remodelling. There is no corresponding abnormality on the endocranial surface, and the lesion is attributed to a healed injury or infection affecting the outer table of the bone.

Conclusion

This part of the Cill Donnain III sequence (above layer 131=162) contains layers with ceramics of which the rims and decorative motifs can be identified as dating to the Middle Iron Age, after AD 100. The sharply everted rims in layers 105 and 190 (see Chapter 9) provide a useful chronological marker for the deposits immediately stratigraphically prior to wheelhouse construction; everted rims were employed as early as the second century AD (Campbell 2002: 141; Campbell *et al*. 2004). Incised decoration in contexts 105, 160, 189 and 190, impressed grooves in context 173, and impressed horizontal cordons in contexts 59, 105, 160, 173 and 190/191 all contribute to this picture of deposition within the later part of the Middle Iron Age.

The radiocarbon date produced by the skull fragment of 710–390 cal BC (95% probability; SUERC-37629, 2385±30 BP) indicates that this is likely to have been a foundation deposit (see Chapter 17 for further discussion).

There is no sign in this phase of any ceramic styles that might be assigned to the end of the Early Iron Age (*cf* Marshall and Parker Pearson 2012) or to the early part of the Middle Iron Age (Campbell 2002). However, the quantities of Late Bronze Age–Early Iron Age pottery, Late Bronze Age clay refractory material for bronze-casting, and the radiocarbon date of the human skull fragment all indicate a degree of mixing or residuality with older material from the first half of the first millennium BC.

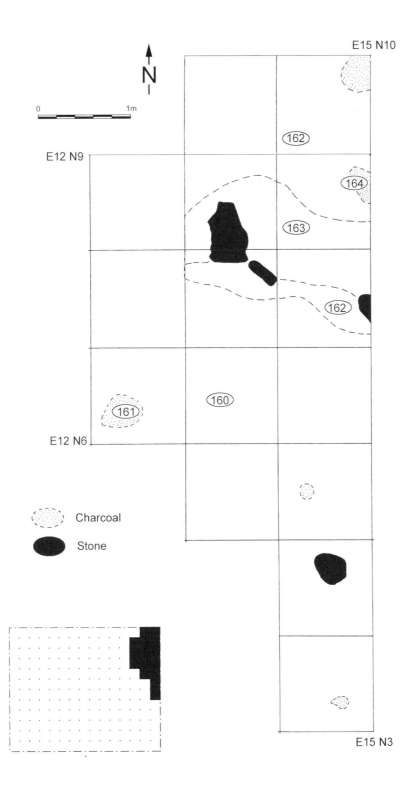

Figure 5.14 The upper part of layer 163 in plan

Figure 5.15 The human skull fragment (SF145) showing evidence of a depressed lesion on top of the head

Chapter 6 Construction and initial use of the wheelhouse (phases 4 and 5)

Mike Parker Pearson and Marek Zvelebil

Introduction

The aisled wheelhouse was constructed in *cal AD 170–360* (*at 95% probability*), probably in the period *cal AD 205–310* (*68% probability*), towards the end of the Middle Iron Age.[1] It is 'aisled' because its stone piers do not reach the outer wall but leave an 'aisle' running around the house's interior perimeter. The wheelhouse consisted of stone uprights forming the outer wall of the circular building, together with piers subdividing the roundhouse into probably six cells and an entrance area encircling a central chamber; remains of four of the probable seven pier bases survived (Figure 6.1).

The house's doorway was located on the southeast side and opened onto stone paving in front of the entrance. Inside the house, a stone-lined hearth was set not in its centre but in its southwest quadrant. Various features identified within the remains of the wheelhouse might have been contemporary with it.

The construction of the wheelhouse (phase 4)

The 1990 sections shown in Figures 8.6–8.10 and the section of the exposed dune face drawn in 1989 (see Figures 2.16–2.18) demonstrate that the wheelhouse was built on a level surface composed of layers 32, 37, 59 and the lower component of 3/1989. The house was not built within a pit set into the sand, as was the case for the Cladh Hallan roundhouses (Parker Pearson *et al.* in prep.) and for some other machair wheelhouses (Armit 1996: 139; 2006). This is demonstrated by the evidence that the paving in front of the entrance of the Cill Donnain III wheelhouse was horizontal and level with the interior floor, indicating that ground level was the same both inside and outside the building.

Rather than lining a pit cut into the sand, therefore, the uprights of the Cill Donnain wheelhouse wall formed the

interior face of a wall wider and higher than those seen in sunken-floored wheelhouses: at Cill Donnain the upper stone courses of the interior wall face would have been bonded into a sand core. This sand core and the exterior wall face are visible in the 1989 long section of the dune face (Figures 2.16–2.18) but left little trace during excavation in plan, owing partly to their poor survival and partly to the excavators' inexperience, leading them to fail to identify these methods of construction in the machair sand.

The stones of the wheelhouse wall, piers and hearth were set into a series of later Middle Iron Age layers (37, 105, 130=187, 173 and 181; phase 3) lying on top of a near-sterile layer of windblown sand (131=162) as described in Chapter 5 (see Figure 5.2 for the stratigraphy of these layers).

At the time of excavation in 1991, it was thought that the wheelhouse sat on top of an earlier roundhouse. In retrospect, it seems quite evident that an arc of pits provisionally identified as the footings of this putative earlier building are simply the holes in which the upright stones of the wheelhouse's inner wall face (169) were set (Figure 6.2). Quite why this confusion arose during excavation is unknown. The most parsimonious interpretation is that these cut features are part of the construction of the wheelhouse, and not the remains of an earlier building. They lie directly under each of the stones of the wheelhouse wall.

Stoneholes for the wheelhouse wall

Thirteen cuts were recorded for the stones forming the wheelhouse's east wall (169). As already mentioned, these stoneholes were initially thought to be postholes belonging to an earlier building but their broadly sub-rectangular shapes and shallow depths indicate that they

---

[1] See Chapter 16 for the model of the wheelhouse chronology and details of radiocarbon dating of specific contexts (phase 5 dated contexts are 177, 179 and 183).

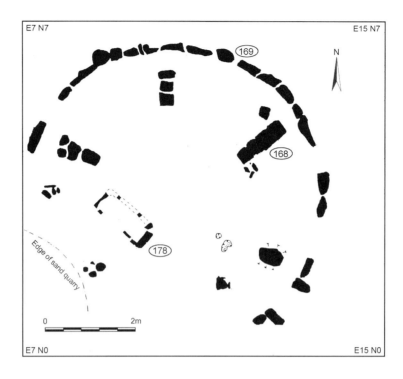

Figure 6.1 Stone structural elements of the wheelhouse in its constructional phase. The dashed line in the bottom left marks the line of part of the 1989 section

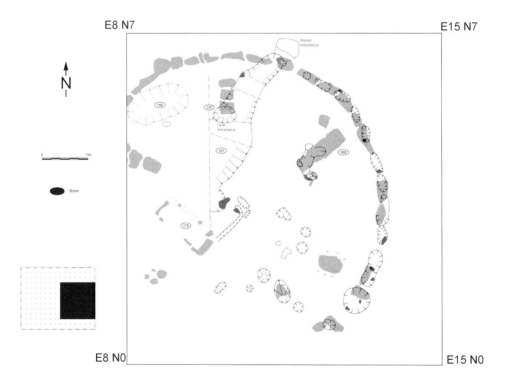

Figure 6.2 Stone structural elements of the wheelhouse superimposed over cut features beneath

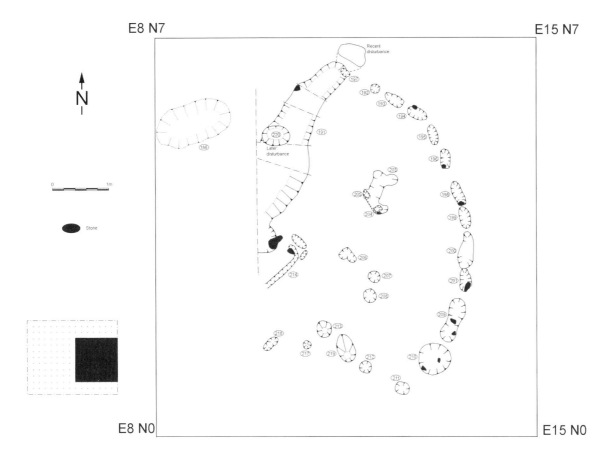

Figure 6.3 Plan of cut features beneath the eastern half of the wheelhouse

are quite certainly stoneholes. It is possible that they represent an initial interior wall face of the wheelhouse, subsequently modified. From north to south in a clockwise direction, these features are numbered as contexts 197, 192–196, 198–201 and 209–211 (Figures 6.3–6.5). Each stonehole has just one context number, indicating both cut and fill.

- Context 197 was a sub-rectangular hollow, 0.26m × 0.20m × 0.06m deep, with a concave base and sides sloping at 60°. It contained some carbonized wood fragments in a light brown sand matrix.
- Context 192 was a shallow circular hollow, 0.20m × 0.20m × 0.05m deep, with a concave base, filled with light brown sand without inclusions.
- Context 193 was a shallow sub-rectangular hole, 0.36m × 0.21m × 0.09m deep, sloping at 45° to a concave base. Its fill of light brown sand contained occasional shells.
- Context 194 was a sub-rectangular hollow, 0.31m × 0.22m × 0.06m deep, sloping at 45° to a concave base, filled with light brown sand, a stone, bone and small stone fragments.
- Context 195 was a sub-rectangular hole, 0.36m × 0.17m × 0.07m deep, with rounded edges and sides sloping at 45°–60° to a concave base. It was filled with light brown sand.
- Context 196 was a sub-rectangular hollow 0.33m ×

0.22m × 0.10m deep, the east and west sides of which sloped to a point at 45°. It was filled with light brown sand and contained pottery fragments, bone and shell.
- Context 198 was a sub-rectangular hollow, 0.51m × 0.30m × 0.18m deep, with sides sloping at 60° towards a concave base. Its light brown sandy fill contained pottery fragments, shell, small stone fragments and a larger stone at the south end of the hole.
- Context 199 consisted of an oval hole, 0.50m × 0.19m × 0.19m deep. Its sides sloped at 60° and it was filled with dark brown sand containing pottery fragments, shell and stone fragments.
- Context 200 was a sub-rectangular hollow, 0.53m × 0.31m × 0.20m deep, with sides sloping at 60°–90° towards an uneven base; its dark brown sand fill contained pottery, bone, shell and occasional stone fragments.
- Context 201 was a sub-rectangular hollow, 0.48m × 0.39m × 0.18m deep, with sides sloping at 60° to a concave base; its light brown sand fill contained pottery, bone and shell with a stone pitched into its southeast end.
- Context 209 was a sub-rectangular hollow, 0.79m × 0.28m × 0.14m deep, with sides sloping at 45° to a concave base filled with dark organic sand with shell and bone inclusions; the hole was divided in two by a centrally placed stone.
- Context 210 was a circular hole, 0.52m × 0.52m ×

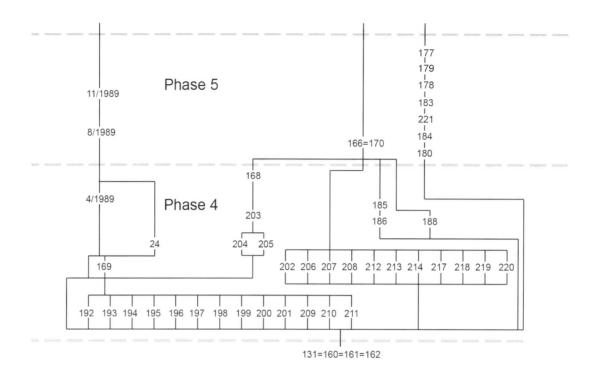

Figure 6.4 Stratigraphic matrix for the Iron Age layers associated with construction and initial use of the wheelhouse

Figure 6.5 Cut features, including stone holes for the inner wall face, viewed from the northeast; gully 191 is visible to the right

Figure 6.6 The northwest sector of the inner wall face, viewed from the northeast (NB to preserve future readers from puzzlement, the possibly mysterious 'object' at the top right is Dave Giles's dreadlocks)

Figure 6.7 The revetted side of the inner wall face in its north sector, viewed from the north

Figure 6.8 The doorway of the wheelhouse, viewed from the east; on the left are stones associated with the building's collapse and dismantling

Figure 6.9 The robbed-out inner wall face in the southwest sector, viewed from the southwest; the wheelhouse interior is to the right of the feature, and the layers above are the midden 5=1/1989 (top) and the windblown sand layer 21=36=2/1989 (middle)

Figure 6.10 The outer wall face in the southwest sector, viewed from the north; the sand wall core is to its left

0.19m deep, with sides sloping at 60° then 45° to a concave base. Its fill consisted of dark brown sand with shell, bone, pottery and stone inclusions, including two larger stones pitched into the southern half of the hole.

- Context 211 was an oval hole, 0.37m × 0.39m × 0.17m deep, with sides sloping at 40°–70° to a concave base, filled with dark brown sand containing pottery, bone and shell.

The walls

The circular wall (169) of the wheelhouse (*i.e.* its interior stone face) consisted of 22 upright slabs forming the interior wall face where it survived on its north and east sides (Figures 6.1–6.2, 6.6–6.7), together with two out-turned upright slabs marking the 0.70m-wide doorway (Figure 6.8). This wall face was entirely missing on the wheelhouse's south and west sides, where any trace of stones or stone holes had been eroded away. In the array of surviving wall stones, there were gaps for missing stones on the east side (two stones missing) and the northwest side (one stone missing). The curve of the surviving wall enables us to calculate the original internal diameter of the wheelhouse as 6.52m, giving an original floor area of 33.4 sq m.

Some of the stone uprights appear to have been roughly dressed. The stones range from medium-sized to fairly large boulders, those in the eastern part of the structure exceeding a height of 0.50m, where they are set

in the underlying sand deposit (131=162). In the western half, the stones are set in a layer of black to dark brown organic sand (59; see Chapter 5).

There was no indication of how the wall's single course of uprights might have supported the upper part of the wall. It would have been difficult to lay upper courses of undressed masonry on top of these uprights without leaving them unstable; either these stones formed the interior face of a wall composed of sand or turf that has left no trace or they constituted the full height of the wall, with the roof beams springing off their tops. The latter arrangement can be discounted because such a roof-pitch would so severely have limited headroom within the house as to make it impossible to use the hearth.

The existence of a sand or turf wall is indicated by the 1989 long section (where it cut through the southwest of the wheelhouse; Figures 2.16–2.18). This reveals that the wheelhouse's walls were about 2m thick and consisted of the inner stone face (169), a sand wall core (layer 4/1989 below 9/1989 below 6/1989 [=2C/1989]) and an outer stone face (no number).

The inner stone wall (169) has been robbed in the two locations where it is visible in the 1989 section. Of the two voids left by robbing of the stones of the inner wall face, the western void (Figure 6.9) looks like a small flat-bottomed, vertically sided pit (phase 9 context 5/1989=2B/1989; 0.55m deep and 0.25m wide; see middle section of Figure 2.16). This void was filled with a lower layer of light grey/brown sand, an intermediate organic layer of dark brown sand containing carbonized wood, and five upper fills of light grey/brown, grey/white and medium brown sand. The wall core in this part of the house wall consisted of a 2m-wide, 0.30m-high layer of sand mixed with organic material (4/1989)[2]. There was no sign of the outer wall face, and context 4/1989 merely fades out (see left side of middle section, Figure 2.16).

Towards the southeast end of the 1989 long section, the appearance of the wall (in the house's southwest sector) shows similar disturbance and robbing. The original position of the inner stone wall face is indicated by three irregular stripes of white windblown sand (context 7/1989) within layer 4/1989. These can be interpreted as being the remains of a robber trench, similar to 5/1989. Three large stones formed a heap immediately east of this suspected robber trench; presumably they are a stockpile of robbed wall stones.

The wall core here on the wheelhouse's southwest side (see bottom section, Figure 2.16) survived to a height of up to 0.60m and consisted of three layers of sand, of which the lowest was 4/1989. Above this, at the outer edge of the wall core, there was a 0.08m-thick lens of dark, humic organic sand with flecks of carbonized wood (9/1989; phase 6); parts of the wall core were thus renovated or rebuilt in this later phase. Layer 4/1989 and layer 9/1989 were both covered by a layer of windblown sand (phase 6) that merged gradually with 4/1989 where the two layers met.

Above the windblown sand, the layer over the wall core consisted of a 0.25m-thick layer of dark, fairly organic sand (6/1989). The layer of windblown sand may derive from an episode of natural accumulation on the top of the initial wall core (4/1989 and 9/1989) that was possibly later enhanced by the addition of layer 6/1989 (a modification assigned to phase 6 or 7; Chapter 7) to raise the height of the wall core from 0.35m to 0.60m; such an operation is likely to have involved repair or replacement of the roof whose rafters would have been sprung from the tops of the wheelhouse wall.

The outer stone face of the wheelhouse wall seems to have survived on the southwest side (see bottom section, Figure 2.16) to two courses high (0.27m; Figure 6.10). Whereas layer 9/1989 extended across the top of the upper course, layer 6/1989 above it stopped abruptly with a steep edge, indicative of later, upper stone courses having been robbed from the wall face. Thin lenses of sand, also numbered as layers 4/1989 (up to 0.06m thick), 9/1989 (0.08m thick) and 6/1989 (0.07m thick), extended beyond the outer wall face and can be interpreted as eroded wall core material spilling from the outer edge of the wheelhouse wall.

The wall core and the external stone face of the wall (or rather its robbed-out remains) went unrecognised during the excavation, and both seem to have been entirely missed along the house's northern, southern and eastern sides. The east–west section from E0/N8 to E10/N8 (the northern edge of the excavation trench, running westwards from the northern edge of wall face 169) seems not to have been drawn or photographed. Fortunately the wall core on the northeast side of the wheelhouse is recognizable as a layer of light sand (24) up to 0.20m thick, banked against the wall 169 and sloping northwards and eastwards (Figures 6.11–6.12, 8.10). It was stained with black and orange peat ash, lying below layer 23 (phase 9; see Chapter 8) and on top of phase 3's layer 32 (in squares 107, 108, 109, 117, 118 and 119). There was no sign of an outer kerb of stones to revet this sand wall core (24), nor of any robbed-out holes for its stones, though this area appears to have been disturbed prior to the accumulation of midden layers in phase 9 by what may be a large scoop into the wall core on its northeast side.

Layer 24 contained a hammerstone, two bone points (SF34 and SF149), three fragments of worked antler (SFs 199–121), a worked ivory tooth (probably walrus; SF32) and Middle Iron Age pottery decorated with applied cordons. The presence of ivory in this and other phases at Cill Donnain III is of interest, since no ivory artefacts were found at the neighbouring sites of Cladh Hallan, Dun Vulan or Bornais mound 1 (see Chapter 12 for discussion).

There may also be surviving traces of the outer stone face on the south side of the wheelhouse, in the southeast corner of the excavations (excavated in 1991). In this corner, the earliest layer (106) equates with layer 162, the sand layer beneath the house. Above it, a thin sand layer (105) could be the lowest surviving deposit within the wall core or the disturbed surface of 106. It was covered with stones, some of which could have formed a small entrance area southeast of the doorway or which could have derived from the house wall. Some of the rubble outside (southeast of) the doorway consists of stones laid flat outside the doorway; these were interpreted by the excavator as a paved area outside the doorway, but they could also derive from the house's abandonment when its stones were robbed (see Chapter 7).

The piers and internal architecture

There were remains of six piers in the house, all surviving as basal courses only (Figures 6.1–6.2). From their layout, it is likely that there was a seventh pier in the south which has left no trace. The three best preserved piers were in the building's northern half.

- The largest of these, the northeast pier base (168; Figure 6.13), consisted of five stones laid flat on the

---

2   The reader should note that this context number of 4/1989 was also given to a deposit that filled the house and which belongs to a later phase.

Figure 6.11 The eroded wall core of sand (layer 24) on the north and east sides of the wheelhouse interior and inner wall face, viewed from the east

sterile sand (131=162) and forming a sub-rectangular, flat-topped platform 1.20m × 0.35m, narrowing to 0.30m wide at its southwest or inward end.

- The north and northwest pier bases were also largely complete in plan, at 0.75m × 0.35m and 1.0m × 0.50m across (Figures 6.14–6.15). The inward ends of these three well-preserved examples were spaced 1.80m apart.

- Four small stones were all that survived of the southwest pier; its west end was presumably removed by recent quarrying and erosion, but there was no sign of its east end, which should have terminated within 0.30m of the stone-lined hearth (178; phase 5).

- The only evidence for piers within the southeast half of the house was the remains of the pair leading to the doorway. All that remained of the pier of the doorway's northeast side was a single slab, whilst that on the southwest side was marked by a setting of four small stones (for stoneholes that belong to the piers, see 'Cut features' below).

These piers originally surrounded a central circular space about 3.30m in diameter (about 8.50 sq m). The stone-lined hearth (178; Figure 6.16) lay just within the south-

west edge of this central space, its southeast end close up against the four small stones which are all that remained of the southwest pier.

Three other stone settings are indicated by the presence of stones set on edge (Figure 6.16). One of these consists of a cluster of four stones close to the west wall, just south of the northwest pier. Another is a setting of three stones immediately south of the northeast pier's inward end, and the third is a pair of stones just north of the same pier's outward end. The purpose of these stone settings is unknown but they might have supported the bottoms of posts.

The 'aisle' running between the outward ends of the piers and the wall was only about 0.40m wide. Although such features were previously considered by early/mid-twentieth-century excavators to be walkways around the internal perimeter of the roundhouses, the role of the 'aisle' is now considered to be architectural and structural rather than for movement within the house.

As Armit (1996: 139–41; 2006) has pointed out in relation to the Cnip (Lewis) wheelhouse, each cell (*i.e.* the area between each pair of wheelhouse piers) might have been corbelled, leaving only the central area beyond the inner ends of the piers (at Cill Donnain only 3.30m in

Figure 6.12 The eroded wall core of sand (layer 24) on the north and east sides of the wheelhouse interior and inner wall face, viewed from the south

diameter) to be roofed using short rafters set at about 45° to form a conical frame for the roof of turf and thatch. Thus the Cill Donnain III wheelhouse would have required roof timbers only 2.3m long (*cf* House 1 of Bornais mound 1; Sharples 2012b: 49, 297). If the piers originally stood as high as those of the Kilpheder wheelhouse (Lethbridge 1952) at 2.30m, then the apex of the roof would have been at almost 4m above the ground. However, given the smaller diameter of the Cill Donnain wheelhouse, the roof apex is more likely to have been just over 2m high (the piers being perhaps about 1.50m high and the central roof space 1.65m high).

The hearth

Within the southwest sector of the house floor there was a hearth (178; Figures 6.16–6.17) and, to its southeast, a pit (184; Figures 6.16, 6.18); although this pit was provisionally interpreted during excavation as being a flue, more careful analysis of the site records shows that it was in fact filled prior to the hearth's construction (Figure 6.19).

The hearth measured 1.52m northwest–southeast × 0.60m northeast–southwest, and lay within a trough-like pit lined with stones (178) on edge. The hearth pit was 0.33m deep, with the top of the stone lining projecting another 0.23m above this. The hearth pit's southeast end cut into the top of pit 184. The bottom 0.25m of the

hearth pit was filled with burnt orange peat ash (179; Figures 6.19–6.20), which produced a piece of worked antler (SF156). Two dates on carbonized grain from 179 were cal AD 260–440 at 95% probability (SUERC-38239; 1660±30 BP) and cal AD 410–560 at 95% probability (SUERC-39426; 1585±30 BP). Hearth layer 179 was covered by a 0.08m-thick layer of black carbonized wood and ash (177) that spilled over the southeast end of the hearth. Radiocarbon dates on carbonized grain from layer 177 indicate that final use of this hearth dates to *cal AD 495–540 at 68% probability*. Both the hearth and pit 184 belong to phase 5.

Pit 184 was a stone-lined oval feature (at right angles to the hearth), 1.25m × 0.78m × 0.35m, with concave sides leading to a flat base. It was lined with stones (180; Figure 6.18) and filled with a basal sand layer (221) and, above it, a dark brown sand fill (183). Two dates on carbonized grain from 183 were cal AD 240–420 at 95% probability (SUERC-38240; 1710±30 BP) and cal AD 340–540 at 95% probability (SUERC-37610; 1630±35 BP). To the east and northeast of the hearth, a deposit of peat ash covered the northern half of the central area of the wheelhouse (2m east–west × 1m north–south; labelled as 'ash spread' in Figure 6.16). This was interpreted as a dump of ash from the hearth, raked out from its east side.

To the east of the hearth lay a linear feature (214; Figures 6.2–6.3), running southwest–northeast for 0.84m

Figure 6.13 The base of the northeast pier, viewed from the southwest

before turning through a 90° angle and running northwest for 0.25m. It was 0.07m–0.12m wide and 0.06m–0.12m deep, and was filled with mottled, dark brown sand containing pottery, bone and shell. It appears to have been a slot (perhaps once containing a stone kerb) that continued the line of the hearth's southeastern side. It may be best interpreted as part of the kerb of an original square hearth (that would have measured 1.50m northwest–southeast × 1.50m northeast–southwest), belonging to phase 4, which was positioned more centrally within the wheelhouse than its later, cut-down form.

Cut features within the house

In the northeast sector, at the inner end of pier 168, the only feature was a shallow hollow (203; Figure 6.3), 0.59m × 0.66m × 0.09m deep, irregularly shaped with an uneven base and containing brown sand and slate fragments. This hollow was presumably the cut in which the northeast pier stood (see Figure 6.2); it overlaid and partially truncated two postholes (204 and 205).

• Posthole 204 was rectangular in plan (0.25m × 0.18m × 0.27m deep) with vertical sides and a 0.03m step to the east. Its base was flat and square (0.12m × 0.12m) and its mottled dark brown sand fill included bone fragments, two hammerstones and stone fragments.
• Posthole 205 was rectangular in plan (0.24m × 0.15m

× 0.21m deep) with near-vertical sides, with a step to the north. Its base was flat and square (0.12m × 0.12m) and its mottled dark brown sand fill contained bone and stone inclusions.

The presence of slate in hollow 203 is unusual, as are the two presumably deliberately placed hammerstones in 204. This might have been a special structure of two upright, dressed wooden or stone posts.

There were eight separate cut features (206–208, 212–213 and 217–219) in the southeast quadrant of the house (Figure 6.3).

• Context 206 was an irregular hollow, 0.40m × 0.35m × 0.10m deep, with an uneven base; its light brown sand fill contained fragments of flint. This is probably two small, inter-cutting features.
• Context 207 was a circular hole, 0.25m × 0.25m × 0.20m deep, with sides sloping at 80° to a concave base, filled with a dark brown, mottled sand fill and a stone pitched into the edge of the hole.
• Context 208 was a hollow, 0.30m × 0.28m × 0.14m deep, with sides sloping at 80° to a concave base, filled with dark brown, mottled sand containing shell and bone inclusions.

Within the entrance area of the house were five features, all described in the excavation records as 'postholes', al-

Figure 6.14 The base of the north pier, viewed from the south

though they are probably the remains of stoneholes.

- Context 212 was a circular hole, 0.22m × 0.22m × 0.10m deep, with sides sloping at 60° to a concave base, 0.12m × 0.12m; its dark brown sand fill contained pottery, bone and shell.
- Context 213 was an oval hole, 0.34m × 0.28m × 0.20m deep, with near-vertical sides and a step on the northwest side. Its base was circular and concave, 0.13m × 0.13m, and it was filled with dark brown, mottled sand containing pottery and bone.
- Context 219 was an oval hole, 0.48m × 0.32m × 0.24m deep, with sides sloping at 45° to a square slot in the base, 0.14m × 0.14m at its southern end. Its fill consisted of several large stones pitched vertically into the top of a dark brown sand matrix containing pottery, bone and shell.

These three holes (212, 213 and 219), together with feature 208, might have formed the bases of the robbed-out walls of an entrance passage leading into the wheelhouse's central space. They are best interpreted as the holes or footings for the bases of piers either side of a 1.80m–long passage from the doorway (Figure 6.2 shows the surviving pier stones overlaid onto these cut features).

West of this line of stoneholes (212, 213 and 219) in the southeast sector were two more cut features:

- Context 217 was a circular hole, 0.17m × 0.17m × 0.17m deep, with sides sloping at 60°–70° to a flat, circular base, 0.08m × 0.08m. It was filled with dark brown sand containing pottery, bone and shell, with a hammerstone pitched vertically.
- Context 218 was a footprint-shaped hollow, 0.36 × 0.16 × 0.06m deep, with sides sloping at 60°–45° to an uneven base. It was filled with light brown sand containing pottery, bone, shell and a hammerstone.

In the north of the house, a small pit (220) was cut into the gully (191) pre-dating the wheelhouse's construction (Figure 6.3). This shallow, oval hollow, 0.50m × 0.30m × 0.19m deep, was filled with mottled, dark brown sand containing pottery, bone and shell (all concentrated in the upper part of the hollow) and a stone pitched at 60° on the pit's southern edge. The coarse nature of the sherds in pit 220 suggests that they are of Late Bronze Age or Early Iron Age date, perhaps disturbed from lower layers when the pit was dug in the Middle Iron Age.

Context 202 was a pit located at about E9.50/N4 (not illustrated).

Pit 186 was an oval feature with slightly bowed edges and rounded ends (Figures 6.2–6.3). Its sides sloped at 60°–70°, to a fairly flat base. It was probably contemporary with the wheelhouse's construction (or earlier) since it appeared to be partially sealed by floor layer 166 (see below). It was filled with mixed dark brown and mid-brown organic sand (185), the darker material being randomly distributed in patches although the upper 0.10m of fill was generally darker. This fill supposedly contained worked antler, a piece of metalworking slag and a 'hone' but none of these items have been found during post-excavation.

'Posthole' 188 appeared as a cluster of stones within dark brown organic sand. The feature, as excavated, was not a cut feature but stood about 0.36m above the basal sand (131=162). It might have been either the eroded remains of stone packing around a post or the remains of a post pad that sat flush on the ground rather than in a hole.

The house floor (phase 5)

Two context numbers (166 and 170) were given to layers interpreted as floors within the wheelhouse (Figures 6.16, 6.21). Although Zvelebil initially interpreted 3/1989 and layer 59 as 'floor layers' of a hypothesised earlier building, they are not (see Chapter 5). In any case, we should not expect to see the wheelhouse's floor layer in the long section (which does not extend any distance into the wheelhouse's interior; Figures 2.16–2.18) since floor layers in Hebridean roundhouses tend not to extend as far as the edges of the walls.

Context 166 was a layer of dark brown, compacted organic sand with very dark brown and mid-brown patches,

Figure 6.15 The base of the northwest pier, viewed from the southeast

forming a floor surface within the wheelhouse (Figures 6.21–6.22). It lay under a dumped deposit (25; see Chapter 7 and Figure 8.10) and abutted the house wall (169) and the large northeastern pier base (168). It was generally thicker near the walls of the house, thinning out towards its centre. This floor layer's darker patches were mostly near the hearth (178) and it was generally lighter near the house's edges. The floor was darkest immediately north of the hearth, extending in a narrowing spread of carbonized wood and peat ash to the inward end of the north pier. Context 170 was a second patch of surviving floor layer in the southern half of the house (Figures 6.21, 6.23).

The floor layers appear not to have covered the entire ground surface of the wheelhouse interior. An area between the southeastern doorway and the northeastern pier (*c.*3.50m east–west × *c.*2.50m north–south) had no floor surface, coming straight down onto the clean sand (162) below. This might have been partly the result of the passage of feet in and out of the house. The floor layer was also absent along the house's western periphery, where deposits were eroded long after the Iron Age. As well as the ash spread in floor 166 running northeast from the hearth, a single burnt patch was also found in floor 170 in the south–southwest sector of the house (visible in Figure 6.21 as a densely shaded area).

The differential wear across the house's floor offers insights into patterns of movement through the house during its occupation as well as into erosion caused dur-

ing later occupation of its ruins (phase 8; see Chapter 7). The excavation was carried out before the publication of what are now well-known ideas about the use of space within Iron Age roundhouses (*e.g.* Fitzpatrick 1994) and so the excavators' identification and recording of this floor layer were not informed by any such hypotheses.

The floor layer (166=170) did not survive across all of the southern part of the house, where a narrow band of erosion (between floor 166 to the north and floor 170 to the south) ran westwards from the doorway towards the south side of the hearth (Figure 6.21). That this erosion is likely to have occurred during the occupation of the house is demonstrated by the fact that this part of the house was covered by a dense layer of rubble (175) after its abandonment; this eroded interior strip is covered by the rubble, and cannot therefore have been created after the house was finally abandoned.

The floor layers cannot be interpreted as revealing any details of lines of movement within the house during its initial period of inhabitation. During that period, the walls of the entrance passage would have guided the visitor directly into the central area of the house towards a square hearth, which was later modified to make more space on its north side.

The floor layer (166) was also absent in the east sector of the house, between the doorway and the northeast pier (Figure 6.21). This was broadly the area in front of the southeast-facing entrance to a bothy-like structure (167)

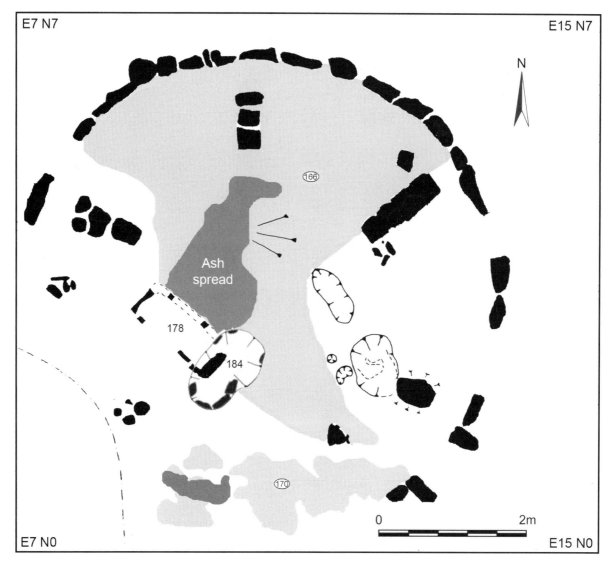

Figure 6.16 Plan of floor layers 166 amd 170 with hearth 178 (and pit 184 beneath it)

that was built within the wheelhouse's ruins in phase 8. This zone was also largely clear of the rubble (175) that accumulated after abandonment of the wheelhouse but before construction of the 'bothy'. It is thus likely that in this part of the building any floor layer associated with the inhabitation of the wheelhouse was eroded by the tramping of feet to and from this secondary structure, well after the wheelhouse in its original form had gone out of use.

There was no evidence of a surviving floor layer in the west of the house, to the west of the hearth and between the remains of the southwest pier and the northwest pier, to about half a metre north of the northwest pier. As with the eastern sector of the wheelhouse, this was an area largely devoid of the rubble (175) deriving from the house's abandonment, and so might have been entered during the structure's re-use through gaps in the west and northwest wall and used in phase 8 as an informal activity area.

The distribution of pottery sherds was plotted within a grid of one-metre squares across floors 166 and 170 (Figure 6.24). This shows a dense concentration in the northern half of the house's central area and in the northeast cell. Fuel ash slag, a flint flake and four pieces of worked antler (SFs 93, 95, 153, 160) came from floor 166.

Accumulation of deposits outside the wall of the wheelhouse (phase 5)

The 1989 long section (Figures 2.16–2.18) shows a series of deposits accumulated on top of layer 3/1989 (which is likely to be contemporary with layers 32, 37 and 59) that pre-dates the wheelhouse's construction (see Chapter 5). The lowest of these was numbered as 4/1989, a mixture of sand and organic material interpreted during excavation by Prof. Dave Gilbertson as containing soil particles blown in from a contemporary soil surface in the vicinity.[3] There

---

[3]   The context number 4/1989 was also used to record a layer within the wheelhouse's wall core (phase 4; see above) and for eroded layers of former wall core material (phase 7) higher up the section.

Figure 6.17 The modified hearth (phase 6) above hearth (178), viewed from the north

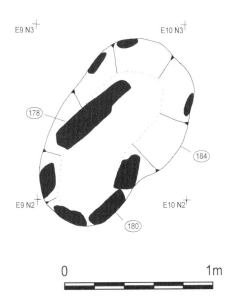

Figure 6.18 Plan of the pit (184) beneath the hearth

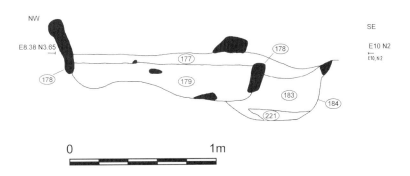

Figure 6.19 Section drawing of the relationship between the hearth (178) and the pit (184) beneath

Figure 6.20 The modified hearth (phase 6) above hearth (178), viewed from the northwest

were streaks of windblown sand (numbered as 7/1989) within this basal layer outside the wheelhouse and, above it, a discontinuous and thin lens of brown-orange sand (11/1989). A 0.12m-thick layer of dark organic sand (8/1989) lay on top of 4/1989 and 11/1989, itself sealed by eroded wall core material (upper component of 4/1989).

Layers 8/1989, 11/1989 and the lower component of 4/1989 are assigned to phase 5: they formed outside the wheelhouse at some time after the house's construction (phase 4) and before the erosion of the wall core (eroded wall core component of 4/1989; phase 7). Their formation also pre-dates the putative construction of a second phase of wall core (layers 9/1989 and 6/1989) and outer wall face that might have constituted the renewal or repair of the building after its initial period of use and which can be assigned to phases 6 or 7 (see 'The walls' above and Chapter 7).

The stone structure in the southern trench

During the 1989 excavation, as well as the main area of excavation located in the central part of the midden, a southern trench, of about 50 sq m, was opened southwards from the southern edge of the eroded area (see

Figures 2.1–2.2). Within the north end of this southern trench, part of a stone structure was encountered but was not fully explored. This consisted of two lines of stones (1.70m and 2.0m long) running southwest–northeast and culminating in a larger mass of laid stone, extending 1.80m east–west and 1.30m north–south, within and just beyond the northeast corner of the trench (Figure 6.25). To the west of this structure, in the northwest corner of the southern trench, was a mass of smaller stones. No context numbers were assigned to these deposits, and it is assumed that no finds were made.

There is no stratigraphic evidence to place this stone structure within the wheelhouse sequence other than that it was buried beneath the same two layers (4/1989=25 under 1/1989=5) that covered the ruins of the wheelhouse (Figures 6.26–6.27). The lower of these (4/1989=25) was a sterile sand that contained small stones (see Chapter 7), possibly some of those shown on Figure 6.26 in the southern trench's northwest corner. The structural stonework is recorded as lying within layer 3/1989, described as a matrix of grey midden deposit with pebbles, and reddish brown and pale mottled patches, and including patches of windblown sand. However, this is the same context number assigned in the 1989 central

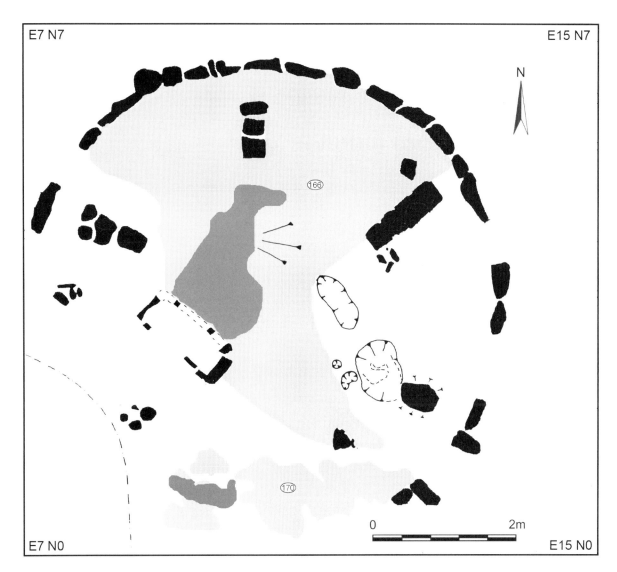

Figure 6.21 Plan of floor layers 166 amd 170 with hearth 178, showing that floor 166 covered pit 184

Figure 6.22 Floor 166, viewed from the east

Figure 6.23 Floor 170, viewed from the east

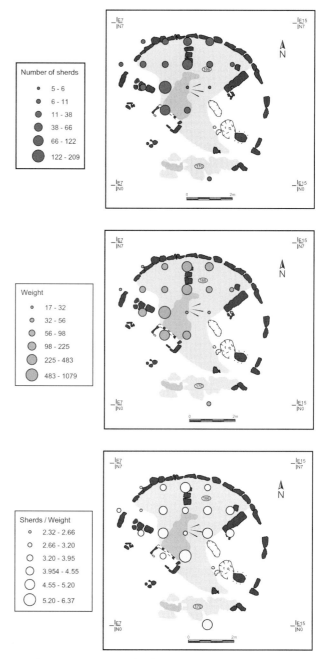

Figure 6.24 Distribution of pottery sherds within floors 166 and 170

excavation area to the layer beneath and beyond the wheelhouse's interior and wall. Since contexts in 1989 were assigned numbers shared on the basis of their type and not their stratigraphic equivalence, we must be wary of equating this layer within the southern trench with either of the layers numbered as 3/1989 in the central trench.

The stone structure in the southern trench would have lain about 5m south-southwest of the outer wall of the wheelhouse, far enough away to belong to a completely different building. Its recorded elements are difficult to interpret as walls or piers, so its likely original form must remain a mystery.

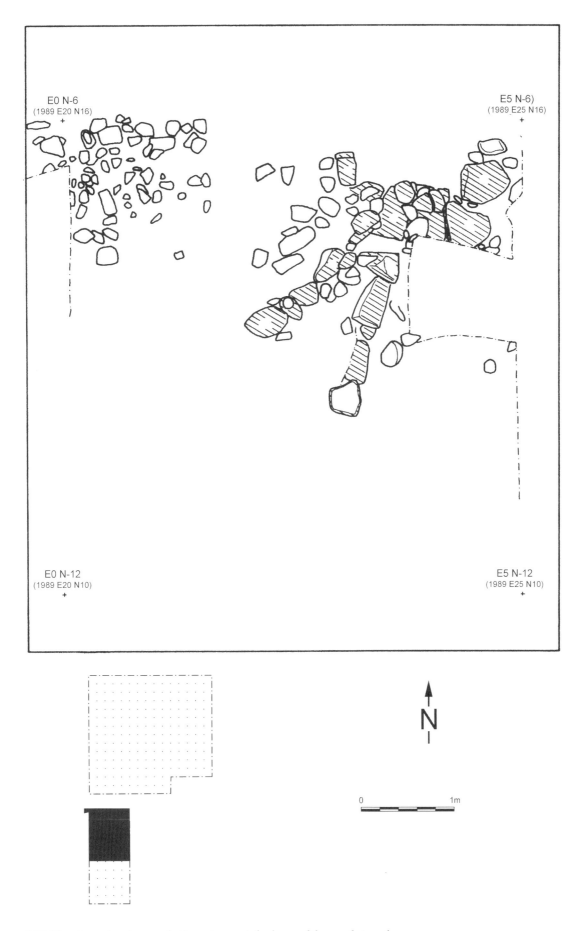

Figure 6.25 The stone structure and other stones at the base of the south trench

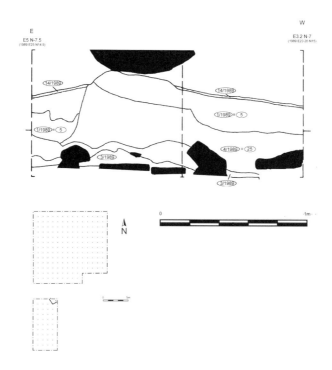

Figure 6.26 Section drawing of the stone structure and layers above it

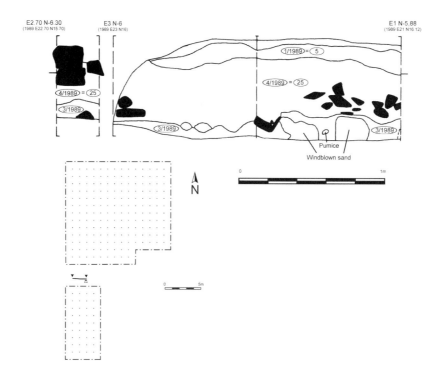

Figure 6.27 Section drawing of layers to the north of the south trench

Chapter 7 Modification and abandonment of the wheelhouse (phases 6–8)

Mike Parker Pearson and Marek Zvelebil

Introduction

Two modifications of the roundhouse interior were detected, both being assigned to phase 6 (Figures 7.1–7.3). The first consisted of a dividing wall extending from the northwestern pier base to the centre of the roundhouse. The second involved restructuring of the hearth – stone uprights were placed above its original lining.

Some time after that, after the wheelhouse had fallen into disuse (phase 7), a smaller, stone-walled round structure (phase 8) was built in the northern sector of the wheelhouse. Its stones, set on edge, were leant against the remains of the northeastern pier base of the original roundhouse and against the phase 6 dividing wall.

Modifications to the wheelhouse interior (phase 6)

The dividing wall

This secondary stone structure (174; Figures 7.4–7.5) was built within the wheelhouse (169) in its northwestern and central area. It was 1.30m long, built of a single course of seven stones on a northwest–southeast axis, and ran southeastwards from the inner end of the house's northwestern pier (Figure 7.6). It thus served to separate the hearth area to its southwest from the northern sector of the house. It appeared to overlie the deposit of carbonized wood and ash (see Figure 6.16) that spread northeastwards from the hearth.

The modified hearth

The hearth was re-built as a sub-rectangular structure, 1.40m northwest–southeast × 1m southwest–northeast, with a kerb of eight surviving flat stones (no context number; Figures 7.2, 7.4–7.6). One of the stones was marked with a zigzag pattern of three chevrons; this is, in fact, a naturally occurring, geological feature within the gneiss and not a humanly created motif (Figure 7.7). Nonetheless, the positioning of this stone within the hearth suggests that this natural pattern might have been noticed and selected for special treatment by the house's Iron Age occupants (Figure 7.8).

This renovated hearth was located on top of the previous hearth (Figure 7.9). Around this hearth in the southwest sector of the wheelhouse, was a dark, black/brown layer with extensive traces of burning (16/1989[1]), revealed beneath a concentration of stones (175; located in squares E9/N0–E9/N3 and E12/N0–E12/N2). Context 16/1989 is described as a 0.15m–0.20m-thick lens of burnt black and orange soil (in squares 59, 58, 49 and 48) found among this rubble (175) infilling the wheelhouse, and extending from the same level as the top of these stones to beneath them. The top of context 16/1989 consisted of burnt black sand, and its bottom of reddish brown/orange peat ash; the few finds consisted of carbonized wood fragments, burnt bone and seven sherds. Context 16/1989 is the topmost layer of the central hearth, the stone lining of which protruded through it.

Gully 182

A small ditch or gully, 0.55m wide, running just south of the hearth, was filled with brown sand rich with flecks of carbonized wood (182) containing mainly shell and some bone. This feature cut into the top of the black fill (177) of the earlier hearth from phase 5.[2]

---

[1] In the site archive this context is occasionally described incorrectly as 170 and 14/1989.

[2] See Chapter 16, Table 16.1 for details of the pair of radiocarbon dates from the fill of gully 182; these contribute to the model shown in Figure 16.2 that dates the construction of the wheelhouse to *cal AD 170–360 (95% probability)*.

Figure 7.1 The wheelhouse early in the 1991 excavation season, viewed from the east; Marek Zvelebil is in the foreground

Accumulation of deposits outside the wall of the wheelhouse (phase 6)

After 0.30m of deposits (4/1989, 11/1989 and 8/1989) accumulated outside the southwest wall of the wheelhouse, probably during its initial use (phase 5), there was a further accumulation of 0.20m–0.30m of sand layers against the outer wall face prior to the robbing of this outer wall face and the deposition in phase 9 of a deep layer of windblown sand (2/1989=36) followed by a midden layer (1/1989=5; see Chapter 8).

The lowest of these sand layers (9/1989 and some of the layers numbered as 7/1989) accumulated on top of the two basal courses of the outer wall face. They appear to be overlain by the cut for an upper section of walling that was later robbed out in phase 9. Layer 9/1989 was a dark, organic lens of sand, flecked with carbonized wood and up to 0.08m thick. Above it lay a thin layer of windblown sand 0.03m thick (7/1989 again). Both layers straddle the wall core, the revetted wall face and the exterior layers beyond the wheelhouse, and are assigned to phase 6 because they appear to represent a modification or re-building of the wheelhouse wall.

The sand layers 9/1989 and 7/1989 lie beneath the uppermost layer of rebuilt wall core material (6/1989, a dark, fairly organic sand layer also belonging to phases 6 and 7). Beyond the robbing trench of the outer wall face (filled with midden material 5=1/1989; phase 9), a lens

of layer 6/1989 is probably the eroded residue from the upper wall core layer 6/1989 that presumably accumulated when the wheelhouse was abandoned.

Abandonment of the wheelhouse (phase 7)

The floor of the wheelhouse was covered by a spread of stones (175) across its interior. These were most numerous in the cells between the northeast, north and northwest piers, and in the southern area immediately west of the doorway (Figure 7.10). Although it is likely that a large proportion of the wheelhouse's stonework was robbed, this surviving distribution of stones supports the notion that the cells were corbelled whilst the central circular area would have been roofed with organic materials of wood, turf and thatch: a reasonable hypothesis is that the rubble derives from the collapsed corbelled roofs of the cells.

The stone spread (175) was covered by a layer of medium-brown sand (25=176) in the central and eastern parts of the wheelhouse, spreading against the inside faces of the circular house wall. This was interpreted as sand dumped to infill the abandoned building. Layer 25 contained a number of bone and antler artefacts, among them a bone spindle whorl (SF30), a bone disc (SF111), a possible whale bone peg (SF135), and two antler objects (SFs 152, 154). It also produced a large quantity of

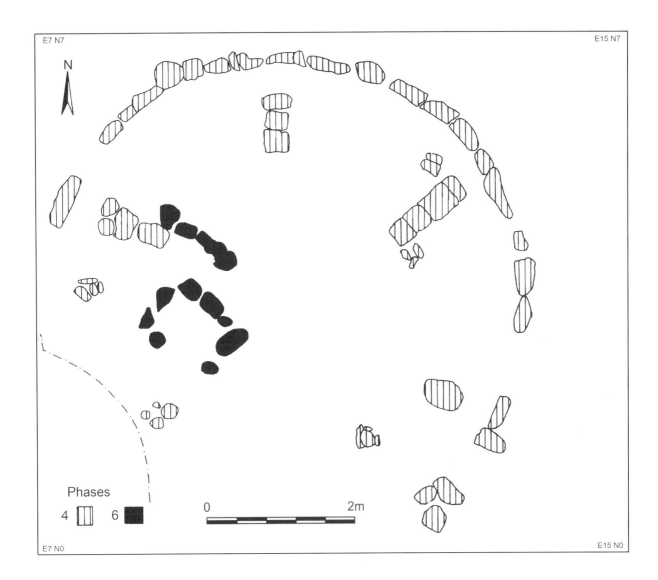

Figure 7.2 Modifications within the wheelhouse (phase 6), consisting of the remodelled hearth and wall (174)

sherds with applied cordons, and two sherds with incised decoration.

Within the top of 25=176, another deposit also numbered as layer 16/1989 formed a lens of burned black and orange sand and carbonized wood fragments found among stones in squares 59, 58, 49 and 48 (see Figure 5.1 for square numbers).

Layer 25=176 can be equated with that part of layer 4/1989 that lay within the interior of the wheelhouse, where it was overlain by a thin layer of white windblown sand (numbered as 7/1989, again) and inter-bedded with localized lenses of windblown sand (also 7/1989). It may consist of the remains of the collapsed turf roof as well as wind-transported and artificially added deposits in amongst fallen masonry on top of the abandoned house's floor. A thin lens of peat ash (12/1989) at the top of layer 4/1989 may signal a brief re-occupation of the wheel-house ruins after the roof was off but before the interior filled with windblown sand (2/1989).

Context 26 was a discrete area of black-stained sand containing carbonized wood, described as below layer

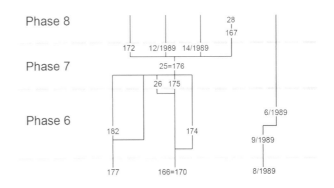

Figure 7.3 Stratigraphic matrix for the Iron Age layers associated with the wheelhouse's modification and abandonment. Several contexts from the 1989 season have had to be omitted, either because their stratigraphic position is unclear or because the same context number was used for multiple contexts

Figure 7.4 Wall 174 with the modified hearth behind it, viewed from the northwest

25, containing much pottery and bone. That would place it within the ruins of the wheelhouse, perhaps amongst or below the stones (175). Another context that may belong to the period of abandonment is layer 172, described as fill in the stone holes of the wheelhouse after the stones were removed, though there is no information in the site archive on this context's location or stratigraphic position or what stone holes it was seen in.

Most of the robbing of the stones from the wheelhouse's inner and outer wall faces did not take place until after abandonment, during phase 7. Robber trenches were dug to remove stones from the revetment walls before the accumulation of layers 2/1989 (=36) and 1/1989 (=5) in phase 9. The piers inside the wheelhouse were removed down to their basal courses during either phase 6 or phase 7, prior to the accumulation of the rubble (175) and the associated sand layer (25=176).

Pottery from layer 25=176 includes flared rims characteristic of the Late Iron Age (AD 300–900); layer 25 also produced metalworking slag. Phase 7 contexts produced a copper-alloy ring (4/1989) and a number of iron objects (see Chapter 10).

The small, stone-walled structure and re-use of the wheelhouse (phase 8)

A circular stone structure (167) was built within the northern half of the abandoned wheelhouse (Figures 7.11–7.12). A hole was dug into the brown sand layer (25=176) and this cut was then lined with stones pitched at 60°–80° with their bases resting on the disturbed remains of the wheelhouse floor (166=170). On its southwestern side, the edging stones of this structure lay at an angle over the remains of the dividing wall (174) although this stratigraphic relationship was not particularly clear.

This circular structure was internally only about 1.30m in diameter, with a 0.90m-wide entranceway to the southeast. The density of masonry and rubble was much lower within this structure and outside its entranceway to the southeast than in other parts of the ruined wheelhouse (Figure 7.13). This suggests that fallen stones were cleared to provide unhindered access into this small building.

It would seem that access towards the small circular structure was not only through the wheelhouse's original doorway but also through two gaps made in the east side of the wheelhouse's interior wall face by the removal of upright stones. One of these gaps was about 0.80m north of the doorway and the other, much narrower, was about a metre further north (Figures 7.11, 7.14). Both of these gaps coincided with the west ends of slight gullies that might have been footpaths leading to the small circular building from the east.

The stone uprights that would have formed the inner face of the wheelhouse's wall were also removed from its

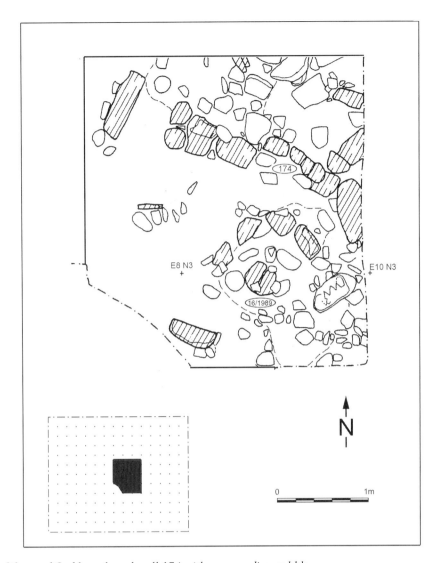

Figure 7.5 Plan of the modified hearth and wall 174 with surrounding rubble

south and west sectors, and it is possible that they were robbed out in this phase, either during the collection of building stone for use elsewhere or for the utilization of these parts of the ruined wheelhouse for some other purpose. It is possible that, between two robbed-out zones, part of the wall in the southwest sector survived into this phase, judging by the large stones (context 10/1989 and four large stones to its north; see Chapter 8) deposited either side of the small sand quarry that encroached into the southwest sector of the former wheelhouse.

The missing stone in the northwest sector of the wheelhouse's inner wall face (the gap is visible in Figures 7.11 and 7.14) coincides with an area of eroded house floor (166; see Figure 6.21), suggesting that it was removed to facilitate access into the wheelhouse ruins in phase 8. The rubble (175) inside the ruined wheelhouse was larger and denser on the north side of this potential line of entry (Figure 7.10). As noted in Chapter 6, the western sector of the wheelhouse, between the bases of the northwest and southwest piers, was largely devoid both of floor layers (166=170) and of rubble (175), indicative of erosion caused by activities possibly more

intense than merely the removal of building stone. In this respect, however, it is unlikely that the modified hearth from phase 6 was re-used in phase 8 since ash and carbonized wood from the hearth were encountered only from the same level as the top of the hearth stones (*i.e.* from amongst the rubble [175] and not from on top of it). Thus the wheelhouse hearth is unlikely to have formed a focus for re-use of this sector of the ruin.

The most likely interpretation of the circular stone structure (167) is that it was a small shieling- or bothy-type building constructed some time after the wheelhouse had been abandoned and filled in. The pitched stones against the wheelhouse's north wall are reminiscent of the lower walling of Structure 4 from the Middle Iron Age cellular phase 2 building at Cnip, Lewis (Harding and Armit 1990: 92–3; Armit 2006) although the Cnip example is much larger.

The small building (167) was filled with a layer of light sand (28), which produced a small assemblage of plain sherds, a piece of worked cetacean bone (SF127) and a fragment of worked antler (SF39). This filling of the structure occurred either when its roof came off or, if

Figure 7.6 The modified hearth, viewed from the south; the 'zigzag' stone is in the centre of the picture

Figure 7.7 Close-up of the modified hearth, viewed from the south-southeast

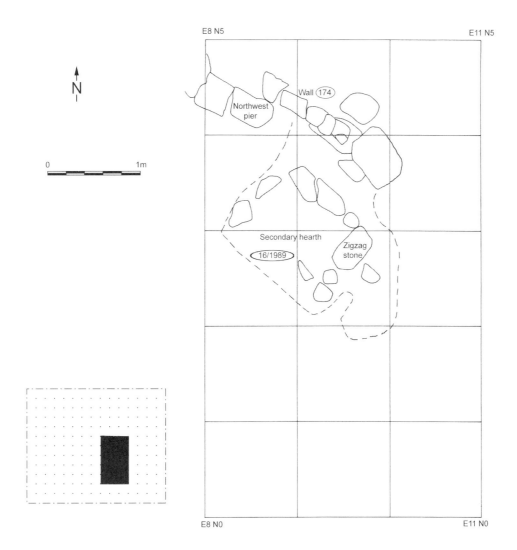

Figure 7.8 Outline plan of the modified hearth, wall 174 and layer 16/1989 as recorded during the 1989 season

the structure was never roofed, during the first major sand blow after construction. The entire area of the wheelhouse and its environs was then covered with a series of midden layers.

Figure 7.9 Stones from the modified hearth and from the original hearth (178) below, viewed from the southeast

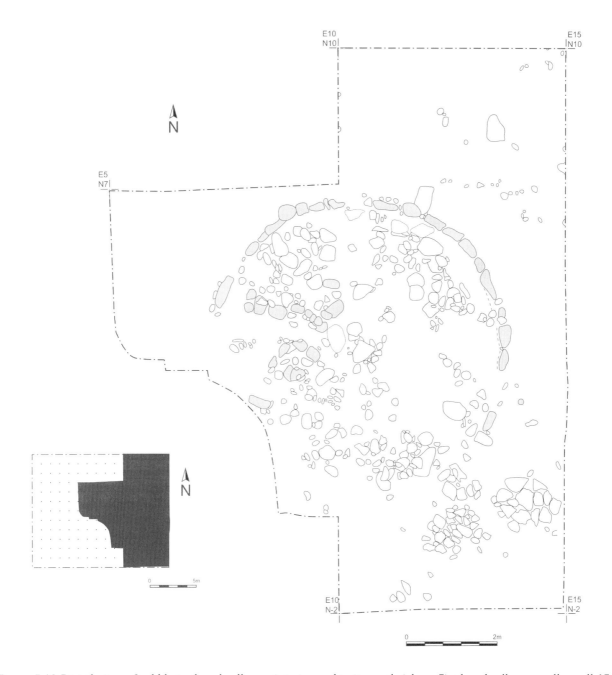

Figure 7.10 Distribution of rubble in the wheelhouse interior and to its south (phase 7); the wheelhouse walls, wall 174 and the modified hearth are shaded

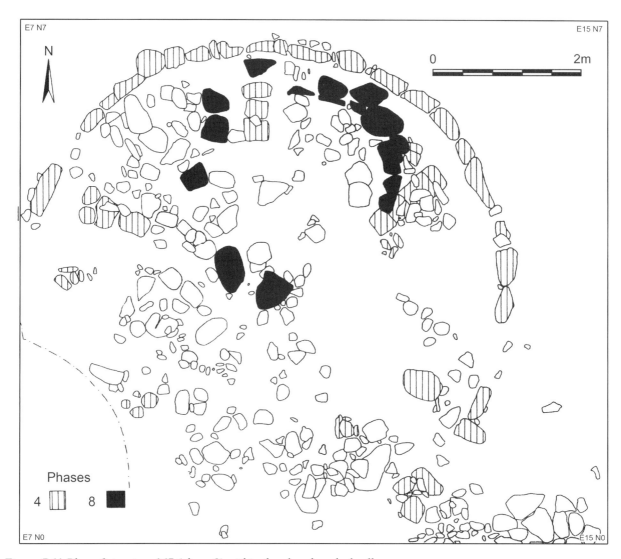

Figure 7.11 Plan of structure 167 (phase 8) within the abandoned wheelhouse

Figure 7.12 Structure 167, viewed from the south

Figure 7.13 The interior of the wheelhouse, viewed from the east, showing the rubble-free areas within

Figure 7.14 Structure 167, viewed from the southeast; the gaps in the wheelhouse wall are visible in the foreground

Chapter 8 The midden overlying the wheelhouse (phase 9)

Mike Parker Pearson

Introduction

A series of midden layers covered the whole wheelhouse. During MPP's work on the excavation archive it became evident that there are some discrepancies between the full range of stratigraphic information available concerning contexts in the midden (Figure 8.1) and the matrix originally drawn up by MZ (Figure 8.2). A second matrix has therefore been created, drawing on all available information in the site archive; both matrices are illustrated but this chapter uses the more detailed matrix in Figure 8.1.

On the house's west side, a thick layer of light brown windblown sand (21=36=2/1989) covered the remains of the building before the midden formed (Figure 8.3). The most extensive of the midden layers (layer 5=1/1989) was a dark, undifferentiated organic layer.

Finds from midden layer 5=1/1989 include eight hammerstones, a cup-marked stone, metalworking slag, worked pumice and eight cetacean bone objects, as well as an ivory object (SF131), worked antler, and 19 bone artefacts, including pins, points, needles and beads (see Chapter 12). Layer 5 also produced a significant number of metal artefacts, including iron objects (among them a ring and a number of nails) and copper-alloy objects such as a belt fitting (SF5) and a Roman plate-headed knee brooch (SF6). The brooch has Continental parallels dating to *c*.AD 150–300 (see Chapter 10), yet radiocarbon dates on carbonized grain date the final activity that created the midden to *cal AD 580–665 (68% probability)*. A further carbonized grain from layer 103 in this midden is dated to cal AD 720–1030 at 95.4% probability (OxA-3353; 1115±70 BP); it is assumed to be intrusive but need not be.

As well as Late Iron Age sherds, the large pottery assemblage from this layer includes residual Middle Iron Age sherds with applied cordons, and impressed and incised decorations. This layer also contained carbonized wood, animal bone, marine shell and burnt bone.

Parts of the midden surface had spademarks and ploughmarks (Figure 8.4). During excavation, this midden deposit was thought to be debris associated with manuring of the machair and its cultivation. However, subsequent experience of similar deposits at Cladh Hallan (Parker Pearson *et al*. 2004: 59–87), Dun Vulan (Parker Pearson and Sharples 1999), Bornais (Sharples 2005; 2012b) and other South Uist sites (Parker Pearson 2012b) makes it more likely that this was a deposit of chronologically mixed domestic waste from an adjacent locale. Such middens might occasionally have been cultivated, even when they lay directly adjacent to domestic structures.

The earliest midden layers

Context 5 (layer 1/1989; also the same as context 51), a dark grey/brown fine sand, was the principal midden layer, stratified beneath the topsoil (contexts 0, 1 and 3) and lying in certain places on windblown sand (2/1989=36) and elsewhere on a whole range of discrete cultural deposits (Figure 8.5), notably those of the abandoned wheelhouse. It lay beneath contexts 2–4, 6–14, and 18–20 but was also judged to be coeval with contexts 14 and 15. Layer 5 and other midden layers are shown in a series of section drawings across the eastern half of the excavation (Figures 8.6–8.10); in Figure 8.11 some are shown in plan.

Layer 5 sloped southwards and, though overlain by these layers, its varying organic content made the transitions between layers so gradual as to make it impossible to distinguish them as clearly separate. The top of layer 5 was approximately level with the top of the wheelhouse's stone uprights. As layer 5 increased in depth, so its organic content decreased and its sand matrix became lighter, with the addition of mottled streaks and larger lenses of clean sand. Layer 5 can be equated with layers 2 and 11 in Quarry Trenches 1 and 2 (see Chapter 3).

Layer 15 was identified as being stratigraphically at the base of layer 5 yet still part of it. Context 15 in the

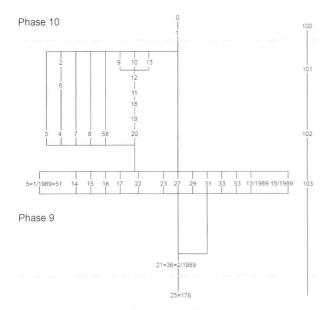

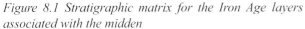

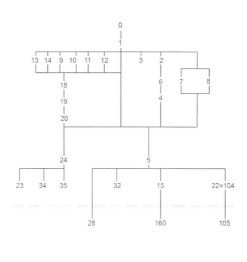

Figure 8.1 Stratigraphic matrix for the Iron Age layers associated with the midden

Figure 8.2 Stratigraphic matrix for the Iron Age layers associated with the midden, as depicted in MZ's original matrix

Figure 8.3 Section showing the midden layer (5=1/1989) on top of windblown sand (layer 21=36=2/1989), viewed from the south

area north of the wheelhouse was arguably a separate deposit to layer 5, containing a greater amount of carbonized wood fragments and small clumps of shell in a red or black matrix of peat ash (0.02m–0.10m thick).[1]

Context 14 was thought originally to be a separate, earlier deposit on the eastern edge of the site (in squares 142, 143, 144, 133, 134; E13–14/N2–4) but was subsequently recognized as a lower component of context 5,

---

[1] Note that context 15 described here (excavated in 1990) is not the same as context 15/1989 described below.

Figure 8.4 Ploughmarks in the tops of layers 102 and 103 in the southeast corner of the main trench, viewed from the east

infilling the uneven and undulating surfaces of deposits beneath, including small gullies (these are visible in Figure 8.5). A copper-alloy tang or shaft (SF7) was found in the top of this context (*i.e.* within the lower part of context 5) in square 144. The deposits in the gullies contained a greater amount of shell and bone, presumably washed into them. Also at the bottom of layer 5, context 53 was a dark orange-brown deposit with occasional darker patches, recognized in the north section of the 1991 extension (Figure 8.12).

North of context 14, in the northeast corner of the site (in squares 138, 139, 148, 149; refer to Figure 5.1 for location of squares), an area of stones (no context number) was found within layer 5; this was possibly destroyed paving (Figures 8.13–8.15). Artefacts embedded amongst and outside the stones included two crushed pots and a collection of hammerstones (SFs 18, 19, 22, 23, 26, 27).

Within layer 5=1/1989, layer 15/1989 was attributed to two separate deposits, one at or near the base of layer 5=1/1989 and the other on top of it:

• The lower of these was an extensive, ill-defined lens of dark, burnt sand outside the wheelhouse along the northern and southern edges of the 1989 long section. Its edges were hard to define but this deposit was

more compacted than layer 5=1/1989. On section drawings it is shown as occurring within the lower component of layer 5/1989 (Figure 8.16) and is described as resting on top of sterile sand layer 2/1989=21=36 and being beneath the main midden layer 5=1/1989 towards the edges of its distribution (*i.e.* square 85). A rich sample of carbonized plant remains (sample 11 from square 16 of layer 15/1989) came from this deposit's southern end.

• Context 15/1989 was also the number assigned to a dark sand layer within the wheelhouse, associated with an accumulation of stones in squares 48, 58 and 68 (Figure 8.11). It is described as found within or on top of layer 5=1/1989, just under the topsoil, with the centre of its distribution amongst stones in squares 68, 58, 67 and 57. The sample of carbonized plant remains from this deposit (sample 16 from square 58) was also rich in barley. A radiocarbon date of cal AD 570–660 (95% probability; SUERC-38628, 1430±30BP) was obtained from carbonized grain in layer 15/1989.[2]

Layer 13/1989 was a small area (0.20m × 0.25m × 0.05m–0.07m thick) of burnt sand on top of layer 2/1989, at the bottom of layer 1/1989 in square 82's southwest corner. Other midden layers excavated in 1989 in the western half of the main trench were 12/1989 and

---

[2]   A further pair of radiocarbon dates for phase 9 comes from layer 1/1989 (see Table 16.1).

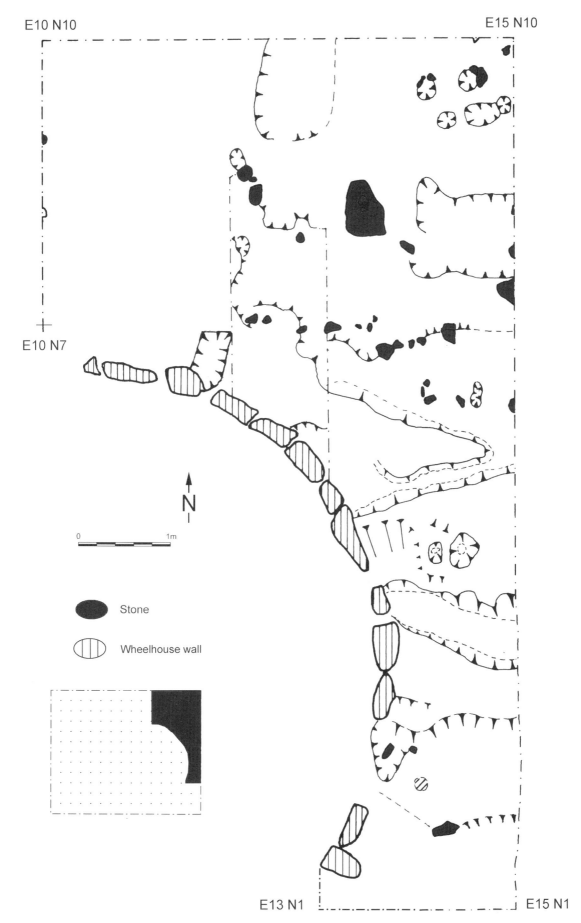

Figure 8.5 Plan of the base of the midden after removal of layer 5=1/1989 in the eastern part of the main trench

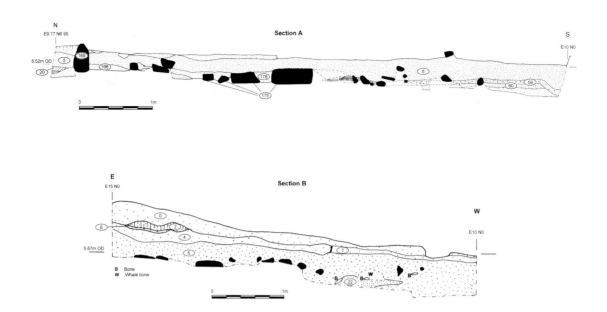

Figure 8.6 Section drawings A and B through the midden layers

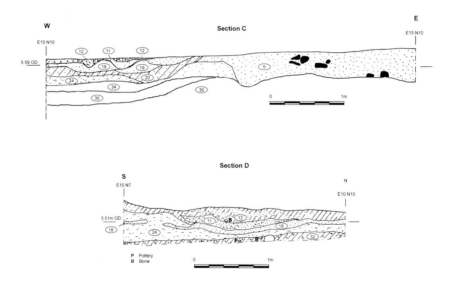

Figure 8.7 Section drawings C and D through the midden layers

17/1989, a 0.02m-thick layer of clean windblown sand settled among the stones of the ruined wheelhouse (Figure 8.17).

Context 12/1989 was assigned to a variety of orange/brown peat ash deposits in several locations in the uppermost part of the midden layers, mostly within layers 5=1/1989, 2/1989 and 3/1989 (Figures 2.16, 8.16–8.18). It was subdivided into 12a/1989 to 12e/1989:

- Context 12a/1989 was assigned to a bowl-shaped deposit in square 37.
- Context 12b/1989 was assigned to a burnt layer in squares 85–65, 86–66 and extending across squares 84, 94–95, on top of 2/1989 (the sand layer beneath the midden).
- Context 12c/1989 was assigned to an orange/brown

and carbonized wood layer within context 15=1/1989, in squares 65–66.

- Context 12d/1989 was assigned to an orange/brown and carbonized wood layer within the top of context 3/1989, in squares 54 and 64.
- Context 12e/1989 was both an indistinct feature of compacted shells embedded in peat ash in the northwest part of the excavation, and also the displaced matrix of peat ash associated with recently tumbled stones from the wheelhouse wall (context 10/1989; see below).

Context 22, a black layer (0.10m–0.20m thick) in squares 110 and 120, just west of the entrance to the roundhouse and lying on sterile sand (layer 36=2/1989), was covered by the main midden (layer 5); a piece of whale bone was

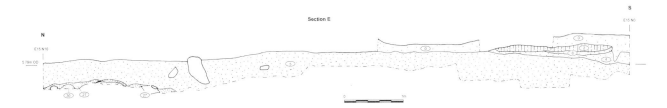

Figure 8.8 Section drawing E through the midden layers

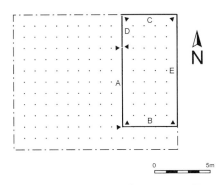

Figure 8.9 Positions of section drawings A–E within the main trench

found at the junction of layers 5 and 22 (Figure 8.6). Context 27 was an ill-defined area with dark stains within the sandy matrix, no more than 0.10m thick, indicating traces of burning, inter-bedded between contexts 5 and 30 (Figure 8.8). It was located in squares 147, 148, 149 and contained plain pottery, carbonized wood, animal bone, a piece of metalworking slag, a bone spatula (SF104) and four further pieces of worked bone and antler. Together with layer 27, layer 22 appears to have been part of an extensive but discontinuous burnt deposit at the base of layer 5.

In the northeast part of the trench, west of the un-numbered spread of stones described above, layer 23 was a discrete, circular spread of orange peat ash (about 0.50–0.60m in diameter in square 108; Figure 8.19) below contexts 12 and 18 and above layer 24 (the sand wall core of the wheelhouse in phase 4).

Context 29 was a burnt layer in squares 100 and 101.[3] Context 31 was an area of light sand (confined mostly to squares 132, 133) inter-bedded between contexts 5, 25 and 30; context 31 resembled context 27. Despite its fairly clean sand matrix, it contained burnt stains, pottery, animal bone, a hammerstone, a piece of metalworking slag, and eight worked bone and antler artefacts. The bottom of this layer was marked by a dense but thin, black layer. Context 33 was a black, burnt layer in the southern area of the trench (squares 101, 102, 111 and 121), about 0.10m thick and containing much pottery, bone and shell.

Windblown sand layers

Much of the site was covered by a layer of windblown sand (2/1989) up to 0.55m thick, on which the midden layer 5=1/1989 had built up. Layer 2/1989 formed an extensive spread of mottled, buff sterile sand. It is equated with context 21, a more-or-less sterile light buff sand located in the northern area of the excavation. Windblown sand was elsewhere found in patches; it is difficult to place these within the stratigraphic sequence but contexts 16 and 17 are described as being within layer 5. Context 16 consisted of lenses of fine windblown sand found in patches in square 120, and also filling between the stone uprights of the wheelhouse. Context 17 was a 0.02m-thick deposit of almost sterile windblown sand between loose stones (in square 147) within layer 5.

Cultivation

In the southern area of the site the surfaces of layers 4 (see below) and 5 bore marks of cultivation. These took the form of two parallel, ephemeral streaks of light sand, produced probably by an ard or hoe, with the furrows having subsequently filled with windblown sand (Figure 8.20). Further south, ploughmarks on the same east–west axis were uncovered in the southeast corner of the trench (Figure 8.4) where they cut across the intersection of layers 102 and 103 (Figure 8.21); layer 103 is equivalent to layer 5. The southeast corner of the excavation was dug as a separate block to the rest of the trench and its contexts were given a separate, unique sequence of numbers (100–106). Layer 103 lay above layers 104–106 (see Chapters 5 and 6). Layer 103 produced two copper-alloy objects, including a penannular brooch (SF26) and a fragment of clay refractory. Above layer 103, context 102 was a layer of sand and context 101 was loose sand above 102 (context 100 was the topsoil above).

Evidence of light burning at the junction between layers 4 and 5 was interpreted by MZ as indicating the burning-off of vegetation, though this seems fanciful. The surface of layer 5 was level with the top of the stone uprights of the wheelhouse, indicating that field cultivation could have been carried out in this soil layer across the entire area of the abandoned house.

---

[3] Square 101 is perhaps marked as context 31: there is ambiguity in the context sheet notes. Context 29 is also described in the excavation records, perhaps mistakenly, as corresponding to context 59 (phase 3) but on the outside of the wheelhouse interior, under the wall core.

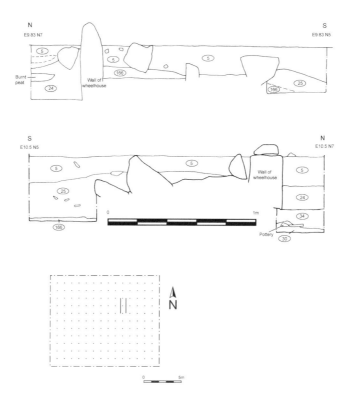

Figure 8.10 Section drawing of both sides of a temporary baulk through the midden and abandonment layers on top of the north side of the wheelhouse

Upper layers of the midden

Midden layer 5 was covered by a series of partial and discrete deposits. Context 4 was a virtually sterile, probably windblown sand layer, up to 0.20m deep, in the southeast part of the site (in squares 140, 141, 142, 130, 131, 132, 120 and 121). As described above, marks probably caused by ard cultivation were noted on the surface of layer 4. Pottery from layers 4 and 5 (and from 103 and 104) includes flared rims dating to the Late Iron Age (AD 300–900). Carbonized grain from layer 103 (equivalent to layer 5) dated to cal AD 720–1030 at 95.4% probability (OxA-3353; 1115±70 BP).

Layer 4 lay on top of layer 5 and beneath layer 6, a coarse, pale buff sand lens only about 0.01m thick, in square 140. Above layer 6 was another layer of windblown sand and organic material (context 2), 0.10m–0.15m thick in the site's southeast corner (square 140; Figures 8.6, 8.8).

Also in the southeast part of the site, to the west of layers 2, 4 and 6, was context 7, a dark grey, silty sand up to 0.10m thick (in squares 100, 101, 110 and 111) that abutted layer 4 and blended gradually into layer 5 (Figure 8.6). In the northwestern part of the site (squares 107 and 117), context 8 was an orange/grey, silty sand forming discrete lenses just 0.04m thick.[4] On the eastern edge of the excavation (squares 145–146) context 3 consisted of a firm, grey midden deposit with pebbles and red-brown and pale mottled patches just 0.03m thick (Figure 8.20).

Abutting layers 4 and 7 was layer 58, a dark brown, speckled sand with the texture of a fine sandy soil, described as a continuation of the main midden layer (*i.e.* layer 5; Figure 8.22).

In the northeast part of the excavation, between the unnumbered area of stones at the eastern edge of the trench and contexts 23 and 24, context 20 (in squares 118, 119 and 129; Figure 8.11) is described variously in the excavation records as *either* a dark mottled greenish-grey silty sand *or* a black/red-brown 'clay'[5] deposit with evidence of burning (the former description is probably a confusion with the layer above it [context 19]; see below). Context 20 is described as very similar to layer 24, the spread of wall core material beneath layer 20 (described in Chapter 6; Figure 8.7), with a thickness of mostly 0.02m–0.03m but ranging up to 0.20m in depth.

Above layer 20 was layer 19, a slightly green-tinged, fine compact sand in squares 119 and 129. It appears to have been a pocket of virtually sterile windblown sand filling a hollow no more than 0.15m deep (Figures 8.7, 8.11). Above it, context 18 consisted of discontinuous stains of orange, brown and black peat ash set in a light sand matrix, abutting and below contexts 11, 12 and 13 (in squares 107–109 and 117–119). Context 18's maximum thickness was no more than 0.20m but in places it was so thin that it appeared as a stain rather than an isolated deposit; it produced two bone points, worked cetacean bone, and a small quantity of residual Middle Iron Age sherds.

---

[4] The lenses of context 8 are probably the areas indicated as 'Grey silty sand' in Figure 8.20.

[5] Given that clay does not occur on the machair, this is likely to be a misidentification of a thick peat ash deposit.

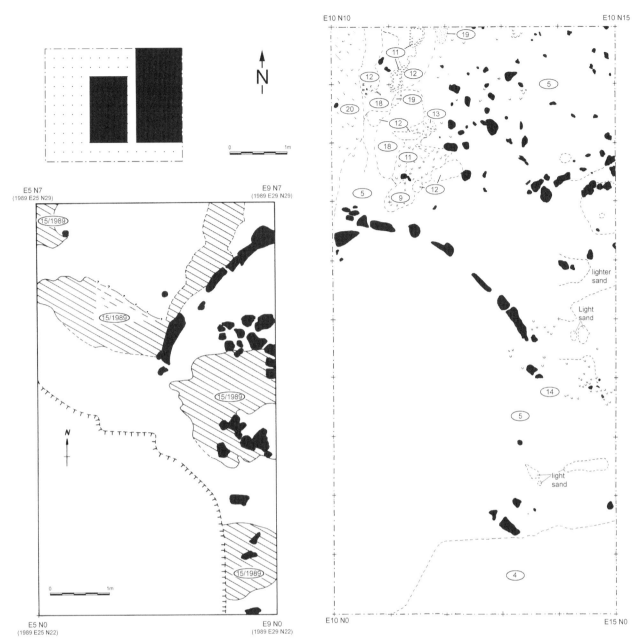

Figure 8.11 Plan of layers within the midden, generally its lower levels; layer 15/1989 inside the abandoned wheelhouse is different from 15/1989 outside it, and those contexts recorded in 1989 (left half of plan) are not necessarily at the same stratigraphic level as those in the right half

A series of layers (contexts 9–14) were later than layer 18 and some could be related stratigraphically to each other. In the northeast part of the site, context 12 was an orange/brown silty deposit (in squares 108, 109, 118 and 119), never exceeding 0.10m in thickness. Layer 12 consisted of a 0.10m-thick deposit in squares 108, 109, 118 and 119 at a depth of 0.02m–0.20m (Figures 8.7, 8.11). This context number was also assigned to two other contexts to the north of the wheelhouse or level with the top of its stone uprights (on both the outside and inside): an orange/grey deposit 0.02m–0.06m thick in squares 107

and 117, and a black ash and carbonized wood deposit within a greenish buff sand in discrete lenses in squares 127, 117, 108 and 118 at the base of layer 5=1/1989.

Above context 12 was a layer of dark red to black peat ash with clumps of shell fragments (13). Also above layer 12, context 10 was an indistinct feature up to 0.60m deep containing a fill (11) of compacted shells within orange peat ash. Although the feature was variably up to 0.60m deep in places, the thickness of fill layer 11 nowhere exceeded 0.20m in thickness.[6] Above layers 11 and 12 was context 9, a deposit of black ash and carbonized wood

---

[6]   There is a numbering difficulty with context 11, however, since photographs of the section identify context 11 as being a midden layer beneath layer 12 and above layer 18 (see Figure 8.7, particularly Section D).

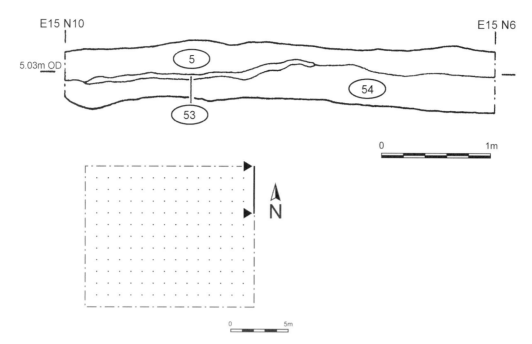

Figure 8.12 Section drawing of layers 53 and 54 in the northeast part of the main trench; the precise position of this drawn section is not known with certainty

Figure 8.13 The spread of stones, with pottery, animal bones and hammerstones, in the northeast corner of the main trench within layer 5=1/1989, viewed from the south

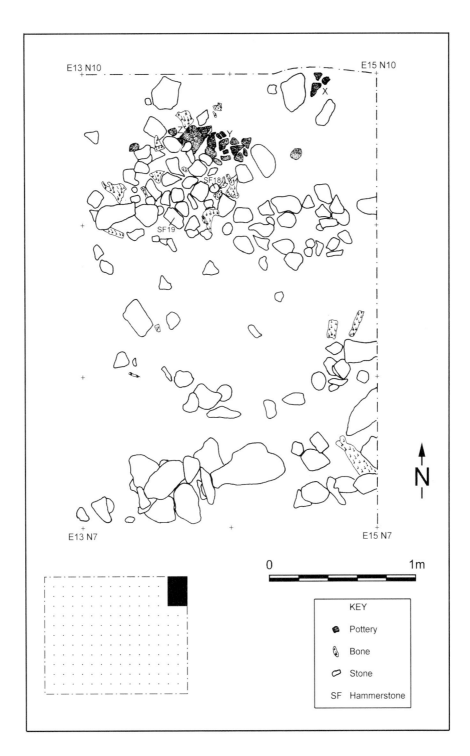

Figure 8.14 Plan of the spread of stones in the northeast corner of the main trench within layer 5=1/1989

Figure 8.15 The spread of stones in the northeast corner of the main trench within layer 5=1/1989, viewed from the east

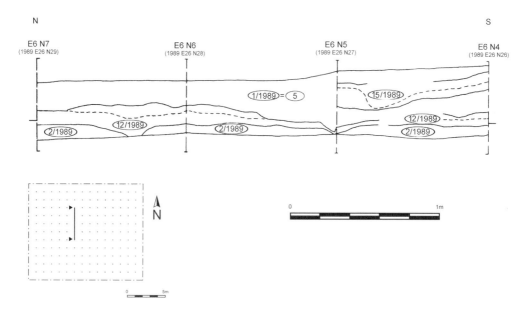

Figure 8.16 Section drawing of midden layers in the western part of the main trench

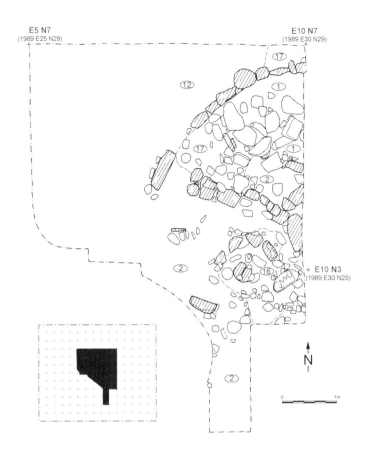

Figure 8.17 Layers 1/1989, 2/1989, 12/1989, 16/1989 and 17/1989 in the central part of the main trench within the ruins of the wheelhouse

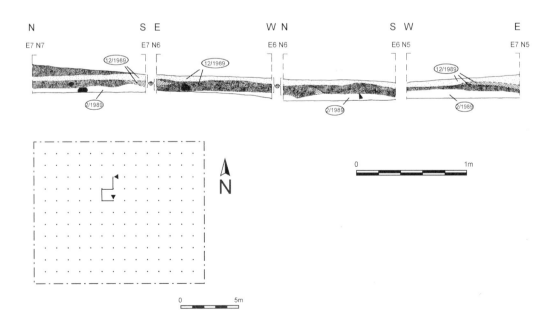

Figure 8.18 Section drawing of layers 2/1989 (=21=36) and 12/1989 in the central part of the main trench

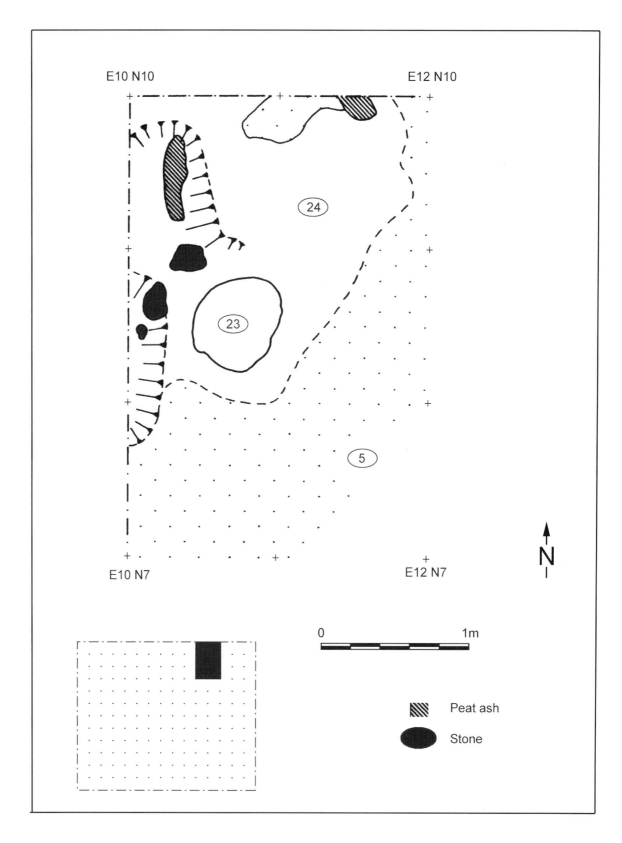

Figure 8.19 Layer of burnt peat ash (23) on top of the sand wall core (24; phase 4) of the wheelhouse

Figure 8.20 Plan of upper layers within the midden deposits; those recorded in 1989 (left half of plan) are not necessarily at the same stratigraphic level as those in the right half

fragments forming discrete lenses within a green/buff sand about 0.07m thick (in squares 127, 117, 108 and 118).

The southern excavation trench

In the southern trench, the stone structure tentatively assigned to phases 4–5 (see Chapter 6) was covered by the same thick layer of light brown windblown sand (21=36=2/1989) that covered the remains of the wheelhouse before the midden formed. This sand layer was encountered across the entire southern trench. It was then partially covered by a midden layer likely to be the

same as 5=1/1989 in the main trench, and given the same context number.

A shelly layer (context 1s/1989) formed the uppermost deposit in the southern trench, partially covering layer 5=1/1989 (Figure 8.23). There were two large stones, one of them a metre across, lying on top of layer 1s/1989.[7]

The top of the stratigraphic sequence (phase 10)

Above all of these midden layers was a very thin cultural

---

[7]   Unfortunately it has not been possible to entirely separate finds from layer 5=1/1989 in the southern trench from those in the central trench because some of the square numbers (50–54, 60–64, 70–74, 80–84, 90–94) are duplicates, occurring in both trenches in 1989 (see Figure 2.15 for square numbers).

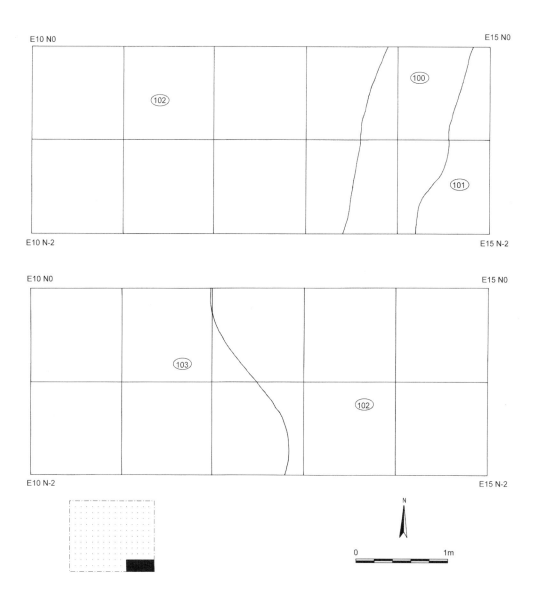

Figure 8.21 Layers 101, 102 and 103 as recorded at different levels in the southeast corner of the main trench; the ploughmarks shown in Figure 8.4 were visible at the level of the lower plan

layer (context 1) just below the topsoil (context 0). Layer 1 was a loose brown sand with buff-coloured patches, containing small quantities of shell, bone and pottery. This context was not sieved: at the time of excavation it was thought to have been the result of recent cultivation. It corresponds with layer 54 in the 1991 east extension, a light grey/brown sand with yellow lenses of sterile sand and a limited amount of organic admixture.

Three groups of stones were encountered within the sand blow-out within the western part of the central excavation, to the west of the wheelhouse. Layers 5=1/1989 and 2/1989=21=36 did not survive in this western part of the trench, as a result of wind erosion and sand-quarrying. The three heaps of stones lay on the eroded surface of the quarried blow-out.

- One heap was a spread of medium-sized gneiss stones (context 10/1989) in the south area of the main excavation trench (in squares 1–6 and 10–16; Figures 2.7,

8.24). These were interpreted as structural remains of the wheelhouse's southern sector, displaced and moved downslope by erosion into the gully between the central and southern excavation trenches. The stones were set within a similarly displaced deposit (context 12e/1989) of compacted sand containing shells and peat ash (presumably the remnants of layer 5=1/1989 moved downslope). Unfortunately, other deposits in different parts of the site were also recorded as context 12/1989 so no finds can be identified specifically as coming from this layer.

- The second stone heap consisted of a north–south line of four large blocks north of the embayment that probably resulted from sand-quarrying towards the western edge of the wheelhouse (Figures 2.7, 8.25). These stones are not commented on in the records and were probably displaced during sand-quarrying in the 1980s prior to archaeological excavation.

- The third stone heap consisted of a small spread of

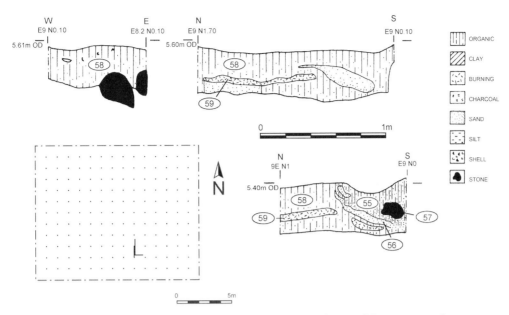

Figure 8.22 Section drawings of contexts 55–59 within the south-central part of the main trench

medium to small-sized stones in the northwest of the central excavation trench (Figure 8.25). They formed an oval ring about 1.30m in diameter, and five stones are drawn as set on edge, as if part of a small structure (Figure 2.7). In the absence of further commentary in the records, these are interpreted as having been displaced and heaped up here during sand-quarrying in the 1980s.

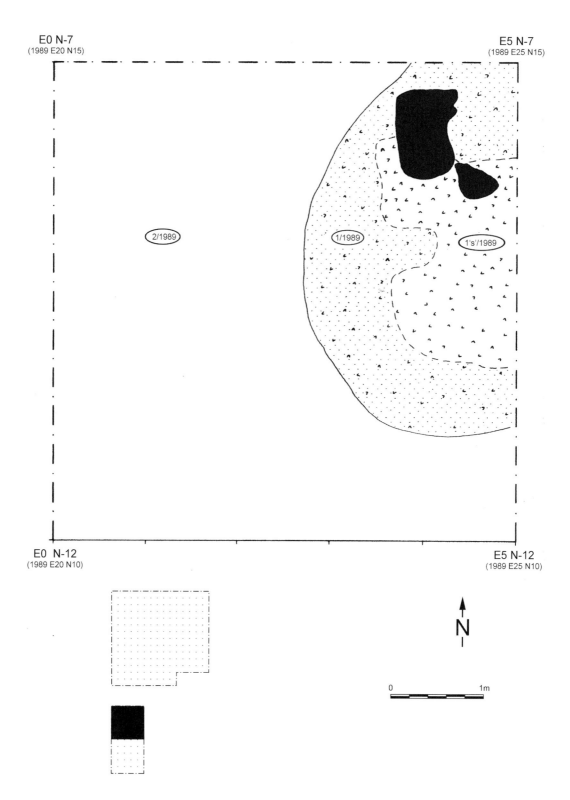

Figure 8.23 Layers 1/1989, 1's'/1989 and 2/1989 within the south trench

Figure 8.24 Heap of disturbed stones in the south area of the main excavation trench (context 10/1989), viewed from the east

Figure 8.25 Four large boulders (right) and a setting of probably disturbed stones (left) within the west half of the main trench, viewed from the south

Chapter 9 The pottery

Chris Cumberpatch

Introduction

The site of Cill Donnain III consists of a series of stratified deposits, spanning about two thousand years from the Early–Middle Bronze Age (phase 1) to the early part of the Late Iron Age (phases 4–9). This is by no means a complete sequence: there are chronological gaps in the pottery assemblage between, for example, the Late Bronze Age (phase 2) and the Middle Iron Age (phase 3), and the Middle Iron Age and the Late Iron Age (phase 4 onwards).

Cill Donnain III's ceramic assemblage consists of 36,450 sherds weighing a total of 158.93kg (Table 9.1). It is thus larger than the assemblages of 19,000 sherds from Dun Vulan (La Trobe-Bateman 1999), 6,980 sherds from Bornais mound 1 (including Norse activity areas; Lane in Sharples 2012b: tab. 61) and, further away, 6,370 sherds from Cnip in Lewis (MacSween 2006). With an average sherd weight of 4.36g, the Cill Donnain assemblage is more heavily fragmented than these comparable sites. Only two sherds from the entire Cill Donnain ceramic assemblage were modified into artefacts, both being circular discs (see 'Ceramic artefacts' at the end of this chapter).

In this report I shall consider the character of the pottery recovered, the light that its condition sheds on the history of the site, its wider position within the Hebridean Iron Age, and its utility in contributing to the solution of problems that surround the later prehistory of the area.

The pottery was examined in four stages.

- The initial analysis dealt with material recovered in 1989 and 1990 and was undertaken by the author in 1992.
- The second stage, involving the remainder of the pottery from 1989 and 1990, together with a small amount recovered in 1991, was carried out in 1993 by Sheffield students Paul Gething and Cornelius Barton, under the guidance of the author and using the principles of classification developed in 1992.

- The third group of material was recorded by extramural studies students and the author in 1993 and 1994.
- A final box of material, excavated in 1991, was recorded in January 1998.

A number of the conclusions reached in the preliminary report (Cumberpatch 1992) have subsequently been modified as a result of the publication of the results of the excavations at Sollas (Campbell 1991). Finally, the report was updated in 2011 and 2012 by Mike Parker Pearson.

The manufacture of the Cill Donnain III pottery

In an important discussion of Hebridean pottery, Alan Lane (1990) has described the later prehistoric and historic pottery sequence as running from at least the Iron Age (from some time in the later first millennium BC) until the nineteenth century AD without any major technological change. All the pottery is handmade and all appears to have been fired in simple clamp kilns or bonfires. Consequently in some parts of the Hebrides there may be at least 2,000 or 2,500 years of handmade pottery production, using similar clay sources and similar production techniques (Lane 1990).

The following discussion will broadly support Lane's arguments, but I hope to amplify some of his comments regarding the manufacturing techniques employed in the production of the pottery and to attempt to describe some of the variations visible in the fabric of the pottery from Cill Donnain.

Fabric

The major difficulty in analyzing the entire Hebridean sequence is that similar gneiss-derived inclusions are found in sherds of widely different dates, and few objectively distinct fabrics can really be defined. Pottery

Phase	Total number of sherds	Total weight (gms)	Average sherd weight	Total number of rims	%age of rims	Number of decorated sherds	%age of decorated sherds
Phase 1	473	3905	8.26	12	2.53	2	0.42
Phase 2	1213	4753	3.92	3	0.25	0	0.00
Phase 3	3649	14384	3.95	39	1.07	20	0.55
Phase 4	946	3669	3.88	10	1.06	27	2.85
Phase 5	1043	4331	4.15	3	0.29	6	0.58
Phase 6	38	100	2.63	0	0.00	3	7.89
Phase 7	6043	33190	5.49	39	0.65	89	1.47
Phase 8	111	1135	10.23	2	1.80	0	0.00
Phase 9	18968	78785	4.15	180	0.95	292	1.54
Phase 10 & U/S	3966	14673	3.69				
Total	36450	158925	4.36	288	0.79	439	1.20

Table 9.1 Total numbers and weights of sherds by phase

of the Iron Age can appear very similar to that of the late Medieval period, and only combinations of form, decoration and fabric allow secure differentiation. The geology of the Hebrides presents a major problem for ceramic analysis given the uniformity of the rock type – Lewisian gneiss – in areas where Hebridean pottery is commonly found. Only in Skye do Tertiary volcanoes provide another rock type as a possible source of tempering material or clay. Although the gneisses are variable in composition, this variation occurs on a scale of metres, and readily distinguishable minerals are only rarely identifiable in pottery fabrics. Pottery from each site can be extremely variable in the nature and amount of mineral inclusions and can usually only be put into broad groups of fabric with no precise provenance other than the Lewisian gneiss (Lane 1990:112).

These features of the pottery fabrics have led both Topping (1986; 1987) and Collins (1981) to conclude that pottery was made locally, the inhabitants of each site presumably making pots either as and when required or at certain times of the year. The Cill Donnain fabrics (Table 9.2) exhibit a range of traits that frequently give a first impression of intra-assemblage distinctiveness but which, when considered in their broader context, fail to maintain their consistency or integrity. Thus, in considering the material recovered from context 1/1989, for example, an initial division was made between coarse-textured, soft, oxidized sherds and coarse-textured, hard, reduced sherds. Although this division could be sustained for several dozen sherds, by the time that several hundred had been examined, it was clear that this differentiation was simply illusory. Individual sherds display a high degree of variability across their surfaces and between the interior and exterior of the vessel.

A number of factors appear to have interacted to produce this degree of irregular variability. These include the use of different manufacturing and decorative techniques, variation in the firing atmosphere of the clamp or bonfire, depositional context, and the post-depositional environment (Swain 1988). To an extent, such variables

affect all ceramic assemblages, but it appears that, in the case of Cill Donnain (and perhaps of Hebridean pottery assemblages generally), these factors, together with the nature of the clays, have interacted to produce a situation of extreme variability that frustrates conventional methods of analysis.

Although the classification of pottery fabrics by macroscopic examination should include a quasi-objective element (the recognition of distinctive mineral or rock fragments), a considerable part of the process depends upon the judgment of the individual analyst and, for this reason, the results of macroscopic examination are ideally to be cross-referenced with some other method of analysis, based upon the determination of the physical or chemical characteristics of the material under consideration. Only two attempts have been made to carry out such analysis on the Hebridean material, by Collins (1981) and Topping (1986; 1987). The latter, which was the most extensive, has been criticized by Lane (1990:116) for failing to begin with a consideration of the mineralogical characteristics of the clays involved. Lane's conclusion, with which I concur, is that we still require a major study of the Iron Age sequence combining basic geological examination with the definition of types, and perhaps wares, by combinations of fabric, form and decorative motifs. That said, research by ceramic specialists on individual Hebridean site assemblages (*e.g.* Campbell 1991; La Trobe-Bateman 1999; Lane in Sharples 2012b; Manley in prep.) along with Campbell's overview of Hebridean ceramics (Campbell 2002) has brought us closer to this goal.

Unfortunately the material from Cill Donnain is not amongst the assemblages best suited to the task of producing such a major study. While the forms and motifs present find parallels on other sites (discussed below) and the fabrics display the variability typical of the area, the fragmentation of the material and the almost complete absence of full vessel profiles render obscure the link between form, decoration and fabric.

Phase	Context number	FABRIC GROUPS														
		1-2		3		4		5		6		7		Other	
		No. of sherds	Weight	No. of sherds	Weight	No. of sherds	Weight	No. of sherds	Weight	No. of sherds	Weight	No. of sherds	Weight	No. of sherds	Weight
Phase 1	140	130	1005											10	320
	149	72	835			28	406								
	153	149	556			9	201							55	376
	157	15	109			3	69							2	27
	Total	366	2505			40	676							67	723
Phase 2	134	171	357			5	28							5	29
	135	516	1869			1	9							4	70
	138	31	120												
	142	421	1471			4	40							55	760
	Total	1139	3817			10	77							64	859
Phase 3	32	119	861	3	26			1	2	100	804	8	43	1	23
	35	3	26												
	52	17	122												
	59	27	103												
	60	219	577	7	22										
	104	172	1018	1	8										
	105	259	628	3	7									1	6
	106	1	27												
	130	14	39											4	8
	131	19	50			1	2							6	6
	132	2	6												
	160	508	2011			11	79	1	4					7	53
	162	6	19												
	163	43	225	1	8	2	12							7	26
	164													71	435
	165	86	276												
	171	1	6												
	173	893	2833			1	3							2	4
	181	94	304												
	187	259	911											6	22
	189	65	261	2	12										
	190	195	834	9	46									2	4
	191	291	1153	4	31	1	3							1	8
	215	22	52												
	222	70	327												
	Total	3385	12669	30	160	16	99	2	6	100	804	8	43	108	595

Phase	Context number	FABRIC GROUPS														
		1-2		3		4		5		6		7		Other	
		No. of sherds	Weight	No. of sherds	Weight	No. of sherds	Weight	No. of sherds	Weight	No. of sherds	Weight	No. of sherds	Weight	No. of sherds	Weight
Phase 4	24	671	2651	6	21			17	101			59	284	2	10
	185	67	225												
	188	4	10												
	196	3	10												
	198	4	20												
	199	6	14												
	200	1	2												
	201	3	8	2	12										
	202	23	73												
	205	1	3			1	2								
	209	9	20												
	210	13	33												
	211	4	10												
	212	10	22												
	213	7	10												
	214	7	6												
	217	2	4												
	218	4	10												
	219	3	8												
	220	4	26											13	74
	Total	846	3165	8	33	1	2	17	101			59	284	15	84
Phase 5	3 [1989]	36	210					6	19						
	8 [1989]	68	249			2	11								
	166	680	2989	7	52	1	3	1	5						
	170	5	19	6	37										
	177	8	31												
	179	16	63												
	183	126	426											1	8
	184	7	25												
	Total	946	4012	13	89	3	14	7	24					1	8
Phase 6	9 [1989]	7	14												
	16 [1989]	7	31												
	182	23	54			1	1								
	Total	37	99			1	1								

Phase	Context number	1-2		3		4		5		6		7		Other	
		No. of sherds	Weight	No. of sherds	Weight	No. of sherds	Weight	No. of sherds	Weight	No. of sherds	Weight	No. of sherds	Weight	No. of sherds	Weight
Phase 7	4 [1989]	2655	13602	18	130	26	159	29	121					1	5
	6 [1989]	2123	10314	64	500	9	32	1	10						
	14 [1989]	38	125	1	2										
	25	852	6883	9	60							22	124	19	194
	172	5	30												
	176	171	911												
	Total	5844	31865	92	692	35	191	30	131			22	124	20	199
Phase 8	28	110	1122	1	13										
Phase 9	1 [1989]	4701	17911	99	536	27	138	48	271	8	66	7	55		
	2 [1989]	677	2344			6	63	2	10						
	12 [1989]	1077	4919	9	296			8	20						
	13 [1989]	8	32												
	15 [1989]	388	1590	14	105			1	5						
	2	1	2												
	4	137	324			1	3								
	5	6858	28620	168	899	3	34	9	28			12	57	95	917
	8	59	109	4	23										
	9	7	14												
	11	118	616					3	14						
	12	241	1145	5	15	4	20	2	7					5	24
	14	538	1781	16	77	1	22					3	10		
	15	359	1481	2	10	2	4	2	17						
	18	278	1619	4	15							18	73		
	19	6	35												
	20	4	15											2	11
	22	32	140												
	23	5	19												
	27	249	1976			1	11								
	29	32	140												
	31	552	2855	95	680	13	60	1	4					1	10
	33	140	467											1	14
	54	4	4												
	58	160	606	2	4	4	22								
	102	152	184												
	103	1559	5355	11	65	2	5								
	Total	18342	74303	429	2725	64	382	76	376	8	66	40	195	104	976
Phase 10	1	2774	9298	243	956							2	24		
	3	1	9												
Unstrat	No context	906	4059	19	248			4	30					1	1
	17 [1989]	15	34	1	14										
U/S & Phase 10	Total	3696	13400	263	1218			4	30			2	24	1	1

Table 9.2 Ceramic fabric groups by context and phase

The pottery assemblage and the fabric classification

The bulk of the pottery assemblage consists of undiagnostic body sherds (Table 9.3). There are relatively few decorated, rim or base sherds and all of these are fragmentary (Tables 9.4–9.7). There are no complete vessel profiles. As described above, classification of the fabrics poses considerable difficulties and correlations between fabric, form and decoration are problematic in the extreme. As a general principle, the approach to the pottery from any site should be guided by the nature of the material and the specific questions raised by the site director after due consideration of regional research priorities.

In the case of Cill Donnain, the nature of the material dictated the adoption of a relatively unsophisticated strategy based upon the determination of the quantities of pottery in each context, sub-divided by sample square. Quantity was measured in terms of the number of sherds and their weight (in grams; average sherd weight in Table 9.1 is rounded to two decimal places), a procedure that has the advantage of giving some measure of the degree of fragmentation of the vessels. This was seen as important because a number of the contexts were initially considered to have been formed as the result of manuring and other practices related to the cultivation of the machair fields, while other contexts were connected with the occupation and abandonment of the wheelhouse.

A number of fabric groups were tentatively identified (Table 9.2). Fabric groups 1–2, 3 and 6 probably do not relate directly to different points of origin of either the clay or the pots, or to different potteries. In particular, fabrics 1–2 and 3 may simply be points on a continuum, distinguished more by manufacturing technique than origin. Sherds belonging to groups 5 and 7, both of which are finer and softer than any others, may be regarded as possible imports or as resulting from different processing and manufacturing techniques. The numbers of sherds of these types are too low to support definite conclusions and they do not appear to be associated with any specific decorative motifs. The similarity of the decorative motifs on sherds in these fabrics (applied cordons with impressed decoration and fine incised lines) to the remainder of the pottery suggests that it is highly unlikely that their origin was outside the Hebridean area.

Fabric group 4 was common in the Bronze Age, with 40 out of a total of 170 sherds in this fabric occurring in phases 1–2. Conversely, fabric groups 3, 5, 6 and 7 do not occur in these Early–Middle and Late Bronze Age assemblages.

The following descriptions of the fabrics are based solely on macroscopic examination and should not be considered a substitute for specialized mineralogical analysis.

Fabric group 1–2

This group of fabrics covers a wide range of variation within a basic group. The texture is coarse and gritty, with abundant angular to sub-angular grains of quartz. Other inclusions include mica (notably biotite) and fragments of igneous rock. Colours vary widely and range from orange-red to black, via dark reds and greys. This is the most common fabric group (34,711 sherds, forming 95% of the assemblage).

Fabric group 3

Basically similar to group 1–2 in terms of the range of inclusions, fabric 3 tends to be somewhat finer in texture. The chief difference lies in the method of manufacture and particularly in the finishing of the surface, which is harder and more resistant to abrasion than that of group 1–2. Typical examples of sherds belonging to this fabric group have a smoothed exterior and a rough but resistant interior. Colours, resulting from firing in a reducing atmosphere, are grey to black. Fabric group 3 (836 sherds) forms 2% of the assemblage.

Fabric group 4

This fabric is distinguished by a general absence of quartz inclusions and the substitution of large angular rock fragments (type undetermined). These inclusions, together with the texture of the clay, give a muddy, homogeneous texture. This fabric forms 8% of the phase 1 assemblage (Cordoned Urns) but is only 0.4% of the total assemblage from all phases.

Fabric group 5

A fine-textured soft fabric containing only fine quartz inclusions and abundant fine mica (principally biotite). The fine texture sets it apart from the bulk of the pottery. The fabric is soft (can be scratched with a fingernail) and dark buff in colour. Fabric group 5 (136 sherds) forms 0.4% of the assemblage.

Fabric group 6

An unusual fabric from context 32 (phase 3, Middle Iron Age), apparently representing only one or two vessels, with a handful of sherds from layer 1/1989 (phase 9, Late Iron Age). A coarse-textured fabric with abundant quartz inclusions of varying sizes and shapes (108 sherds forming 0.3% of the assemblage). Fabric group 6 is distinguished from group 1–2 by its hardness and the smoothed (when wet) exterior.

Fabric group 7

This is a distinctive fabric group resembling group 5 in some respects, being soft and dark buff in colour. It differs in that it includes medium–coarse grains of quartz. The surface of sherds belonging to this fabric group is characterized by impressions apparently from vegetable matter (grass stems). It is not, however, a grass-tempered fabric. It consists of 131 sherds only.

Other fabrics

During the course of the examination of the pottery a number of unclassifiable fabrics were encountered (380 sherds, forming 1% of the assemblage). These sherds generally differed from the commoner fabric types in having a coarser texture, but were similar in that they contained the same range of inclusions.

Manufacturing techniques

The pottery from Cill Donnain, in common with that from other sites in the Hebrides, was made using hand-modelling techniques, and only the simplest of tools appear to have been employed. As physico-chemical analysis of the pottery appears unlikely to offer any very profound insight into the organization of pottery production, it may be useful, at some stage in the future, to consider the manufacturing techniques themselves in greater detail. In principal, comparison of assemblages from different sites could allow the products of individual potters or groups of potters to be differentiated. Unfortunately the Cill Donnain III assemblage is ill-suited to this method of investigation given its highly fragmented character. A number of points, however, can be made that have relevance both to the assemblage itself and to wider issues.

Lane has noted that the Late Iron Age pottery from the Udal is characterized by a lack of decoration and by a distinctive method of construction, based on coil-building, which he terms 'tongued and grooved' (1990: 117; for similar construction at Bornais mound 1, see Lane in Sharples 2012b: 174, 258). I feel this analogy, drawn from carpentry, is inappropriate in the context of the manufacture of pottery, a subject with a vast and subtle terminology of its own. Abundant evidence of this (or a similar) method of construction can be seen in the Cill

Phase	Context	Total number of sherds	Total weight (gms)	Average sherd weight	Total number of rims	%age of rims	Number of decorated sherds	%age of decorated sherds
Phase 1	140	140	1325	9.46	4	0.70	0	
	149	100	1241	12.41	5	0.36	0	
	153	213	1133	5.32	1	0.54	1	0.54
	157	20	206	10.30	2	0.10	1	0.05
	Total	473	3905	8.26	12	0.55	2	0.09
Phase 2	134	181	414	2.29	1	0.55	0	
	135	521	1948	3.74	0		0	
	138	31	120	3.87	0		0	
	142	480	2271	4.73	2	0.42	0	
	Total	1213	4753	3.92	3	0.25	0	
Phase 3	32	232	1763	7.60	4	1.72	1	0.43
	35	3	26	8.67	0		0	
	52	17	122	7.18	1	5.88	0	
	59	27	103	3.81	0		1	3.70
	60	226	599	2.65	2	0.88	0	
	104	173	1026	5.93	11	6.36	0	
	105	263	642	2.44	4	1.52	2	0.76
	106	1	27	27.00	0		0	
	130	18	47	2.61	0		0	
	131	26	58	2.23	0		0	
	132	2	6	3.00	0		0	
	160	527	2148	4.08	4	0.76	3	0.57
	162	6	19	3.17	0		0	
	163	53	272	5.13	0		0	
	164	71	435	6.13	0		0	
	165	86	276	3.21	0		0	
	171	1	6	6.00	0		0	
	173	896	2840	3.17	4	0.45	5	0.56
	181	94	304	3.23	0		0	
	187	265	933	3.52	0		0	
	189	67	273	4.07	1	1.49	1	1.49
	190	206	885	4.30	6	2.91	6	2.91
	191	297	1195	4.02	0		1	0.34
	215	22	52	2.36	0		0	
	222	70	327	4.67	2	2.86	0	
	Total	3649	14384	3.95	39	1.07	20	0.55

Phase	Context	Total number of sherds	Total weight (gms)	Average sherd weight	Total number of rims	%age of rims	Number of decorated sherds	%age of decorated sherds
Phase 4	24	755	3067	4.06	10	1.32	27	3.58
	185	67	225	3.36	0		0	
	188	4	10	2.50	0		0	
	196	3	10	3.33	0		0	
	198	4	20	5.00	0		0	
	199	6	14	2.33	0		0	
	200	1	2	2.00	0		0	
	201	5	20	4.00	0		0	
	202	23	73	3.17	0		0	
	205	2	5	2.50	0		0	
	209	9	20	2.22	0		0	
	210	13	33	2.54	0		0	
	211	4	10	2.50	0		0	
	212	10	22	2.20	0		0	
	213	7	10	1.43	0		0	
	214	7	6	0.86	0		0	
	217	2	4	2.00	0		0	
	218	4	10	2.50	0		0	
	219	3	8	2.67	0		0	
	220	17	100	5.88	0		0	
	Total	111	1135	3.88	10	9.01	27	24.32
Phase 5	3 [1989]	42	229	5.45	0		0	
	8 [1989]	70	260	3.71	1	1.43	0	
	166	762	3233	4.24	1	0.13	4	0.52
	170	11	56	5.09	0		0	
	177	8	31	3.88	0		0	
	179	16	63	3.94	0		0	
	183	127	434	3.42	0		2	1.57
	184	7	25	3.57	1	14.29	0	
	Total	1043	4331	4.15	3	0.29	6	0.58
Phase 6	9 [1989]	7	14	2.00	0		0	
	16 [1989]	7	31	4.43	0		3	42.86
	182	24	55	2.29	0		0	
	Total	38	100	2.63	0	0.00	3	7.89
Phase 7	4 [1989]	2729	14017	5.14	22	0.81	28	1.03
	6 [1989]	2197	10844	4.94	9	0.41	14	0.64
	14 [1989]	39	127	3.26	0		0	
	25	902	7261	8.05	8	0.89	40	4.43
	172	5	30	6.00	0		1	20.00
	176	171	911	5.33	0		6	3.51
	Total	6043	33190	5.49	39	0.65	89	1.47

Phase	Context	Total number of sherds	Total weight (gms)	Average sherd weight	Total number of rims	%age of rims	Number of decorated sherds	%age of decorated sherds
Phase 8	28	111	1135	10.23	2	1.80	0	0.00
Phase 9	1 [1989]	4792	18851	3.93	52	1.09	89	1.86
	2 [1989]	685	2418	3.53	5	0.73	4	0.58
	12 [1989]	1094	5028	4.60	18	1.65	28	2.56
	13 [1989]	8	32	4.00	0		2	25.00
	15 [1989]	403	1701	4.22	0		6	1.49
	2	1	2	2.00	0		1	100.00
	4	138	327	2.37	0		0	
	5	7147	30644	4.29	55	0.77	92	1.29
	8	63	132	2.10	0		0	
	9	7	14	2.00	0		0	
	11	121	630	5.21	3	2.48	2	1.65
	12	257	1212	4.72	9	3.50	6	2.33
	14	559	1893	3.39	5	0.89	6	1.07
	15	365	1512	4.14	3	0.82	12	3.29
	18	300	1707	5.69	0		14	4.67
	19	6	35	5.83	0		1	16.67
	20	6	26	4.33	0		0	
	22	32	140	4.38	3	9.38	0	
	23	5	19	3.80	0		0	
	27	250	1987	7.95	4	1.60	1	0.40
	29	32	140	4.38	1	3.13	1	3.13
	31	662	3609	5.45	5	0.76	19	2.87
	33	141	481	3.41	1	0.71	4	2.84
	54	4	4	1.00	0		0	
	58	166	632	3.81	1	0.60	1	0.60
	102	152	184	1.21	0		0	
	103	1572	5425	3.45	15	0.95	3	0.19
	Total	18968	78785	4.15	180	0.95	292	1.54

Table 9.3 Sherd numbers, weights, rims and decorated sherds by context and phase

Donnain assemblage and it is consequently appropriate to describe it in some detail:

- A number of the larger sherds in the assemblage show clear breaks along lines of weakness caused by the joining of two pieces of clay. Such breaks are not uncommon in hand-modelled pottery and are the result of the inadequate merging of the two masses (Rye 1981).
- The Cill Donnain III material is characterized by the enclosure of one element by the other, giving an effect

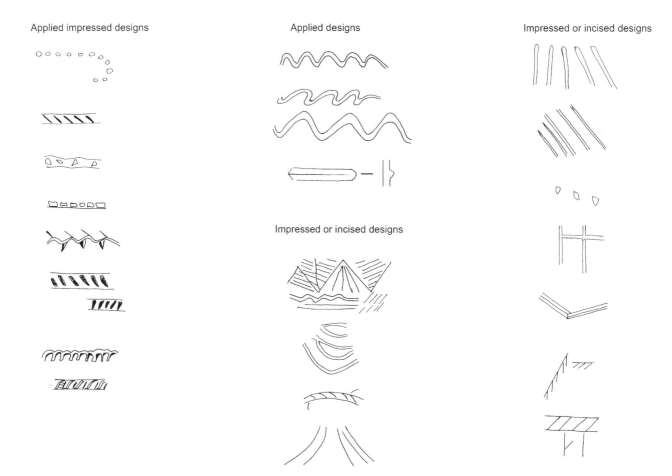

Figure 9.1 Impressed, applied and incised motifs on ceramics

superficially similar to that of tongued and grooved planks. However striking this is when compared to wheel-thrown or moulded ceramics, it is simply a secondary effect contingent upon the method of constructing the body of the vessel.

- It appears that the vessels were built of slabs, or broad ribbons, of clay butted together and sealed by smoothing clay from one over the other.
- In some cases, extra clay might have been added to reinforce the join and this has resulted, in some examples, in a thickening of the vessel wall at this point.
- While it is possible that such a technique could also have been employed with coil- or ring-built vessels, the absence of evidence of coils, as opposed to slabs, within the assemblage suggests that the latter was the commoner technique. Examples of the technique include sherds from context 4/1989 (square 7) and context 5 (squares E14/N9 and E13/N9).
- This distinctive method of manufacture was also noted at Sollas (Campbell 1991: microfiche), and has been distinguished from the 'tongue and groove' technique (*ibid.*: 150, microfiche), although the grounds for this distinction are not clear.

Lane has linked this method of construction to undecorated post-Roman pottery but it (or a similar technique) occurs at Cill Donnain in conjunction with decorative motifs, particularly applied wavy cordons. If such a correlation can be sustained, it would appear that there were changes in the degree of elaboration of pottery vessels (a decline in decoration), while the same basic techniques and traditions of construction were maintained.

The firing of the pottery was most probably carried out in simple clamps or bonfires. Apart from the apparent absence of kilns in the area, this is also indicated by wide variations in colour across the surface of the vessels and between the interior and exterior surfaces. Colours range from a bright orange-red to black, via a range of browns and greys, typical of the effect of a variable firing atmosphere such as may be expected in the absence of a kiln structure.

Decorative techniques and motifs

Topping (1986: fig. 2) has presented a simple descriptive classification of the range of motifs employed in the decoration of Hebridean ceramics, and this forms the basis of the analysis presented in Tables 9.4–9.6 (Figure 9.1).

The decorative techniques employed can be divided broadly into

- those involving the application of clay to form cordons or other projections, and
- those based on incisions and impressions into the body of the vessel.

Phase	Context	1	2	3	4	5	6	7	8	9	10	11	12	Other
								Incised decoration						
Phase 3	32	1												
	105								1					
	160								1					
	189	1												
	190												1	
	Total	2							2				1	
Phase 7	25				1						1			
Phase 9	1 [1989]	0	0		0						0	0	0	0
	4 [1989]												2	
	5 [1989]	0	0		0						0	0	0	
	12 [1989]				0				0	0			0	
	5		0								0	0		
	11	1									1			
	15				1						2			
	18	1									2			
	103			1						1				
	Total	2	0	1	1				0	1	5	0	2	0
	Grand total	8	0	1	2				3	1	6	0	10	0

Table 9.4 Incised decoration by context and phase. For the key, see Figure 9.2

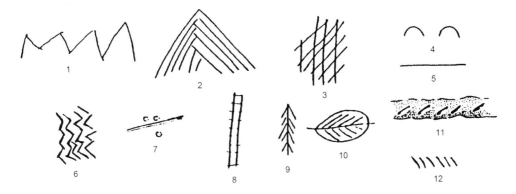

Figure 9.2 Incised decorative motifs represented at Cill Donnain III; this is the key to Table 9.4

This is reflected in the division of the tables into that dealing with incised decoration (Table 9.4), with impressed and stamped decoration (Table 9.5) and with applied and impressed decoration (Table 9.6).

There have long been indications that some of the decorative motifs have chronological implications, and Lane has suggested that the incised motifs may be earlier than the 'channelled' motifs of the Clettraval style (Lane 1990: 113; Lane in Sharples 2012b: 21). Until recently, however, the complexities of the data and the invalid assumptions that directed a large part of the early research on Hebridean Iron Age pottery made it all but impossible to draw any firm conclusions as to the relationship between the various motifs and other aspects of the archaeological record. As Lane (1990: 115) has commented: 'Only when the pottery has been analysed, the significance of the undoubted stylistic changes evaluated, and the whole sequence independently dated are we likely to be able to make use of the pottery in wider cultural analysis'.

The publication by Ewan Campbell (1991) of the results of Atkinson's excavations at Sollas has provided a framework for the interpretation of the decorative motifs in chronological terms. The fragmentary nature of the material from Cill Donnain does not permit the use of the assemblage to evaluate the scheme set out in the Sollas report, but the latter is of considerable value for the interpretation of the Cill Donnain pottery, as is Lane's report on the Bornais mound 1 Late Iron Age pottery (Lane in

Sharples 2012b). The chronological issues will be discussed further below.

The treatment of the surfaces of the vessels from Cill Donnain is highly variable. In some cases, an effort has clearly been made to produce a smooth finish (particularly, but not exclusively, associated with fabric group 3), and this probably involved the smoothing of the surfaces when soft. Scratches and drag-marks, which would inevitably have resulted from attempts to burnish the pottery when dry, are rare. In almost all cases, the interior of the vessels has been left rough, both in terms of the protrusion of quartz grains and of lumps resulting from the joining of the slabs or ribbons of clay. Good examples of this technique can be seen in sherds from context 5 (squares E10/N4, E11/N0 and E11/N1).

It should be noted that there appears to be a correlation between the occurrence of flaky black carbon-like deposits on the outside of sherds and the wavy cordon decoration (*e.g.* context 11, square E10/N9). The extent and significance of this occurrence requires further investigation.

Chronology of and parallels for the Cill Donnain III assemblage

It is only in the last 30 years that the study of Hebridean ceramics began to emerge from the fog of fallacious assumptions regarding connections between pottery production and ethnicity. Topping (1986) and Lane

Phase	Context	Impressed and stamped decoration					
		1	2	3	4	5	Other
Phase 3	173				1		
Phase 5	166				1		
Phase 9	2 [1989]						1
	12 [1989]	1					1
	5	1	2	2	1	1	1
	18	2					
	33	1					
	103				1		
	Sub-total	5	2	2	2	1	3
Total		5	2	2	4	1	3

Key		
1	Channels (channelled arches)	
2	Fingernail impressions	
3	Angled impressions (some overlap with incisions)	
4	Ring-headed pin	
5	Impressed grooves	

Table 9.5 Impressed decoration by context and phase

(1990; see also Lane in Sharples 2012b: 20–1) have noted the problems associated with attempts, such as those of MacKie (1974), to date the pottery by association with pottery from southern Britain and France. In addition, Topping (1987) has pointed out the problems involved in the dating of the pottery by association with specific artefact types (including glass beads and ring-headed pins), or with the sparse series of radiocarbon dates then in existence. As Lane's review of MacKie's work is both concise and readily available, there seems little point in repeating the details here.

Lane's position, that significant stylistic variations do occur and may provide some form of chronological framework for the area, is entirely reasonable, but has to be taken together with his plea for a comprehensive review of the whole subject, involving: 'a number of site sequences and several sets of calibrated C-14 dates' (1990:113; see also Lane in Sharples 2012b: 220–1, 257–8).

In broad terms, the material from Cill Donnain phases 3–9 can be said to be of Iron Age date. The range of decorative motifs and vessel forms closely resembles that set out by Topping (1986; 1987) based on his work on assemblages from a number of sites in the Western Isles, and parallels for both rim shapes and decorative motifs can be found on many sites in the area (including Allasdale and Dun Cuier [Barra; Young 1953; 1956], A' Cheardach Mhor [South Uist; Young and Richardson 1960], Dun Carloway [Lewis; Tabraham 1979], Dun Cul Bhuirg [Iona; Ritchie and Lane 1981; Topping 1985], and Dun Vulan [South Uist; Parker Pearson and Sharples

1999]). The question of whether there are differences relating to social status between the pottery assemblage from Cill Donnain and those from other sites (as postulated in Zvelebil 1990: 5) is likewise a question that requires consideration in a wider framework.

The publication of dated ceramic sequences from excavations at Sollas (Campbell 1991), Dun Vulan (Parker Pearson and Sharples 1999), Cnip (Armit 2006) and Bornais mound 1 (Sharples 2012b) has consolidated our understanding of the chronological changes in decorative motifs during the Middle and Late Iron Age. In addition, the analysis of a large assemblage of Bronze Age–Early Iron Age Plain Wares at Cladh Hallan (Parker Pearson and Parsons in prep.) allows the earlier phases at Cill Donnain to be assessed against a well-dated ceramic sequence from that site. These sequences offer the opportunity to place Cill Donnain within a chronological framework of Hebridean ceramic change and innovation (Campbell 2002; Parker Pearson 2012d: 402–9).

The sequence at Cill Donnain III begins with a small assemblage of Cordoned Urn wares (in phase 1). Such ceramics are normally found in Britain and Ireland as cremation containers, although similar domestic assemblages are known from nearby Cladh Hallan in South Uist (Parker Pearson *et al.* in prep.) and from Downpatrick in Ireland (Pollock and Waterman 1964). Radiocarbon dates for Cordoned Urns from funerary contexts place their use within the period *c.*1900–1400/1300 BC (Sheridan 2003: 207), the later part of the Early Bronze Age and the Middle Bronze Age.

Phase	Context	Applied and applied/impressed decoration											
		1	2	3	4	5	6	7	8	9	10	11	Other
Phase 1	153								1				
	157	1											
Phase 3	59				1								
	105						1						
	160				1			1					
	173				1	1			1		1		
	190	4	1										
	191					1							
Phase 4	24	6		5	9		4					2	1
Phase 5	166				2		1						
	183		2										
Phase 6	16 [1989]	1											2
Phase 7	4 [1989]			6	8		1		4			3	6
	6 [1989]			4	5		1					2	2
	25			6	19		3		1	2			7
	172							1					
	176	1	5										
Phase 9	1 [1989]			13	35		2		3	1		20	3
	2 [1989]								2				1
	12 [1989]				3	1	1		3	2		4	1
	13 [1989]				2								
	15 [1989]				5								1
	2						1						
	5	1	3	21	21	2	8	1	7	9	1	1	5
	11				2								
	12				3		2					1	
	14				2		1				3		
	15						2		5		1	1	
	18						2		2			1	4
	19												1
	27				1								
	29			1									
	31				17				1			1	
	33		1									2	
	58			1									
Total		14	12	57	137	5	30	3	30	14	6	38	34

	Key			
1	Plain cordon, horizontal		7	Impressed cordon, sub-circular, vertical
2	Plain cordon, large wave shape		8	Tool impressed cordon, indeterminate
3	Zig-zag cordon, angular		9	Impressed cordon, finger nail
4	Zig-zag cordon, rounded		10	Impressed cordon, lines (vertical)
5	Impressed cordon, circular		11	Impressed cordon, lines (angled)
6	Impressed cordon, sub-circular, angled			

Table 9.6 Applied decoration by context and phase

The second phase at Cill Donnain comprises a small assemblage of Late Bronze Age–Early Iron Age Plain Ware, dated to the eighth–early sixth centuries BC and closely comparable with similar material from Cladh Hallan phases 12–13.

Phase 3 at Cill Donnain is dated to the mid-first–early third century AD, falling within the period of the Middle Iron Age (*c*.200 BC–AD 300) when decorated ceramics were manufactured in the Western Isles. These are known from many sites within the region, and chronological sequences of these decorated styles have been derived from key sites such as the wheelhouses at Sollas (Campbell 1991) and Cnip (Armit 2006) and the broch of Dun Vulan (Parker Pearson and Sharples 1999).

The chronology at Sollas can be summarized as follows:

- Period A1: late first millennium BC to first century AD
- Period A2: late first millennium BC to first century AD

Chris Cumberpatch

Phase	Context	Rim form									
		1	2	3	4	5	6	7	8	9	Other
Phase 1	140	2	2								
	149	3	2								
	153		1								
	157		1							1	
	Total	5	6							1	
Phase 2	134		1								
	142	1									1
	Total	1	1								1
Phase 3	32		4								
	52			1							
	60	1			1						
	104	4		1			1	1	1	0	
	105	1	1	1						1	
	160	2	2								
	173	3									1
	189	1									
	190	1	1				1			3	
	222	1								1	
	Total	14	8	3	1		2			5	1
Phase 4	24	8				1	1				
Phase 5	8 [1989]	1									
	166										1
	184	1									
	Total	2									1
Phase 7	4 [1989]	10	1	4	1	2	1	2	1		
	6 [1989]	3	1	3					1		1
	25	3	2	1			1	1			
	Total	16	4	8	1	2	2	3	2		1
Phase 8	28		1		1						
Phase 9	1 [1989]	15	10	16		6	4			1	
	2 [1989]		2		2	1					
	12 [1989]	11	3			1	2	1			
	5	21	10	7	9	1	4	1	2		
	11	2					1				
	12	6	1	2							
	14	5									
	15		3								
	22			3							
	27	3			1						
	29		1								
	31		3	2							
	33	1									
	58	1									
	103	10						1	3	1	
	Total	75	33	30	12	9	11	3	5	2	
	Grand Total	121	53	41	15	12	16	7	8	11	4

	Rim types	
	1	Unidentifiable
	2	Flat-topped rim (= Topping type 1)
	3	Vertical rim probably on a round bodied vessel (= Topping type 2)
	4	Round-topped rim (= Topping type 3, orientation variable)
	5	Thick, rounded rim (= Topping type 4)
	6	Pointed-topped rim (Topping type 5)
	7	Flared neck and rim (= Topping type 6)
	8	Flat-topped rim with everted beading (no parallel)
	9	Sharply everted rim (no parallel)

Table 9.7 Rim types by context and phase

- Period B1: first to second century AD
- Period B2: later first to second century AD

This has been refined by later work (Campbell 2002; MacSween 2006) to identify chronologically significant changes in the character of the pottery assemblage:

1. Everted rim vessels appeared suddenly and did not evolve from earlier forms. These forms appeared in the Uists in the later first or second century AD (Sollas period B2) at around the same time as channelled decoration (Campbell 2002: 141; Campbell *et al.* 2004). In Lewis, however, sharply everted rims were present from the first century BC at the Cnip wheelhouse site (MacSween 2006: 101).
2. Earlier forms continued to be made during period B2 although in smaller quantities than previously.
3. Incised decoration continued from the earlier period and there was a substantial increase in the frequency of decoration.
4. Decorative motifs, other than applied horizontal cordons, went out of use in the third century AD.

A number of the incised motifs found at Cill Donnain III (Figure 9.2) are similar to those identified in period B at Sollas. Cill Donnain types 2 (triangles, formed of parallel hatchings) and 3 (diamond lattices, sometimes filling triangles) can be linked generally to Sollas period B, while types 6, 8, 9 and possibly 10 are similar to those characteristic of period B2. Impressed channels are typical of period B, and are not apparently found in period A.

Stamped decoration is limited to period A at Sollas. Applied decoration, including the wavy cordons which are by far the commonest decorative feature in the Cill Donnain assemblage, is rarer in period A than in B, but is nevertheless present in the earlier period.

Hebridean pottery of the Late Iron Age consists of bucket-shaped, cordon-decorated vessels with flaring or upright rims (Lane 1990; Lane in Sharples 2012b). In the early part of this period (AD 300–600), known as Late Iron Age I, these vessels were decorated with applied horizontal cordons, normally on the shoulder or neck of the pot. These are known as Dun Cuier ware (Campbell 2002: 142) and are found within the nearby occupation site of mound 1 at Bornais (Lane in Sharples 2012b: figs 52–53, 68–69, *etc.*). Thereafter (AD 600–800), in the period known as Late Iron Age II, these pots were no longer decorated and are known as Plain Ware; they occur in quantity at the Udal in North Uist (Lane 1990).

Flaring rims are dated as early as AD 200–250 at Cnip (MacSween 2006: 101–2) and elsewhere in the region (MacKie 1974) but continued into the pre-Viking Late Iron Age (AD 600–800) – Late Iron Age II – when they were still used on Plain Ware (Lane 1990).

Most of the deposits at Cill Donnain (phases 5–9, including the wheelhouse's occupation, and subsequent layers) date to the Late Iron Age (AD 300–800). Construction of the wheelhouse in phase 4 is radiocarbon-dated to *cal AD 205–310 (68% probability*; see Chapter 16). The wheelhouse's occupation (phase 5) ended probably in the early sixth century AD.

The dating of the final midden deposit in phase 9 is not clear-cut but it appears to contain residual material from several centuries earlier. If the late radiocarbon date from phase 9 of cal AD 720–1030 at 95% probability (from context 103, equivalent to layer 5) is rejected as being intrusive, then phase 9 dates to *cal AD 580–665 (68% probability*). If the late date is not rejected, then phase 9's midden might not have been deposited until the second part of the Late Iron Age (c.AD 600–800), when undecorated Plain Ware with flaring rims was the predominant ceramic style (Lane 1990: 117).

The stratigraphic phases and their ceramic associations

Tables 9.4–9.7 present the basic decorative motif and rim form data arranged in sequence by phase and by context number. Figures 9.1 and 9.2 illustrate the decorative motifs.

Early–Middle Bronze Age contexts containing Cordoned Urn pottery (Phase 1)

This assemblage is mostly plain (Figure 9.4), with examples of applied horizontal cordons from contexts 153 and 157. Identifiable rims are mostly flat-topped, with one example of a sharply everted rim. A partial profile was obtained for one of the vessels. Whilst fabrics 1–2 dominate this assemblage, 8% and 14% of the sherds contain large, angular rock fragments (fabric 4) and other, similarly coarse fabrics respectively.

Late Bronze Age–Early Iron Age contexts containing Plain Ware (Phase 2)

This assemblage is entirely plain (Figure 9.5). Rims include one flat-topped example. There is the same range of fabrics as in phase 1 but fabrics 1–2 now form 94% of the assemblage.

Middle Iron Age contexts containing decorated wares (Phase 3)

Incised and impressed decorations on sherds first appear in this phase (Figures 9.6–9.7) yet decorated sherds make up only 0.5% of the assemblage. Decorative motifs include three types of incised decoration, a ring-headed pin impression, and eight varieties of applied decoration: plain cordon, large wave-shaped cordon, zigzag cordon, and impressed cordons. Rims are mostly flat-topped or sharply everted, with examples of round-topped, pointed-topped and vertical rims. All eight fabric groups are represented in phase 3.

Layer 104 is radiocarbon-dated to cal AD 70–240 (at 95% probability). Other phase 3 deposits are dated to the mid-first–early third century AD, comparable with the midden and wall chamber pottery assemblages from the nearby broch of Dun Vulan; these include decorative motifs such as ring-headed pin impressions (Parker Pearson and Sharples 1999: fig. 4.13.11) similar to those seen at Cill Donnain, but decorated sherds form 7%–8% of these broch assemblages.

In comparison with the wheelhouse assemblage from Cnip, with a good proportion of decorated sherds and dating to around the same period, the Cill Donnain III phase 3 pottery stands out as unusually plain. Just why the Cill Donnain assemblage has so few decorated sherds by comparison is mysterious. This discrepancy may be due, in part, to formation processes of deflation and cultivation, introducing residual Late Bronze Age Plain Ware from lower layers or 'contaminant' Late Iron Age Plain Ware from higher layers. Nonetheless, over 4% of the Late Iron Age sherds (fifth–sixth centuries AD) from Bornais mound 1 were decorated with cordons (Lane in Sharples 2012b: tab. 61), so contamination from higher levels is unlikely to explain the low number of decorated sherds in phase 3 at Cill Donnain. Nor can the lack of motifs be explained by excessive erosion of sherd surfaces. It is most likely that the lack of decoration on the pots from Cill Donnain phase 3 is due to a high degree of mixing with residual Late Bronze Age sherds. This is corroborated by the majority of Late Bronze Age ceramic moulds for metalworking coming from phase 3 contexts (see Chapter 10).

End of Middle Iron Age and Late Iron Age I contexts associated with wheelhouse construction (Phase 4)

The pottery from this phase is made of a wide range of fabrics (only fabric group 6 is absent) and possesses a wide range of rim forms (sharply everted, pointed-topped, vertical, thick rounded, flared and flat-topped with beading). Decorated sherds compose 2.9% of the assemblage, entirely applied cordons (plain, zigzag and impressed) with no incised or impressed motifs. This assemblage compares well with that from Bornais mound 1 (Lane in Sharples 2012b) and the absence of Middle Iron Age decorated styles in these contexts suggests that there is little or no residual material incorporated into these layers.

Late Iron Age I contexts associated with occupation of the wheelhouse (Phase 5)

The pottery from this phase is very similar to that from phase 4, and is likely to be only slightly later in date. The range of fabrics is slightly narrower (fabric groups 6 and 7 are absent) and there are very few rims, none of them distinctive. Decorated sherds form only 0.5% of the assemblage, all applied cordons (plain, zigzag and impressed) except for a single ring-headed pin motif

from the floor (context 166) of the wheelhouse; this style dates to the first two centuries AD and thus the sherd is presumably residual (Figure 9.8).

Late Iron Age I contexts associated with re-occupation of the wheelhouse (Phase 6)

The small number of sherds (38) from phase 6 makes characterization useless; suffice to say, the sherds include one with cordon decoration.

Late Iron Age I contexts associated with abandonment of the wheelhouse (Phase 7)

The pottery from this phase is made of a wide range of fabrics (only fabric group 6 is absent) and possesses a wide range of rim forms; whilst sharply everted rims are entirely absent, vertical, flat-topped and flaring rims are common. Decorated sherds compose 1.5% of the assemblage, consisting almost entirely of sherds with applied cordons (plain, zigzag and impressed; Figure 9.9), with two examples of incised motifs. The latter are presumably residual.

Late Iron Age contexts associated with the small stone-walled structure within the wheelhouse (Phase 8)

This assemblage of 111 sherds is too small for meaningful analysis. There are only two rim sherds (one flat-topped and the other round-topped) and none of the sherds is decorated.

Late Iron Age II contexts associated with the midden covering the wheelhouse (Phase 9)

The midden layers of phase 9 contain the largest quantities of sherds of any phase, more than half of the entirety from the whole excavation. All fabric groups are represented, with fabric 3 being the most common after fabrics 1–2. All rim types are present, especially flat-topped and vertical rims (Figures 9.10–9.11). Surprisingly, flaring rims are among the least common; it is possible that the small average sherd size has reduced the possibility of identifying these from among the other rim sherds.

The presence of a wide range of motifs on the 311 decorated sherds from phase 9 (forming 1.6% of the total number of sherds in phase 9) implies the incorporation of a fair quantity of residual Middle Iron Age and Late Iron Age I sherds. These include the full range of cordons, incised lines, and impressed and stamped decorations. Phase 9 contexts contain material typical of Campbell's periods A and B (including stamp-decorated sherds), indicating that some five or more centuries of ceramic styles have been mixed into this midden. Given that phases 4–8 show nothing like this level of residuality, it is likely that mixing occurred outside the excavated area. Other finds indicative of residuality in phase 9 layers

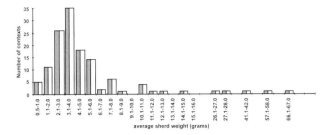

Figure 9.3 Average ceramic sherd weights

include a Roman plate-headed knee brooch dating to the mid-second to third century AD (see Chapter 10).

The fragmentation of the pottery assemblage

In Table 9.1 the average sherd weight for each phase has been calculated in an attempt to provide data for an exploration of the processes involved in the formation of the site. Figure 9.3 shows the distribution of the average weights of sherds. With the exception of Cordoned Urn contexts from phase 1, these approximate to a normal distribution around a modal weight of between 3g and 4g. The truncation of the graph at the lower end of the range is best explained by the bias in recovery through the loss of very small sherds falling through the 10mm mesh of the sieves.

By and large, the Cill Donnain III assemblage is heavily fragmented, more so than other assemblages from wheelhouses and other Iron Age sites on the machair of South Uist and the Western Isles more generally (Dun Vulan [La Trobe-Bateman 1999], Bornais mound 1 [Lane in Sharples 2012b: tabs 8, 22, 32, 61] and Cnip [MacSween 2006]). This is curious, especially since the heavily fragmented material from Cill Donnain spans a long period from the Late Bronze Age to the Late Iron Age and thus results from different depositional processes.

The considerable degree of fragmentation of the Late Bronze Age assemblage in phase 2 (average sherd weight 3.9g) is probably due to the layers belonging to this phase forming a well-used cultivation horizon; the heavily abraded ceramic mould fragments from these layers (see Chapter 10) also attest to the degree of erosion in this ancient ploughsoil. Similar fragmentation in phase 3 (4g average sherd weight; deposits formed prior to construction of the wheelhouse) is also likely to be due to long-term disturbance within a plough soil.

Average sherd weights of 3.9g, 4.2g and 2.6g from phases 4, 5 and 6 respectively are from assemblages associated with the use of the wheelhouse: its construction, initial occupation, and re-use. Sherds were larger (average sherd weight 5.5g) in the abandonment levels of the wheelhouse (phase 7), presumably because of less trampling on surfaces. The same is also likely to have been the case with the infilling of the bothy-like structure (context 28 in phase 8) within the wheelhouse ruins although the average of 10.2g is derived from only 111 sherds.

The midden deposits of phase 9 that covered the wheelhouse ruins have an average sherd weight of 4.2g, similar to the ceramics of phases 4 and 5 from the floors of the wheelhouse. Whilst some at least of these phase 9 contexts were subjected to ploughing, it is likely that the small sherd sizes relate as much to trampling underfoot on an internal floor surface prior to deposition in this midden; we can only assume that this refuse was created within one or more as yet unexplored buildings to the east of the excavated area. In spatial terms, there is little indication of any marked internal differentiation within the Late Iron Age midden assemblage.

The larger sherds from phase 1 (the Cordoned Urn assemblage) as well as from later contexts 25 (phase 7), 28 (phase 8), 32, 35, 52 and 164 (phase 3) require explanation within the context of the character of the deposits concerned:

- The pottery from the Cordoned Urn layers (phase 1) is from in and around structures that were probably dwellings. These deposits have not been subjected to erosive processes such as subsequent cultivation or heavy trampling of floor surfaces within domestic interiors.
- Contexts 25, 28 and 52 were all sand fills, not subjected to trampling and presumably containing sherds from relatively freshly broken vessels.
- Context 164 was a burnt peat ash deposit but little more is known about it.

Conclusion

In spite of the large quantity of excavated pottery, it is highly unlikely that Cill Donnain III holds the key to any of the problems that surround the later prehistory of the Hebrides, but the pottery assemblage is distinctive enough for the results of its study to link the site into the wider picture of settlement and society in South Uist and the Hebrides generally. Armit (1990: 206) has noted that material culture, including pottery, has traditionally been considered principally as a dating tool. As should be clear from the details of this report, this is a role for which the Cill Donnain pottery, in particular, is singularly ill-suited.

Questions of greater importance, to which study of the pottery may offer solutions, concern the role of material culture in the constant renegotiation of social relationships and the changing roles of particular types of artefact. The characteristics of Hebridean pottery (in particular the persistence of certain manufacturing techniques, and of continuity and change in design and in decoration) should be considered in relation to other aspects of the archaeological record, especially architecture and personal ornamentation (Armit 1990: 206).

Although most of the Cill Donnain III ceramic assemblage is heavily fragmented, it provides a small but important collection of domestic Cordoned Urn pottery from the end of the Early Bronze Age/Middle Bronze

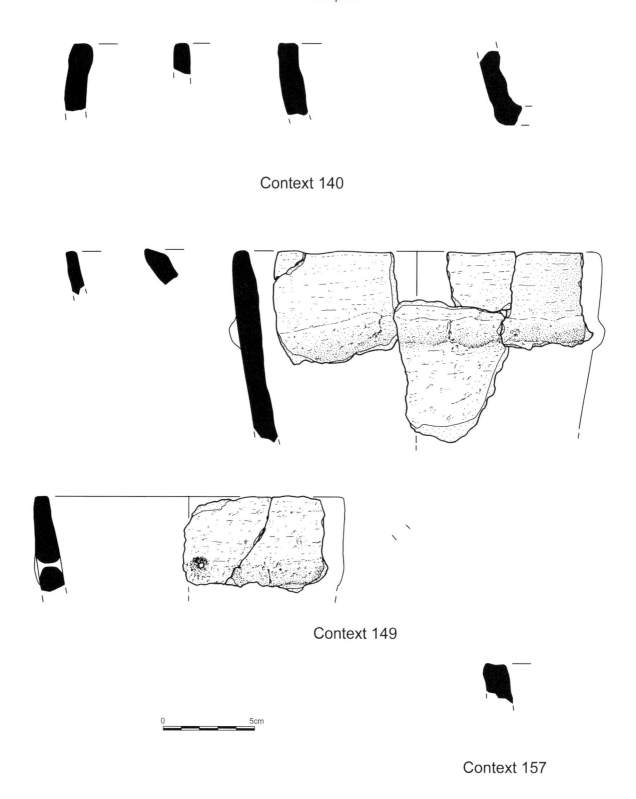

Context 140

Context 149

0 _____ 5cm

Context 157

Figure 9.4 Collared Urn ceramics from phase 1

Age. Such ceramics are normally known in Britain only from funerary contexts, in which they were used as containers of cremated bones; in Ireland, they are now well-known from settlement contexts too (Grogan and Roche 2010). The decoration on these Cordoned Urn vessels from Cill Donnain is limited to horizontal cordons; this contrasts with the presence of incised, cord-impressed and other impressed motifs on similar

Cordoned Urn ceramics from the nearby settlement site at Cladh Hallan (Parker Pearson and Parsons in prep.).

Late Bronze Age–Early Iron Age ceramics are attested at Cill Donnain III by the presence of heavily fragmented Plain Ware in association with fired-clay refractory material for bronze-casting (see Chapter 10) and carbonized plant remains of the early first millennium BC. Some of this pottery forms a relatively discrete horizon within ploughed

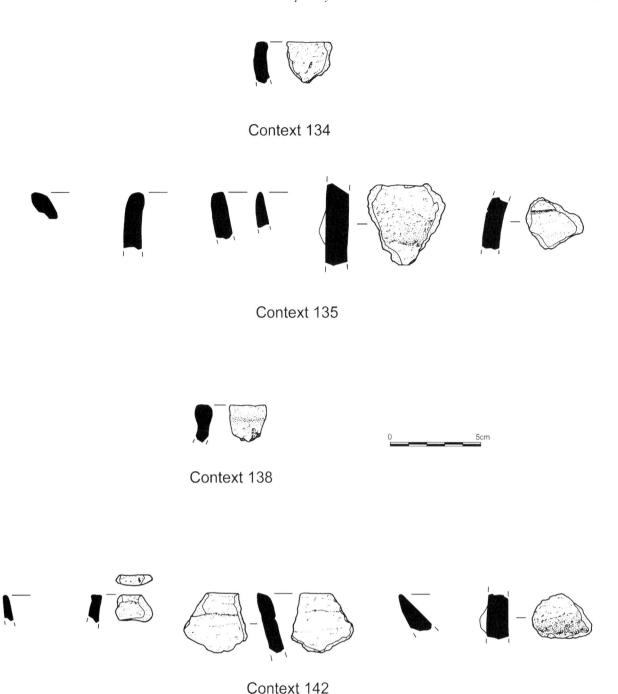

Context 134

Context 135

Context 138

0   5cm

Context 142

Figure 9.5 Late Bronze Age ceramics from phase 2

layers assigned to phase 2. However, a substantial proportion of Late Bronze Age–Early Iron Age pottery is mixed in with Middle Iron Age ceramics in the layers above (phase 3).

The wheelhouse was constructed and used (phases 4 and 5) after Middle Iron Age incised and impressed decoration had gone out of use at the end of the third century AD (Figure 9.12). Radiocarbon dates on carbonized grain place the wheelhouse's occupation during the fourth–sixth centuries AD, a period characterized by Dun Cuier-style ceramics with applied horizontal cordons (Figure 9.13). The ceramics from within the deposits formed during the wheelhouse's abandonment (phase 7)

are similarly consistent with Dun Cuier style and presumably date to the sixth or even seventh century AD.

Diagnostic artefacts and radiocarbon-dated carbonized plant remains from the midden covering the wheelhouse's ruins in phase 9 indicate a good deal of residuality in these final deposits. These appear to have been laid down within the sixth–seventh centuries AD, if not even later. The pottery in use in that period was Plain Ware (Figure 9.14), thus by definition difficult to differentiate within a chronologically mixed assemblage such as that typified by the midden layers of phase 9.

Chris Cumberpatch

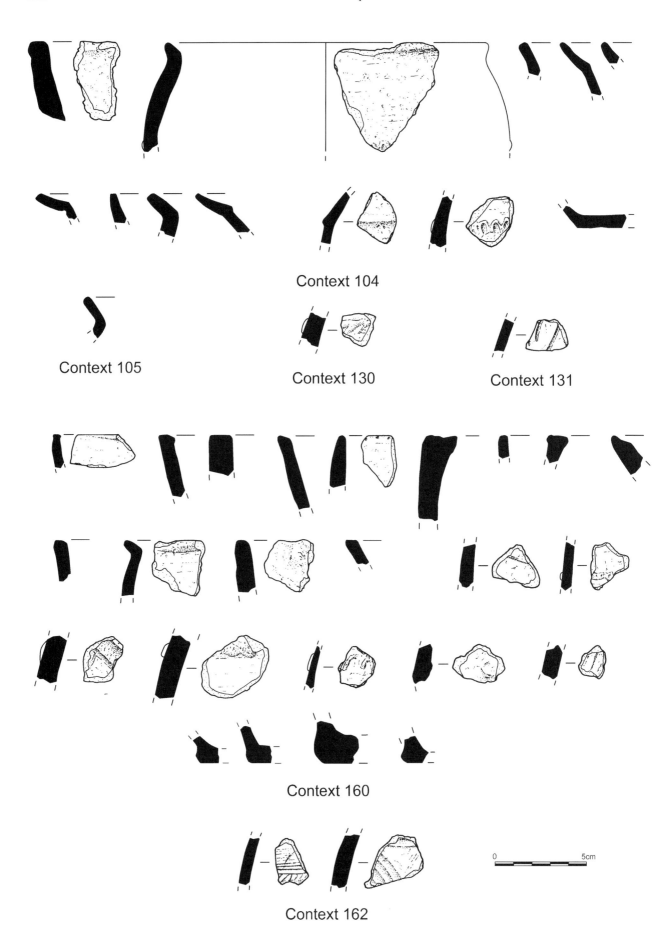

Context 104

Context 105

Context 130

Context 131

Context 160

Context 162

0 ———— 5cm

Figure 9.6 Middle Iron Age ceramics from phase 3, contexts 104–162

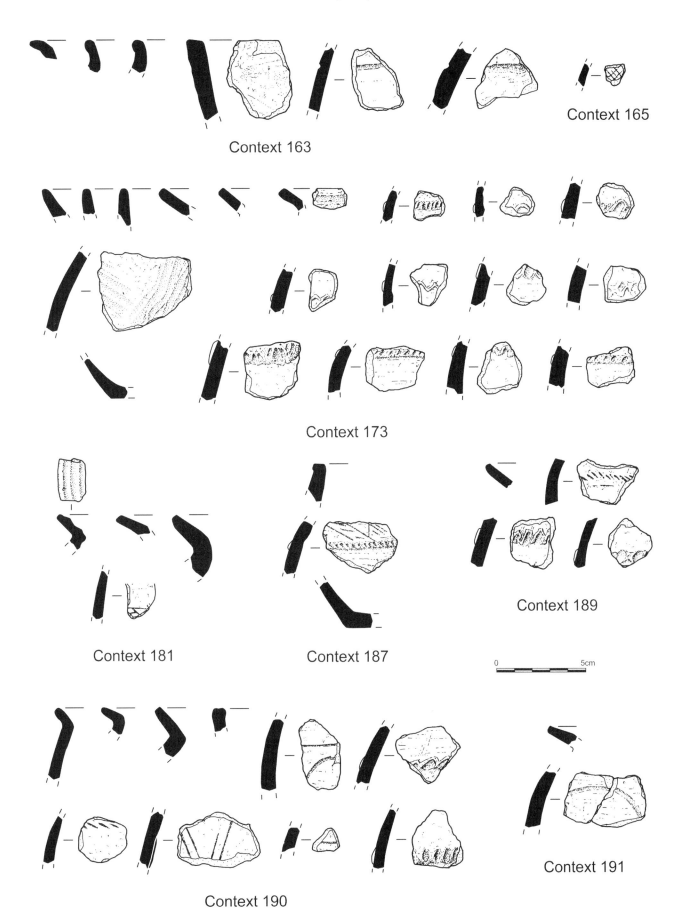

Figure 9.7 Middle Iron Age ceramics from phase 3, contexts 163–191

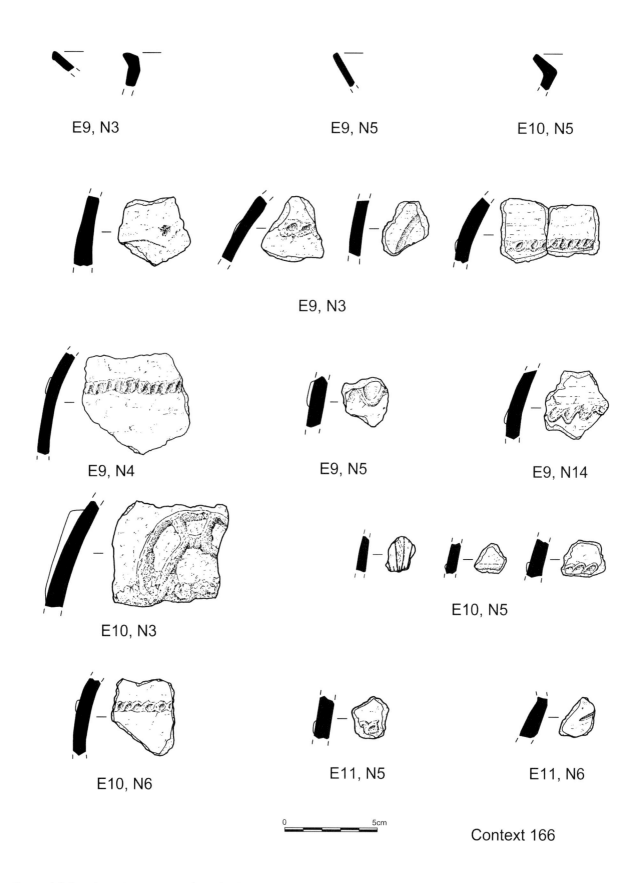

Figure 9.8 Late Iron Age ceramics from the floor (166) of the wheelhouse

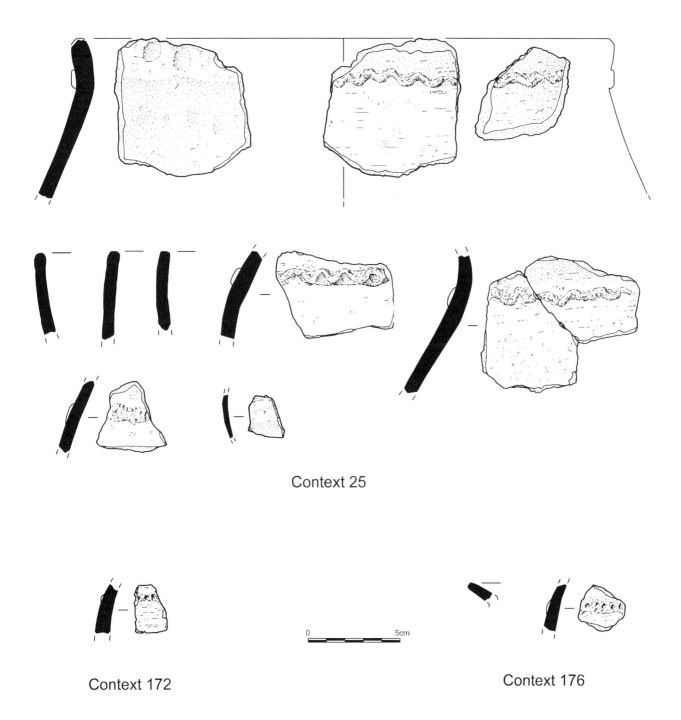

Context 25

Context 172

Context 176

0   5cm

Figure 9.9 Late Iron Age ceramics from the abandonment phase of the wheelhouse

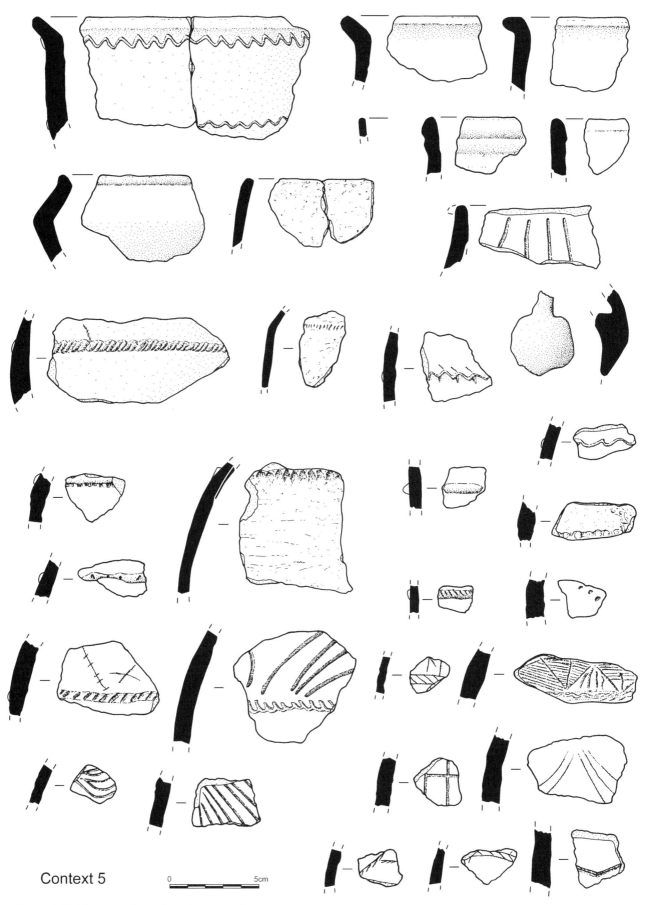

Context 5   0 _____ 5cm

Figure 9.10 Ceramics from phase 9, context 5

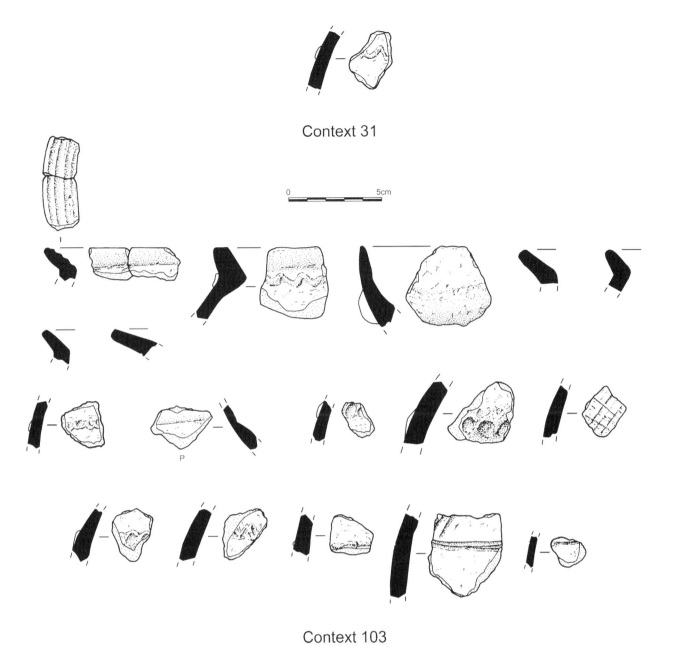

Figure 9.11 Ceramics from phase 9, contexts 31 and 103

Figure 9.12 Reconstructions of Middle Iron Age pottery (c. 100 BC-AD 300) from South Uist

Figure 9.13 Reconstructions of Late Iron Age pottery (c.AD 300-600) from South Uist

Figure 9.14 Reconstructions of Late Iron Age pottery (c.AD 600-900) from South Uist

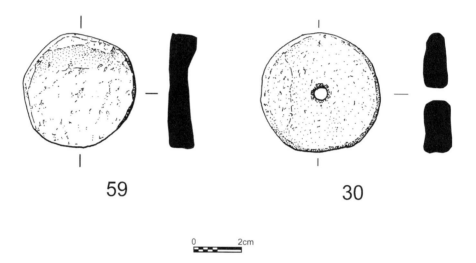

Figure 9.15 Ceramic artefacts SF30 and context 59

Ceramic artefacts

Mike Parker Pearson

Context 59 (E9/N6; phase 3) produced a circular disc (46mm dia., 10mm thick), made from a pottery sherd (Figure 9.15). Such discs can be interpreted as either gaming counters or unfinished spindle whorls. The occurrence of spindle whorls on Iron Age sites in the Western Isles is discussed in Chapter 11.

SF30 (unstratified). Spindle whorl (48mm dia., 10mm thick) with an hourglass-sectioned hole (6.5mm in diameter) at its centre. The whorl is made from the body sherd of a broken pot (Figure 9.15).

Chapter 10 The metal finds and industrial debris

Martin Dearne and Mike Parker Pearson

The copper-alloy artefacts

Martin Dearne

The majority of the copper-alloy objects appeared to be in a relatively stable condition when they were examined for this report in 1997, although one or two showed initial signs of surface flaking. Of the 22 copper-alloy artefacts from Cill Donnain III, three came from phase 3 contexts, one probably from phase 7, eleven from phase 9, and seven were unstratified (phase 10).

The relative quantity of copper-alloy items in relation to the stratified iron artefacts – of which there are 20 – is surprisingly high. Even though iron is relatively scarce in pre-Viking contexts on settlements in the Western Isles, copper alloy is normally even scarcer. The pre-Norse Late Iron Age contexts at Bornais mound 1 produced only nine iron and five copper-alloy items (Sharples 2012b: tab. 62). Similarly, Middle–Late Iron Age contexts at Dun Vulan yielded only 13 iron artefacts and a single fragment of copper-alloy sheet (Parker Pearson and Sharples 1999: 228–30).

The two artefacts from phase 3 at Cill Donnain III (Middle Iron Age, pre-dating the wheelhouse) are from different contexts and both consist of fragments of copper-alloy sheet or strip; phase 4 also produced a fragment of copper-alloy sheet. The remainder of the copper-alloy metalwork came from deposits likely to post-date the wheelhouse. One of these is a ring from context 4/1989 (a context number used to identify wall core and a deposit within the house and a deposit outside the house) that can be assigned to phase 4, 5 or 7. The rest of the stratified finds were recovered from layers associated with the midden (phase 9) covering the site. They consist of brooches (or fragments of brooches), rings, a possible belt fitting, strips, bars, sheets, a molten lump, and other items.

Since the midden dates to the Late Iron Age, the Roman plate-headed knee brooch (see below) is considerably earlier than its context, confirming other lines of dating evidence which indicate that the phase 9 midden incorporated material that was already of some antiquity at the time of its deposition on the site of the wheelhouse.

Brooches
SF1, context 8 (1990; E14.38/N1.87). Pin shank. This thin shank (6.4mm × 3.5mm max. width × 2.5mm max. thickness) is the pin for a brooch, from which it has become detached (Figure 10.1, labelled as 1 [1990]).

SF6, context 12 (1990; E10.65/N7.45). Plate-headed knee brooch (44mm × 24mm × 18mm). This has a large rectangular plate at its head with a rear ridge, three frontal grooves and a small, un-removed casting blemish. There is no trace of a pin mechanism or of its seating but the widely and deeply hollowed back implies a sprung mechanism. The bow curves down and in from the plate to an abrupt downturn, marked by a frontal flattened circle. The main bow is slightly baluster-shaped with angled sides and tapering frontal flattening. The large circular foot is deeply cupped for a missing gem (or enamel). The triangular catchplate continues in vestigial form on the back of the bow as far as the plate head (Figure 10.1, 6 [1990]).

This brooch is clearly Roman and amongst the knee tradition, but it is difficult to parallel. Nothing even vaguely similar is known from Roman Britain and the parallels are exclusively Continental, and then they apply only to the head plate and, in very general terms, the bow (Böhme 1972: taf. 8, nos. 411–16 and especially 414; Jobst 1975: taf. 18–20). A mid-second to third century AD date may be appropriate, possibly in the later part of this bracket, but there is no real evidence to cite and the opinion is based purely on typological grounds.

The occurrence of an evidently Continental brooch in the Western Isles is of some interest. A 'drift' of Romano-British objects into Scotland beyond the Antonine Wall and Hadrian's Wall is well established (*e.g.* Robertson 1970), and some clearly reached the Western

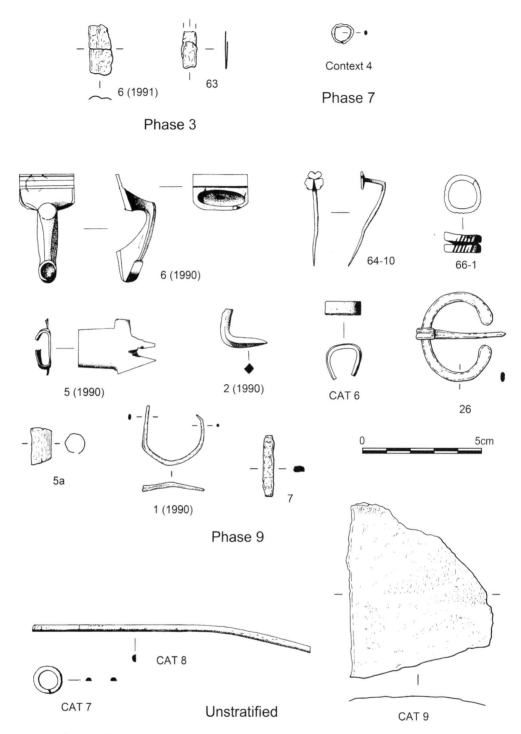

Figure 10.1 Copper-alloy artefacts from Cill Donnain III

Isles (Richardson 1960), particularly in and after the third century (Robertson 1970: figs 1–4). However, as this brooch has no parallel south of the walls, it is entirely conceivable that it was traded or brought directly from the Continent and not via the province of Britannia.

SF26, context 103 (1991; E10/N0). Penannular brooch (36mm × 29mm) of oval section (2mm × 1.5mm) with flattened, spatulate ends (4mm wide) and a 37mm-long pin (of circular section) whose head attachment is cast as two conjoined circular-sectioned wires (Figure 10.1, 26).

It is recorded as 'lying loose on the 1990 excavation surface; might have fallen out of section or from underneath stone of the structure [wheelhouse]'. Thus its context is uncertain.

Pins and a belt fitting
SF5, context 5 (1990; E13/N5; CAT 4, labelled No. 5). Belt fitting (length 33.55mm). This is made from a 0.8mm-thick sheet, cut at a slight angle either side of part of its length, giving two 'wings' folded back to make a

slightly tapering, interrupted 'tube'. Beyond the rectangular lug on one side and the slight projection on the other, it forms part of the base of one of two triangular prongs with a groove-bounded (incompletely cut-out) area at the base between them. No parallel has been noted but the 'tube' probably fitted over the end of a belt, and the prongs might have been intended to keep the belt end tidy by pushing them into clothing (Figure 10.1, 5 [1990]).

SF64-10, context 5=1/1989 (1989). Pin (37mm long). This is cast with a shamrock head (8mm dia.) and a sharp angular turn in its shank. It is probably a tie-pin or a lapel stick pin. It would be considered to be of nineteenth-century date except that its context is Late Iron Age (Figure 10.1, 64-10).

Rings

SF66-1, context 1. Finger ring (external dia. 16mm, internal dia. 12mm). This ring has two spiralled turns of rectangular-sectioned bar with two zones of angled grooves on its outer face. The grooves conceivably imitate later Roman braided wire forms but a very wide date range is possible (Figure 10.1, 66-1).

Context 0 (1990; CAT 7, labelled Sq. 58.15 and 1.58/2). Ring (diameter 12.5mm). This is a small ring of 1.7mm-wide D-section, with a crack across one point (Figure 10.1, CAT 7).

Context 4/1989 (1990; recovered from section of 1989 excavation). Ring (9mm × 8mm oval). This tiny ring is made from a looped flat strip (28mm × 2mm × 0.5mm), with both ends slightly overlapping (Figure 10.1, context 4).

Rods, strips and bars

SF2, context 5 (1990; E14.28/N3.69; CAT 5, labelled No. 2 and 0/0/2). Tip of a hook or bent rod (length 20.7mm). This broken, circular-sectioned rod (4.3mm dia.) turns at right angles, becoming lozenge-sectioned and tapering to a point (Figure 10.1, 2 [1990]).

SF5a, context 5 (1990; E13/N5). Strip folded to form a tube. A trapezoidal strip (28mm long × 15mm–9mm wide × 0.2mm thick) has been rolled to form a 14mm-long penannular tube up to 10mm in diameter (Figure 10.1, 5a).

SF7, context 14 (1990; E13.92/N4.64). Bar (14mm long × 4mm × 3mm). This fragment of a rectangular-sectioned bar appears to have breaks at both ends. It is presumably a tang or shaft for some implement rather than a pin shank (Figure 10.1, 7).

SF63, context 181 (1991; E12/N0). Strip (originally 28mm × 5mm × 0.5mm) folded in half and now in three pieces (Figure 10.1, 63).

Context 0, square 197 (1990; CAT 8). Strip (length 112.1mm). Three conjoining fragments of 2.35mm-wide, 11.05mm-thick, D-sectioned strip. It is now bent in plan and profile, and has possible evidence of decorative trim or inlay (Figure 10.1, CAT 8).

Context 0 (1990; CAT 11, labelled No.1 and 0/0/1). Semi-cuboid block (7mm × 5.7mm × 6.1mm). Its six faces are smooth except that one is uneven and another has a breakage scar. It is conceivably a tooth from a small tumbler lock key (not illustrated).

Context 1 (1990; CAT 6, labelled 83/31). Clip or strip (length 15.5mm; max. width 14.6mm). A piece of a *c*.1.5mm-thick, 5.2mm-wide strip that is flat-backed, convex-fronted, chamfer-edged and bent at both ends to give unequal legs turning inwards (Figure 10.1, CAT 6)

Context 103 (E11/N-2). Small fragment, perhaps the end of a triangular-sectioned bar (4mm × 3mm × 3mm; not illustrated)

Sheet fragments and other pieces

SF6, context 0 (1990; CAT 10). Sheet fragment (7mm × 6mm × 0.3mm), folded over (not illustrated).

SF6, context 160 (1991; E14/N7). Sheet fragment (18mm × 10mm × 1mm), originally folded but now broken across the fold. (Figure 10.1, 6 [1991])

SF131, context 104 (1991). Small fragment of sheet (10mm × 7mm × 0.5mm; not illustrated).

Context 0 (1989; CAT 9). An approximately triangular sheet fragment (81mm × 68mm × 0.6mm) with two approximately straight edges but all ragged. There is a slight crease running down from its 'apex' (Figure 10.1, CAT 9).

Context 5=1/1989, square 65 (1989; CAT 25, labelled No. 7). A small, irregular lump of molten copper alloy (4g).

Context 58 (1990; E9/N0). Three tiny fragments of copper-alloy plate, smaller than 3mm across and 0.5mm thick.

The lead object

Mike Parker Pearson

There was a single lead object from Cill Donnain:

Unknown context or year (CAT 35, labelled as No. 4). A small, triangular lump of molten and deformed lead (6g).

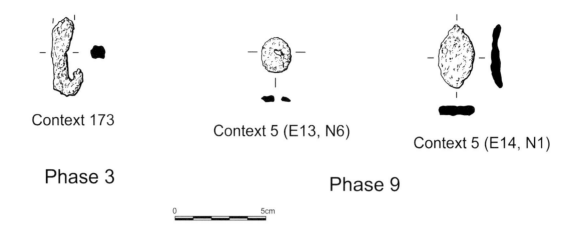

Context 173   Context 5 (E13, N6)

Context 5 (E14, N1)

Phase 3   Phase 9

0   5cm

Figure 10.2 Iron artefacts from Cill Donnain III

The iron objects

Martin Dearne

All objects were identified solely by eye, no facilities for x-radiography being available, but in no case would such examination appear to be desirable. No cleaning was undertaken. The ferrous finds are in an advanced state of decay, many pieces having already fragmented and all having flaked and/or split; indeed most had to be assessed by re-assembling fragments and few are sufficiently intact to illustrate. Conservation of the ironwork was considered pointless given its poor state.

Twenty-nine iron objects or concretions with iron cores/staining were recovered (nine of them, including two modern tin cans, in topsoil or unstratified). The only certainly identifiable pieces are six nails with circular heads and circular-sectioned shanks or rectangular-sectioned shanks. An extremely corroded object (SF 49-1, context 5=1/1989) has been tentatively identified as the tang end of a small knife. The remainder of the iron objects consists of short strips, a long strip, rings and small plate fragments. Most came from the Late Iron Age layers at the end of the sequence (phase 9). Only two items date to the Middle Iron Age (phase 3) prior to the wheelhouse's construction, and seven pieces came from layers relating to the building's abandonment in the early Late Iron Age (phase 7).

Although this is a small assemblage, it is larger than the quantities of pre-Norse Middle–Late Iron Age ironwork from the neighbouring, broadly contemporary sites of Dun Vulan (Parker Pearson and Sharples 1999: 228–30) and Bornais mound 1 (Sharples 2012b: tabs 62, 109), both of which were more extensively excavated. This raises the possibility that iron, as well as copper alloy, was more plentiful at Cill Donnain III, a scenario supported by the evidence for working of both iron and copper alloy (see below).

Nails
Context 1, square 59 (1989; CAT 22). Possible nail (length 20.6mm). This concretion has an iron core or is iron-stained.

Context 1, square 113 (1990; CAT 19, labelled (1)-113-1). Nail fragment (length 17.25mm; head diameter 20.8mm). This consists of the circular head and stub of a probably rectangular-sectioned shank.

Context 1, square 121 (1990; CAT 17). Nail fragment (reconstructed length 17.8mm; head diameter 17.5mm). This nail fragment consists of a circular head and the stub of a circular-sectioned shank.

Context 4, square 5 (1989; CAT 24). Uncertain object (length 20.5mm). This is a corroded and concreted fragment, possibly a nail head.

Context 4, square 7 (1989; CAT 21). Possible nail fragment (length c.25.5mm). This is a fragment of a bent, circular-sectioned shank.

Context 5 (1990; E13/N8). Nail head (20mm dia.) with the 15mm-long stump of a rectangular shank.

Context 6, square 17 (1989; CAT 18). Nail fragment (length 32.5mm). This is a fragment of a shank.

Context 12, square 86 (1989; CAT 20). Nail fragment (length 26mm). This is a fragment of a shank.

Knife fragments
Context 1, square 49 (1990; CAT 12, labelled (1)-49-1). Possible knife fragment (reconstructed dimensions: length 21mm; max. width 17.5mm; thickness less than 1.5mm). This was shattered before submission to the author but is probably a badly corroded thick strip with one tapered end. It is possibly the tang end of a small knife.

Context 1, square 57 (1989; CAT 23, labelled (1)-57-1). Uncertain object (length 29.5mm). This concretion has an iron core, and is irregular with a narrower projection at one end. It is just conceivably the tang end of a small knife.

Strips and bars

Context 0, square 66 (1989; CAT 13, labelled 66-(0)). One or more strips. A nearly straight, 165mm-long strip, probably originally of 5mm × 3mm rectangular section, with an irregular surface resulting from corrosion flaking. It was bagged with a hooked strip (length 106.7mm; estimated straightened length 160mm) in similar condition and probably of similar form, together with several short fragments of similar form.

Context 0, square 70 (1989; CAT 14, labelled as 1-2). Strip (reconstructed length 42mm; reconstructed width 15.4mm; thickness not measurable). This was shattered before submission to the author but is small and sub-rectangular with a concretion or protrusion on one face.

Context 1, square 28 (1989; CAT 15, labelled 1.28/1). Strip. This object is beyond reconstruction but was probably a small, narrow, rectangular strip.

Context 1, square 124 (1990; CAT 16,). ?Strip (length 15.9mm). Small, concreted piece of ?rectangular strip.

Context 165 (1991; E10/N5). Fragment of a rectangular strip (33mm × 11mm × 4mm).

Context 173, SF54 (1991; E10/N0). Hook or bar with curved end (39mm × 7mm × 6mm); this could be a broken slotted fitting and is unlikely to be a bent nail shank (Figure 10.2).

Plate fragments

Context 5 (1990; E11/N0). Riveted plate fragment (40mm × 21mm × 5mm). This plate-like fragment, now in pieces, appears to have had a circular rivet head (15mm dia.) associated with it. The rivet presumably fitted in a curved indentation on one side of the plate.

Context 5 (1990; E11/N5). Unidentified fragments. Seven pieces of corroded iron plate, of which the largest is 28mm × 9mm × 3mm.

Context 5 (1990; E14/N1). Lozenge-shaped plate (31mm × 19mm × 4mm); this resembles a rove but there is no central hole (Figure 10.2).

Context 25 (1990; E12/N3). Plate fragment (19mm × 16mm × 2mm).

Rings

Context 5, SF45 (1990; E11/N0). 'Iron ring.' Described in the site finds inventory but not found in the archive.

Context 5 (1990; E13/N6). Oval ring (18mm × 15mm across and 3mm thick) with copper alloy stain on one edge (Figure 10.2).

Other objects

Context 5 (1990; E11/N4). Unidentified lump (18mm × 16mm × 11mm).

Context 22, SF28 (1990; E11/N0). 'Two iron bits.' Described in the site finds inventory but not found in the archive.

Context 25 (1990; E12/N2). Unidentified lump (17mm × 15mm × 7mm).

Context 25 (1990; E13/N3). Unidentified lump (49mm × 32mm × 28mm). This heavily corroded lump is too dense to be a nail.

Context 100, SF1 (1991; E14/N-1). Tin can (modern).

Context 100, SF2 (1991; E14/N-2). Tin can (modern).

Context 176 (1991; E16/N3). Unidentified lump (25mm × 16mm × 10mm). This is possibly the tapering tip of a tool such as a chisel.

Bronze-casting clay refractories

Mike Parker Pearson

Eighteen fragments (105g) of clay refractory for casting implements of copper alloy were recovered from the excavations (Table 10.1), mostly from layer 160 and with smaller quantities from layers 103, 142, 163, 191, and layer 4 in Quarry Trench 1 (see Chapter 3). They were recognized in 2011 by this author, after the pottery report had been written, during its checking and editing.

All the fragments are heavily abraded, with none of their original surfaces surviving, but their distinctive red and red/grey fabric allows them to be positively identified as broken mould fragments from Late Bronze Age metal-casting (Figure 10.3). The largest surviving piece (context 160; E14/N6) is identifiable as a fragment of inner valve with a layer of wrap from a mould for a bronze sword, perhaps the proximal end of the handle.

Their fabric is comparable to the clay refractory fragments from Cladh Hallan (Cowie in prep.) and other Bronze Age assemblages. It consists of a relatively fine clay, mixed with fine sand and moderately well fired. Most of the fabric is oxidized to orange except for what

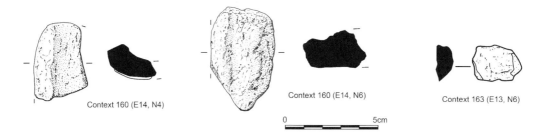

Figure 10.3 Clay refractory fragments from contexts 160 and 163

Phase	Context	Easting	Northing	Weight (g)	Observations
Phase 2	142	7	4	3	Unidentifiable
	4 (QT1)	1	8	1	Unidentifiable
Phase 3	160	14	6	33	Valve and wrap for a probable sword handle
	160	14	6	14	Valve possibly for the same item
	160	14	6	9	Valve
	160	14	6	2	Unidentifiable
	160	14	6	1	Unidentifiable
	160	14	3	14	Valve?
	160	14	3	4	Valve
	160	13	6	2	Unidentifiable
	160	14	4	2	Unidentifiable
	160	14	4	1	Unidentifiable
	163	13	6	5	Valve
	163	13	6	5	Unidentifiable
	163	13	6	2	Unidentifiable
	163	13	6	1	Unidentifiable
	191	10	5	3	Unidentifiable
Phase 9	103	10	-2	3	Valve

Table 10.1 Clay refractory debris from Cill Donnain III

remains of the contact faces, which have grey surfaces because of their predominantly oxygen-free environment.

Two of the fragments come from Late Bronze Age layers (phase 2): one is from a pit fill (142) and the other is from layer 4 in Quarry Trench 1. All but one of the remainder are from contexts in phase 3 (Middle Iron Age prior to the construction of the wheelhouse), dating to well after the Bronze Age. All but one of these phase 3 fragments are from layers 160 and 163, located within an area outside the northeast wall of the later wheelhouse (E13–14/N3–6). Pre-Iron Age layers beneath 160 and 163 were not excavated in this part of the site. It is likely that these mould fragments have been disturbed from lower layers by Iron Age cultivation (or other disturbance) to become residual within layers 160, 163 and 191, and layer 103 (belonging to phase 9). The tight spatial cluster within layers 160 and 163 suggests the possibility of either a metalworking focus surviving unexcavated in the Late Bronze Age layers beneath, or that this is a deposit at some distance from the metalworking site itself, as was found in a house entrance at Cladh Hallan (Parker Pearson *et al.* 2004: 76–9).

This small collection of Late Bronze Age refractories from Cill Donnain III is significant, even though most have come from residual contexts. The closest comparable assemblage is of more than 400 pieces from nearby Cladh Hallan, just five miles to the south; this includes

fragments from moulds for swords, spears, ornaments and tools (Cowie in prep.). The possibility that one of the Cill Donnain fragments is from the mould for a sword is particularly interesting because it indicates that sword-making residues were deposited not just at Cladh Hallan but also at neighbouring settlements. This makes it likely that the manufacture of swords and other artefacts was carried out at adjacent Late Bronze Age settlements in South Uist, rather than being restricted to just one settlement at the top of a local hierarchy. Thus bronze-casting might have been more widely distributed in the Western Isles (and perhaps western mainland Scotland) than previously thought, whether practised by travelling smiths or by craft-workers within each community.

The crucible

Mike Parker Pearson

A single rim sherd of a crucible (Figure 10.4), initially identified as a sherd of glazed pottery, was found in layer 187 (E9/N5), a deposit of sand beneath the wheelhouse, dating to the Middle Iron Age, prior to its construction (phase 3). The sherd has a glassy, bubbled surface on both interior and exterior and its fabric is hardened from exposure to high temperatures. It derives from a crucible

Figure 10.4 Crucible fragment from context 187

that was originally about 110mm in diameter. It may be residual from earlier layers dating to the Late Bronze Age, similar to the clay mould fragments also found in phase 3 deposits (see above).

The metalworking slag

Martin Dearne and Mike Parker Pearson

Almost a kilo of metalworking slag (951g) was recovered from stratified contexts, together with a further 44g from topsoil layers of the site (Table 10.2). The slag was analysed using English Heritage's criteria for distinguishing different types of metalworking debris (see Dungworth in prep.). There was no investigation for the presence of hammerscale in soil samples or flotation residues.

The identified categories of slag found at Cill Donnain III are smithing-hearth bottoms and undiagnostic iron-working slags; no slags diagnostic of iron-smelting were identified (Tables 10.3–10.4). The absence of hearth linings, the generally small quantities of material, and the small size of the fragments (average weight 10.6g) suggest that iron-smithing took place not within the excavated area but at a location elsewhere, and that the material is re-deposited. A single piece of copper-alloy slag was found in layer 5=1/1989 (phase 9) though its context is not wholly certain.

Most of the metalworking slag was deposited during the abandonment of the wheelhouse (phase 7; Table 10.5) and within the mixed deposits of the midden (phase 9; Table 10.6). Small quantities were found in layers relating to before the wheelhouse's construction in the Middle Iron Age (phase 3), its construction (phase 4), and its initial occupation (phase 5). However, the attribution of three pieces (18g) to phase 3 is problematic because the slag is recorded from that part of layer 165 that lay within the wheelhouse, and they might therefore have been deposited in phase 5.

The metalworking slag exhibits a degree of spatial patterning in its distribution. The nine pieces from phases 3–5 were concentrated in the northwest and west/central part of the wheelhouse. The higher quantities from phase 7 were concentrated in the eastern part of the wheel-house, by now becoming abandoned. By phase 9, most of the slag was deposited across the top of the filled-in ruins of the wheelhouse in its southern and central area with a second smaller spread north of the abandoned building. These are all likely dumps of material rather than residues of *in situ* metalworking, which did not take place within the Cill Donnain III wheelhouse or immediately in its vicinity but probably somewhere to its east within the larger, adjacent unexcavated settlement complex now covered by a large dune.

Comparison with neighbouring, contemporary Late Iron Age settlements shows that only two fragments of possible iron-smithing slag were found at Dun Vulan (Dungworth 1999) and none from the Late Iron Age wheelhouse at Bornais (see Young in Sharples 2012b: 289–95). Nor was any industrial debris found at the nearby Middle Iron Age settlements of Upper Loch Bornais (Marshall and Parker Pearson 2012) or Sligeanach mound 27, further west on Cill Donnain machair (Sharples 2012a). This raises the possibility that not all Middle–Late Iron Age settlements in the Cill Donnain–Bornais region of South Uist engaged in iron-smithing, and that it was restricted to certain groups within the community. A Late Iron Age high-status metalworking site, broadly contemporary with the upper component of the Cill Donnain sequence, was excavated at Eilean Olabhat in North Uist (Armit *et al.* 2008). Surface remains of another Late Iron Age metalworking site are known at Machair Mheadhanach (site 141) near the north end of South Uist (Parker Pearson 2012c).

Fuel ash slag

Mike Parker Pearson

Nine pieces of fuel ash slag, weighing 36g in total, were also recovered (Tables 10.7–10.8). Six of these (weighing 26g) came from the midden layer (5=1/1989) in phase 9, and the others were single pieces found in layers 24 and 31 (phase 9) and 166 (phase 5). Layer 166 is the floor of the wheelhouse, where a 2g-piece was found in the vicinity of the north pier. Fuel ash slag is a glassy silicate compound produced by high temperatures. It is not a by-product of metalworking but is normally associated with temperatures higher than those for peat fires, such as those produced by pyres and bonfires. No analysis has been made of this material; the thorough report by Young on the non-metallurgical slag from Bornais mound 1 describes the possible formation processes and chemistry of similar slags from the comparable machair environment at Bornais (Young in Sharples 2012b: 289–95).

Catalogue of metalworking slag			
Context	Location (year)	weight (g)	notes
0	square 5 (1989)	9	
	E9/N2 (1990)	3	
1	square 58 (1989)	7	
	square 58 (1989)	8	
	square 85 (1989)	7	
	square 114 (1990)	9	
	square 152 (1991)	23	
5	E10/N1	24	smithing-hearth bottom
	E10/N1	3	
	E10/N1	10	
	E10/N1	7	
	E10/N1	5	
	E10/N1	15	
	E10/N5	14	
	E11/N1	26	
	E11/N1	9	
	E11/N4	8	
	E12/N2 (1990)	18	(two pieces)
	E12/N4 (1990)	30	(four pieces)
	E12/N4	9	(three pieces)
	E12/N7, square 127 (1990)	6	
	E12/N8	29	
	E12/N8	2	
	E13/N2	14	
	E13/N4	7	
	E14/N5	7	
	E14/N8	5	
18	E11/N9	8	
25	E11/N3, square 113 (1990)	10	(two pieces)
	E11/N3, square 113 (1990)	10	(two pieces)
	E12/N1	11	(two pieces)
	E12/N2	49	smithing-hearth bottom
	E12/N2	28	smithing-hearth bottom
	E12/N2	100	(15 pieces)
	E12/N2	4	
	E12/N3	130	smithing-hearth bottom
		142	(25 pieces)
27	E13/N3	6	
31	E12/N2	5	
32	E10/N9 (1990)	3	
58	E9/N1	33	
165	E10/N5	18	(three pieces)
166	E9/N3	72	(five pieces)
	E10/N3	16	
176	E10/N3, SF44	34	(two pieces)
185	E8/N5	2	
Total weight		995	

Table 10.2 Metalworking slag from Cill Donnain III

Slag Type	Weight (g)
Smithing-hearth bottoms	231
Vitrified hearth-lining	0
Non-diagnostic iron-working slag	764
Total weight	**995**

Table 10.3 Quantities of different types of metalworking slag

Phase	1	2	3	4	5	6	7	8	9	u/s
Non-diagnostic iron slag			18	2	88		311		301	44
Smithing-hearth bottoms							207		24	

Table 10.4 Weight (g) of types of iron-working slag, by phase

Metalworking slag from Phase 7		
Easting	**Northing**	**Weight (g)**
12	2	182
12	3	272
12	1	11
11	3	20
10	3	34
Total weight		519

Table 10.5 Contextual distribution of metalworking slag from phase 7

Metalworking slag from Phase 9		
Easting	**Northing**	**Weight (g)**
5	6	7
8	3	15
9	1	33
10	1	64
10	5	14
10	9	3
11	1	35
11	4	8
11	9	8
12	8	31
12	4	39
12	7	6
12	2	23
13	2	14
13	4	7
13	3	6
14	8	5
14	5	7
Total weight		325

Table 10.6 Contextual distribution of metalworking slag from phase 9

Catalogue of fuel ash slag			
Context	Location (year)	weight (g)	notes
1	square 48 (1989)	13	(two pieces)
	square 58 (1989)	6	
	square 65 (1989)	1	
	square 75 (1989)	3	
	square 76 (1989)	3	
24	E10/N9 (1990)	4	
31	E10/N3 (1990)	4	
166	E10/N5 (1991)	2	
Total weight		36	

Table 10.7 Contextual distribution of fuel ash slag from Cill Donnain III

Fuel ash slag in Phase 9		
Easting	Northing	Weight (g)
10	9	4
6	4	3
10	3	4
8	3	6
5	5	3
5	4	1
8	2	13
Total weight		34

Table 10.8 Spatial distribution of fuel ash slag in phase 9

Chapter 11 The stone tools

Mike Parker Pearson

Introduction

The worked stone assemblage from Cill Donnain III consists of coarse stone tools (mostly hammerstones made from beach cobbles or pebbles), flint tools and debitage, and pumice. The excavation records indicate that fragments of quartz pebbles were kept but these have not been analysed. One of the problems in reporting on the stone tools is that examination of the site archive reveals uncertainty about standards of retrieval and about recovery of such items. For example, some coarse stone tools are mentioned in the paper records but cannot be found in the finds archive. Since all stratified deposits were sieved, it is likely that most stone tools were recognized during excavation, but it may be that certain categories (especially pumice and coarse stone tools) were less systematically recovered, especially in the first two excavation seasons when experience in recognizing such materials was limited.

All stones on the site can be considered as manuports; nearly all of the assemblage, including the flint pebbles, is likely to have come from the beach along South Uist's west coast, just a few hundred metres away from the wheelhouse. The only evidence of exploitation of sources on the east coast of South Uist is a small piece of green slate from the island of Stulaigh (Stulay), south of Loch Aoineart.

The coarse stone tools

Fifteen coarse stone tools from Cill Donnain III have been located in the finds archive; a further eight are mentioned in the site records but are not available for analysis. It is possible that these mislaid objects were later found not to be artefacts and were therefore discarded, but there is no way of knowing. All but three of the stone tools – a cup-marked stone and two missing objects recorded as 'worked stones' – have been used as hammerstones; of these, one has been used additionally as a rubber and two as grinders (Table 11.1). Most of these hammerstones are from contexts associated with the midden (phase 9). The close spatial patterning of many of them in context 5 (five being found in squares E13/N8–E13/N9; Figures 8.13–8.15) suggests that some might have been dumped together in this midden layer.

The small number of stone tools associated with the wheelhouse (phases 4–8) accords well with previous observations that wheelhouse assemblages from the Western Isles are generally restricted in the number and range of coarse stone tools (Parker Pearson and Sharples 1999: 230–1). In contrast, however, a large assemblage was recovered from the Late Iron Age wheelhouse at Bornais mound 1 (Sharples 2012b: 85, 284–8). This moderately large assemblage of hammerstones from the Late Iron Age midden (phase 9) at Cill Donnain III compares well with other large Late Iron Age assemblages at Dun Vulan and Bornais although the range of tools is more restricted: there were no quernstones, whetstones or stone discs at Cill Donnain in contrast to Dun Vulan.

Phase	1	2	3	4	5	6	7	8	9	u/s
Hammerstones	1		1	5			1		11	1
Cup-marked stone									1	
Worked stone	2									

Table 11.1. Coarse stone artefacts from Cill Donnain III

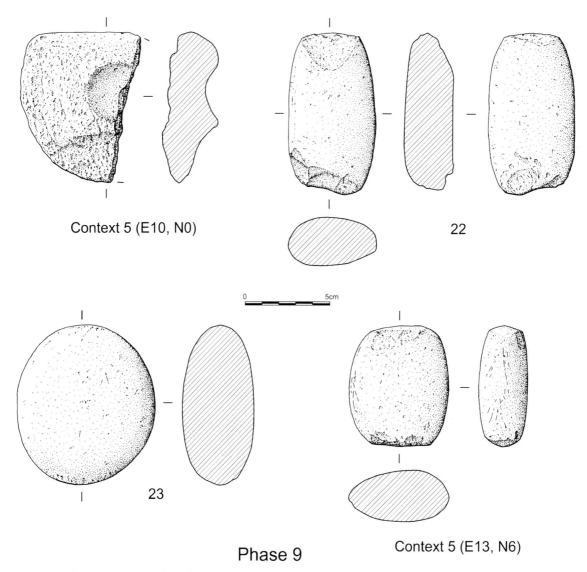

Context 5 (E10, N0)

22

23

Phase 9

Context 5 (E13, N6)

Figure 11.1 Coarse stone artefacts from Cill Donnain III

Catalogue of the coarse stone tools
Phase 1
Context 140. 'Hammerstone'. Recorded in the site finds inventory but not found in the archive.

Context 149. 'Two worked stones'. Recorded in the site finds inventory but not found in the archive.

Phase 3
SF49, context 32 (E10/N6). Elongated oval grinding stone and hammerstone made from a gneiss pebble, with three grinding facets at one end and a small pecked facet at the other; there is slight damage along the long sides (117mm × 51mm × 26mm; 320g).

Phase 4
Context 24 (E10.05/N10.00). Oval hammerstone made from a quartzite pebble, with a small pecked facet at one end and a large flake scar at the other (84mm × 53mm × 46mm; 362g).

Context 204. 'Two hammerstones'. Recorded in the site finds inventory but not found in the archive.

Context 217. 'Hammerstone'. Recorded in the site finds inventory but not found in the archive.

Context 218. 'Hammerstone'. Recorded in the site finds inventory but not found in the archive.

Phase 7
SF43, context 25 (E12.54/N3.53). 'Hammerstone'. Recorded in the site finds inventory but not found in the archive.

Phase 9
SF18, context 5 (E13/N9). Oval hammerstone made from a sandstone pebble, with a pecked facet at one end and a polished facet with transverse striations on one flat side (104mm × 67mm × 44mm; 543g).

Phase	1	2	3	4	5	6	7	8	9	us
Scraper	1	3								
Core		2								
Retouched piece					1					
Blade		1								
Flake		3	1	1					4	
Chunk or spall	2	1							1	1

Table 11.2. Worked flint from Cill Donnain III

SF19, context 5 (E13/N9). Elongated oval hammerstone made from a quartzite pebble, with pecked and flaked facets at each end, a small pecked facet along one narrow side and a slight polished facet on one flat side (183mm × 99mm × 48mm; 1741g).

SF22, context 5 (E13/N6; square 149). Elongated oval hammerstone made from a quartzite pebble, with a pecked and flaked facet at one end and a small lightly pecked facet at the broader end (90mm × 49mm × 24mm; 206g; Figure 11.1).

SF23, context 5 (E13/N9). Oval hammerstone made from a quartzite pebble with two angled pecked facets at each end (87mm × 78mm × 38mm; 456g; Figure 11.1).

SF26, context 5 (E13/N8; square 138). Oval flat hammerstone made from a metamorphic rock pebble, with pecked facets at opposite ends and light pecking on its long edges; its flat sides might have been artificially polished (90mm × 63mm × 24mm; 274g).

SF27, context 5 (E13/N6). Broken end fragment of an elongated oval hammerstone of metamorphic rock, exhibiting a pecked facet at one end, broken across the middle and split laterally through its centre (67mm × 53mm × 21mm; 150g).

Context 5 (E10/N0). Broken flat gneiss pebble with cup-marks on opposed sides, one well-preserved (31mm dia. × 7mm deep) and the other damaged by flaking; the stone has broken across the centres of the two cup-marks (85mm × 62mm × 29mm; 260g; Figure 11.1).

Context 5 (E13/N6). Oval grinder and hammerstone made from a sandstone pebble, with a pecked facet at one end and three ground facets at the other; both ends are slightly damaged by small flake scars (66mm × 56mm × 30mm; 205g; Figure 11.1).

Context 5 (E13/N8). Broken end of an oval hammerstone made from a quartzite pebble, with a lightly pecked facet at its end (55mm × 56mm × 36mm; 163g).

Context 18 (E11/N9). Sub-rectangular hammerstone made from a metamorphic rock pebble, with small pecked facets at opposite ends, one of them damaged by a large flake scar (87mm × 51mm × 30mm; 280g).

SF46, context 31 (E12/N3). Elongated oval hammerstone made from a quartz pebble, with pecked and flaked facets at each end and a polished flat facet on one flat side (79mm × 41mm × 30mm; 175g).

Context 58 (E9/N1). Round hammerstone made from a quartz pebble, with pecked facets at each end, one of them flaked (62mm × 55mm × 29mm; 174g).

Unstratified/phase 10
Context 0. Triangular hammerstone made from a basalt pebble, with three pecked facets at one end and three small pecked facets at the other (82mm × 59mm × 36mm; 334g).

The flint tools
The small assemblage of 22 pieces of worked flint (Table 11.2) is derived entirely from raw materials found as water-worn beach pebbles; only four pieces exhibit no cortex. It is likely that these pebbles were found locally in beach deposits, and the small sizes of the tools, cores and flakes indicate the limitations dictated by such raw material. Most of the flint assemblage derives from Early–Middle Bronze Age and especially Late Bronze Age/Early Iron Age deposits (phases 1 and 2); the flakes, chunks and spalls found in later contexts dating to the Middle and Late Iron Age are likely to be residual.

The flakes are small, between 32mm and 15mm long, except for the single retouched flake (46mm × 25mm); the blade is also small (34mm × 13mm). The two cores (one measuring 28mm × 12mm × 6mm and the other 25mm × 12mm × 11mm) exhibit bi-polar working and are small and worked-out, having been used to detach flakes and blades.

The four thumbnail scrapers are very small, with retouch forming rounded distal ends. The scrapers' working edges, moderately to steeply angled, have been created through regular semi-invasive retouch. The retouched flake has unifacial retouch along one lateral edge.

The lithics from Cill Donnain III compare well with the other Early Bronze Age assemblages of similar size from the immediate vicinity of the site, a few hundred metres to the west at Sligeanach (Pannett in Sharples 2012a: 237–8) and Cill Donnain I (Pollard in Hamilton and Sharples 2012: 207, fig. 10.7), although these date to a slightly earlier period of the early second millennium BC, being associated with Beakers and Food Vessels.

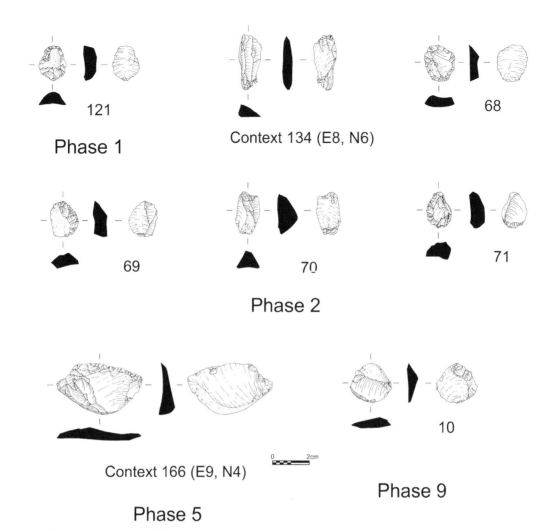

Figure 11.2 Flint artefacts from Cill Donnain III

In contrast to the contemporary assemblages from Cladh Hallan (Edmonds and Martin in prep.), Cill Donnain I and Sligeanach, there is no evidence at Cill Donnain III of Early Bronze Age quartz-working. Some six quartz flakes were recovered during the 1990 excavation season: all were from phase 9 (contexts 4, 5, 18 and 20). With a complete absence of quartz flakes from earlier levels at Cill Donnain III, it is highly likely that these phase 9 quartz flakes are accidental debris from broken quartz hammerstones of the Late Iron Age, rather than residual flakes from a Bronze Age industry.

Catalogue of the worked flint
Flakes and blades
SF10, context 5 (E13/N7). Flake (Figure 11.2).

Context 5 (E10/N4). Flake.

Context 5 (E12/N0). Flake.

Context 24 (E11/N9). Flake.

Context 142 (E8/N5). Blade.

Context 142 (E8/N5). Flake.

SF6, context 135 (E5/N5). Flake.

Context 135 (E9/N5). Broken flake.

Context 166 (E9/N4). Retouched flake (Figure 11.2).

SF132, context 191 (E11/N6). Flake.

SF36, context 206 (E11/N3). Flake.

Cores
Context 134 (E8/N6). Blade core fragment (Figure 11.2).

SF70, context 135 (E3/N5). Core fragment (Figure 11.2).

Scrapers
SF68, context 135 (E4/N5). Thumbnail scraper (Figure 11.2).

SF69, context 135 (E4/N5). Thumbnail scraper (Figure 11.2).

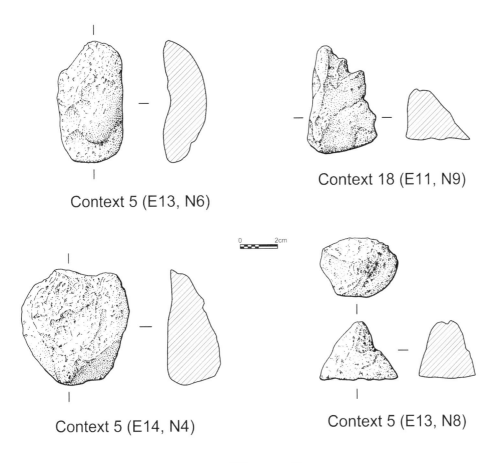

Context 5 (E13, N6)

Context 18 (E11, N9)

Context 5 (E14, N4)

Context 5 (E13, N8)

Phase 9

Figure 11.3 Pumice artefacts from Cill Donnain III

SF71, context 135 (E3/N5). Thumbnail scraper (Figure 11.2).

SF121, context 149 (E4/N4). Thumbnail scraper (Figure 11.2).

Chunks and spall
SF123, unstratified. Spall.

Context 33 (E11/N1). Chunk.

Context 140 (E8/N16). Chunk.

Context 142 (E8/N5). Chunk.

Context 149 (E4/N4). Chunk.

The pumice
The finds archive contains just 17 pieces of unworked pumice (weighing 82g) and 12 worked or shaped pieces (weighing 138g). The largest piece is 32g in weight, and the average weight of the 29 pieces is 7.7g. All the worked fragments came from the Late Iron Age levels (phase 9), so there might well have been material of

earlier date either missed during excavation or subsequently mislaid. Two unworked pieces came from context 24, the phase 4 wall core; the remainder of the unworked fragments also came from phase 9 (Table 11.3). No small finds numbers were assigned to the pumice fragments.

Bearing in mind the caveat that the surviving pumice assemblage from Cill Donnain III may be incomplete, this is one of the smaller assemblages of worked and unworked pumice from the Western Isles, smaller than the 55 pieces from the Neolithic site of Allt Chrisal on Barra (Branigan and Foster 1995: 144–8), the 43 pieces from Early and Middle Iron Age Baile Sear (Newton and Dugmore 2003: 135) and the 42 pieces from Middle and Late Iron Age Dun Vulan (Parker Pearson and Sharples 1999: 232), and much smaller than the 632 pieces from Bronze Age and Early Iron Age Cladh Hallan (Parker Pearson *et al.* in prep.). The pumice assemblage from Bornais mound 1 is also very small, at just 12 fragments (Sharples 2012b: tab. 110; this useful table gives pumice quantities for a number of other Iron Age sites of the Western and Northern Isles).

Unfortunately the Dun Vulan pumice was not weighed but comparisons of average pumice weight can be drawn between Cladh Hallan (10.1g) and the Allt Chrisal (22.9g) and Baile Sear (6.1g) assemblages. This shows

Context	total no. fragments	location	weight (g)
Unstratified	2		6
5	10	E10/N1	6
		E10/N2	20
		E11/N0	3
		E12/N1	3
		E12/N7	6
		E13/N8	4
		E13/N2	14
		E13/N9	3
		E14/N3	3
		E14/N9	3
7	1	E10/N0	3
24	2	E10/N8	2
		E11/N8	1
31	1	E12/N3	3
32 (or 12? Labelling unclear)	1	E11/N8	2
TOTAL	**17**		**82**

Table 11.3 Catalogue of the unworked pumice

that average pumice weight declined gradually through time from the Neolithic to the Iron Age. However, within the Iron Age, quantities of pumice are small, with the assemblage at Cill Donnain III being smaller than the Middle Iron Age assemblage from Baile Sear.

The proportions of worked to unworked pieces are also different on each site: 12:17 at Cill Donnain, 21:34 at Allt Chrisal, 172:453 at Cladh Hallan, 3:40 at Baile Sear, and 10:32 at Dun Vulan. Cill Donnain has the highest proportion of worked to unworked pieces, although again this may be the result of a bias in retrieval or retention.

The Cill Donnain III pumice is brown and black in colour, with the former predominating, as is also seen in the Dun Vulan, Cladh Hallan, and Baile Sear assemblages; it differs from the entirely brown assemblage from Allt Chrisal. Newton and Dugmore (2003) correlate this brown and black dacitic pumice to tephra layers from the Icelandic Katla volcanic system, originating before 4500 BC.

Catalogue of the worked pumice
Context 5 (E11/N3). A broken triangular piece (29mm × 17mm × 17mm) with a concave worn facet (3g).

Context 5 (E11/N3). A broken sub-rectangular piece (18mm × 16mm × 8mm) with a concave worn facet on one side and a 1.5mm groove on the other (1g).

Context 5 (E12/N2). An oval piece (18mm × 14mm × 9mm) with a concave facet (1g).

Context 5 (E12/N3). A broken oval piece (37mm × 27mm × 15mm) with a flat, stepped facet on one face and a flat, bevelled facet on one side (7g).

Context 5 (E13/N6). A sub-rectangular piece (60mm × 34mm × 19mm) with a concave facet on which there are two slight grooves 2mm wide (23g; Figure 11.3).

Context 5 (E13/N8). An oval piece with a triangular profile (39mm × 28mm × 27mm), with a concave base and a groove 6mm wide and 4mm deep in one side (13g; Figure 11.3).

Context 5 (E14/N2). A flat, rectangular piece (35mm × 33mm × 15mm) with a flat facet on one side (10g).

Context 5 (E14/N4). A round piece (59mm × 58mm × 25mm) with a flat facet on one face (32g; Figure 11.3).

Context 18 (E10/N9). A triangular piece (59mm × 43mm × 23mm) with a groove 7mm wide and 3mm deep (4g).

Context 18 (E11/N9). A triangular piece (53mm × 40mm × 30mm) with a scalloped edge along one side, produced by five grooves (3mm–6mm wide); one flat side has a concave worn facet (21g; Figure 11.3).

Context 24 (E10/N8). A triangular-sectioned and triangular-shaped piece (41mm × 38mm × 27mm) with a concave facet on one side (9g).

Context 31 (E12/N3). A triangular-sectioned piece (38mm × 35mm × 23mm) with a flat facet on one side (14g).

The slate
A fragment of green slate (18mm × 13mm × 2mm) came from context 5 (E13/N8). A nearby source of slate is known on the small island of Stulaigh, off the east coast of South Uist.

Chapter 12 Bone, ivory and antler tools and ornaments

Mike Parker Pearson

with species identifications by

John Hamshaw-Thomas and Kim Vickers

Discussion

There are 94 pieces of worked bone and antler recorded from Cill Donnain III (Tables 12.1–12.2). Some of the objects recorded in the field during the 1990 excavation could not be traced in the finds archive during post-excavation; they are listed in the catalogue below as registered but not examined so their identifications must be regarded as provisional. Two-thirds of the assemblage came from the phase 9 midden layers covering the Middle–Late Iron Age wheelhouse and earlier deposits. Since these midden deposits appear to have mixed contents from a long period of over 500 years (as indicated by the wide date range of the pottery and other small finds from these layers), it must be assumed that the bone and antler tools from phase 9 represent a similarly chronologically mixed assemblage. The same is likely to be true of the Middle Iron Age finds from phase 3 that derive from deposits containing residual Late Bronze Age material.

Within the phases unlikely to contain chronologically mixed assemblages, there are several notable finds. The incomplete ivory pin (SF158; Figure 12.1) from pit 142, dating to the Late Bronze Age (phase 2), is exceptional in its fineness; not one of the 31 pins from Cladh Hallan (Davies and Slater in prep.) is made of ivory, and none are as finely crafted as this pin from Cill Donnain III. Its headless style is one of two types common at Cladh Hallan during the Late Bronze Age (*ibid.*) so there is no reason to suspect that this item has been introduced to pit 142 from a later context.

From layers associated with construction of the Cill Donnain III wheelhouse (phase 4), the sawn tip of a marine mammal's tooth (SF32) provides evidence for ivory-working, alongside antler-working. The remaining bone artefacts from this phase consist of points.

Material from the floor (166) of the wheelhouse includes a small assemblage of antler artefacts and manufacturing debris, scattered in the north, west and central (hearth) parts of the wheelhouse's interior. One of these objects is a detached tine and the remaining three are worn-down antler rings made of narrow, hollowed segments of beam (Figure 12.3). Two more examples of these were found in contexts from phases 7 and 9. Such antler artefacts are not known from Dun Vulan. Bornais mound 1 has three from its Late Iron Age layers (Sharples 2012b: 368, tab. 98, figs 57, 80), and others have been found in the Western Isles at Bac Mhic Connain, North Uist (Hallén 1994: 221) and Dun Cuier, Barra (Young 1956: 321). Further afield, examples are known from the Northern Isles (cited in Hallén 1994: 221). Additionally, Bornais mound 1's Late Iron Age layers have also produced six similarly cut sections of cattle long bone, interpreted as possible rough-outs for parallelopiped dice (Sharples 2012b: 253–4, fig. 156).

Unfortunately, the distribution of antler material on the floor (166) of the Cill Donnain wheelhouse cannot be compared with that of the unworked bone found in floor 166 because the spatial provenance of the animal bones was lost during faunal analysis in 1991.

Artefacts from the abandonment of the wheelhouse

	Phase 1	Phase 2	Phase 3	Phase 4	Phase 5	Phase 7	Phase 8	Phase 9
	EBA-MBA	LBA	MIA	Construction	Occupation	Abandonment	Bothy	Midden
Bone tools or working	1		1	2		5		37
Worked cetacean bone				1		2	1	11
Ivory		1		1				2
Antler artefacts			2		3	2		3
Antler manufacturing			1	3	2		1	11
Total	**1**	**1**	**4**	**7**	**5**	**9**	**2**	**64**

Table 12.1 Bone, ivory and antler artefacts by phase

	Phase 1	Phase 2	Phase 3	Phase 4	Phase 5	Phase 7	Phase 8	Phase 9	Unstratified	Total
Point	1		1	2				7		11
Blunt point								1		1
Pin		1						2		3
Peg			1	1		1		2		5
Needle								3		3
Modelling tool						1				1
Spatula								3		3
Weaving beater								1		1
Pierced disc						2		1		3
Tube						1				1
Socket/handle						1		2		3
Bow-drill bit						1				1
Chopping board								1		1
Bead								3		3
Segment ring					3	1		1		5
Miniature comb								1		1
Toggle								2		2
Other			1			1	1	22		25
Working debris			1	4	2		1	12	1	21
Total	**1**	**1**	**4**	**7**	**5**	**9**	**2**	**64**	**1**	**94**

Table 12.2 Bone, ivory and antler artefact types by phase

(phase 7) include a modelling tool, a pierced disc, a socket, a possible peg and a possible rotary quern handle or bow-drill bit. A bone spindle whorl (SF30) was recorded during excavation but could not be found in the archive during post-excavation; it could be the same object as the pierced disc (SF111) from similar co-ordinates in the same layer. One fragment of worked cetacean bone and one fragment of antler were found in association with the bothy-like structure built in the wheelhouse's ruins in phase 8.

Because the material from phase 9 is chronologically mixed, it does not warrant analysis separate from the remainder of the assemblage. Instead, it can be considered within an overview of the entire Cill Donnain III assemblage of worked bone and antler.

The most numerous bone tools from Cill Donnain III are 11 bone points and a blunt point, found in contexts from phases 1, 3, 4 and 9 (Table 12.2). Otherwise, different tool types are represented by between one and three examples only:

- Evidence of textile-working is provided by a weaving beater (SF151) and a spindle whorl (SF30), though neither of these is identified with certainty.
- With just one ceramic spindle whorl (unstratified) from the site (see Chapter 9), the evidence for spinning at Cill Donnain is much less than that for neighbouring Dun Vulan (Parker Pearson and Sharples 1999: 126, fig. 5.31) or Bornais mound 1 (Sharples 2012b: 275, tabs 109, 110; Sharples's tables give comparative data for spindle whorls from other sites in the Western and Northern Isles).

- Three needles indicate sewing of leather or textiles.
- The miniature long-handled comb (SF142; Figure 12.1) could not have functioned as a weaving comb and might well have been a child's toy (see catalogue below for comparison to combs from Bornais mound 1).

A variety of other domestic activities are indicated at Cill Donnain by examples of a wide range of bone tools: peg, modelling tool, spatula, tube, socket, pierced disc, chopping board, and a rotary or bow-drill bit. The latter could be a rotary quern handle although it is smaller than the examples from Dun Vulan (Parker Pearson and Sharples 1999: 220–7, figs 5.32, 6.31, 6.33, 7.15) where the number of quernstones and quern handles suggests that milling of grain was a significant economic activity, in contrast to Cill Donnain.

Ornaments are restricted to a small range of bone pins, beads and toggles. The antler segment rings could be components of a composite artefact and their heavy wear suggests that they might have formed decorative parts of composite handles (as suggested for examples from Midhowe, Orkney, by Foxon [1991: 202]). Otherwise, the remainder of the assemblage consists of unidentifiable fragments and manufacturing waste. The latter consists mostly of red deer antler off-cuts of tines and beam segments, in smaller quantities than the Late Iron Age layers at Bornais mound 1 (Sharples 2012b: 366–8; tab. 110) and especially Dun Vulan (Parker Pearson and Sharples 1999: 219–27).

One aspect of the assemblage that differentiates the settlement of Cill Donnain III (but not so much the wheelhouse itself) from other Bronze Age and Iron Age

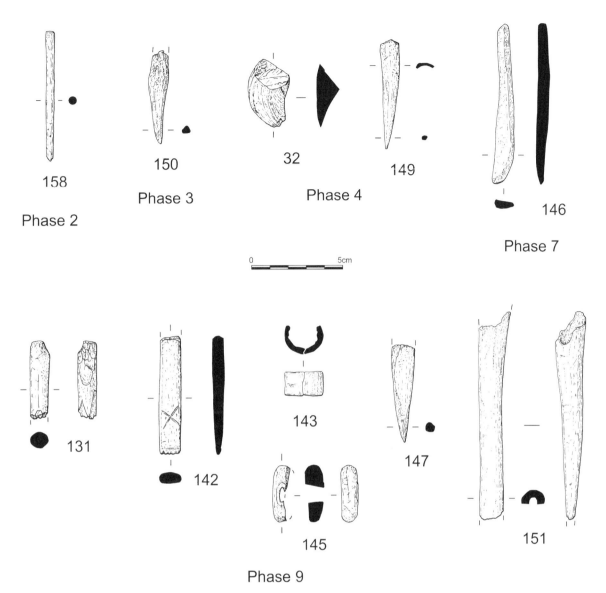

Figure 12.1 Bone and ivory artefacts from Cill Donnain III

settlements in the Western Isles is the presence of ivory, both as an off-cut (SF32) and as finished artefacts (SF158, SF131 and SF145; Figure 12.1). Such material is rare in Scotland before the Norse period (Trevor Cowie and Fraser Hunter pers. comm.), known from sites such as Neolithic Skara Brae (Childe 1931) and Ashgrove, Fife (Henshall 1964) where a sperm whale tooth was fashioned into an Early Bronze Age dagger pommel. Iron Age finds of ivory include a disc bead from Sandwick, Unst, dating to 400–200 BC, along with beads, pin heads, gaming pieces and sword fittings from a variety of sites such as Midhowe (Callander and Grant 1934: 490) and Mine Howe in Orkney (Jane Downes pers. comm.), Caird's Cave, Rosemarkie (Foster 1990: ill. 9.2.21) and High Pasture Cave in Skye (Fraser Hunter pers. comm.).

No such finds of ivory were made at Cill Donnain's neighbouring sites of Cladh Hallan, Dun Vulan or Bornais mound 1, suggesting that the presence of ivory artefacts and possibly even manufacturing of ivory products was a special aspect of life at Cill Donnain III in

both the Late Bronze Age and the Late Iron Age. Although the Cill Donnain wheelhouse itself shows no indication of elevated social status, it might have formed part of a larger complex that included individuals with access to marine mammal ivory, a commodity that did not become commonly exploited in the North Atlantic zone until the Viking period.

Catalogue of the worked bone, ivory and antler

Phase 1

Bone

SF2, context 15/2003 (Quarry Trench 2). Bone point (172mm long × 15mm wide), made from a cattle rib that has been split in half longitudinally. The sharp point has been formed by trimming the sides along the last 30mm of the distal end.

Phase 2
Ivory
SF158, context 142 (1991). Incomplete polished ivory headless pin (68mm × 4mm dia.), with its tip broken off; the pin has a flat top that gradually tapers along the circular-sectioned shank to just 2mm diameter, where it is broken (Figure 12.1).

Phase 3
Bone
SF150, context 32 (1990; E10/N8). Small bone point (49mm × 10mm × 4mm). Its proximal end has been broken off recently and is missing (Figure 12.1).

Antler
SF133, context 32 (1990; E11/N7). Fragment of antler beam segment (35mm × 21mm × 5mm) split longitudinally along both edges but with a curved, sawn end. The other end is snapped. It might originally have been a semicircular-ended artefact about 30mm across.

SF114, context 61 (1990). Antler tine (54mm) detached by chopping around its circumference.

SF41, context 173 (1991; E9/N1). Antler peg (73mm × 14mm dia.) with a swollen mid-shank, tapering to crudely snapped ends; whittling marks are visible beneath the slight surface polish (Figure 12.3).

Phase 4
Bone
SF34, context 24 (1990; E10.4/N8.65). Bone point. Registered but not examined. Recorded in the site finds inventory but not found in the archive.

SF149, context 24 (1990; E11/N9). Small bone point (57mm × 11mm × 2mm) made from a splinter of an ovicaprid longbone. It is heavily worn along 25mm from its tip (Figure 12.1).

Cetacean bone
SF157, context 188 (1991). Broken tip of a whale bone peg or blunt point (63mm × 15mm × 11mm), with slight damage to its point (Figure 12.2).

Ivory
SF32, context 24 (1990; E10/N8). Sawn and snapped tip of an ivory tooth (37mm × 21mm × 8mm). The tooth, presumably that of a walrus, was 24mm in diameter at the sawn section although one side of the tusk is worn flat from contact with the other tusk while the animal was still alive. This tip can be considered manufacturing

debris, discarded whilst keeping the higher-quality ivory lower down the tusk for the manufacture of ivory artefacts (Figure 12.1).

Antler
SF119, context 24 (1990; E11/N7). Antler beam segment (26mm long × 35mm across) heavily worn at one end and sawn across the other, split longitudinally in half.

SF120, context 24 (1990; E10/N7). Antler beam segment (79mm long × 32mm across) sawn across one end and broken at the other.

SF121, context 24 (1990; E10/N7). Antler beam segment (31mm long × 35mm across) at the junction with a sawn and snapped tine, sawn across both ends and split longitudinally.

Phase 5
Antler
SF93, context 166 (1991; E7/N4). Antler tine (108mm long × 18mm dia.) with four sets of parallel cut-marks chopped circumferentially around the snapped proximal end where it has been roughly snapped from the beam.

SF95, context 166 (1991; E10/N6). Antler beam segment (32mm × 32mm × 28mm), sawn at each end and hollowed through its centre to provide an oval hole (15mm × 11mm dia.), giving this artefact the appearance of a modern napkin-ring or fig roll. Both ends are heavily worn, removing all traces of saw-marks. With the other hollowed antler segments (SF153 and SF160 from context 166, and SF152 [phase 7, below] and SF141 [phase 9, below]) this might have formed part of a composite artefact (Figure 12.3).

SF153, context 166 (1991). Antler beam segment (24mm × 31mm × 26mm), sawn at each end and hollowed through its centre to provide a circular hole (11mm dia.), giving this artefact the appearance of a modern napkin-ring or fig roll. This artefact's exterior surfaces, including the saw-marks, are heavily worn through subsequent use (Figure 12.3).

SF160, context 166 (1991; E10/N5). Antler beam segment (19mm × 44mm × 32mm), sawn at each end and hollowed through its centre to provide an oval hole (16mm × 11mm dia.), giving this artefact the appearance of a modern napkin-ring or fig roll. Both ends are lightly worn but the saw-marks are still visible. This is most similar in size and treatment to SF141 (see below); the two pieces might have been cut from the same beam but not consecutively (Figure 12.3).

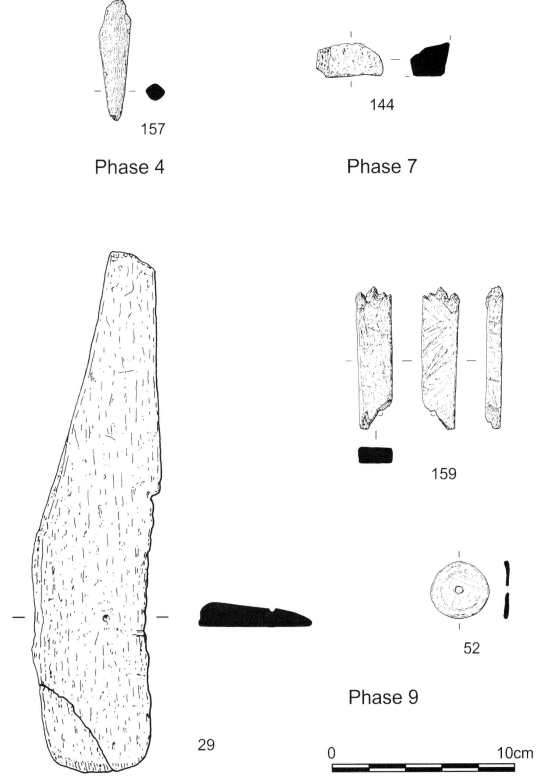

157

Phase 4

144

Phase 7

159

52

Phase 9

0   10cm

Figure 12.2 Whale bone artefacts from Cill Donnain III

29

SF156, context 179 (1991). Antler tip (50mm × 13mm × 11mm) detached by knife-cutting and snapping. There is a knife slice along one side near the point and most of the surface has been subsequently blackened by burning, except for the point (Figure 12.3).

Phase 7
Bone
SF146, context 6 (1989; E6/N-2). Bone modelling tool (84mm × 9mm × 6mm), highly polished, with a spatulate, flattened and curved end, the other terminating in a slightly flattened blunt point. Similar examples are

known from Cnip (Hunter 2006: 143) and are interpreted as tools for forming wax models for lost-wax bronze casting or for shaping and decorating pottery (Hallén 1994: 207) (Figure 12.1).

SF129, context 14 (1989). Hollow bone tube (65mm × 11mm dia. with a hole 8mm dia.), highly polished, with one end worked smooth and worn and the other snapped. It is made from a bird long bone. Similar bone tubes were common at Dun Vulan (Parker Pearson and Sharples 1999: 218).

SF30, context 25 (1990; E11.22/N3.73). Bone spindle whorl. Registered but not examined. Recorded in the site finds inventory but not found in the archive.

SF111, context 25 (1990; E12/N4). Fragment of a bone disc (39mm × 28mm × 4mm) snapped across a formerly central hole (6mm diameter). The disc was probably originally oval in shape, about 50mm across.

SF124, context 25 (1990; E12/N4). Ovicaprid metatarsus (115mm) with one end sawn to form a socket 8mm in diameter.

Cetacean bone
SF144, context 14 (1989). Fragment of whale bone (34mm × 18mm × 14mm), sawn on two sides to produce flat surfaces perpendicular to each other (Figure 12.2).

SF135, context 25 (1990; E1/N3). Fragment of cetacean bone (25mm × 11mm × 12mm), with two opposite flat, polished surfaces terminating at a rounded and bevelled edge. It may be one end of a whale bone peg.

Antler
SF152, context 25 (1991). Antler beam segment (26mm × 39mm × 29mm), sawn at each end and hollowed through its centre to provide an oval hole (15mm × 12mm dia.), giving this artefact the appearance of a modern napkin-ring or fig roll. This artefact's exterior surfaces, including the saw-marks, are heavily worn through subsequent use (Figure 12.3).

SF154, context 25 (1991). Antler tine (67mm × 14mm dia.), sawn and snapped at one end and tapering to a blunt, circular point at the other. It has been ground to form grooves in a rotary pattern along 32mm of the shaft's length. This is slightly larger than a similar example in bone (SF1387) from Bornais mound 1, interpreted as a thong-stretcher or bow-drill (Clarke *et al.* in Sharples 2012b: 280). Larger examples are known from Dun Vulan where they are described as quern handles (Parker Pearson and Sharples 1999: 220 [SF1043], 225 [SF1285; SF1115], 227 [SF1054]). This

example is probably too small to be a quern handle; no rotary querns or fragments were recovered from Cill Donnain III, in contrast to Dun Vulan (Figure 12.3).

Phase 8
Cetacean bone
SF127, context 28 (1990; E11/N5). Fragment of cetacean bone (49mm × 31mm × 11mm) in which one external surface survives, terminating at a chamfered and polished end.

Antler
SF39, context 28 (1990; E10.98/N4.58). Worked antler. Registered but not examined. Recorded in the site finds inventory but not found in the archive.

Phase 9
Bone
SF142, context 1 (1989; E6/N3). A long-handled, miniature bone comb (61mm × 12mm × 6mm), broken and blackened at one end but with a flat, denticulated end at the other. The flat end has five short but complete triangular teeth, each 1.5mm long. The comb is decorated on one side with a transverse incision 2mm from the denticulate end and with an angled cross incised further along the shaft. It has the appearance of a miniature long-handled comb, of which there are full-sized examples from Bornais mound 1 (Clarke *et al.* in Sharples 2012b: 277) and Cnip (Hunter 2006: 143). It could be a toy since its teeth are too short to have been very effective, except for impressing denticulate motifs. Its decoration is most closely paralleled by the grooves on weaving comb SF1437 from Bornais mound 1 (Clarke *et al.* in Sharples 2012b: fig. 179) (Figure 12.1).

SF2, context 5 (1990; E14.28/N3.69). Bone needle. Registered but not examined. Recorded in the site finds inventory but not found in the archive.

SF3, context 5 (1990; E14.5/N6.46). Worked sheep's tibia. Registered but not examined. Recorded in the site finds inventory but not found in the archive.

SF4, context 5 (1990; E11.93/N3.83). Bone pin. Registered but not examined. Recorded in the site finds inventory but not found in the archive.

SF8, context 5 (1990; E14/N9). Bone toggle/pendant. This may be the same as SF143 (see below). Registered but not examined. Recorded in the site finds inventory but not found in the archive.

SF11, context 5 (1990; E13.42/N7.64). Worked bone/antler. Registered but not examined. Recorded in the site finds inventory but not found in the archive.

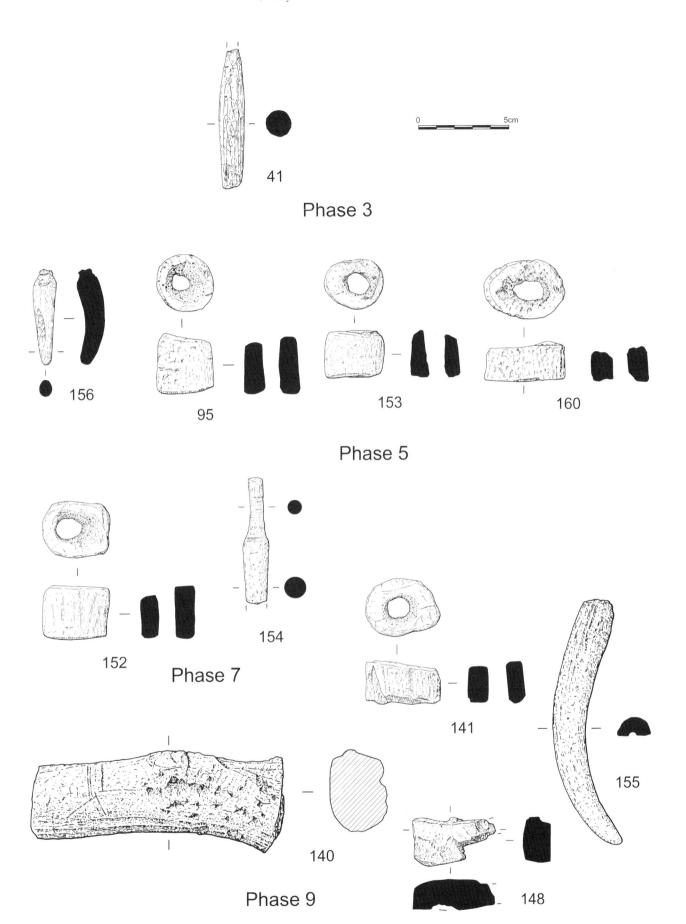

Phase 3

Phase 5

Phase 7

Phase 9

Figure 12.3 Antler artefacts from Cill Donnain III

SF12, context 5 (1990; E12.42/N9.5). Bone needle. Registered but not examined. Recorded in the site finds inventory but not found in the archive.

SF13, context 5 (1990; E13/N1). Worked bone. Registered but not examined. Recorded in the site finds inventory but not found in the archive.

SF20, context 5 (1990; E14.53/N9.8). Worked bone. Registered but not examined. Recorded in the site finds inventory but not found in the archive.

SF21, context 5 (1990; E14/N9). Bone needle. Registered but not examined. Recorded in the site finds inventory but not found in the archive.

SF24, context 5 (1990; E11.07/N5.82). Worked bone. Registered but not examined. Recorded in the site finds inventory but not found in the archive.

SF37, context 5 (1990; E14.5/N6.35). Bone pin. Registered but not examined. Recorded in the site finds inventory but not found in the archive.

SF38, context 5 (1990; E14.29/N2.64). Bone point. Registered but not examined. Recorded in the site finds inventory but not found in the archive.

SF101, context 5 (1990; E12/N0). Fragment of worked long bone (44mm × 20mm). One end has been whittled with a knife to create four shallow facets on its exterior.

SF106, context 5 (1990; E11/N6). Sawn end of an ovicaprid tibia (32mm × 11mm) that has been split longitudinally.

SF107, context 5 (1990; E14/N9). Maxillary cattle molar with longitudinal splitting that could be the result of working or abnormal wear.

SF112, context 5 (1990; E10/N10). Bone bead (14mm × 18mm dia.; with an internal diameter of 12mm), snapped in half.

SF122, context 5 (1990; E14/N6). Broken tip of a blunt bone point (36mm × 10mm × 4mm) with a slightly damaged tip.

SF123, context 5 (1990; E14/N6). Broken tip of a bone spatula (28mm × 18mm × 5mm) made from the rib of a large mammal.

SF143, context 5 (1990; E14/N9). Two fragments of a bone cylinder or bead (13mm × 18mm dia. with a circular hole 13mm dia.), cut and hollowed as a section from an ovicaprid-sized longbone. Its external surfaces are worn (Figure 12.1).

SF109, context 14 (1990; E13/N4). Heavily worn proximal end of a snapped cattle metapodial (36mm × 18mm).

SF14, context 18 (1990; E11.08/N9.08). Bone point. Registered but not examined. Recorded in the site finds inventory but not found in the archive.

SF16, context 18 (1990; E10.8/N8.88). Bone point. Registered but not examined. Recorded in the site finds inventory but not found in the archive.

SF31, context 22 (1990; E12.14/N0.46). Bone point. Registered but not examined. Recorded in the site finds inventory but not found in the archive.

SF36, context 27 (1990; E14.7/N9.5). Worked bone. Registered but not examined. Recorded in the site finds inventory but not found in the archive.

SF44, context 27 (1990; E14/N7). Worked bone. Registered but not examined. Recorded in the site finds inventory but not found in the archive.

SF103, context 27 (1990; E14/N7). Trimmed off-cut of bone (34mm × 10mm × 2mm). It has been cut along one long side.

SF104, context 27 (1990; E14/N1). Broken end of a bone spatula, made from the rib of a large mammal (75mm long × 14mm wide × 6mm thick). The rib has split longitudinally through the spatulate end which has been ground to a blade-end on both sides.

SF47, context 31 (1990; E11/N3). Bone bead. Registered but not examined. Recorded in the site finds inventory but not found in the archive.

SF48, context 31 (1990; E12/N4). Bone point. Registered but not examined. Recorded in the site finds inventory but not found in the archive.

SF136, context 31 (1990; E12/N3). Splinter of long bone (45mm × 10mm × 6mm) with one longitudinal edge sawn.

SF137, context 31 (1990; E12/N3). Tip of a bone point (40mm × 10mm × 6mm) with a slightly curving tip similar in shape to a scalpel blade.

SF138, context 31 (1990; E12/N3). Cattle long bone with both ends removed by sawing and snapping. There are more than 20 transverse cut-marks, typically 5mm–10mm long, circumferentially along the bone. It can be interpreted as a chopping board; a very similar example is known from Cnip (Hunter 2006: 144, fig. 3.22b, SF149).

SF139, context 31 (1990; E11/N2). Distal end of a cattle metatarsal (71mm long) sawn through the shaft. There are no further signs of wear but examples from other sites (*e.g.* SF1191 from Dun Vulan; Parker Pearson and Sharples 1999: 224) have been modified into sleeves for blades or points. This could be an unfinished rough-out for a sleeve-type handle.

SF147, context 58 (1990; E9/N1). Small bone point (50mm × 11mm × 6mm). It is heavily worn along 20mm from its tip, which is slightly damaged (Figure 12.1).

SF151, context 103 (1991). Distal end of a right sheep/goat tibia (110mm long), the proximal end of which has been cut at an angle, presumably to create a spatulate or blunted point, and is heavily polished. The tip has been broken off recently and is missing. Polish on the exterior of the bone, opposite the cut face, indicates that this artefact might have been a beater used in weaving (Figure 12.1).

Cetacean bone

SF15, context 5 (1990; E11.8/N4.7). Worked whale bone. Registered but not examined. Recorded in the site finds inventory but not found in the archive.

SF25, context 5 (1990; E14.59/N8.85). Worked whale bone. Registered but not examined. Recorded in the site finds inventory but not found in the archive.

SF29, context 5 (1990; E13.9/N8.44). Spatula (273mm × 57mm × 12mm) made from a whale rib, with a 53mm-wide, flat blade bevelled on both sides; the handle's edges are worn smooth through use (Figure 12.2).

SF35, context 5 (1990; E13.82/N7.94). Worked whale bone. Registered but not examined. Recorded in the site finds inventory but not found in the archive.

SF117, context 5 (1990; E13/N2). Fragment of cetacean bone (26mm × 17mm × 11mm) sawn at one end.

SF130, context 5 (1990; E10/N5). Fragment of cetacean bone (26mm × 10mm × 4mm) sawn on two sides at right angles.

SF132, context 5 (1990; E11/N6). Fragment of cetacean bone (26mm × 18mm × 13mm) sawn on two sides at right angles.

SF159, context 5 (1990; E10/N0). Fragment of a whale bone bar or peg (74mm × 18mm × 8mm) broken at both ends, with a rectangular section; trimming marks are visible on both flat sides, and one end is polished (Figure 12.2).

SF110, context 14 (1990; E13/N4). Splinter of cetacean bone (22mm × 11mm × 4mm) with three smoothed facets on one side.

SF161, context 14 (1990; E13/N0). Fragment of whale bone plate (35mm × 21mm × 9mm); this might have been part of a straight-sided bar- or plate-like artefact.

SF118, context 18 (1990; E11/N9). Fragment of cetacean bone (48mm × 17mm × 9mm) sawn on two sides at right angles. It may be a fragment of a rectangular-sectioned whale bone peg.

SF52, context 103 (1991; E10/N-1). Pierced disc (29mm dia., 2mm thick) made from an epiphysis of a small cetacean, with a central hole 3mm in diameter (Figure 12.2).

Ivory

SF131, context 5 (1990; E14/N8). Ivory shank or shaft (41mm long) with an oval cross-section (10mm × 8mm). One end is snapped and the other has the remains of a squared-off terminal. Both ends are damaged by flake beds. This is too thick to have been a pin but could be the remains of a peg, point or modelling tool (Figure 12.1).

SF145, context 12 (1989; E7/N6). Broken ivory toggle (29mm × 9mm × 8mm), highly polished, with a central slot (7mm × 1.5mm). It has split longitudinally along the slot and also perpendicular to this along one side. On the other side, where the surface of the slot is undamaged, it is surrounded by a 1.5mm-wide surround raised 0.3mm from the surface of the toggle. The artefact would have measured 29mm × 10mm × 9mm when complete (Figure 12.1).

Antler

SF128, context 1 (1989; E7/N2). Antler tine tip (27mm × 11mm across) that has been whittled to a point and detached from the rest of the tine by snapping.

SF141, context 1 (1989; E7/N6). Antler beam segment (20mm × 40mm × 30mm), sawn at each end and hollowed through its centre to provide an oval hole (12mm × 10mm dia.), giving this artefact the appearance of a modern napkin-ring or fig roll. This artefact's exterior surfaces, including the saw-marks, are worn through subsequent use but not as heavily as SF152 and SF153. Although one of five similar artefacts from Cill Donnain (SF95, SF141, SF152, SF153 and SF160), none of them conjoin (Figure 12.3).

SF148, context 1 (1989; E3/N6). Antler burr heavily modified by sawing into an almost rectangular block (44mm × 25mm × 16mm). Part of the burr, heavily worn, survives on one face where it has been partially removed by sawing. This appears to be manufacturing waste rather than a crafted artefact (Figure 12.3).

SF134, context 4 (1990; E11/N7). Fragment of antler

beam segment (15mm × 20mm × 7mm) sawn at both ends.

SF108, context 5 (1990; E13/N6). Antler splinter (77mm × 14mm × 7mm) that has been sawn at one end and longitudinally down one side. It could be a crudely made peg.

SF113, context 5 (1990; E10/N10). Antler tine (57mm × 18mm × 6mm), split longitudinally and sawn and snapped at the proximal end.

SF116, context 5 (1990; E14/N9). Antler tine (60mm) detached by sawing (from opposite directions) and snapping. The tip has been snapped off.

SF125, context 5 (1990; E11/N0). Antler beam fragment (25mm × 15mm × 7mm), sawn across one end.

SF140, context 5 (1990; E14/N7). Antler beam segment (132mm × 42mm × 29mm) that has been sawn and snapped at both ends. A tine has been sawn and snapped midway along the shaft, and there are four cut-marks, each about 15mm long, transversely across the segment. About 5mm from the basal end, there are saw-marks where sawing was commenced but abandoned. One side of the segment is pock-marked with 30 holes punched with a pointed implement with a tip 2mm–4mm across (Figure 12.3).

SF17, context 11 (1990; E10.3/N8.3). Worked antler tip. Registered but not examined. Recorded in the site finds inventory but not found in the archive.

SF105, context 27 (1990; E14/N1). Antler tine (125mm × 27mm × 21mm), detached by sawing and snapping. Its tip is heavily worn.

SF102, context 31 (1990; E12/N5). Antler beam segment, worn, with ends sawn (101mm × 40mm × 27mm). Its surface has been trimmed along one side, suggesting that it might have been shaped to fit the hand, and there are two chop-marks at one end.

SF126, context 31 (1990; E11/N2). Antler beam segment (38mm × 23mm across) sawn at one end and longitudinally down opposing sides. It has snapped longitudinally across a drilled hole about 12mm in diameter. More complete examples are known from Dun Vulan (Parker Pearson and Sharples 1999: 227, fig. 9.3.1168) and Cnip (Hunter 2006: 144, fig. 3.21g) where they are described as a handle to hold a bar and a socketed tool head (?), respectively. This could, however, be a broken toggle.

SF155, context 103 (1991). One half of an antler tip (131mm × 20mm × 9mm) split laterally through the centre of the tine. The fresh edges at the point are worn, indicating that this was used as a tool (Figure 12.3).

Unstratified

SF115, unstratified (1990). Shed antler base and brow tine (114mm) with circumferential saw-marks and snapping where the beam has been removed.

Chapter 13 The faunal remains

Kim Vickers with Saleem ul Haq and John Hamshaw-Thomas

Introduction

The animal bone assemblage from Cill Donnain III is one of a number of such assemblages from Iron Age deposits in the Western Isles (*e.g.* Cartledge *et al.* in Sharples 2012b; Mulville and Powell in Sharples 2012b; Mulville 1999; Halstead 2003; Finlay 1991; Clarke 1962). The majority of these published assemblages are relatively small, but together they build a picture of animal husbandry and exploitation at a variety of different settlements within a challenging environment (Parker Pearson *et al.* 1996).

The assemblage from Cill Donnain III complements and adds to the existing body of data. It was initially analysed by ul Haq (1989) and Hamshaw-Thomas (1991). These reports, along with recent analysis of the assemblage deriving from the 1990 excavation season, are integrated in this chapter. Ul Haq's (1989) report does not treat contexts separately and so cannot be included in any discussion of phasing (although most of the 1989 material, which is the subject of his report, derives from the Late Iron Age midden of phase 9). The only quantitative information provided by Hamshaw-Thomas (1991) concerns NISP by species and element.

Excavation methods and fish bone

The assemblages analysed were retrieved both by hand collection and systematic sieving of spoil from all contexts using a 10mm mesh. Although the site records indicate that the flotation of environmental samples produced heavy residues that included fish bone, these residues have subsequently been lost. As a result, the only surviving fish bones are a handful of remains, mostly vertebrae of Gadiformes, hand-collected during excavation or retrieved from the 10mm-mesh sieves on site. Most of these fish bones come from context 5 (phase 9), with the remainder from contexts 14, 58 and 103 (phase 9), and context 32 (phase 3). The species identified are saithe (*Pollachius virens*), plaice (*Pleuronectes*

platessa) and ballan wrasse (*Labrus bergylta*). Crab claws were recovered from context 135 (phase 2).

Because of the small size of the surviving fish bone assemblage, little can be inferred from Cill Donnain III's fish remains. On the basis of comparison with similar but larger assemblages from broadly contemporary sites at Dun Vulan, Bornais mound 1 and Cnip, we can only surmise that fishing at Cill Donnain is likely to have been small-scale and domestic in nature, using the technique of fishing from craig seats along the immediate coastline (Cerón-Carrasco and Parker Pearson 1999: 282; Cartledge *et al.* in Sharples 2012b; Cerón-Carrasco 2006: 179).

Laboratory methods

Animal bone fragments were identified to taxon using the reference collection at the Department of Archaeology, University of Sheffield.

Recording of the 1989 and 1991 assemblages

The 1989 assemblage was recorded by ul Haq, and the 1991 assemblage by Hamshaw-Thomas, for MSc dissertations at the University of Sheffield.

For both the 1989 and 1991 assemblages, all identifiable post-cranial elements were recorded (*cf* Watson 1979). Proximal and distal sections of long bones (divided mid-shaft) were counted as different elements. Scapula, pelvis, ulna, calcaneus, astragalus, and phalanges I, II and III were considered as single units. Fragments that could not be assigned to either proximal or distal zones were disregarded. No attempt was made to identify any vertebrae (with the exception of the atlas and axis), ribs, carpals, tarsals (with the exception of the astragalus and calcaneus), fibulae, lateral metapodials or lateral phalanges. Cranial elements counted were antlers, horn cores, maxillae, mandibles and loose premolars and molars.

Excavation year		Phase									Total
		1	2	3	4	5	6	7	8	9	
		EBA-MBA Cordoned Urn layers	LBA/EIA layers	Late MIA pre-wheelhouse layers	Late MIA wheelhouse construction	Late MIA wheelhouse initial occupation	Late MIA wheelhouse modification	Early LIA wheelhouse abandonment	Early LIA bothy-type structure	LIA midden	
1989	No. contexts			3				2		7	12
	NISP	Information unavailable									1731
	Total no. fragments	Information unavailable									13988
1990	No. contexts			6	1			1	1	18	27
	NISP			56	14			105	2	2725	2902
	Total no. fragments										14757
1991	No. contexts	5	4	16	8	4	1	3		5	46
	NISP	57	159	246	86	140	2	99		124	913
	Total no. fragments	Information unavailable									

Table 13.1 Summary of contexts and number of specimens by excavation year, and phase

In the 1989 assemblage, for each recorded fragment, sex, side, age, fragmentation, preservation, burning, gnawing and butchery were recorded where available.

The distinction between sheep and goat was made using Boessneck (1969) and Payne (1985). Differences in sex were recorded following criteria from Boessneck (1969) and Grigson (1982).

Recording of the 1990 assemblage
Because of the highly fragmented nature of the assemblage, a 'diagnostic zones' approach was used to record the 1990 assemblage, in an attempt to minimize bone interdependence and any bias as a result of differential inter-specific or inter-element fragmentation. The recording method used in the analysis of the animal bones recovered in 1990 follows a modified version of that outlined by Davis (1992) and Albarella and Davis (1994). Briefly, the elements included as 'countable' are: loose upper and lower teeth (in mammals), jaws with at least one tooth in place; cranium (complete or partial zygomaticus), atlas, axis, scapula (glenoid cavity), coracoid (in birds), distal humerus (at least half of articular surface), distal radius (at least half of articular surface), proximal ulna, distal metacarpal (at least half of articular surface), carpometacarpus (in birds), pelvis (ischial part of the acetabulum), distal tibia (at least half of articular surface), calcaneus, scaphocuboid, distal metatarsal (at least half of articular surface), and phalanges 1, 2, and 3. Wherever possible, fragmented bones with clearly matching edges were reconstructed.

In addition to these 'countable' elements, other 'non-countable' specimens were recorded. These include horn core, antler, all bones with evidence of butchery, bone-working or pathology, and ribs and vertebrae (recorded as belonging to a small-, medium- or large-sized mammal). The state of preservation of the material from each context was also noted, fragmentation as a percentage of the entire element was estimated for each bone recorded, and any occurrence of gnawing or burning was recorded.

The distinction between sheep and goats has only been attempted on the following elements: horn core (non-countable), dP_3 and dP_4, permanent lower molars (when a row is present), humerus, radius, metacarpal, tibia, astragalus, calcaneus and metatarsal. The criteria of Boessneck (1969), Payne (1985), Prummel and Frisch (1986), and Halstead et al. (2002) were used to separate sheep from goats.

Mandibular wear stages were recorded for cattle and pig following the criteria of Grant (1982) and for sheep/goat following Payne (1973). Epiphysial fusion state was recorded wherever possible. Analysis of mandibular wear stages follows Payne (1973) for sheep/goat, and the groupings of O'Connor (1989) and Halstead (1985) for cattle and pig. Epiphysial fusion data were analysed using groupings of elements derived from Silver's (1969) fusion tables.

Measurements were taken as defined in von den Driesch (1976), Payne and Bull (1988) and Davis (1992). In addition, the central cusp of the pig third molar was measured and is defined as M3WC.

Overview
A total of 5,546 bones (NISP) was recorded from 85 contexts spanning nine site phases. The proportions of the assemblage represented by each phase at Cill Donnain III can be seen in Table 13.1. In addition, more than 28,000 unidentifiable bone fragments were recovered during excavation: these are predominately skull, rib, and long bone fragments measuring less than 20mm.

The bulk of the assemblage derives from phase 9, the Late Iron Age midden overlying the wheelhouse, although (for the 1990 and 1991 material) phases 2, 3, 4, 5

Taxa	Phase												TOTAL		
	3			4			7			9					
	No fragments <10% of whole element	Total number of recorded fragments	% <10% of complete bone	No fragments <10% of whole element	Total number of recorded fragments	% <10% of complete bone	No fragments <10% of whole element	Total number of recorded fragments	% <10% of complete bone	No fragments <10% of whole element	Total number of recorded fragments	% <10% of complete bone	No fragments <10% of whole element	Total number of recorded fragments	% <10% of complete bone
Cow	14	41	34.1%	18	73	24.7%	10	43	23.3%	235	1121	21%	277	1278	21.7%
Sheep/goat	8	27	29.6%	16	61	26.2%	10	61	16%	245	920	26.7%	279	1069	26.1%
Pig	0	4	0	2	10	20.0%	1	16	6%	28	244	11.5%	31	274	11.3%
Large mammal	121	132	91.7%	83	93	89.2%	48	58	82.8%	1104	1339	82%	1356	1614	84.0%
Medium mammal	121	152	79.6%	158	195	81.0%	62	91	68.1%	1336	1646	81.2%	1677	2084	80.5%
TOTAL	264	356	74.2%	277	432	64.1%	131	269	48.7%	2948	5270	56%	3620	6319	57.3%

Table 13.2 Distribution of fragments making up less than 10% of a complete element in the 1990 assemblage by phase and taxa

and 7 also contain more than 100 recorded fragments. No articulated bone associations were observed in the assemblage.

Preservation

Preservation of the bone recovered in all three seasons was good, with very little evidence of bone reworking or diagenesis.

The bulk of the assemblage is very highly fragmented, with 57% of the 1990 recorded assemblage represented by bone fragments making up less than 10% of the element when complete (Table 13.2). When all unidentified fragments are considered, over 83% of the assemblage consists of fragments representing less than 10% of the complete element. The 1989 assemblage is also heavily fragmented and, in the assemblages from both years, denser elements such as phalanges, carpals, tarsals and loose teeth (which also contain relatively little marrow or bone grease; Binford 1978) are the most frequently complete elements recovered, while long bones, mandibles, ribs and vertebrae are highly fragmented.

There is very little difference in fragmentation between the large mammal (cattle-sized) and medium-sized mammal (sheep/goat/pig-sized) categories, although pig bone tends to be proportionally less fragmented than sheep/goat or cattle bones. Almost all of this fragmentation represents ancient breakage, and very little newly broken bone was recorded. The 1991 assemblage would appear to be less fragmented than either the 1989 or 1990 assemblages, but quantitative data is unavailable.

Of the bone recovered in 1989 just 12% shows evidence of canid gnawing. In the 1990 assemblage just 8% of bone shows canid gnawing and 0.6% has been gnawed by rodents. A small number of sheep/goat carpals, tarsals and phalanges show signs of having been digested (Table 13.3). The relatively low level of gnawing observed may indicate that bone was buried soon after disposal, and it is likely that evidence for gnawing is under-represented as a result of the complete destruction of some bone by dogs, although dog bones are themselves very rare within the assemblage,

Around 20% of the bone recorded in the 1990 assemblage is burnt (Table 13.4). There is nearly twice as much burning observed on the bones recorded as cattle and large mammal compared with those recorded as sheep/goat, pig and medium mammal; the majority of burnt fragments are unidentifiable fragments of long bone or rib. The relatively small sample size of each element for each species means that patterns of burning associated with particular elements cannot be identified.

Species representation
The mammals
Taxa identified at Cill Donnain III across all three years' assemblages include cattle (*Bos*), sheep (*Ovis*), sheep/goat (*Ovis/Capra*), pig (*Sus*), red deer (*Cervus elaphus*), dog (*Canis*), cat (*Felis*), otter (*Lutra lutra*), seal (*cf Halichoerus grypus*), cetacean (indeterminate) and rabbit (*Oryctolagus cuniculus*). All of the sheep/goat specimens that could be identified to species were sheep, and no goat was positively identified in the assemblages, so it is likely that the remaining specimens identified as sheep/goat represent sheep.

All three assemblages, and all site phases, show a similar pattern of relative species abundance. Overall, cattle specimens are more frequent than sheep/goat but this varies according to phase, probably as a result of the relatively small sample sizes for some of the phases, and MNI (minimum number of individuals) calculations

Excavation year/phase	COW CANID N	%	RODENT N	%	TOTAL N	SHEEP/GOAT CANID N	%	RODENT N	%	DIGESTED N	%	TOTAL N	PIG CANID N	%	RODENT N	%	DIGESTED N	%	TOTAL N	RED DEER CANID N.	%	RODENT N.	%	TOTAL N
1989: TOTAL	116				638	79						423	19						120					
1990 ph 3	5	12.8			39	2	9.1					22							3					6
1990 ph 4	5	6.8			73	4	6.5	1	1.6			62							12					9
1990 ph 7	3	7.0			43	7	11.5					61	1	0.1	1	6.3			16					5
1900 ph 8												1												
1990 ph 9	84	7.5	9	0.8	1127	81	8.8	8	0.9	4	0.4	919	20	0.1	3	1.2	1	0.4	246	6	6.7	1	1.1	89
1990: TOTAL	97	7.6	9	0.7	1282	94	8.8	9	0.8	4	0.4	1065	21	7.6	4	1.4	1	0.4	277	6	5.5	1	0.9	109

Excavation year/phase	LARGE MAMMAL CANID N.	%	RODENT N.	%	TOTAL	MEDIUM MAMMAL CANID N.	%	RODENT N.	%	DIGESTED N.	%	TOTAL	TOTAL CANID N.	%	RODENT N.	%	DIGESTED N.	%	TOTAL
1989: TOTAL													214						1181
1990 ph 3	5	3.9			128	3	2.0					147	15	4.0					345
1990 ph 4	5	5.4			93	2	1.0					196	16	3.6	1	0.2			445
1990 ph 7	2	3.3			60	7	7.3					96	20	7.1	1	0.4			281
1900 ph 8					1														2
1990 ph 9	72	5.4	10	0.8	1330	66	66.0	4	4.0	2	2.0	10	329	8.8	35	0.7	7	0.1	3721
1990: TOTAL	84	5.2	10	0.6	1612	78	17.4	4	0.9	2	0.4	449	379	7.9	37	0.6	7	0.1	4794

Table 13.3 Occurrence of gnawed bone in the 1989 and 1990 assemblages (information for the 1991 assemblage unavailable)

Phase	Cow N. Burnt	Total N. frags	% Burnt	Sheep/goat N. Burnt	Total N. frags	% Burnt	Pig N. Burnt	Total N. frags	% Burnt	Red Deer N. Burnt	Total N. frags	% Burnt
1990 ph 3	4	41	9.8	4	27	14.8		4	0	1	6	16.7
1990 ph4	7	73	9.6	11	61	18		10	0		9	0
1990 ph 5		1	0									
1990 ph 7	1	43	2.3	0	61	0		16	0		5	0
1990 ph 8				0	1	0						
1990 ph 9	150	1121	13.4	57	920	6.2	6	244	2.5		83	0
1990 ph 10		20	0	1	25	4		4	0			0
1990:TOTAL	162	1299	12.5	73	1095	6.7	6	278	2.2	1	103	1
1989 TOTAL	30	608	4.9	32	389	8.2	4	116	3.4			

Phase	Large Mammal N. Burnt	Total N. frags	% Burnt	Medium Mammal N. Burnt	Total N. frags	% Burnt	Total assemblage N. Burnt	Total N. frags	% Burnt
1990 ph 3	83	132	62.9	54	152	35.5	146	362	40.3
1990 ph4	42	93	45.2	34	195	17.4	94	441	21.3
1990 ph 5								1	0
1990 ph 7	10	58	17.2	9	91	9.9	20	274	7.3
1990 ph 8		1	0					2	0
1990 ph 9	466	1339	34.8	300	1646	18.2	979	5353	18.3
1990 ph 10	10	17	58.8	25	21	119	36	87	41.4
1990:TOTAL	611	1640	37.3	422	2105	20	1275	6520	19.5

Table 13.4 Frequency of burning by phase and taxa. (NB No information is available for the 1991 assemblage. 1989 percentages are calculated on the basis of identified fragments; the 1990 percentages are calculated on the basis of the entire assemblage)

EXCAVATION YEAR	PHASE	Cow				Sheep/goat				Pig				Red deer				Seal				Dog				Cat				Rabbit				Otter				TOTAL NISP	TOTAL MNI
		NISP	%	MNI	%	NISP	%	MNI	%	NISP	%	MNI	%	NISP	%	MNI	%	NISP	%	MNI	%	NISP	%	MNI	%	NISP	%	MNI	%	NISP	%	MNI	%	NISP	%	MNI	%		
1991	1	20	35.1	1	20	34	59.6	2	40	2	3.5	1	20	1	1.8	1	20																					57	5
	2	56	35.2	3	30	83	52.2	3	30	8	5	1	10	8	5	1	10	3	1.9	1	10	1	0.6	1	10													159	10
	3	90	36.6	3	25	123	50	6	50	23	9.3	1	8.3	9	3.7	1	8.3	1	0.4	1	8.3																	246	12
	4	64	74.4	2	33.3	19	22.1	2	33.3	2	2.3	1	16.7	1	1.2	1	16.7																					86	6
	5	53	37.9	3	27.3	75	53.6	6	54.5	8	5.7	1	9.1	4	2.9	1	9.1																					140	11
	6	1	50	1	50	1	50	1	50																													2	2
	7	46	46.5	2	33.3	44	44.4	2	33.3	6	6.1	1	16.7	3	3	1	16.7																					99	6
	9	60	48.4	4	44.4	59	47.6	3	33.3	4	3.2	1	11.1	3	0.8	1	11.1																					126	9
	?																													1		1		1	?	1	?	2	2
	TOTAL	390	43	4	21	438	47.9	6	31.6	53	5.8	3	16	29	3	2	11	4	0.4	1	5.3	1	0.1	1	5.3					1	0.1	1	5.3	1	0.1	1	5.3	917	19
1990	3	35	62.5	2	40	18	32.1	2	40	3	5.4	1	20																									56	5
	4	6	42.9	2	33.3	1	7.1	2	33.3	6	42.9	1	16.7	1	0.1	1	16.7																					14	6
	7	36	34.3	1	12.5	57	54.3	6	75	12	11.4	1	12.5																									105	8
	8					1	100	1	100																													1	1
	9	1746	64.1	25	48.1	773	28.4	21	40.4	172	6.3	5	9.6	28	1	1	2					2	0	1	2													2721	53
	TOTAL	1824	63.1	26	46.4	850	29	24	42.9	193	6.7	5	8.9	29	1	1	2					2	0	1	2													2897	56
1989	TOTAL	701	53	22	43.1	486	37	20	39.2	134	10	6	11.8	4	0.8	1	2					2	0.2	1	2	2	0.2	1	2									1329	51

Table 13.5 NISP and MNI quantification of the species present at Cill Donnain III

Taxa	Phase	ZY	X	Z	LT	LTX	LTN	AT	SC	PHU	DHU	PRA	DRA	UL	PE	PFE	DFE	PTI	DTI	PMT	DMT	PMC	DMC	PMP	DMP	SCU	AS	CA	PH1	PH2	PH3	Total
Cow	1						5		1						1	1			2				1		1			1	2	2	1	19
	2			1			9		2			2	2	1	5		1	1	2	1	1				2		5	3	12	5	1	56
	3			1			4		4			5	5	4	2	6	1	3	1	2	4	2	4	1			7	3	16	12	2	90
	4			6			1		2	1		2			1		1	1	4	2	1	3	1		1			2	13	11	7	62
	5						2		1			5	2	1	1			2	2		1	4	2	2			5	5	10	4	4	53
	6																													1		1
	7			3					4	2	3		1		2	1	2	2					1		4		2	2	6	6	5	46
	9						1		3		2	1	2	2		1				6	4	7	2		2		3	1	7	11	5	60
	TOTAL			11			22		17	3	19	11	8	7	14	7	9	8	6	16	12	16			11		22	17	67	51	25	387
Sheep/goat	1			4			2			2	2	3	3	2	1	1	1	1	1	1	1	1			3			2		3	3	34
	2			2			10		4	2	5	1	3	4	5	5	5	1	4	1	1				1	5	11	3	5	1	1	80
	3			1			6		5		6	10	8	2	12	3	3	2	1	12	10	4	7	1	7		2	3	6	7	2	120
	4											1	1		3			1	2			2	2				3	1	1	1	1	19
	5			6			2		1	3	6	5	4		2		3	6	12	6	5	1					4	2	1	5	1	75
	6																									1						1
	7						1			1	2	2	2		4	3	3	2		4	2	3	1		3		5	2	2	2		44
	9			2			3		2	1	3	4	5		6	1	1	2	3	3	1	2	2		1		8		2	2	2	54
	TOTAL			15			24		12	9	24	26	26	8	31	15	17	15	22	27	20	13	14	1	20		33	13	17	21	4	427
Pig	1															1	1															2
	2										1				1				2				1		1					1	1	8
	3						2					2	1	2	2			1	1	1	1	2								6	2	23
	4						0										1													1		2
	5						1							1	1			2	1								1			1		8
	7						0											2									1		2		1	6
	9						3											1														4
	TOTAL						6				2	2	2	3	2	1	1	6	4	1	1	1			3		1	1	10	3	2	53
Red deer	2						1		1		1																			2	2	7
	3																		1										1	4	1	7
	4																										1					1
	5																										1					1
	7						1																		1		1					3
	9																							1								1
	TOTAL						2		1		1								1					1	1		3	1	2	6	1	20
Seal	2									1	1																			1		3
	3																													1		1
	TOTAL									1	1																			2		4
Dog	2								1										2													3
Rabbit	?			1								1																				2
TOTAL				27			55		30	13	48	39	36	18	47	23	27	31	33	44	33	31	25	1	33		59	32	98	81	32	896

Table 13.6i Element representation by phase for the 1991 assemblage (based on NISP)

Taxa	Phase	ZY	X	Z	LT	LTX	LTN	AT	SC	PHU	DHU	PRA	DRA	UL	PE	PFE	DFE	PTI	DTI	PMT	DMT	PMC	DMC	PMP	DMP	SCU	AS	CA	PH1	PH2	PH3	Total
Cattle	3	2		1		1	8		1	3	1	3	1				3	1	1		1		1		1			1		5	1	35
	4					2																							2	1	1	6
	7			2	7	7			1		1	1	2			1					2				2				3	4	3	36
	9	11	8	14	86	364	278	5	25	19	36	36	37	26	39	39	19	31	46	49	15	38	29	7	46	11	35	36	148	148	73	1754
	TOTAL	13	8	17	86	374	293	5	27	22	38	40	40	26	39	40	22	32	47	51	15	39	29	8	48	11	35	37	153	158	78	1831
Sheep/goat	3			1		5	1		1		1	1	1	1	3		1	1			1				1				1	1		19
	4		1	1		7	8		4		1	2	1	2	2	2		2	2			1			4	3		1	1	1	1	46
	7	2				5	6			1	1	7	2	2	2		1	3	3	3	3	4	1		2	1	1	4			1	55
	8															1																1
	9	5	10	13	22	117	113	1	11	14	30	24	24	21	30	24	13	21	31	22	5	16	18	4	29	10	12	24	35	19	13	731
	TOTAL	7	11	15	22	134	128	1	16	15	33	34	28	27	37	26	15	27	36	25	8	21	20	4	36	10	16	25	40	20	15	852
Pig	3				1	2																							1	1		5
	4					1				1				1												1			1	1		6
	7			2		1			1	2		1					1	1							2					1	12
	9		2	3	18	13	32		4	2	4	10	5	8	2	2	5	1	5	5	1	13	8		2	1	3	5	4	6	8	172
	TOTAL		2	3	21	13	36		4	3	7	10	6	9	2	3	6	2	5	5	1	13	8		2	1	6	6	4	8	9	195
Red Deer	4										1																					1
	9			1	2		4		1		1	2	2	1				1					1				4		3	5	2	30
	TOTAL			1	2		4		1		1	3	2	1				1					1				4		3	5	2	31
Dog	9				1				1																							2
TOTAL		20	21	36	132	521	461	6	49	40	79	87	76	63	78	69	43	61	89	81	24	73	58	12	86	22	61	68	200	191	104	2911

Table 13.6ii Element representation by phase for the 1990 assemblage (based on NISP)

Taxa	Element																													Total
	ZY	X	Z	LT	LTX	LTN	AT	SC	PHU	DHU	PRA	DRA	UL	PE	PFE	DFE	PTI	DTI	PMT	DMT	PMC	DMC	PMP	DMP	SCU	AS	CA	PH1	PH2	PH3	
Cow		3	30		231	131	2	30	23	34	26	14	20	25	20	24	25	17	32	35	20	34	8	41		19	26	90	79	54	1093
S/G		6	1		117	99	1	24	10	31	31	23	6	39	24	10	31	28	23	18	23	25	6	30		25	15	34	18	9	707
Pig		15	8		14	21		6		1	2	2	1	1	3	4	3	6					22	25		6	5	21	17	9	192
Red Deer																							1						1	2	4
Dog									1	1																					2
Cat															1	1															2
TOTAL		24	39		362	251	3	60	34	67	59	39	27	65	48	39	59	51	55	53	43	59	37	96		50	46	145	115	74	2000

Table 13.6iii Element representation for the 1989 assemblage (based on NISP, phasing information not available)

suggest the two taxa were present in similar proportions. Pig is present in much smaller numbers. Red deer is present sporadically throughout all three assemblages, and probable grey seal, dog, cat and otter are represented by a handful of specimens. Table 13.5 provides the NISP and MNI counts for each species in each site phase.

Although the proportions of sheep/goat and cattle suggest similar numbers of these animals on the site, their size relative to each other would usually suggest that cattle were the primary contributors to the meat diet. At Cill Donnain, however, it would appear that a large proportion of the cattle present were very young when they were killed, and therefore unlikely to have provided large quantities of meat per head.

Although dogs were clearly present in and around the site, as shown by the presence of gnawed bones, dog remains are very scarce at Cill Donnain. Wild animals do not appear to have contributed to the inhabitants' diet to any great extent, although seal (phases 2 and 3) and cetacean bones are present in very small numbers (Tables 13.6–13.7). It is likely that the unstratified rabbit bones derive from intrusive animals, as is seen on other machair sites. Similarly, the unstratified otter remains may indicate the later use of the site as an otter holt rather than the hunting of the animal by the site's inhabitants.

The birds

Very few bird bones were recovered from Cill Donnain III. Of the 11 fragments of bird bone in the assemblage (from phases 3, 4 and 9) only one could be identified; this is a humerus of *Laurus* sp., either a herring gull or a lesser black-backed gull. The remainder of the fragments were unidentifiable pieces of sacrum (2), skull (5), vertebra (1), and shafts of goose-sized ulna (1) and tibiotarsus (1).

Element representation
Cattle
In all phases, the different cattle body parts are relatively evenly represented (Tables 13.6–13.7), and it would seem that whole animals were brought to the site and butchered *in situ*. The assemblage is dominated by loose teeth and phalanges, and this is partly due to the number

of these elements present in an individual skeleton, in comparison with other body parts. However, it is also a reflection of taphonomic processes at work as these elements are some of the most robust in the body. There is little other evidence for the under-representation of elements as a result of differential preservation, and the remainder of the assemblage shows no correlation with bone density (*cf* Brain 1981).

Although the relatively small sample sizes mean that identifying characteristics of different site phases should be tentative, it would seem that phase 4 (Middle–Late Iron Age transition with wheelhouse construction) is dominated by primary butchery waste, and the majority of this assemblage is made up of head and foot bones. Phase 9 (the Late Iron Age midden) also contains more foot bones in comparison with other phases than would be expected on the basis of their presence in the skeleton, suggesting that primary butchery waste was an important contributor to this deposit. Other skeletal elements associated with secondary butchery are also present in some numbers, however, and indicate that waste from both stages of butchery was deposited in the phase 9 midden.

Sheep/goat
Because of the relatively small number of bones identified to sheep, both sheep and sheep/goat are treated together in this section.

As with cattle, in all phases there is a relatively even representation of skeletal elements, and whole animals were brought to the site for butchery. There is no evidence for the separation of primary and secondary butchery waste. A comparison of element robustness and density within the assemblage shows no clear patterning and it would seem that the bulk of the assemblage does not reflect taphonomic bias. This said, across all phases, there is an under-representation of smaller elements such as phalanges, the astragalus and the calcaneus. This is often attributed to recovery bias (Payne 1972), but for Cill Donnain III this is unlikely, given the sieving program implemented during excavation; the relatively high number of sheep/goat loose teeth (of a similar or smaller size to the missing foot bones) that were recovered indicates no recovery bias. It is likely that the under-representation of the smaller elements is a result of

Phase	Cetacean	Antler	Horn Core		Rib			Vertebrae		Skull fragment	TOTAL
		Red deer	Cow	Sheep	Large Mammal	Medium Mammal	Small Mammal	Large Mammal	Medium Mammal		
1990 ph3		5			13	71		8	22	40	**159**
1990 ph4	1	5	3	1	19	53	2	2	18	80	**184**
1990 ph7	1	3	1		17	37		4	18	29	**110**
1990 ph8	1										**1**
1990 ph9	10	25	24	2	252	662	2	122	218	619	**1936**
1990:?		1			1	1		1	2	2	**8**
TOTAL	**13**	**39**	**28**	**3**	**302**	**824**	**4**	**137**	**278**	**770**	**2398**
1991 ph1		1	1								**2**
1991 ph2		1		1							**2**
1991 ph3		2		1							**3**
1991 ph4			2								**2**
1991 ph5		3									**3**
1991 ph9				1							**1**
TOTAL		**7**	**3**	**3**							**13**
1989		11	3	2							**16**

Table 13.7 Frequency of element fragments not recordable under the 1990 recording scheme (NISP)

canid activity, and a number of small bones showed evidence of having been digested (Table 13.3). Canid gnawing and consumption of bone can have a very detrimental effect on the preservation of the bones of smaller animals (Payne and Munson 1985) and this may also account for the virtual absence of bird bone from the site, in contrast to the assemblage from nearby Bornais mound 1 (Cartledge and Serjeantson in Sharples 2012b).

Pig

Pig bone was recovered in much smaller numbers than cattle and sheep/goat bone, making interpretation of body-part representation difficult. Overall, pigs are represented by all body parts and whole animals were probably present on the site; the abundance of the different skeletal elements, though sporadic, is even in all site phases. As with the sheep/goat assemblage, phalanges are under-represented, probably as a result of canid activity. In the phase 9 assemblage, denser skeletal elements are marginally more frequent than those that are less robust, suggesting that some of the pig bone at the site might have been lost through taphonomic processes. The trend for higher numbers of pork front-leg joints identified at nearby Dun Vulan and associated with high-status activity (Mulville 1999) was not observed at Cill Donnain III.

Other species

The occurrence of other species in the assemblage is sporadic. Although not all bones in the red deer skeleton have been recovered from the site, the range of skeletal elements present does not suggest the import to the site solely of cuts of meat or of partially butchered animals. Antler is relatively frequent (57 fragments from all years) and many antler fragments show clear signs of having been worked. A single piece of antler has been shed, but this was recovered from an unstratified context.

Because the cetacean bones present are heavily worked and highly fragmented, it has been impossible to identify these to either element or species. They might have derived from beached or hunted whales or dolphins, used for meat, oil and blubber; alternatively these bones might have been recovered from beaches as drift bone and used as raw material for bone-working, as tools, or as fuel (Mulville 2002), although none of the cetacean bone recovered from Cill Donnain III was burnt. Dog, cat, otter and seal bones are too few to draw conclusions regarding body-part representation.

Ageing
Cattle

Because of the highly fragmented nature of the assemblage, very few ageable mandibles were recovered. Only three mandibles from the 1990 assemblage were ageable from the mandibular tooth row; two mandibles belonged to animals between *c*.1–18 months of age and one to a senile animal. This small sample provides very little information about the age structure of the cattle population at Cill Donnain III, but analysis of the loose mandibular teeth recovered in 1990 may be instructive:

- Eleven of the loose mandibular dP4 teeth present were unworn, indicating that around 33% of the assemblage derived from neonatal calves less than 1 month old when they died.
- Another 18 teeth (52%) exhibit wear recorded as between stages b–f (Grant 1982), suggesting that 85% of the dP4s present come from animals less than 3 months old.
- Thirty-five per cent of loose M1/M2 teeth were unworn and these derive from animals killed before they reached 30 months of age
- The presence of a small number of heavily worn mandibular M3 teeth indicates that at least some individuals reached a relatively old age.

The majority of the sample of loose teeth in the 1990 assemblage derives from phase 9, the LIA midden deposit; other phases contained teeth in numbers too small to show any clear spatial or temporal patterns in cattle population structure.

This pattern is reflected in the 1989 assemblage, where 84% of mandibular dP_4 teeth were unworn, and a small number of heavily worn mandibular M_3 teeth were recovered. Ageing data is unavailable for the 1991 assemblage.

Fusion of long bones can also provide information about the age profile of an animal population and, in general, the available fusion evidence at Cill Donnain (Table 13.8) supports that of the tooth-wear:

- In the 1990 assemblage, 7% of bones that fuse before birth are unfused (Silver 1969), indicating that a small number of foetal animals were present.
- In addition, 98 elements were recorded that represent very young or foetal cattle on the basis of their small size and unconsolidated bone matrix. The presence of foetal and neonatal cattle indicates that the site was a production site as well as a consumer site.
- In the 1990 data set, of the bones that fuse within the first year of an animal's life, 50% are unfused; of the bones that fuse in the second year of life, 38% are unfused; of the bones that fuse during the third year of life, 54% are unfused; and of the bones that fuse during the fourth year of life, 69% are unfused.
- This suggests that around half of the animals present were killed as calves within their first year but, following this, few cattle were killed until they reached around four years old.
- Around 32% of the herd reached full skeletal maturity and were killed when they were over 3½ years old.

The 1989 cattle assemblage (made up primarily of material from phases 6 and 9) shows a slightly different pattern:

- Of the bones that fuse within the first year of an animal's life, 25% are unfused.

- 81% of the bones that fuse in the second year of life are unfused.
- 46% of the bones that fuse during the third year of life are unfused.
- Of the bones that fuse during the fourth year of life, 49% are unfused.
- Although there is a relatively high level of infant mortality, with cattle being killed in their first year, the majority of cattle appear to have been killed between their first and second years of age.

This is in contrast to the tooth-wear evidence from the loose dP_4 teeth in this 1989 assemblage, which indicates a very high mortality of calves in the first few months of life. This discrepancy is probably due to the differential preservation of post-cranial elements and teeth, with the bones of young animals being more prone to taphonomic processes than fused bone, an effect less apparent in the teeth since they are more robustly structured. It is likely that, in both assemblages, younger animals are under-represented as a result of taphonomy.

Sheep/goat

There were five ageable sheep/goat mandibles in the 1990 assemblage. Using the criteria set out in Payne (1973), two of these derive from animals killed in their second year, two are from animals killed in their third year, and one belongs to an animal that reached 4–6 years of age.

- Only 17 loose dP4 teeth are present; of these, two (12%) are unworn indicating animals that died before they reached two months of age.
- The remainder of the dP4 loose teeth are heavily worn and indicate animals that died between 1 and 3 years of age.
- Loose M1 and M2 teeth are difficult to separate, but heavily worn examples are rare, indicating that the majority of animals (89%) were killed between the ages of 1 and 6 years (Payne 1973).
- Of the 18 loose M3 teeth present, 39% indicate animals that died at 2–3 years of age, 6% animals that died in their third year, 50% that died between the ages of 4 and 8 years, and 6% that died between 8 and 10 years of age.

No tooth-wear information is available for the 1989 or 1991 assemblages from Cill Donnain.

The 1990 post-cranial assemblage shows a very even kill-off pattern for the sheep/goat in the assemblage (Table 13.8):

- 6% of the proximal metapodials which fuse before birth are unfused, indicating that lambs were born at or very near the site.
- A further 34 bones were recorded as foetal/neonatal on the basis of bone characteristics.

Taxa	Phase	Approximate age of element fusion (Silver 1969)															Total
		F	U	% U	F	U	% U	F	U	% U	F	U	% U	F	U	% U	
		Year 3-4			Year 2-3			Year 1-2			<1 year			Foetal			
Cattle	1990 ph3	1	3	75	1	1	50	2	5	71.4				1		0	14
	1990 ph4				2		0	4	3	42.9				2		0	11
	1990 ph7	1	2	66.7	1	1	50	4	3	42.9				2		0	14
	1990 ph9	14	29	67.4	20	25	55.6	91	57	38.5	4	5	80	46	4	8	295
	1990 ph10		1	100		1	100	3		0	1		0	1		0	7
	1990 TOTAL	16	35	68.6	24	28	53.8	104	68	38.2	5	5	50	52	4	7.1	341
	1989: TOTAL	25	24	49	25	21	45.7	23	96	80.7	540	181	25.1				935
	TOTAL	41	59	59	49	49	50	117	164	56.8	545	186	25.8	52	4	7.1	1276

Taxa	Phase	F	U	% U	F	U	% U	F	U	% U		F	U	% U	Total
		36-42 months			15-36 months			3-16 months				Foetal			
Sheep/goat	1990 ph3		3	100		1	100	3	1	25					8
	1990 ph4	1	5	83.3		3	100	4	5	55.6					18
	1990 ph7	2	7	77.8	3	5	62.5	11		0		6		0	34
	1990 ph9	19	47	71.2	41	36	46.8	74	26	26		38	3	7.3	284
	1990 ph10		1	100	1	2	66.7	1		0		1		0	6
	1990:?	1	1	50				1		0					3
	1990: TOTAL	23	64	73.6	45	47	51.1	94	32	25.4		45	3	6.3	353
		36-42 months			30-36 months			13-28 months			6-10 months	Foetal			Total
	1989	7	21	75	13	19	59.4	54	42	43.8	62	15	19.5	469	17	3.5	719

Taxa	Phase	F	U	% U	F	U	% U	F	U	% U		F	U	% U	Total
		Year 3-4			Year 2-3			Year 1-2				Foetal			
Pig	1990 ph3								1	100					1
	1990 ph4								5	100					5
	1990 ph7		4	100					4	100					8
	1990 ph9	1	16	94.1	6	16	72.7	13	35	72.9		18		0	105
	1990: TOTAL	1	20	95.2	6	16	72.7	13	45	77.6		18	0	0	119
	1989 TOTAL	0	6	100	14	35	71.4	13	6	31.6		130	1	0.76	205
	TOTAL	1	26	96.3	20	51	71.8	26	51	66.2		148	1	0.67	324

Taxa	Phase	F	U	% U	F	U	% U	F	U	% U		F	U	% U	Total
		Late fusing			Middle fusing			Early fusing				Very early fusing			
Red deer	1990 ph9		2	100	1	1	50	9		0					13

Table 13.8 Fusion data from the 1989 and 1990 assemblages at Cill Donnain III

- 25% of the bones that fuse between 3 and 16 months of age are unfused.
- 51% of animals appear to have died before they reached 36 months.
- 74% of animals were killed before they reached 42 months of age.

The 1989 dataset shows a very similar pattern (Table 13.8). Based on Silver's (1969) fusion ages:

- 3.5% of proximal metapodials represent foetal/neonatal lambs.
- 19.5% of sheep/goat were killed before they reached 10 months of age.
- 44% before they reached 28 months.
- 59% before they reached 36 months.
- 75% before they reached 42 months of age.

Pig

Only one ageable pig mandible was recovered in the 1990 assemblage, and this was from an immature animal according to the criteria of O'Connor (1989). Just 30 loose mandibular teeth of pig were recovered:

- The proportion of unworn to worn M1/M2 teeth indicates that around 35% of these M1/M2 teeth come from animals in O'Connor's (1989) juvenile and immature categories.
- A very small number of M3s derive from the adult and sub-adult categories.

From the 1989 assemblage, very few pig teeth were recovered, just two loose dP_4s (one worn, one unworn), and four loose M_3s (three unworn and one worn), indicating the presence of one very young animal and three animals that died before reaching adulthood.

Phase	Species	Element	Pathology	Number of specimens
1990 ph9	Cow	Tarsal	Eburnation	1
		PE	Eburnation, pitting and grooving on acetabulum	2
		PMC	Pitting and grooving on distal articulation	1
		PMT	Eburnation of the proximal articulation	1
		PMT	Pitting on proximal articulation	1
		PH1	Pitting on distal articulation, grooving on proximal articulation	1
		PH1	Pitting on distal articulation	2
		PH1	Pitting on proximal articulation	1
		PH1	Eburnation and grooving on proximal articulation	1
		PH2	Pitting on distal articulation	1
		Loose M_3	Missing hypocondulid cusp	2
		Loose P_4	Abnormal wear	1
		Loose $M_{1/2}$	Abnormal wear	1
1990 ph10		PE	Pitting on articulation	1
1991 ph3		PH1	Type I depressions in the distal articular surface (Baker & Brothwell 1980)	1
		PH2	Type I depressions in the distal articular surface (Baker & Brothwell 1980)	1
1990 ph9	Sheep/goat	PE	Eburnation on acetabulum	1
1991 ph1		Mandible	Severe periodontal disease (distinct swelling and surface modification P_4; M_1 abnormally inclined in a forward direction).	1
1990 ph9	Pig	PH2	Extra bone growth lateral side	1

Table 13.9 Recorded pathologies in the 1990 and 1991 assemblages

Eighteen pig bones from the 1990 assemblage were recorded as deriving from neonatal or foetal pigs on the basis of their size and porosity. The 1989 data also suggest neonatal mortality of around 3%, indicating that pigs were bred at or near the site.

Fusion of post-cranial elements in the 1990 assemblage indicates that a high proportion (78%) of pigs at Cill Donnain III were killed before they were 2 years old and, by 4 years of age, 95% of animals had been killed (Table 13.8). The 1989 assemblage shows a more steady mortality for pigs, with around 32% of pigs killed before their second year, and 71% killed before they reached 3 years of age. No fused late-fusing pig bones were recovered from these contexts, suggesting that the majority of pigs were killed before they reached 42 months of age.

Other species
Deer teeth are very rare in the assemblage but one M_1/M_2 was recovered with very superficial wear, and an unworn dP_4 was also present in phase 9. These teeth indicate the presence of some very young deer in the assemblage, suggesting that deer-hunting was not restricted to the recovery of antler. A mandible exhibiting a moderate wear stage and a handful of unfused middle- and late-fusing elements indicate that immature or sub-adult animals were also present.

Of the two dog elements recovered in the 1990 assemblage, one was a foetal/neonatal scapula.

Sex
The highly fragmented nature of the assemblage precluded any attempt to ascertain sex using the pelvis or metapodials of the cattle and sheep/goat present. Nine mandibular and four maxillary pig canines were recovered from the 1990 assemblage, giving a male to female ration of 2:1 and 1:3 respectively.

Pathology
Evidence for pathology within the assemblage was rare, with just 22 specimens exhibiting lesions. These are predominantly arthropathies of the cattle foot, although some cattle and sheep/goat dental pathologies were also recorded. Details can be seen in Table 13.9. When pathologies of cattle foot bones appear consistently in an assemblage, they may sometimes be used to identify the use of cattle for traction. While the arthropathies observed at Cill Donnain may possibly result from traction stress, the small numbers involved cannot be used to in-

		Cow										Sheep /goat									Pig						
	Phase	Dismembering	Filleting	Horn working	Skinning	Bone working	Other	Uncategorized	TOTAL	Total no. Cow	% butchered	Dismembering	Filleting	Skinning	Bone working	Other	Uncategorized	TOTAL	Total no. Sheep/Goat	% butchered	Dismembering	Filleting	Other	Uncategorized	TOTAL	Total no. Pig	% butchered
Chopped	3	1						11	12	41	29.3							0	27	0					0	4	0
	4		1					1	2	73	2.7							0	61	0		1	1		2	10	20
	7	1				1			2	43	4.7							0	61	0			1		1	16	6.3
	8																	0	1	0							
	9	7	3				3	11	24	1121	2.1	5	1			2	1	9	920	1	1				1	244	0.4
	TOTAL	9	4	0	0	1	4	22	40	1278	3.1	5	1	0	0	2	1	9	1070	0.8	1	1	2	0	4	274	1.5
Cut	3								0	41	0							0	27	0					0	4	0
	4						1		1	73	1.4	2					2	4	61	6.6					0	10	0
	7								0	43	0	2						2	61	3.3	1				1	16	6.3
	9	8	2	2	2		10	7	31	1121	2.8	17	1			10	5	33	920	3.6	6		2		8	244	3.3
	10								0	20	0							0	25	0					0	4	0
	TOTAL	8	2	2	2	0	10	8	32	1298	2.5	21	0	1	0	12	5	39	1094	3.6	7	0	2	0	9	278	3.2
Sawn	3								0	41	0							0	27	0					0	4	0
	4								0	73	0							0	61	0					0	10	0
	7					1			1	43	2.3							0	61	0					0	16	0
	9							3	3	1121	0.3	1					2	3	920	0.3					0	244	0
	TOTAL	0	0	0	0	1	0	3	4	1278	0.3	1	0	0	0	0	2	3	1069	0.3	0	0	0	0	0	274	0
other working	3								0	41	0							0	27	0					0	4	0
	4								0	73	0							0	61	0					0	10	0
	7								0	43	0				1			1	61	1.6					0	16	0
	9								0	1121	0							0	920	0					0	244	0
	TOTAL	0	0	0	0	0	0	0	0	1278	0	0	0	0	1	0	0	1	1069	0.1	0	0	0	0	0	274	0

		Red Deer			Cetacean			Large Mammal							Medium Mammal							Overall assemblage		
	Phase	Antler working	Total antler	% worked	Bone working	Total Cetacean	% worked	Dismembering	Horn working	Bone working	Other	TOTAL	Total no. LM	% butchered	Uncategorized	Bone working	Other	Uncategorized	TOTAL	Total no. MM	% butchered	TOTAL	Total No.	% butchered
Chopped	3		5	0								0	132	0	3				3	152	2	15	361	3.8
	4	1	5	20	1	1	100					0	93	0	2				2	195	1	8	438	1.8
	7	1	3	33.3	1	1	100					0	58	0	1		2		3	91	3.3	8	273	2.9
	8				1	1	100					0	1	0								1	3	50
	9	3	25	12	10	10	100	2		2		4	1339	0.3	23		3	8	34	1646	2.1	85	5305	1.5
	TOTAL	5	38	12.8	13	13	100	2	0	2	0	4	1623	0.2	29	0	3	10	42	2084	2	**117**	**6380**	**1.7**
Cut	3		5	0								0	132	0	12				12	152	7.9	12	361	3.1
	4		5	0	1	1	100		1		1	2	93	2.2	3		4	4	11	195	5.6	19	438	4.3
	7		3	0	1	1	100					0	58	0	3		3	3	9	91	9.9	13	273	4.7
	9	1	25	4	10	10	100	3		1	4	8	1339	0.6	39		8	79	126	1646	7.7	217	5305	3.8
	10											0	17	0	1		2		3	21	14.3	3	87	2.5
	TOTAL	1	38	2.6	12	12	100	3	1	1	5	10	1639	0.6	46	0	15	100	161	2105	7.6	**264**	**6464**	**4**
Sawn	3	1	5	20								0	132	0					0	152	0	1	361	0.3
	4	3	5	60								0	93	0					0	195	0	4	438	0.9
	7	1	3	33.3	1	1	100				2	2	58	3.4					0	91	0	5	273	1.8
	9	6	25	24	10	10	100				5	5	1339	0.4	7		2	2	11	1646	0.7	38	5305	0.7
	TOTAL	11	38	28.9	12	12	100	0	0	0	7	7	1622	0.4	7	2	0	2	11	2084	0.5	**48**	**6377**	**0.8**
other working	3	3	5	60							1	1	132	0.8					0	152	0	4	361	1
	4		5	0	1	1	100					0	93	0					0	195	0	1	438	0.2
	7	1	3	33.3	1	1	100				2	2	58	3.4					0	91	0	4	273	1.5
	9	3	25	12	10	10	100				3	3	1339	0.2		1			1	1646	0.1	17	5305	0.3
	TOTAL	6	38	15.8	12	12	100	0	0	0	6	6	1622	0.4	0	1	0	0	1	2084	0	**26**	**6377**	**0.4**

		Cow										Sheep/goat									Pig						
Phases 3,4,5,7,8,9,10		Dismembering	Filleting	Horn working	Skinning	Bone working	Other	Uncategorized	TOTAL	Total no. Cow	% butchered	Dismembering	Filleting	Skinning	Bone working	Other	Uncategorized	TOTAL	Total no. Sheep/Goat	% butchered	Dismembering	Filleting	Other	Uncategorized	TOTAL	Total no. Pig	% butchered
TOTAL BUTCHERY		17	6	2	2	2	14	33	76	1299	5.9	27	1	1	1	14	8	52	1095	4.7	8	1	4	0	13	278	4.7

		Red Deer			Cetacean			Large Mammal							Medium Mammal							Overall assemblage		
Phases 3,4,5,7,8,9,10		Antler working	Total antler	% worked	Bone working	Total Cetacean	% worked	Dismembering	Horn working	Bone working	Other	TOTAL	Total no. LM	% butchered	Uncategorized	Bone working	Other	Uncategorized	TOTAL	Total no. MM	% butchered	TOTAL	Total No.	% butchered
TOTAL BUTCHERY		23	39	59	[49]	13	100	5	1	16	5	27	1640	1.6	82	3	18	112	215	2105	10.2	458	6467	7.1

NB The total 'bone working' for cetacean bone is greater than the number of fragments, as each fragment has more than one type of bone working.

Table 13.10 Occurrence of butchery in the 1990 assemblage (percentages are calculated on the basis of the entire assemblage; butchery-mark category based on Lyman 1994)

Taxa	Butchered		Total
	No.	%	
Cattle	93	13.3	698
Pig	3	2.5	120
Sheep/Goat	54	12.8	423
TOTAL	**150**	**12.1**	**1241**

Table 13.11 Occurrence of butchery in the 1989 assemblage (percentages are calculated on the basis of identified fragments)

dicate that this was an important aspect of cattle exploitation at the site.

Butchery and bone-working

Around 6% of the cattle bone from Cill Donnain's 1990 assemblage exhibits butchery-marks (Table 13.10). Both chop-marks and cut-marks are evident in relatively equal proportions (3% and 2.5% of the assemblage respectively) and a few cattle bones have been sawn. Of the butchery-marks found on the cattle bone, 22% are associated with dismemberment of the carcass, while just 8% are associated with filleting (Lyman 1994). A relatively large proportion (47%) of the butchery-marks on cattle bone are either not characteristic of any particular butchery activity or were recorded on bones too fragmentary to assign to a butchery category. In the 1989 data set, 13% of cattle bone has butchery-marks (Table 13.11).

Around 5% of the sheep/goat bone in the 1990 assemblage carries butchery-marks. As is often the case with sheep/goat butchery, these are overwhelmingly cut-marks (75%) although a small number of bones exhibit chop-marks and three bones have been sawn. Fifty-two per cent of butchery-marks on sheep/goat bones are associated with dismemberment, and very small numbers of bones provide evidence for filleting and skinning. In the 1989 data set, 13% of sheep bone has butchery-marks (Table 13.11).

Only 13 pig bones in the 1990 assemblage exhibit butchery-marks, making up around 5% of the pig assemblage. Both chop-marks and cut-marks were recorded. In the 1989 data set, just 2.5% of pig bone has butchery-marks.

In addition to identified specimens, a relatively high number of sheep/goat/pig-sized rib fragments exhibit cut-marks at right angles to the rib shaft.

The very high levels of fragmentation in the assemblage (Table 13.2), with 57% of the 1990 assemblage being made up of bone fragments less than 10% of their original size, is highly suggestive of either the deliberate and consistent processing of bone (in which bone is smashed and/or boiled to release marrow and fat) or the subjecting of the assemblage to intense taphonomic damage (such as ploughing). Phases 2 and 9 (and possibly phase 3) include some cultivation layers (see Chapters 4,

5 and 8), and therefore plough damage may be a possible explanation of the fragmentation of the bone in these contexts, but the material from the other site phases is also very fragmented. Highly fragmented assemblages appear to be a feature of Iron Age bone assemblages from the Outer Hebrides (Mulville 1999) and it is likely that intensive use of all parts of the animal was a cultural trend in this region.

Tarsals, carpals and phalanges were the least fragmented post-cranial elements in the 1989 and 1990 assemblages. These elements are some of the densest in the skeleton (Brain 1981), making them more time-consuming to process and less likely to be affected by taphonomy. These elements also produce relatively small amounts of bone marrow and grease (Binford 1978; Morin 2007) and might therefore not have been selected as frequently for processing. The high levels of fragmentation of other dense elements that contain more marrow and grease, such as the mandible, support the interpretation that the bulk of the assemblage was deliberately smashed during marrow-fat and grease extraction. Elsewhere, the intensive and comprehensive processing of animal carcasses in this way has been used as an indicator of resource stress (*e.g.* in Norse Greenland; see Outram 1999; Buckland *et al.* 1996) although this kind of butchery is also characteristic of other cultures with no perceived increased resource pressure (*e.g.* in Roman Britain; see Albarella *et al.* 2008).

In addition to bone that has been processed for food, a number of elements also show evidence of bone-working and industry. In the 1990 assemblage, two cattle-sized horn cores had cut-marks around the base of the horn associated with horn removal, and two cattle metapodia and one sheep bone had cut-marks characteristic of skinning activity (Table 13.10).

The use of a saw in animal butchery is relatively rare in Britain until the late Medieval or post-Medieval periods, and where it does occur in prehistoric contexts it is often associated with bone-working (Rixson 1989). This seems to be borne out in the Cill Donnain III assemblage where a large proportion of the bones that have been sawn are unidentifiable bone-working waste, and are evidently off-cuts from large mammal (probably cow) long bones.

Around 60% of the antler recovered in 1990 exhibits chop-marks, and most of the antler present consists of tine tips, representing antler-working waste. Other fragments of worked bone include a sheep/goat tibia with a hole bored down the centre, and a prepared cattle tibia shaft with the articular ends sawn off ready for bone-working. Further information on antler-working waste and worked bone is to be found in Chapter 12.

Biometry

Because of the highly fragmented nature of the assemblage and the frequency of unfused elements, relatively few bones can provide biometrical data, re-

Phase	Context	Element	Taxa	Measurement (mm)																		
				GL	GLl	GLm	GB	BP	DP	Bd	BT	Dd	HTC	LAR	SD	BATF	DL	a	b	1.00	3.00	4.00
9	5	AS	B		63.62	58.25		40.11		39.31												
9	31	AS	B		62.57	57.48		43.35		42.66												
9	31	AS	B		52.80	49.77		34.64		34.03							27.06					
9	27	AS	B		57.47	52.92		34.83		35.70							31.42					
9	5	AS	B		55.27	47.85		36.69		37.19							32.96					
9	31	AS	B		60.81	53.02		38.31		37.78							31.23					
9	5	AS	B		58.70	51.89		37.35		36.60							33.68					
9	31	AS	B		60.70	55.50		37.99		37.46							32.94					
9	5	AS	B		58.68	53.70		40.02		38.82							32.47					
9	5	AS	B		60.77	55.24		38.96		37.33							36.39					
9	5	AS	B		60.67	55.25		40.31		39.72							33.48					
9	31	AS	B		58.63	53.23		40.15		41.55							32.17					
9	22	CALC	B	119.36																		
9	5	HU	B							47.40												
9	5	HU	B							60.06		29.32										
9	5	HU	B							65.06		30.96										
9	22	HU	B							65.69		30.47										
9	5	HU	B							68.46		31.06										
9	5	HU	B							76.46		30.36										
9	31	MC	B							49.71								23.67	23.62	20.38	25.08	21.27
9	5	MC	B	168.00						52.01						46.82		23.92	25.19	19.60	25.17	21.37
9	5	MC	B	185.00						49.93					26.32			23.64	23.22	22.31	25.67	20.23
9	5	MC	B	186.00						53.15					27.88	49.15		25.96	24.32	22.56	27.31	21.09
9	4	MC	B					48.40														
9	5	MC	B					52.91														
9	22	MC	B					49.44							26.77							
9	5	MC	B					49.41	30.65													
9	5	MC	B					50.41	33.66													
9	18	MT	B						27.30	48.95												
9	31	MT	B							45.31							41.99	20.59	21.65	19.69	27.32	20.54
9	5	MT	B							48.74							45.23	22.07	23.04	19.74	25.80	21.28
9	5	MT	B					41.54	39.31													
9	5	MT	B					41.41	39.73													
9	31	MT	B					43.68	41.31													
9	18	MT	B	190.00				41.08	40.34						21.69							
9	5	TI	B							51.90	40.15											
9	5	AS	CERVUS		46.72	43.44		29.05		29.62												
9	5	AS	CERVUS		43.91	41.91		28.48		27.86							23.78					
9	27	AS	CERVUS		46.95	44.76		30.02		30.10							26.32					
9	5	AS	CERVUS		47.09	44.58		30.41		31.12							26.60					
9	13	HU	CERVUS								46.06	26.66										
4	24	RA	CERVUS					42.85														
9	5	AS	O							18.20												
9	15	AS	O		24.69	23.64		15.49		15.54							14.35					
9	31	AS	O		25.59	23.93		16.60		16.78							14.61					
9	5	AS	O		26.72	25.49		16.41		16.85							15.46					
9	27	AS	O		27.49	25.60		17.02		17.97							15.72					
10	1	AS	O		23.81	22.81		15.68		15.24												
9	5	CALC	O	47.40																		
9	5	CALC	O	47.43																		
9	5	CALC	O	52.60																		
9	5	CALC	O	51.42			18.65															
9	5	FE	O							34.74												
9	13	HU	O								22.46	10.49										
9	5	HU	O								22.61	11.89										
9	5	HU	O	130.00							26.87	12.98		12.42								
7	25	MC	O							23.40						22.98		10.70	10.60	9.11	12.81	9.81
7	25	PE	O										26.28									
7	25	RA	O					27.33														
7	25	RA	O					27.64														
9	14	RA	O							25.14												
9	27	RA	O					28.23														
9	5	RA	O					29.20														

stricting the potential for analysis of animal size and shape from the site. Information from the 125 bones in the 1990 assemblage that were measured is provided in Table 13.12, and tooth measurements can be found in Table 13.13.

All of the measurements taken fall within the range of those observed at other contemporary sites in the Hebrides (Mulville 1999; Mulville and Powell in Sharples 2012b; Clarke 1962). While most of the measurements at Cill Donnain fall in the middle of the range observed in the region, for both sheep/goat and cattle, astragalus measurements fall at the top of this range.

Discussion

The species present

The dominance of cattle and sheep at Cill Donnain III is mirrored at other Iron Age sites in the Western Isles although, in contrast to Cill Donnain, the majority of these sites have a higher relative proportion of sheep/goat to cattle, which has been attributed to the greater suitability of sheep for a challenging farming environment (Clarke 1962; Finlay 1991; Mulville 1999; Halstead 2003; Cartledge *et al.* in Sharples 2012b; Mulville and Powell in Sharples 2012b). There are, however, some exceptions and, as at Cill Donnain, the assemblages from Cnip,

9	5	RA	O					24.54											
9	5	RA	O					26.75											
9	5	RA	O					27.91											
9	31	RA	O					28.39				15.75							
9	5	TI	O						19.89										
9	5	TI	O						21.64										
9	5	TI	O						18.81	17.40									
9	31	TI	O						20.72	15.96									
9	31	TI	O						18.84	19.28									
9	5	TI	O						23.32	17.73									
9	31	TI	O						23.58	18.18									
9	5	TI	O						24.22	19.44									
4	24	AS	O/C		21.97	22.08		13.97	14.15						12.33				
7	25	AS	O/C		23.61	24.28		15.39	16.30						14.88				
9	31	AS	O/C						15.86										
9	31	AS	O/C		26.79			16.02											
9	5	AS	O/C		26.91	26.78		17.96											
9	5	AS	O/C		24.54	24.17			15.39						14.29				
9	31	AS	O/C						15.99						14.41				
9	31	AS	O/C		26.09	25.25		17.30							14.19				
9	5	AS	O/C		24.92	23.99		17.08							14.81				
9	5	AS	O/C		25.08	23.44		16.26	15.72										
9	18	AS	O/C		25.44	24.40		15.91	15.66						13.63				
9	31	AS	O/C		25.75	24.78		16.79	15.97						14.61				
9	5	AS	O/C		25.76	25.06		17.82	16.24						15.25				
9	58	CALC	O/C	47.38															
9	5	FE	O/C	166.00								14.17							
3	32	HU	O/C						20.91		11.26								
9	5	HU	O/C						25.57										
9	5	HU	O/C						25.53		12.74								
9	13	HU	O/C						27.91		14.51								
9	58	HU	O/C						23.91	20.64	13.32								
9	31	HU	O/C						24.91		12.95								
9	5	HU	O/C						28.19	22.03	13.11								
9	5	HU	O/C						25.25		12.71								
9	5	HU	O/C	124.00					25.15		12.46		12.74						
9	5	MC	O/C					15.36	20.85										
9	5	MC	O/C												9.50	8.77	9.61	12.15	9.29
9	5	MC	O/C						20.04						9.22	8.26	9.72	11.26	9.13
9	31	MC	O/C						25.03						10.52	11.47	11.33	14.33	11.34
9	5	MC	O/C						20.48					21.43	9.73	8.89	9.76	12.64	9.42
9	31	MC	O/C						21.75					21.44	10.33	8.97	9.66	12.69	9.95
9	5	MC	O/C						22.08					22.34	9.92	8.09	9.02	14.32	9.98
9	5	MC	O/C						23.95					23.53	11.07	11.25	9.95	12.83	10.45
9	15	MC	O/C					14.24	21.66					21.71	9.32	10.16	10.07	12.46	9.47
9	5	MC	O/C	117.20			21.27	15.67	23.60				12.75	23.93	10.78	10.00	9.81	12.72	9.30
9	5	MC	O/C					19.58	13.65										
9	5	MC	O/C					23.10	15.46										
9	5	RA	O/C						25.68										
9	5	RA	O/C					26.92											
7	25	TI	O/C						24.70										
9	5	TI	O/C						20.37	17.32									
9	5	TI	O/C						22.12	17.27									
9	27	TI	O/C						23.29	17.13									
9	5	TI	O/C					36.94											
7	25	AS	S					16.80											
7	25	AS	S		38.29	35.93		19.64	20.98					20.61					
9	5	AS	s		34.81	32.41		18.74											
9	5	AS	S		36.92	35.10		18.18	23.36										
9	5	MC	S						14.41										
9	5	MC	S	71.08					15.80										
9	5	RA	S						31.11										

Table 13.12 Measurements taken on the 1990 postcranial assemblage

Lewis (McCormick 2006), Sollas midden, North Uist (Finlay 1991) and Kilellan, Islay (Serjeantson *et al.* n.d., cited in Mulville 1999) contain a slightly higher NISP for cattle than for sheep/goat.

At Cill Donnain, the dominance of cattle over sheep/goat is much less obvious when MNI is calculated and, although the use of diagnostic zones to record the 1990 assemblage should preclude any individual element from having been counted twice for that data set, the predominance of cattle in the total NISP counts may, to some extent, be an artefact of the high levels of fragmentation in the 1991 and 1989 assemblages.

Alternatively, the apparent dominance of cattle may reflect a higher rate of taphonomic loss for the smaller sheep/goat foot bones across the whole assemblage.

Proportions of pig in the Cill Donnain III assemblage are comparable with other contemporary sites in the islands where, with a few exceptions, pig represents less than 12% of the assemblage (Clarke 1962; Finlay 1991; Halstead 2003; Mulville and Powell in Sharples 2012b). Parker Pearson *et al.* (1996) have suggested that the slightly more common occurrence of pigs at broch sites as opposed to other settlements may be an indicator of elite status; pig at Cill Donnain is considerably less fre-

Kim Vickers with Saleem ul Haq and John Hamshaw-Thomas

Phase	Context	Taxa	Measurement (mm)										
			DP4L	DP4W	M1WP	M1L	M1WA	M2WA	M2WP	M2L	M3L	M3WA	M3WC
4	24	B	35.05	10.58									
4	24	B			12.33	23.25	11.95						
7	25	B			13.9	20.29	13.37						
9	5	B	30.34										
9	5	B	32.19										
9	5	B	34.23										
9	5	B	30.51	10.8									
9	5	B	29.94	11.58									
9	5	B	31.51	10.97									
9	5	B	31.64	12.28									
9	5	B	34.28	10.9									
9	12	B	28.04	11.39									
9	14	B	22.16	11.81									
9	33	B	34.04	10.39									
9	5	B			14.61	24.25		14.72					
9	22	B			13.77			14.34	14.49	21.53	34.31	15.11	13.95
9	5	B										14.03	12.33
9	5	B									25.87	15.31	13.55
9	5	B									34.55	14.78	13.64
9	5	B									35.14	14.77	13.44
9	5	B									36.9	16.3	14.11
9	11	B									30.36	13.79	12.52
9	14	B									30.77	15.3	14.28
9	15	B									33.22	15.3	14.15
9	15	B									33.85	15.01	14.32
9	29	B									34.59	15	15.1
9	5	CERVUS									27.22	12.13	11.86
3	60	O/C									21.58	7.85	7.5
4	24	O/C	15.65										
4	24	O/C	18.73	6.08									
7	25	O/C	15.66										
7	25	O/C									18.78	7.92	7.42
7	25	O/C									20.59	7.78	7.17
9	5	O/C	14.99	5.85	6.9	12.79	6.76	7.01	6.81	16.7	18.2	7.41	6.93
9	31	O/C		5.82	7.02	14.01	6.64	7.05	6.93	16.29			
9	5	O/C	15.43										
9	5	O/C	16.28	5.65									
9	5	O/C	16.56	5.49									
9	5	O/C	17.65	5.96									
9	5	O/C	17.86	6.07									
9	14	O/C	16.37	5.3									
9	14	O/C	16.36	6.35									
9	14	O/C	17.35	6.19									
9	18	O/C	15.16	5.62									
9	31	O/C	14.83	5.59									
9	12	O/C			6.19	11.47	6.04						
9	12	O/C			7.01	13.46	6.9						
9	15	O/C				11.51		6.31	6.89				
9	4	O/C									19.8	7.84	7.75
9	5	O/C										7.12	6.47
9	5	O/C										7.92	7.38
9	5	O/C									18.57	7.09	6.61
9	5	O/C									18.86	7.33	6.94
9	5	O/C									18.77	7.38	7.03
9	5	O/C									19.93	8.11	6.41
9	12	O/C									19.16	6.75	6.52
9	13	O/C									21.5	7.88	7.65
9	14	O/C									20.14	7.8	7.1
9	15	O/C									19.36	7.07	7.15
9	15	O/C									20.05	7.75	7.14
9	27	O/C									22.33	8.48	7.89
9	5	S			10.67		9.68	11.33	12.68	21.33			
9	5	S		8.35									
9	5	S	18.94	7.84									
10	3	S											13.81

Table 13.13 Measurements taken on the 1990 tooth assemblage

quent than at the nearby broch of Dun Vulan (Mulville 1999), while comparable to the nearby farmstead of Bornais mound 1 (Mulville and Powell in Sharples 2012b: tab. 111).

As at Cill Donnain, dog is present in very small numbers at other contemporary sites in the Western Isles, and cats are rare on the islands, with the only other examples being recovered from Dun Vulan (Mulville 1999).

Red deer were probably introduced to the Western Isles during the Neolithic (Serjeantson 1990) and appear to have had a ritual and social significance beyond that of a meat and antler source throughout the prehistory of the islands. The presence of very young red deer in the Cill Donnain tooth assemblage indicates that there was a breeding population of deer in the islands, and this is borne out by evidence from other sites (Smith and Mulville 2004; Mulville in Sharples 2012b: 341–2, tab. 111). Red deer remains have been recovered from a handful of special deposits on Iron Age sites at Northton, Harris (Simpson *et al.* 2006) and A'Cheardach Bheag, South Uist (Fairhurst 1971) and pictorial representations have been identified at Kilpheder wheelhouse (Lethbridge 1952; Morris 2005).

In the Early and Middle Iron Age red deer would appear to have been an important source of meat, but the quantities of red deer bone decline during the Late Iron Age (Morris 2005). Deer also appear to be less well represented on prehistoric sites in the Uists than they are on other Hebridean islands, probably because suitable habitats for deer were less extensive, and there was possibly less need to supplement agricultural food production with wild resources on the Uists than on other islands (McCormick 2006). That said, red deer form a relatively substantial proportion of the faunal assemblage at Bronze Age–Iron Age Cladh Hallan nearby (Jacqui Mulville pers. comm.; Mulville and Powell in prep.).

The deer assemblage from the majority of phases at Cill Donnain III is too small to identify any temporal trends in deer numbers. As is seen at other Iron Age sites in the Outer Hebrides, the deer assemblage at Cill Donnain is dominated by antler fragments and limb extremities (partially because these are numerous in the skeleton, relatively dense and useful as raw materials); other post-cranial elements are, however, also present in small numbers. The presence of foot bones with low meat-bearing potential at the majority of sites indicates that whole animals were probably brought in to be butchered, suggesting some use of these animals' hides as well as meat and antler (*cf* Mulville and Powell in Sharples 2012b: 306).

As is the case at other Iron Age sites in the Western Isles, imported minor species are rare at Cill Donnain. Although imported wild species are uncommon at almost every site, hare, badger, pine marten and roe deer were recovered from Dun Vulan, where they were associated with the broch inhabitants' likely high status (Mulville 1999: tables 10.36, 10.38). Native wild species such as otter, seal and whale are sporadically present in small numbers on the majority of contemporary settlements, but do not appear to have made up an important part of the economy at any site in the region (Clarke 1962; Mulville 1999; Halstead 2003; Cartledge *et al.* in Sharples 2012b; Mulville and Powell in Sharples 2012b).

The paucity of birds at Cill Donnain III is in sharp contrast to the relatively large number of bird bones recovered from nearby Dun Vulan (Cartledge and Grimbley 1999), Bornais mound 1 (Cartledge in Sharples 2012b: 195–6), and Baile Sear, North Uist (Serjeantson 2003), although smaller numbers were recovered at Cnip, Lewis (Hamilton Dyer 2006) and Hornish Point, South Uist (Serjeantson 2003).

These differences in bird-bone assemblage size may, to some extent, be due to differing recovery practices, in particular the loss in the years since the Cill Donnain excavations took place of the heavy residues from the flotation of environmental samples. Even so, a large proportion of the sea and wetland birds typically recovered from contemporary sites in the Hebrides (such as gannets, gulls, geese, cormorants, shags, ducks, swans, and great auks) have bones of a size that would have been retrieved by the systematic dry-sieving on site during each excavation season. It is, therefore, likely that the lack of bird bone from Cill Donnain is a result of differential deposition of bird remains or of taphonomy.

Age at death

High rates of infant mortality for cattle appear to be a characteristic of Iron Age sites in the Hebrides. At Dun Vulan (Mulville 1999), Bornais mound 1 (Mulville and Powell in Sharples 2012b: 233–9), Cnip (McCormick 2006), Baile Sear and Hornish Point (Halstead 1998), as at Cill Donnain III, a large proportion of the cattle were killed in the first few months of life. Traditionally, the occurrence of high levels of cattle infant mortality on settlements has been interpreted as evidence of an economy organized to optimize milk production and dairying (Payne 1973; Legge 1981). Logically, in a milk-based economy, animals not required for breeding or milk production (*i.e.* primarily males) would be killed as early as possible to minimize unnecessary costs, while milk-producing and breeding females would be killed at the end of their useful lives.

A dilemma arising from this model is whether or not primitive cattle breeds required their calves to be present during milking to stimulate milk let-down (McCormick 1992; McCormick 2006). Although historical and pictorial evidence of milking in the presence of calves from Near Eastern and European contexts has been used in support of the argument that calves were essential, other authors have suggested various techniques early farmers might have used to circumvent this problem (Sherratt 1981; Clutton-Brock 1981); for example, Martin Martin (1703 [1989]), writing about Skye in the late seventeenth/early eighteenth century, describes the practice of manipulating cows to allow milking by covering a substitute calf with the skin of their own slaughtered calf. Some Roman and English Medieval historical sources advocate a cull of infant animals (goat and cattle) to optimize milk production (Halstead 1998).

Halstead (1998) has suggested that these apparent discrepancies in the potential for milk let-down in primitive breeds, with or without a calf present, may be attributed to differing husbandry conditions and levels of nutrition in different farming contexts; milk let-down is easier for animals with good nutrition and shelter, but needs external stimulus under less ideal conditions. While it may be expected that the Western Isles would have posed a challenging environment for cattle-farming, the true impact of the islands' climate and resource availability cannot be unpicked without further evidence of the conditions in which cattle were kept and of their nutritional constraints.

Further support for the occurrence and/or importance of dairying in the Iron Age economy on the islands comes from the analysis of lipid and protein residues on pottery sherds from the Bronze Age–Early Iron Age site at Cladh Hallan and the Iron Age broch at Dun Vulan, where numerous vessels have been found to contain cattle milk residues (Craig *et al.* 2005); however, Mc-Cormick (2006) points out that the scale of dairying activity is difficult to assess using these techniques.

Halstead (1998) and Mulville (1999) also explore the possibility that the high level of infant cattle deaths at Iron Age sites in the Outer Hebrides may be a result of high levels of natural infant mortality brought on by poor living conditions. They conclude that the difference between mortality patterns for sheep/goat and cattle at these sites suggests a deliberate cull of neonatal animals, although they concede that differences in sheep/goat and cattle mortality may derive from variations in husbandry or disposal practices (*e.g.* the stalling of cattle and open grazing of sheep), which would have led to differences in mortality rate, and would mean that neonatal calves were more likely to be disposed of on site.

Although winter-stalling of cattle is mentioned in post-Medieval ethnographic accounts from the region (Smith 2012; Carmichael 1884; Fenton 1986), evidence for stalled cattle in the form of shed deciduous teeth is relatively scarce, having been recovered only at Baile Sear (Halstead 2003) and Dun Vulan (Mulville 1999). Evidence for at least one very young calf having been eaten at Cill Donnain can be seen in filleting butchery-marks on a neonatal proximal tibia and femur.

An alternative reason for a cull of very young cattle may be a deficit in winter fodder supplies or limited grazing resources. If a farmer has only enough resources to feed a limited number of cattle year-round, it is economically rational to dispose as soon as possible of those animals that cannot be supported in the long term, to avoid draining the resources available to feed the sustainable cattle population. The level of resource stress

experienced by the Iron Age inhabitants of Cill Donnain is difficult to assess, although the ability to produce enough hay to over-winter livestock is a common feature of ethnographic accounts throughout the North Atlantic region (Amorosi *et al.* 1998).

A relatively short growing season and the scarcity of leaf fodder in the Western Isles might have restricted fodder production, and eighteenth-century accounts from the islands support this (McCormick 1998). Abundant seaweed resources are likely to have been available to contribute to the diet of livestock although this was also an important fertilizer and fuel resource (Martin 1703 [1989]; Carmichael 1884; Fenton 1986; Smith 2012); a sample of Late Iron Age cattle, sheep and pig bone from Bornais subjected to C/N isotopic analysis does not demonstrate a significant marine element in the animals' diet (Mulville *et al.* 2009).

A third and final interpretation of the high proportion of very young cattle at these sites is that older cattle were removed from the settlement and their bones were deposited elsewhere. Halstead (1998) has identified some evidence that special deposits from settlements in the islands (though rare) tend to contain bones of sub-adult and adult cattle, and he has speculated that this could point to animals of this age group having been treated differently to others; however, he also points out that the apparent meaning attributed to these animals might have related to their rarity within the animal population.

Parker Pearson *et al.* (1996) and Mulville and Powell (in Sharples 2012b: 236) consider that a level of infant mortality as high as that observed at Dun Vulan (75%) and Bornais mound 1 (90% dead by the age of 8 months) is too extreme to maintain a sustainable herd of cattle, and suggest that the animals recovered must have formed only part of the animal population raised on these settlements. This has been shown to be the case at Late Iron Age Bornais, where spatial analysis of cattle bones indicates that bones within house floors from mound 1 are mostly of animals over 2 years of age (Cartledge *et al.* in Sharples 2012b: 101–2; *i.e.* those that are missing from most other Iron Age deposits from the islands) while, elsewhere at Bornais, infant cattle dominate during this period (Mulville and Powell in Sharples 2012b).

The fusion and tooth-wear data for sheep/goat at Cill Donnain suggest that sheep/goat were farmed using a very different husbandry regime to the cattle. Although there is evidence for some infant mortality, there seems to be a much steadier attrition of the population, with similar numbers of animals being killed for each year of life up to around 4 years of age, with a few animals surviving well into old age. This pattern would usually be interpreted as evidence for a meat-optimizing husbandry strategy, where the majority of animals are killed between *c.*18 and 30 months of age, with a breeding population of ewes being maintained into old age (Payne 1973). This does not preclude the use of these animals for milk and wool production (or indeed some culling of surplus animals), but these products were not necessarily the primary reason for rearing sheep/goats.

A similar meat-based economy has been observed in sheep/goat mortality profiles from Dun Vulan (Parker Pearson *et al*. 1996; Mulville 1999), Sollas (Finlay 1991), Cnip (McCormick 2006), Hornish Point and Baile Sear (Halstead 2003), while the evidence from Iron Age Bornais suggests an economy focusing on both meat and wool production (Mulville and Powell in Sharples 2012b).

Pigs provide no secondary products, and the main function of pig farming is to produce meat and fat; it is therefore unremarkable that the vast majority of pigs at Cill Donnain were killed before they reached skeletal maturity, a pattern that is mirrored at contemporary sites across the Western Isles such as Sollas (Finlay 1991), Dun Vulan (Mulville 1999) and Bornais mound 1 (Mulville and Powell in Sharples 2012b: 238–9).

The presence of infant, neonatal and foetal cattle and sheep/goat indicates that, like other comparable Iron Age sites in the Western Isles (Mulville 1999; Parker Pearson *et al*. 1996), Cill Donnain was certainly occupied during the spring and summer months.

Conclusion

Animal husbandry and exploitation at Cill Donnain III appear to be consistent with that observed on other con-temporary settlements in the Outer Hebrides. The Cill Donnain assemblage also appears to be relatively consistent between the site phases, with no clear spatial or temporal differences observed. However, the small numbers of bones from the Bronze Age levels (phases 1 and 2) at Cill Donnain makes it difficult to say much about these early phases with any confidence.

The bulk of the bone material from all phases is domestic in character. No specialized butchery practices were apparent and, for all of the main taxa present, whole animals were brought to the site for butchery. The main food animals were sheep and cattle, supplemented by small amounts of pig. Sheep were probably kept primarily for their meat, although this does not preclude their use in wool or milk production. The large number of cattle killed in the first few months of life suggests that dairy activities were an important aspect of the economy, although relatively frequent butchery-marks on cattle bones indicate that cattle were also eaten. Wild species breeding along the islands' coastline, such as seal and otter, are present, as are red deer, but the exploitation of wild animals for food appears to have been minimal. In contrast, red deer antler and cetacean bone, as well as the long bones of domesticates, were an important raw material for bone-working.

Chapter 14 The carbonized plant remains

Pam Grinter and Soultana-Maria Valamoti

Introduction

This report examines material extracted from samples taken during the 1989 and 1991 seasons of excavations at Cill Donnain III. The material recovered from samples taken during the 1990 season has not been located and is probably lost. It was decided at the beginning of the excavation, in 1989, that samples would be taken on a judgmental basis from sealed contexts that appeared to contain charred material. This decision was necessary given the limitations on time and labour.

The aims of examining the plant remains were:

- to ascertain the species of any cultivated plants found;
- to see if cultivated crops formed part of the economy of the site;
- to look for evidence of early stages of crop-processing.

In addition to these aims, when analyzing the 1991 season's material, we also hoped:

- to determine any changes in species composition over time;
- to attempt to identify any spatial differences in use of the areas between the piers of the wheelhouse.

Methodology

All samples were processed on site by water flotation, using a mesh of 1mm aperture to retain the residues. The flots were collected in two successive sieves of 1mm and 0.3mm mesh sizes and were then air-dried. A total of 18 samples from the 1989 season and 14 from the 1991 season were available to the authors for examination. The coarse flots were sub-sampled randomly using a riffle box; the resultant fractions were sorted progressively until 500 crop items were reached where possible. Fine flots were sorted in their entirety. Sorting and identification were carried out using a low-power binocular microscope at magnifications of ×10–×40.

Soil volume was recorded during the flotation process for the samples taken during the 1989 season and has been used to estimate the density of carbonized material, and to enable comparisons to be made between samples. This information was unavailable for the 1991 samples.

Quantification and identification

To avoid problems when quantifying broken cereal grains, it was decided to count cereal grains as single examples only if the embryo or embryo end was present. Each weed seed has been counted as whole unless the seed has split into clear halves, as with some legumes, in which case two halves have been treated as one seed. Where a single half survives, this has been counted as one seed.

Identifications were made according to the following criteria:

- Barley (*Hordeum* sp.) grains were identified by their shape from above, which is narrow at both ends and widest in the middle. Only where ridges were visible on the dorsal surface, or where hulls still adhered to grains, were they counted as hulled barley.
- Quantification of straight and asymmetrical barley grains was attempted for the 1989 material but this was not carried out for material from the 1991 season given its poor preservation and distortion of grains from charring.
- It is sometimes possible, when preservation is good, to attempt to determine quantities of two- or six-row barley (*Hordeum distichon* or *Hordeum vulgare*); this is normally done by calculating the ratio of straight to asymmetrical grains, this being 2:1 in six-row barley (*Hordeum vulgare*). However, because much of the material from both seasons was poorly preserved, eroded or distorted, this was not attempted.
- Weed seeds were identified by use of various illustrations in botanical atlases (Beijetinck 1947; Berggren 1969; 1981). The taxonomy and habitat information used in this report follows Stace (1991).

Context number	1				2	3	4				6		7	8	9	12	15	
Square number	81	83	15	68	46	55	15	15	60	16	15	16	16	15	16	85	58	16
Sample number	2	3	4	12	6	1	7	10	11	15	5	9	13	8	14	19	16	17
Volume of soil floated (l)	40	60	45	20	45	20	28	50	50	40	25	50	8	30	8	43	40	50
Fraction	1	1	1	1	1	1	1	1	1	1	1	1	1	1	1	1	1/16	1/8
Hordeum hulled asymmetric grains	1	0	1	0	0	0	0	0	0	1	0	0	0	0	0	1	16	46
Hordeum hulled symmetric grain	0	0	0	1	0	0	0	0	0	0	0	0	0	0	0	0	3	48
Hordeum hulled indet grains	0	4	11	0	0	0	2	2	17	12	14	31	3	4	0	33	295	358
Hordeum naked grains	0	0	0	0	0	0	0	0	0	0	0	0	0	0	0	0	1	0
Hordeum indet. grains	9	41	39	32	0	0	16	9	41	26	27	68	7	17	3	100	416	355
Triticum/Hordeum grains	1	2	1	1	0	0	0	0	2	4	3	0	0	1	0	5	6	4
Cereal grains indet.	0	1	8	2	0	0	0	0	2	8	0	4	2	2	0	12	2	12
Internodes	0	0	0	0	0	0	0	0	0	0	0	2	0	0	0	4	0	1
Ranunculaceae *Ranunculus* sp.	0	0	0	0	0	0	0	0	0	0	0	0	0	0	0	2	0	0
Caryophyllaceae/Chenopodiaceae	0	0	0	0	0	0	0	0	0	0	0	1	0	0	0	0	0	0
Polygonaceae *Rumex* sp.	1	0	0	0	0	0	0	0	1	3	0	6	0	1	0	2	0	0
Polygonaceae *Polygonum* sp.	0	0	1	0	0	0	1	4	0	0	0	4	0	0	0	14	0	0
Polygonaceae	0	0	1	0	0	0	0	0	1	0	0	1	0	0	0	0	0	0
Brassicaceae *Brassica/Sinapis*	0	0	0	0	0	0	0	0	1	2	0	1	0	0	0	6	0	0
Brassicaceae cf *Brassica/Sinapis*	0	0	0	0	0	0	0	0	0	0	0	1	0	1	0	0	0	0
Convolvulaceae *Convulvulus* sp.	0	0	0	0	0	0	0	0	0	0	1	0	0	1	0	3	0	0
Rubiaceae *Galium* cf *aparine* L.	0	0	1	0	0	0	0	0	1	0	0	0	0	1	0	0	0	0
Rubiaceae *Galium* cf *palustre* L.	0	0	0	0	0	0	0	2	0	4	0	2	0	1	0	0	1	0
Cyperaceae	0	0	4	1	0	0	0	1	0	3	0	2	0	0	1	1	0	0
Cyperaceae/Polygonaceae	0	0	0	0	0	0	2	1	4	2	0	4	0	0	0	4	0	0
Poaceae sp.	1	1	3	1	0	0	2	2	2	3	2	13	0	0	0	1	0	0
Wild species indet.	0	0	2	0	0	0	3	1	5	1	1	8	2	1	1	6	0	3

Table 14.1 Samples of carbonized plant remains from Cill Donnain III (1989)

Context	Square no.	Sample no.	% wild species per total number of seed & chaff
1	83	3	2%
1	15	4	17%
1	68	12	5%
4	15	7	30%
4	15	10	50%
4	60	11	19%
4	16	15	26%
6	15	5	8%
6	16	9	29%
8	15	8	42.8%
12	85	19	20%
15	58	16	0.1%
15	16	17	0.4%

Samples with fewer than 20 seeds are excluded.

Table 14.2 Percentage of wild species per total number of seeds and chaff from Cill Donnain III (1989)

Results from the 1989 material

Of the 18 samples examined from the 1989 season (Table 14.1), two contained no charred seeds (context 2/1989, sample 6; context 3/1989, sample 1). However, two samples (context 15/1989, samples 16 and 17) were rich in barley *(Hordeum* sp.). Five samples contained relatively low quantities of barley and some weed seeds (context 1/1989, sample 4; context 4/1989, samples 11 and 15; context 6/1989, sample 9; context 12/1989, sample 19). The remaining nine samples contained fewer than 50 seeds.

In the case of context 15/1989 (samples 16 and 17) the samples certainly represent a cleaned crop of barley, given the absence of other species. The high density of barley grains in these samples indicates that they derive from a major processing accident, perhaps associated with parching. Context 1/1989 (samples 3 and 12) con-tained seeds in much lower densities but these were also almost exclusively barley grains.

Context 1/1989 (sample 4), context 4/1989 (samples 7, 10, 11 and 15), context 6/1989 (sample 9), context 8/1989 (sample 8) and context 12/1989 (sample 19) are all of similar composition. They contain both barley and wild species, the latter in all cases being more than 17% of the sample (Table 14.2).

Results from the 1991 material

Of the 14 samples examined from the 1991 season (Table 14.3), two contained no charred seeds (context 103, sample 3; context 135, sample 5), three were found to be rich in barley (context 177, sample 10; context 179, sample 11; context 182, sample 11 [*sic.*]). The remaining nine samples contained fewer than 50 seeds.

Context Number	103	104	134	135	142	142	166	173	177	179	182	183	185	190
Sample Number	3	6	4	5	17	18	9	2	10	11	11	12	16	15
Fraction	1	1	1	1	1	1	1	1	1/8	1/4	1	1	1	1
Hordeum hulled indet. grains	[1]	3	4	0	2	3	2	0	354	179	183	17	7	4
Hordeum hulled indet. sprouted grains	0	0	0	0	0	0	0	0	0	1	0	0	0	0
Hordeum hulled indet. *cf* sprouted grains	0	0	0	0	0	0	0	0	0	4	0	0	0	0
cf Hordeum indet. grains	0	11	2	0	3	4	0	16	404	385	328	16	16	0
Cereal grains	0	0	1	0	2	9	3	2	32	10	4	0	2	7
Detached plumules (sprouting embryos)	0	0	0	0	0	0	0	0	0	1	0	0	0	0
Internodes	0	0	0	0	0	0	0	0	0	0	2	0	0	0
Chenopodiaceae	0	0	0	0	0	0	0	0	2	0	0	0	0	0
Caryophyllaceae *cf Stellaria*	0	0	0	0	0	0	0	0	1	0	0	0	0	0
Fabaceae (spherical type)	0	0	0	0	0	0	0	0	2	0	0	0	0	0
Polygonaceae *Rumex* sp.	0	3	0	0	0	4	0	0	0	0	0	6	3	0
Rubiaceae *Galium cf aparine* L.	0	0	0	0	0	0	0	0	0	0	3	2	1	0
Rubiaceae *Galium cf palustre* L.	0	2	0	0	0	0	0	1	4	0	3	0	0	0
Cyperaceae	0	1	0	0	0	7	0	0	0	0	0	0	2	0

Note: the carbonized barley grain sent for radiocarbon-dating from layer 103 (OxA-3355) was hand collected during the 1991 excavations, as was one of the dated grains from layer 177 (OxA-3356)

Table 14.3 Samples of carbonized plant remains from Cill Donnain III (1991)

The only cereal identified from the samples was hulled barley *(Hordeum* sp.). Preservation of grains was generally poor, perhaps as a result of the intense nature of the fire in which they were charred or because of post-depositional erosion of their surfaces. This poor preservation of the grains has affected recording of the ratio of symmetrical to asymmetrical grains. However, some asymmetrical grains were present in the material from both seasons and it is therefore possible that both six-row barley *(Hordeum vulgare)* and two-row barley *(Hordeum distichon)* were present.

Sample 11 from context 179 contained a detached plumule (sprouting embryo) and five grains of barley that appear to exhibit signs of sprouting. Such a small quantity of sprouted grain is unlikely to be an indication of malting in the process of beer-making (Hillman 1982) and is more likely to represent a crop that has begun to germinate in the field as a consequence of a wet summer *(ibid.:* 137). In such cases, in order to try to salvage the crop it would have been necessary to dry the cereal heads prior to storage, in order to reduce their moisture content. Fenton (1978: 375) cites three main reasons for parching grain:

- when the summer is short and moist, a crop may never ripen properly;
- kilns are required for drying malt, for stopping germination in the seed once it has started, as part of the process of making ale;
- to prepare the grain for grinding.

These illustrate some of the reasons that grain would have been put into close contact with fire. It is possible that, during activities at Cill Donnain such as drying or preparation for grinding, accidents resulted in the charring of grains. It is also possible that accidental burning took place during grain storage, or that grain was destroyed intentionally because of insect infestation.

However, in this instance, no insect damage was noted on the grains, so this possibility can be discounted.

The samples examined contained no rachis fragments and had very few weed seeds. No large weed seeds were found in the cereal-rich samples, and this would appear to indicate that the samples represent grain that had gone through the final hand-picking stage of crop-processing to become a stored crop or one being prepared for use (Hillman 1981). Of the weed seeds present, only cleavers *(Galium* cf *aparine* and cf *palustre)* are sometimes classed as a weed of cultivation. The other weeds present include small weeds of the goosefoot family (Chenopodiaceae), stitchworts *(Stellaria* sp.), and dock *(Rumex* sp.). These plants have a range of habitats that include disturbed ground and waste areas. They could have been brought into contact with fire as part of the fuel that might have consisted of peat, turf or dung (Fenton 1978).

Plant husbandry, land use and subsistence

The evidence from these samples indicates that barley was the major (and, possibly, the only) crop exploited by the occupants of the site at Cill Donnain III. Archaeological evidence for barley in Scotland dates from the Neolithic onwards (Dickson and Dickson 2000; Edwards and Ralston 2003). The small number of samples from Cill Donnain does not allow for the exclusion of other potential crops such as oats, rye or wheat. However, the archaeobotanical evidence from other Iron Age sites in the Uists at Baile Sear and Hornish Point (Jones 2003) has shown the same dominance of barley, with the persistent absence of oats and rye. Similar findings have come from Cnip, Lewis (Church and Cressey 2006) and Dun Bharabhat, Lewis (Church 2000).

The consistent occurrence of barley in samples from Bronze Age and Iron Age sites in the Outer Hebrides probably derives from a subsistence strategy chosen to cope with the edaphic and climatic conditions of the region. Barley has a preference for calcareous soils, although it is not restricted to them, and the existence of the machair must have provided suitable conditions for this crop. Nevertheless, cultivation of the machair is not an easy task; fields are exposed to wind, thus putting seed beds at risk, and additional nutrients are required on a regular basis, rendering rotation and fertilization crucial factors for maintaining the potential of arable land (Grant 1979).

Conclusion

Of the 32 samples examined from the 1989 and 1991 seasons at Cill Donnain, only five were rich in charred plant remains. The only cereal present was hulled barley, possibly both two-row and six-row types (*H. distichon* and *H. vulgare*). The lack of rachis fragments and large weed seeds indicates that charring of the cereal occurred in a fully cleaned crop. It would seem likely that this crop was being prepared for human consumption at the time of charring, as it would be unnecessary to process the cereal to this advanced stage for animal consumption. Therefore this would indicate that the grain came into contact with fire during one of the processes cited by Fenton (1978) or during an accidental blaze whilst the grain was in storage.

The quantities of cereal involved do not indicate large-scale crop storage. More likely, they represent the remains of domestic debris or small-scale parching accidents.

The 18 samples that contained fewer than 50 grains may be representative of 'background noise' on the site. Areas that were in regular use by people would have accumulated a few charred fragments, representing the various activities going on in the surrounding area. Sweepings from fire- or hearth-sides would have contained charred fragments of seeds both from food preparation and from the contents of fuel for the fire.

No samples contained evidence for the early stages of crop-processing. If those early stages of crop-processing were taking place on or near the site, it is probable that the processing waste was subsequently used in some way that prevented it from coming into contact with fire.

Hulled barley formed an important part of the economy for the people of Cill Donnain III throughout the site's occupation from the Early Bronze Age to the Late Iron Age. There would appear to have been no change over time between the Bronze Age phases and the later 'midden' phases of the site.

A number of samples come from likely primary contexts within Cill Donnain. Those from the phase 5 hearths within the wheelhouse (177 and 179) are particularly rich in carbonized barley grains. A sample from an unknown location within the wheelhouse floor (166; phase 5) is also a likely primary context but included only five cereal grains. The remaining samples come from contexts that can be regarded as secondary:

- midden (1/1989, 15/1989, 103),
- wall core (4/1989, 6/1989, 9/1989),
- possible wall core/possible pre-wheelhouse midden (104)
- fills (8/1989, 134, 173),
- pits (142, 183, 185),
- gullies (182, 190),
- a peat ash spread (12/1989),
- windblown sand (2/1989, 7/1989, 135),
- possible pre-construction levelling layer (3/1989).

Of the secondary contexts, high concentrations of barley grains were obtained from the midden layers, the peat ash spread, wall cores (4/1989, 6/1989) and a gully (182). The latter is cut into hearth 177, and the carbonized grain may be residual from that context.

Unfortunately, no insights can be gained into spatial patterning within the wheelhouse floor because only one sample (position unknown) appears to have been taken from floor 166.

Finally, the Cill Donnain III assemblage permits useful comparisons with other Bronze Age and Iron Age settlements in the site's vicinity. Cill Donnain was excavated before these other sites so its judgmental sampling strategy limits full comparison with the more systematic strategies employed at Dun Vulan (Smith 1999), Sligeanach (Smith in Sharples 2012a) and Bornais mound 1 (Colledge and Smith in Sharples 2012b; Summers and Bond in Sharples 2012b).

At Early Bronze Age Sligeanach and Late Bronze Age Cladh Hallan, cereals are dominated by hulled six-row barley (*Hordeum vulgare* L.; Smith in Sharples 2012a; Smith in prep.). These sites reflect the general pattern that is seen at other Scottish sites (Dickson and Dickson 2000) and elsewhere in Britain (van der Veen 1992).

At the Middle Iron Age wheelhouse at Sligeanach mound 27 (Sharples 2012a) and the Middle Iron Age broch of Dun Vulan (Smith 1999), hulled six-row barley (*Hordeum vulgare* L.) was the dominant cultivated species. The same is true of Late Iron Age levels at Dun Vulan and Bornais mound 1. At Dun Vulan other cereals were represented by a few grains of wheat, oat and a possible rye grain (*ibid.*: 298). At Bornais mound 1, oats were found in much lower quantities than barley but became more common during the Late Iron Age (Summers and Bond in Sharples 2012b: 230–1). It seems that wheat and rye were not cultivated at Late Iron Age Bornais; flax was present at mound 1 but it is not possible to be certain that it was being deliberately cultivated before the Norse period (Summers and Bond in Sharples 2012b: 231–2).

Thus the Cill Donnain III assemblage closely matches adjacent contemporary sites in its dependence on hulled barley, but it differs in having no other cultigens, notably lacking oats. Whether this is a reflection of the more limited sampling of deposits at Cill Donnain or a real difference in subsistence practices between adjacent settlements is difficult to say.

Chapter 15 Marine mollusca

Sean Bell and Karen Godden

Introduction

Quantities of shells of both marine and land species were recovered during the three seasons of archaeological excavation at Cill Donnain III. ARCUS (Archaeological Research Consultancy University of Sheffield) was commissioned by Sheffield University's Department of Archaeology to undertake an analysis of the shell material retrieved.

Methodology

All the shell material recovered was recorded in the field by its context number and location within the site grid; the shell fragments were cleaned and identified (generally to genus level) on South Uist, and then discarded. The assemblage was not, therefore, available during the course of the analysis undertaken by ARCUS. As marine snails were identified on site, it has been assumed that results marked simply as 'snail' in the primary archive were land snail species.

A total of 127,705 fragments of marine shell from 1989–1991 were identified, of which 125,044 came from stratified contexts (Table 15.1). For each context, the numbers of fragments recorded by individual grid points

Year	Limpet	Common periwinkle (winkle)	Flat periwinkle	Dog whelk	Common whelk	Cockle	Mussel
1990-91	24742	97197	43	330	20	368	17
1989	226	1969		7			
TOTAL	24968	99166	43	337	20	368	17

Year	Topshell	Scallop	Razorshell	Oyster	Cowrie	Indet.	Rissoa parva
1990-91	47	15	1	2	29	29	1
1989		1					
TOTAL	47	16	1	2	29	29	1

Table 15.1 Total numbers of marine shell fragments recovered from Cill Donnain III, by species

has been combined to give a total number of marine shell fragments for each context. These totals form the basis of the analysis. Spatial distributions within single contexts have not been considered. Tables 15.2 and 15.3 summarize the assemblage by context.

Scientific nomenclature and biotope information is sourced from Beedham (1972), Hayward and Ryland (1990), and MarLIN (the Marine Life Information Network for Britain and Ireland).

Results from the 1989 excavations

A total of 2,203 shell fragments were recovered during the excavations undertaken in 1989. These are summarized in Table 15.4.

A total of 1,947 shell fragments were recovered from context 1/1989, the Late Iron Age midden (phase 9). Of these fragments, a total of 1,738 (89%), were identified as common periwinkle (*Littorina littorea*).[1] The remainder of the assemblage consisted mainly of limpets (*Patella vulgata*) with a few examples of dog whelk (*Nucella lapillus*) and one fragment of scallop shell (*Pecten maximus*).

A total of 185 fragments were recovered from context 3/1989, a context number used for a layer predating the wheelhouse's construction (phase 3; see Chapter 5) and also for a layer in the southern trench probably belonging to phase 4 (see Chapter 6). This assemblage was also dominated by common periwinkle, with occasional examples of limpet and a single fragment of dog whelk.

Results from the 1990 and 1991 excavations

The excavations focused on the wheelhouse, whose construction dates to the late Middle Iron Age, and on the Late Iron Age midden deposits by which it was ultimately covered in the centuries following its abandonment. The

---

[1] *Littorina littorea* has the English name of 'common periwinkle', but is more often referred to as 'winkle' in ordinary speech. *Littorina obtusata* has the common name 'flat periwinkle' and in ordinary speech is usually called simply 'periwinkle'.

Context	Limpet	Common periwinkle (winkle)	Flat periwinkle	Topshell	Dog whelk	Common whelk	Cowrie	Rissoa parva
0 [U/S]	167	2358	0	0	3	0	0	0
100 [U/S]	32	98	0	2	1	0	0	0
1989								
1 [1989]	203	1738	0	0	5	0	0	0
2 [1989]	7	63	0	0	1	0	0	0
3 [1989]	16	168	0	0	1	0	0	0
1989 total	*226*	*1969*	*0*	*0*	*7*	*0*	*0*	*0*
1990								
4	167	1747	0	0	9	1	1	1
5	7184	42135	0	6	101	11	8	0
6	4	31	0	0	0	0	0	0
7	10	176	0	0	0	0	0	0
8	186	1136	0	0	6	0	2	0
11	881	3999	0	0	3	2	0	0
12	224	404	0	0	4	0	0	0
13	351	1217	0	0	3	0	0	0
14	422	1674	0	0	5	1	3	0
15	447	1394	0	0	9	0	0	0
16	1	16	0	0	0	0	0	0
18	390	1887	0	1	5	0	2	0
20	19	112	0	0	0	0	0	0
22	134	141	0	0	0	0	0	0
24	1224	4597	0	2	23	0	1	0
25	599	2687	1	2	11	1	3	0
27	149	530	0	0	3	0	0	0
28	74	277	0	0	1	0	0	0
29	170	553	0	0	5	0	0	0
31	305	1038	0	0	6	0	1	0
32	386	1365	0	0	10	0	0	0
33	337	553	0	0	3	1	0	0
34	3	12	0	0	1	0	0	0
54	5	74	0	0	0	0	0	0
58	1214	3570	0	0	25	1	1	0
59	34	104	0	0	0	0	0	0
60	94	273	0	0	3	0	0	0
61	39	82	0	0	1	0	0	0
101	9	20	0	0	0	0	0	0
102	269	1200	0	3	4	0	1	0
103	1338	7933	0	2	19	0	2	0
104	544	533	0	0	7	0	0	0
105	138	218	0	0	1	0	0	0
106	11	17	0	0	0	0	0	0
130	32	61	2	0	7	0	0	0
131	412	114	4	1	1	0	0	0
132	9	8	0	0	0	0	0	0
134	198	555	1	0	1	0	0	0
135	1264	2584	6	1	8	0	0	0
140	275	928	0	0	3	1	0	0
142	716	1404	0	0	4	0	0	0
149	701	964	1	0	0	0	0	0
153	175	589	1	0	0	0	0	0
157	25	36	0	0	1	0	0	0
160	717	978	7	12	9	0	0	0
162	9	11	0	0	1	0	0	0
163	46	186	0	1	0	0	0	0
165	51	378	0	0	0	0	0	0
166	676	1868	9	12	10	1	0	0
168	39	174	0	0	0	0	0	0
172	33	110	0	0	0	0	0	0
173	800	1575	4	0	1	0	0	0
174	15	51	0	0	0	0	0	0
176	156	434	3	1	2	0	4	0
177	8	28	0	0	1	0	0	0
179	17	34	0	0	0	0	0	0
181	42	133	0	0	0	0	0	0
182	33	104	0	0	0	0	0	0
183	111	287	0	0	0	0	0	0
185	93	173	0	0	0	0	0	0
187	208	446	3	1	2	0	0	0
188	16	14	0	0	0	0	0	0
189	89	112	0	0	1	0	0	0
190	109	242	0	1	2	0	0	0
191	69	144	1	1	0	0	0	0
193	33	88	0	0	0	0	0	0
196	0	7	0	0	0	0	0	0
198	4	43	0	0	0	0	0	0
199	1	10	0	0	0	0	0	0
200	1	10	0	0	0	0	0	0
201	7	42	0	0	0	0	0	0
202	8	15	0	0	0	0	0	0
204	2	6	0	0	0	0	0	0
208	3	4	0	0	0	0	0	0
209	7	25	0	0	0	0	0	0
210	19	61	0	0	0	0	0	0
211	5	14	0	0	0	0	0	0
212	9	10	0	0	0	0	0	0
213	7	16	0	0	0	0	0	0
214	10	4	0	0	0	0	0	0
215	8	15	0	0	0	0	0	0
217	1	2	0	0	0	0	0	0
218	3	8	0	0	0	0	0	0
219	0	9	0	0	0	0	0	0
220	2	5	0	0	0	0	0	0
222	106	373	0	0	8	0	0	0
1990 total	24742	97197	43	47	330	20	29	1

Table 15.2 Sea snails recovered from Cill Donnain III, by context

Context	Cockle	Mussel	Scallop	Oyster	Razorshell	Indeterminate	Land snails
0 [U/S]	0	0	0	0	0	0	4
100 [U/S]	0	0	0	0	0	0	24
1989							
1 [1989]	0	0	1	0	0	0	0
2 [1989]	0	0	0	0	0	0	0
3 [1989]	0	0	0	0	0	0	0
total	*0*	*0*	*1*	*0*	*0*	*0*	*0*
1990							
4	0	0	0	0	0	1	0
5	9	2	8	0	0	8	72
6	0	0	0	0	0	0	0
7	0	0	0	0	0	0	0
8	0	0	0	0	0	2	1
11	0	0	0	0	0	0	0
12	0	0	0	0	0	0	1
13	0	0	0	0	0	0	0
14	0	0	0	0	0	3	0
15	1	1	0	0	0	0	16
16	0	0	0	0	0	0	0
18	0	0	0	0	0	2	6
20	0	0	0	0	0	0	2
22	0	0	0	0	0	0	0
24	2	0	1	0	0	1	47
25	12	1	2	0	0	3	27
27	0	0	0	0	0	0	7
28	0	1	0	0	0	0	8
29	0	0	0	1	0	0	0
31	0	1	0	0	0	1	27
32	0	0	0	0	0	0	1
33	0	0	1	0	0	0	3
34	0	0	0	0	0	0	0
54	0	0	0	0	0	0	0
58	0	1	1	1	0	1	32
59	0	0	0	0	0	0	0
60	0	0	0	0	0	0	0
61	0	0	0	0	0	0	0
101	0	0	0	0	0	0	2
102	7	1	0	0	0	1	2
103	7	2	0	0	0	2	4
104	1	0	0	0	0	0	0
105	0	0	0	0	0	0	0
106	1	0	0	0	0	0	1
130	0	0	0	0	0	0	5
131	0	2	0	0	0	0	34
132	0	0	0	0	0	0	0
134	7	0	0	0	0	0	0
135	98	0	1	0	0	0	3
140	17	0	0	0	0	0	1
142	131	0	0	0	0	0	5
149	66	2	0	0	0	0	2
153	0	0	0	0	0	0	1
157	0	0	0	0	0	0	0
160	7	0	0	0	0	0	5
162	0	0	0	0	0	0	0
163	0	0	0	0	0	0	0
165	0	0	0	0	0	0	0
166	0	2	1	0	0	0	4
168	0	0	0	0	0	0	0
172	0	0	0	0	0	0	0
173	0	0	0	0	0	0	3
174	1	0	0	0	0	0	0
176	0	0	0	0	0	4	0
177	0	0	0	0	0	0	0
179	0	0	0	0	0	0	0
181	0	0	0	0	0	0	0
182	0	0	0	0	0	0	30
183	0	0	0	0	0	0	2
185	0	0	0	0	0	0	1
187	0	0	0	0	1	0	1
188	1	0	0	0	0	0	1
189	0	1	0	0	0	0	0
190	0	0	0	0	0	0	0
191	0	0	0	0	0	0	0
193	0	0	0	0	0	0	0
196	0	0	0	0	0	0	0
198	0	0	0	0	0	0	0
199	0	0	0	0	0	0	0
200	0	0	0	0	0	0	0
201	0	0	0	0	0	0	0
202	0	0	0	0	0	0	0
204	0	0	0	0	0	0	0
208	0	0	0	0	0	0	1
209	0	0	0	0	0	0	0
210	0	0	0	0	0	0	0
211	0	0	0	0	0	0	0
212	0	0	0	0	0	0	1
213	0	0	0	0	0	0	0
214	0	0	0	0	0	0	0
215	0	0	0	0	0	0	0
217	0	0	0	0	0	0	0
218	0	0	0	0	0	0	1
219	0	0	0	0	0	0	0
220	0	0	0	0	0	0	0
222	0	0	0	0	0	0	4
1990 total	368	17	15	2	1	29	364

Table 15.3 Marine bi-valves and land snails recovered from Cill Donnain III, by context

Context	Limpet	Common periwinkle (winkle)	Dog whelk	Scallop	Total
1	203	1738	5	1	1947
2	7	63	1	0	71
3	16	168	1	0	185
Total	226	1969	7	1	2203

Table 15.4 Marine shell recovered in 1989, by context

Context	Limpet	Common periwinkle (winkle)	Flat periwinkle	Dog whelk	Common whelk	Cockle	Mussel	Topshell	Scallop	Cowrie	Oyster	Indet./Other	Total
4	167	1747	0	9	1	0	0	0	0	1	0	2	1927
5	7184	42135	0	101	11	9	2	6	8	8	0	8	49472
6	4	31	0	0	0	0	0	0	0	0	0	0	35
7	10	176	0	0	0	0	0	0	0	0	0	0	186
8	186	1136	0	6	0	0	0	0	0	2	0	2	1332
11	881	3999	0	3	2	0	0	0	0	0	0	0	4885
12	224	404	0	4	0	0	0	0	0	0	0	0	632
13	351	1217	0	3	0	0	0	0	0	0	0	0	1571
14	422	1674	0	5	1	0	0	0	0	3	0	3	2108
15	447	1394	0	9	0	1	1	0	0	0	0	0	1852
16	1	16	0	0	0	0	0	0	0	0	0	0	17
18	390	1887	0	5	0	0	0	1	0	2	0	2	2287
20	19	112	0	0	0	0	0	0	0	0	0	0	131
22	134	141	0	0	0	0	0	0	0	0	0	0	275
27	149	530	0	3	0	0	0	0	0	0	0	0	682
29	170	553	0	5	0	0	0	0	0	0	1	0	729
31	305	1038	0	6	0	0	1	0	0	1	0	1	1352
33	337	553	0	3	1	0	0	0	1	0	0	0	895
54	5	74	0	0	0	0	0	0	0	0	0	0	79
58	1214	3570	0	25	1	0	1	0	1	1	1	1	4815
101	9	20	0	0	0	0	0	0	0	0	0	0	29
102	269	1200	0	4	0	7	1	3	0	1	0	1	1486
103	1338	7933	0	19	0	7	2	2	0	2	0	2	9305
Total	14216	71540	0	210	17	24	8	12	10	21	2	22	86082

Table 15.5 Marine shell recovered in 1990 and 1991 from the Late Iron Age midden (phase 9), by context

Context	Limpet	Common periwinkle (winkle)	Flat periwinkle	Dog whelk	Common whelk	Cockle	Mussel	Topshell	Scallop	Cowrie	Indet.	Total
25	599	2687	1	11	1	12	1	2	2	3	3	3322
28	74	277	0	1	0	0	1	0	0	0	0	353
166	676	1868	9	10	1	0	2	12	1	0	0	2579
172	33	110	0	0	0	0	0	0	0	0	0	143
174	15	51	0	0	0	1	0	0	0	0	0	67
176	156	434	3	2	0	0	0	1	0	4	4	604
177	8	28	0	1	0	0	0	0	0	0	0	37
179	17	34	0	0	0	0	0	0	0	0	0	51
182	33	104	0	0	0	0	0	0	0	0	0	137
183	111	287	0	0	0	0	0	0	0	0	0	398
Total	1722	5880	13	25	2	13	4	15	3	7	7	7691

Table 15.6 Marine shell recovered in 1990 and 1991 from deposits associated with the occupation and abandonment of the wheelhouse (phases 5–8), by context

wheelhouse overlay Early–Middle Bronze Age and Late Bronze Age/Early Iron Age deposits and cut features.

The Late Iron Age midden

A total of 86,082 marine shell fragments were recovered from contexts interpreted as forming part of the midden (phase 9) that post-dated the abandonment of the wheel-house (Table 15.5). Of these fragments, a total of 71,540 (83%) were identified as common periwinkle (*Littorina littorea*). The remainder of the assemblage consisted almost entirely of limpets (*Patella vulgata*), with a few examples of dog whelk (*Nucella lapillus*); unidentified land snails were also present. Other marine species were identified, but these constituted only 116 fragments within the midden assemblage.

Context	Limpet	Common periwinkle (winkle)	Flat periwinkle	Dog whelk	Cockle	Mussel	Topshell	Scallop	Cowrie	Indet./Other	Total
24	1224	4597	0	23	2	0	2	1	1	1	5851
32	386	1365	0	10	0	0	0	0	0	0	1761
34	3	12	0	1	0	0	0	0	0	0	16
59	34	104	0	0	0	0	0	0	0	0	138
60	94	273	0	3	0	0	0	0	0	0	370
61	39	82	0	1	0	0	0	0	0	0	122
104	544	533	0	7	1	0	0	0	0	0	1085
105	138	218	0	1	0	0	0	0	0	0	357
106	11	17	0	0	1	0	0	0	0	0	29
130	32	61	2	7	0	0	0	0	0	0	102
131	412	114	4	1	0	2	1	0	0	0	534
132	9	8	0	0	0	0	0	0	0	0	17
160	717	978	7	9	7	0	12	0	0	0	1730
162	9	11	0	1	0	0	0	0	0	0	21
163	46	186	0	0	0	0	1	0	0	0	233
165	51	378	0	0	0	0	0	0	0	0	429
168	39	174	0	0	0	0	0	0	0	0	213
173	800	1575	4	1	0	0	0	0	0	0	2380
181	42	133	0	0	0	0	0	0	0	0	175
185	93	173	0	0	0	0	0	0	0	0	266
187	208	446	3	2	0	0	1	0	0	1	661
188	16	14	0	0	1	0	0	0	0	0	31
189	89	112	0	1	0	1	0	0	0	0	203
190	109	242	0	2	0	0	1	0	0	0	354
191	69	144	1	0	0	0	1	0	0	0	215
193	33	88	0	0	0	0	0	0	0	0	121
196	0	7	0	0	0	0	0	0	0	0	7
198	4	43	0	0	0	0	0	0	0	0	47
199	1	10	0	0	0	0	0	0	0	0	11
200	1	10	0	0	0	0	0	0	0	0	11
201	7	42	0	0	0	0	0	0	0	0	49
202	8	15	0	0	0	0	0	0	0	0	23
204	2	6	0	0	0	0	0	0	0	0	8
208	3	4	0	0	0	0	0	0	0	0	7
209	7	25	0	0	0	0	0	0	0	0	32
210	19	61	0	0	0	0	0	0	0	0	80
211	5	14	0	0	0	0	0	0	0	0	19
212	9	10	0	0	0	0	0	0	0	0	19
213	7	16	0	0	0	0	0	0	0	0	23
214	10	4	0	0	0	0	0	0	0	0	14
215	8	15	0	0	0	0	0	0	0	0	23
217	1	2	0	0	0	0	0	0	0	0	3
218	3	8	0	0	0	0	0	0	0	0	11
219	0	9	0	0	0	0	0	0	0	0	9
220	2	5	0	0	0	0	0	0	0	0	7
222	106	373	0	8	0	0	0	0	0	0	487
Total	5450	12717	21	78	12	3	19	1	1	2	18304

Table 15.7 Marine shell recovered in 1990 and 1991 from pre-wheelhouse Middle Iron Age layers (phases 3–4), by context

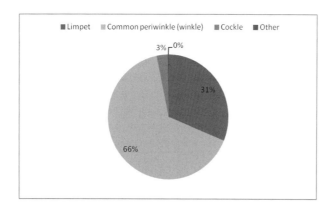

Figure 15.1 Summary of marine shell fragments recovered from Bronze Age deposits (phases 1–2) at Cill Donnain III, based on 10,764 identified fragments

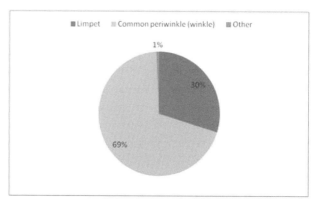

Figure 15.2 Summary of marine shell fragments recovered from phases 3 and 4 at Cill Donnain III, based on 18,304 identified fragments

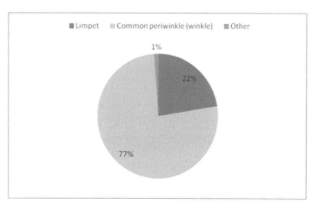

Figure 15.3 Summary of marine shell fragments from phases 5 to 8 at Cill Donnain III, based on 7,691 identified fragments

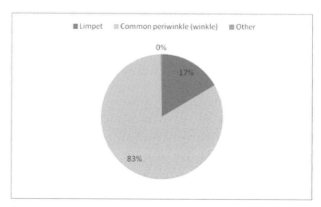

Figure 15.4 Summary of marine shell fragments from phase 9 at Cill Donnain III, based on 86,082 identified fragments

The Middle–Late Iron Age wheelhouse

The wheelhouse was associated with a number of deposits both within it and outside, including context 166, the main floor layer of the wheelhouse. For the purpose of this analysis, all deposits associated with the use, modification and abandonment of the building have been considered as a single assemblage (phases 5–8), summarized in Table 15.6.

A total of 7,691 shell fragments were recovered from contexts associated with the wheelhouse. Of these fragments, a total of 5,880 (76%) were identified as common periwinkle (*Littorina littorea*). The remainder of the assemblage consisted mainly of limpets (*Patella vulgata*), with a few examples of dog whelk (*Nucella lapillus*); unidentified land snails were also present. Other marine species were identified, but these constituted fewer than 100 fragments within this portion of the assemblage.

Middle Iron Age layers pre-dating the wheelhouse

A number of features and deposits underlay the wheelhouse, including pits and postholes sealed by the floor of the wheelhouse. For the purpose of this analysis, all these deposits (phase 3) and those belonging to the construction of the wheelhouse (phase 4) have been considered as a

single assemblage, summarized in Table 15.7. A total of 18,304 marine shell fragments were recovered from contexts interpreted as belonging to the Middle Iron Age cultural layers (and cut features) deposited before and during the construction of the wheelhouse. Of these fragments, a total of 12,717 (69%) were identified as common periwinkle (*Littorina littorea*). The remainder of the assemblage consisted almost entirely of limpets (*Patella vulgata*) with a few examples of dog whelk (*Nucella lapillus*); unidentified land snails were also present. Other marine species were identified, but these constituted fewer than 100 shell fragments within this assemblage.

Bronze Age layers

For the purpose of this analysis, all deposits within this lowest part of the sequence (phases 1–2) have been considered as a single assemblage, summarized in Table 15.8.

A total of 10,764 marine shell fragments were recovered from contexts belonging to the Bronze Age. Of these fragments, a total of 7,060 (66%) were identified as common periwinkle (*Littorina littorea*). The remainder of the assemblage consisted almost entirely of limpets (*Patella vulgata*), with a significantly greater number of

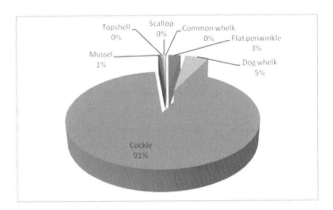

Figure 15.5 Summary of marine shell fragments excluding common periwinkle and limpet from phases 1 and 2 at Cill Donnain III, based on 350 identified fragments

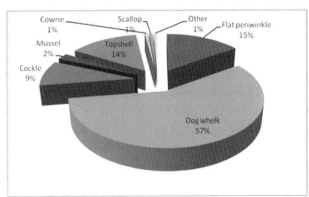

Figure 15.6 Summary of marine shell fragments excluding common periwinkle and limpet, from phases 3 and 4 at Cill Donnain III, based on 137 identified fragments

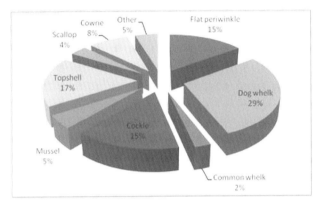

Figure 15.7 Summary of marine shell fragments excluding common periwinkle and limpet from phases 5 to 8 at Cill Donnain III, based on 89 identified fragments

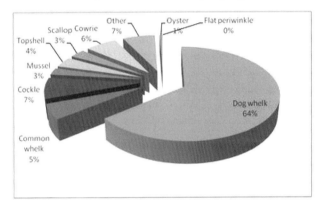

Figure 15.8 Summary of marine shell fragments excluding common periwinkle and limpet from phase 9 at Cill Donnain III, based on 326 identified fragments

cockle fragments (*Cerastoderma edule*) than is seen in any other phase. Other marine species were identified, but these constituted fewer than 50 fragments within this assemblage.

Discussion

The assemblage is dominated by common periwinkle throughout all phases (Figures 15.1–15.4), with the majority of the remainder of the assemblage consisting of limpets. Both species are found on rocks and stones on both the high shore and the sub-littoral fringe. As such, they would have been plentiful and easily observed on the beaches of South Uist. Common periwinkles are also found in sandy and muddy habitats associated with estuaries and mud-flats, and are fairly tolerant of brackish water. This wider habitat range may be the reason for their abundance within the assemblage, rather than an indication of preference by the inhabitants of Cill Donnain.

The proportion of common periwinkles within the assemblage increases over time when comparing the Bronze Age and pre-wheelhouse Middle Iron Age assemblages with those from the occupation of the wheelhouse and the Late Iron Age midden. However, this may be the result of differing sample sizes. The deposits

associated with the midden and the wheelhouse together account for 69% of the marine shell fragments forming the assemblage.

Within the individual deposits forming the Bronze Age assemblage (phases 1–2; Table 15.8, Figure 15.1), the proportion of common periwinkle is generally consistent throughout. Those deposits constituting the pre-wheelhouse Middle Iron Age stage (phases 3–4; Table 15.7, Figure 15.2) have a proportion of common periwinkle generally lower than the overall site figure of 80%; from this stage there are two deposits (contexts 131 and 132; phase 3) in which common periwinkles constitute less than 50 % of the molluscan assemblage.

There is some variation in the proportion of common periwinkles within the deposits associated with the wheelhouse's occupation and abandonment (phases 5–8; Table 15.6, Figure 15.3), from 66% to 80%. This reflects the varied nature of the deposits included in the assemblage. These include deposits from both outside and inside the structure, as well as structural features where deposition was presumably of a more accidental nature within the fabric of the building.

The variation in proportions of common periwinkles within the individual deposits of the Late Iron Age midden (phase 9) is greater (between 51% and 95%), with an

Context	Limpet	Common periwinkle (winkle)	Flat periwinkle	Dog whelk	Common whelk	Cockle	Mussel	Topshell	Scallop	Total
134	198	555	1	1	0	7	0	0	0	762
135	1264	2584	6	8	0	98	0	1	1	3962
140	275	928	0	3	1	17	0	0	0	1224
142	716	1404	0	4	0	131	0	0	0	2255
149	701	964	1	0	0	66	2	0	0	1734
153	175	589	1	0	0	0	0	0	0	765
157	25	36	0	1	0	0	0	0	0	62
Total	3354	7060	9	17	1	319	2	1	1	10764

Table 15.8 Marine shell recovered in 1990 and 1991 from Bronze Age deposits (phases 1–2), by context

overall proportion of common periwinkle (Figure 15.4) greater than that of the deposits associated with the wheel-house (phases 5–8). A midden deposit, however, must not be regarded solely as a definitive reflection of the mollusc-based element of the diet of the population that created the midden. The midden will contain only those shells which, after consumption of the organism, were discarded. Certain shells might have been re-used as a resource, for decoration, trade or utilitarian uses, resulting in deposition away from the midden. Though this is unlikely to drastically alter the marked dominance of common periwinkle, it is a point that must be considered when evaluating the less frequent species within the assemblage (Figures 15.5–15.8). No finds of perforated or decorated shells are recorded in the Cill Donnain site archive, in contrast to Bornais mound 1, where examples were found of scallop, whelk and topshells modified for use as tools or ornaments (Sharples 2012b: 262, 271, 368–9, figs 166, 174).

The proportion of species other than common periwinkle and limpet within the assemblage remained fairly constant over the lengthy period of the site's occupation.[2] The exception is the occurrence in the Bronze Age assemblage of a significant number of cockles (3% of the phase 1–2 assemblage; Figures 15.1, 15.5), whilst the later phases have greater proportions of whelks, with cockles being rare (although never entirely absent). Cockles are often abundant in estuaries and sheltered bays with clean sand, muddy sand, mud or muddy gravel. This contrasts with the majority of other species identified within the assemblages, such as limpets, dog whelks and mussels, which are indicative of rocky shorelines. This marked change in the discarded shell population may be due to a number of factors:

- The Iron Age inhabitants of Cill Donnain III might have chosen not to exploit estuarine habitats, since the common periwinkles could have been collected from other habitats where cockles do not occur.

- If common periwinkles were collected from estuarine habitats, then this may be an expression of a human preference for winkles rather than cockles.
- Alternatively, the common periwinkle population might have expanded at the expense of cockles in these estuarine habitats.
- It is also possible that changes in the local environment reduced the number of estuarine habitats along the local shoreline.

The latter hypothesis, of local environmental change, has been suggested for the disappearance of cockles in settlements between the Middle Iron Age and the Norse period at Cille Pheadair (Parker Pearson *et al.* forthcoming). In that situation, six miles south of Cill Donnain, it seems likely that the freshwater loch east of the Iron Age and Norse settlements on Cille Pheadair machair was once tidal, forming an estuarine environment of sand and mud flats until the mid-first millennium AD. It is possible that Loch Chill Donnain experienced a similar sequence of events, changing from a tidal estuary to a freshwater loch as machair sand encroached eastwards. That change might have occurred at some point between the Late Bronze Age and the Middle Iron Age.

In contrast to the preponderance of common periwinkle in all phases at Cill Donnain III, the Late Iron Age phases at Bornais mound 1 show a preference for limpet; in the Norse phases at Bornais (mound 1 and mound 3), the common periwinkle becomes dominant over limpet (Sharples 2005; Sharples and Light in Sharples 2012b: 201–3). At Sligeanach limpets dominate, except in the mound 16 samples belonging to the Middle Iron Age, where common periwinkles dominate (Law in Sharples 2012b: tab. 11.9).

The available data are, therefore, contradictory:

- at Cill Donnain III, there is a predominance of common periwinkle in all phases (Early–Middle Bronze

---

[2] The occurrence of land snails has been ignored entirely in this discussion: in the absence of systematic collection of land snails from flotation samples, a specialist report on the land snails has not been feasible. The only available data (shown in Table 15.3) are total quantities of land snail shells <10mm in size per phase, which tells us nothing about the site, its economy or its inhabitants.

Age to Late Iron Age), coupled with a declining percentage of limpet over time;

- this is not echoed at Bornais mound 1, where there is a predominance of limpet in the Late Iron Age activity areas;
- Sligeanach shows common periwinkle as the dominant species in the Middle Iron Age.

For all sites, however, we must be aware of the varying strategies for collection and identification of marine shell during both excavation and post-excavation.[3] This means that these comparative results must be treated with some caution. There is, however, a suggestion that the inhabitants of the wheelhouse at Cill Donnain had a different shellfish preference or foraging strategy to the inhabitants of the wheelhouse at Bornais mound 1. The decline of cockles on all sites during the Iron Age is, however, incontrovertible.

Most of the shells recovered at Cill Donnain III and the nearby comparable sites are not bivalves, but limpets and common periwinkles. To eat such shellfish, the flesh can be prised out to be eaten raw, prised out to be subsequently cooked, or the entire shell can be cooked and the meat prised out after cooking. Bivalve shellfish can be processed either by prising open the shell and eating the contents raw, or by heating the shell and allowing it to open as the organism dies and the muscle tension relaxes. We can hypothesize that the cooking of shellfish is more likely to be undertaken close to dwellings, whereas the eating of raw shellfish could occur at any point from the place of collection. The composition of this Cill Donnain assemblage may, therefore, be affected by locational differences in deposition of shells, dependent on whether the shellfish were eaten raw or cooked.

The importance of mollusca within the diet of populations is difficult to assess and is often exaggerated given the size and durability of the residues in contrast to their contents' calorific value (Shackleton 1988). The collection of shellfish is often a seasonal activity, and fluctuations in the assemblage over time may reflect changes in seasonal and exploitative strategies. Seasonal data or size variations through time for the molluscan species from Cill Donnain are not available because of on-site recording and discard of the assemblage.

---

[3] At Bornais mound 1, for example, the majority of the shell data derives from material recovered from the heavy residues produced by a very intensive flotation programme, sorted off-site, with the retrieved shells being taken to Cardiff University for analysis (see Sharples 2012b: 34 for strategy); in contrast the marine shell at Cill Donnain was collected by hand from the 10mm sieve on site, sorted in the site hut at Cill Donnain Museum, and discarded immediately.

Chapter 16 Radiocarbon dating

Peter Marshall and Gordon T. Cook

Introduction

Twenty-eight radiocarbon samples were submitted from Cill Donnain III. They comprised carbonized plant remains (barley, *Hordeum vulgare*) and a single human skull fragment. Charred residue adhering to the interior of sherds of earlier Bronze Age Cordoned Urn pottery proved too small to submit for analysis.

In 1992, two radiocarbon measurements (OxA-3355 and OxA-3356) were obtained from the Oxford Radiocarbon Accelerator Unit (Hedges *et al.* 1992) on samples of carbonized seeds from the 1991 excavations.

A further 26 samples were submitted to the Scottish Universities Research and Reactor Centre (SUERC) for dating in 2011–12, from which 17 radiocarbon determinations were obtained; nine samples failed and are identified by the laboratory code GU in Table 16.1.

Methods

The two samples dated at Oxford were pre-treated as outlined in Hedges *et al.* (1989) and measured on the CO_2 gas ion-source (Bronk Ramsey and Hedges 1989).

The single human bone sample processed at SUERC was pre-treated using a modified Longin method (Longin 1971), and the carbonized seeds using the acid-base-acid protocol (Stenhouse and Baxter 1983). The samples were all converted to carbon dioxide in pre-cleaned sealed quartz tubes (Vandeputte *et al.* 1996), and graphitized as described by Slota *et al.* (1987). They were measured by Accelerator Mass Spectrometry (AMS) as described by Freeman *et al.* (2010).

Both laboratories maintain continual programmes of quality assurance procedures, in addition to participation in international inter-comparisons (Rozanski *et al.* 1992; Scott 2003; Scott *et al.* 2010). These tests indicate no laboratory offset and demonstrate the validity of the precision quoted.

Results

The radiocarbon results in Table 16.1 are quoted in accordance with the international standard known as the Trondheim convention (Stuiver and Kra 1986). They are conventional radiocarbon ages (Stuiver and Polach 1977).

The calibration of the results, relating the radiocarbon measurements directly to calendar dates, is given in Table 16.1 and in Figure 16.1. The radiocarbon determinations have been calibrated with data from Reimer *et al.* (2009) using OxCal (v4.1) (Bronk Ramsey 1995; 1998; 2001; 2009). The date ranges have been calculated according to the maximum intercept method (Stuiver and Reimer 1986), and are cited at two sigma (95% confidence). They are quoted in the form recommended by Mook (1986), with the end points rounded outwards to 10 years. The ranges in Figure 16.2 quoted in italics are *posterior density estimates* derived from mathematical modelling of archaeological problems (see below). The probability distributions (Figures 16.1 and 16.2) are derived from the usual probability method (Stuiver and Reimer 1993).

Stable isotopes

Carbon and nitrogen stable isotope analysis was applied to the human bone sample, as the potential for diet-induced radiocarbon offsets if a person has taken up carbon from a reservoir (*i.e.* the sea) not in equilibrium with the terrestrial biosphere (Lanting and van der Plicht 1998) might have implications for the chronology of the site and the date of the death of the individual.

The stable isotope result (Table 16.1) indicates that the person consumed a diet predominantly based upon temperate terrestrial C_3 foods (Schoeninger and DeNiro 1984; Katzenberg and Krouse 1989).

The C:N ratio suggests that bone preservation was sufficiently good for us to have confidence in the accuracy of the radiocarbon determination (Tuross *et al.* 1988)

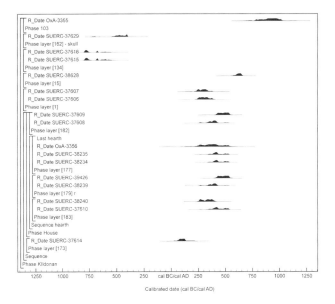

Figure 16.1 Probability distributions of dates from Cill Donnain III. Each distribution represents the relative probability that an event occurred at a particular time. These distributions are the result of simple radiocarbon calibration (Stuiver and Reimer 1993)

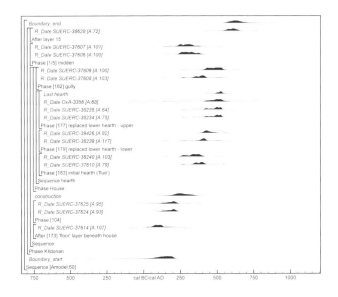

Figure 16.2 Probability distributions of dates from Cill Donnain III: each distribution represents the relative probability that an event occurs at a particular time. For each of the radiocarbon dates two distributions have been plotted, one in outline, which is the result of simple calibration, and a solid one, which is based on the chronological model used. Figures in brackets after the laboratory numbers are the individual indices of agreement which provide an indication of the consistency of the radiocarbon dates with the prior information included in the model (Bronk Ramsey 1995). The large square brackets down the left-hand side along with the OxCal keywords define the model exactly

and it is within the range usually quoted as being indicative of good-quality collagen preservation (2.9–3.6; DeNiro 1985)

Methodological approach

A Bayesian approach has been adopted for the interpretation of the chronology of the site (Buck *et al.* 1996). Although the simple calibrated dates are accurate estimates of the dates of the samples, this is usually not what archaeologists really wish to know. It is the dates of the archaeological events, which are represented by those samples, that are of interest. In the case of the wheelhouse, it is the chronology of the activity that is under consideration, not the dates of the individual samples. The dates of this activity can be estimated not only using the absolute dating information from the radiocarbon measurements on the samples, but also by using the stratigraphic relationships between samples.

Fortunately, methodology is now available which allows the combination of these different types of information explicitly, to produce realistic estimates of the dates of archaeological interest. It should be emphasized that the *posterior density estimates* produced by this modelling are not absolute. They are interpretative *estimates*, which can and will change as further data become available and as other researchers choose to model the existing data from different perspectives.

The technique used is a form of Markov Chain Monte Carlo sampling, and has been applied using the program OxCal v4.1 (http://c14.arch.ox.ac.uk/). Details of the algorithms employed by this program are available from the on-line manual or in Bronk Ramsey (1995; 1998; 2001; 2009). The algorithm used in the models described below can be derived from the structures shown in Figure 16.2.

The samples

The samples from the 2011–2012 dating programme were all single entity (Ashmore 1999), short-lived material. Given the paucity of samples that are demonstrably not residual in the context from which they were recovered (see Bayliss *et al.* 2011), where possible duplicate samples from a context were submitted to test the statistical consistency of results (Ward and Wilson 1978). The duplicate samples from layers 1/1989, 104, 134, 177, 179, 182, and 183 all produced statistically consistent results (see Table 16.2), implying that they contain material of the same actual age. The determinations from contexts with only single samples (layers 15/1989 and 173) have been treated as providing *termini post quos* for their contexts.

The sequence

The stratigraphically earliest layer to be dated was a sand layer (context 134) deposited before the wheelhouse was

Laboratory Number	Sample reference	Material	Radiocarbon Age (BP)	δ¹³C (‰)	δ¹⁵N (‰)	C:N ratio	Calibrated date range (95% confidence)
SUERC-37606	Layer 1 - 1	Carbonised grain, *Hordeum vulgare*	1735±30	-24.3			cal AD 230–400
SUERC-37607	Layer 1 - 2	Carbonised grain, *Hordeum vulgare*	1755±30	-23.6			cal AD 210–390
SUERC-38628	Layer 15 - 3	Carbonised grain, barley	1430±30	-25.0*			cal AD 570–660
GU25702	Layer 15 - 3	Carbonised grain, *Hordeum vulgare*	failed insufficient carbon				-
GU25703	Layer 15 - 4	Carbonised grain, *Hordeum vulgare*	failed insufficient carbon				-
OxA-3355	103	Carbonised seeds	1115±70	-23.4			cal AD 720–1030
SUERC-37624	104	Carbonised grain, *Hordeum vulgare*	1865±25	-20.0			cal AD 70–240
SUERC-37625	104	Carbonised grain, *Hordeum vulgare*	1865±30	-22.2			cal AD 70–240
SUERC-37615	Layer 134 - 15	Carbonised grain, *Hordeum vulgare*	2550±30	-23.8			800–550 cal BC
SUERC-37616	Layer 134 - 15	Carbonised grain, *Hordeum vulgare*	2560±30	-26.1			810–590 cal BC
SUERC-37629	Layer 162 -17	Human bone, skull fragment	2385±30	-20.6	9.5	3.4	710–390 cal BC
SUERC-37614	Layer 173 - 13	Carbonised grain, *Hordeum vulgare*	1900±30	-24.3			cal AD 20–220
GU25713	Layer 173 - 14	Carbonised grain, *Hordeum vulgare*	failed insufficient carbon				-
GU25706	Layer 177 -7	Carbonised grain, *Hordeum vulgare*	failed insufficient carbon				-
SUERC-38234	Layer 177 -7 (replacement for GU25706)	Carbonised grain, barley	1630±30	-23.9			cal AD 340–540
GU-25707	Layer 177 -8	Carbonised grain, *Hordeum vulgare*	failed insufficient carbon				-
SUERC-38235	Layer 177 -8 (replacement for GU25707)	Carbonised grain, barley	1635±30	-24.1			cal AD 340–540
GU-25708	Layer 177 -9	Carbonised grain, *Hordeum vulgare*	failed insufficient carbon				-
OxA-3356	177	Carbonised seeds	1670±75	-24.2			cal AD 210–560
SUERC-39426	Layer 179 – 9 (replacement for GU26746)	Carbonised grain, Barley	1585±30	-24.7			cal AD 410–560
GU26746	Layer 179 - 9	Carbonised grain, barley	failed insufficient carbon				-
GU25709	Layer 179 - 10	Carbonised grain, barley	failed insufficient carbon				-
SUERC-38239	Layer 179 – 10 (replacement for GU25709)	Carbonised grain, barley	1660±30	-24.5			cal AD 260–440
SUERC-37608	Layer 182 - 5	Carbonised grain, *Hordeum vulgare*	1660±30	-25.0*			cal AD 260–440
SUERC-37609	Layer 182 - 6	Carbonised grain, *Hordeum vulgare*	1585±30	-25.0*			cal AD 400–560
SUERC-37610	Layer 183 - 11	Carbonised grain, *Hordeum vulgare*	1630±35	-24.7			cal AD 340–540
GU25711	Layer 183 - 12	Carbonised grain, *Hordeum vulgare*	failed insufficient carbon				-
SUERC-38240	Layer 183 – 12 (replacement for GU25711)	Carbonised grain, barley	1710±30	-24.6			cal AD 240–420

*assumed value

Table 16.1 Cill Donnain III radiocarbon results

Context	Radiocarbon Age (BP)	Chi-square test
Layer [1]	SUERC-37606 SUERC-37607	T'=0.2; T' (5%)=3.8; v=1
Layer [104]	SUERC-37624 SUERC-37625	T'=0.0; T' (5%)=3.8; v=1
Layer [134]	SUERC-37615 SUERC-37616	T'=0.1; T' (5%)=3.8; v=1
Layer [177]	SUERC-38234 SUERC-38235 OxA-3356	T'=0.2; T' (5%)=6.0; v=2
Layer [179]	SUERC-38239 SUERC-39426	T'=3.1; T' (5%)=3.8; v=1
Layer [183]	SUERC-37610 SUERC-38240	T'=3.0; T' (5%)=3.8; v=1
Layer [182]	SUERC-37608 SUERC-37609	T'=3.1; T' (5%)=3.8; v=1

Table 16.2 Cill Donnain III chi-square test results

built. The next layer dated was a shell and carbonized wood deposit (173) above this sand layer but beneath the wheelhouse.

Above these, layer 104 was an organic layer of sand and carbonized wood fragments forming a deposit outside and against the inner wall face of the wheelhouse; it was initially interpreted as being part of the sandy wall core of the wheelhouse, deposited during the building's construction. However, the unexpectedly early dates for the charred plant remains from this layer raise the possibility that it formed a midden layer pre-dating the building of the wheelhouse (see Chapter 5). Either way, the charred plant remains from context 104 provide a TPQ for the construction of the wheelhouse.

The period of occupation of the wheelhouse can be dated from samples of charred plant remains found in hearths and related structures positioned in a stratigraphic sequence within the house. The earliest of these was the fill (183) of a pit, filled in before the construction of the wheelhouse's hearth. Two layers above this – the basal hearth deposit (179) and the hearth deposit above it (177) – were dated with charred plant remains. A gully cut through this hearth and its brown sand rich in carbonized wood fragments (182) contained a deposit of charred plant remains.

In 1992, a single barley grain from layer 177 produced a determination of cal AD 210–560 (95% confidence; OxA-3356; 1670±75 BP; Hedges *et al.* 1992: 338).

After the wheelhouse was abandoned, a thick deposit of dark brown, organic-rich sand containing quantities of pottery, animal bone and marine shell was deposited across the entire site. This midden layer (5=1/1989) consisted of a series of lenses and discrete layers that were also given separate context numbers. One of these was layer 103, from which a carbonized barley grain was dated in 1992 to cal AD 720–1030 (95% confidence; OxA-3355; 1115±70 BP). Another was 15/1989, a particularly dark brown layer of organic-rich sand. It is not possible to demonstrate a stratigraphic relationship between the samples from 5=1/1989 and 103, except to

note that they come from broadly similar contexts in different parts of the site. Context 103 lay in the southeast corner of the excavation trench (at about E12/N-1; see Figure 8.21), south of the doorway of the wheelhouse, whereas the sample (environmental sample number 4) from 5=1/1989 came from square 15 (E5/N-1) in the southwest area of the excavation, southwest of the wheelhouse (see Figure 5.1).

Context 15/1989 was assigned to two separate layers within the main midden layer 5=1/1989. One of these was at the base of 5=1/1989 to the west of the ruined wheelhouse and the other was from the top of 5=1/1989 within the wheelhouse. The dated sample (environmental sample number 16) from 15/1989 came from square 58 (E8/N3) within the western sector of the wheelhouse; thus it should be stratigraphically later than layer 5=1/1989.

The chronology of Cill Donnain III

The model shown in Figure 16.2, that excludes the Late Bronze Age dates from layers 134 and 162 and the intrusive later seed (OxA-3355) from layer 103, shows good agreement between the radiocarbon dates and stratigraphy (Amodel=60%).

- The model provides an estimate for construction of the wheelhouse of *cal AD 170–360* (*95% probability; construction*; Figure 16.2) and probably *cal AD 205–310* (*68% probability*).
- The last use of the repositioned lower hearth (layer 177) probably took place in the late fifth or early sixth centuries cal AD (*cal AD 495–540; 68% probability; Last hearth*; Figure 16.2).
- This last use of the lower hearth therefore occurred a little time before the end of dated activity in *cal AD 580–665* (*68% probability; Boundary_end*; Figure 16.2).

Chapter 17 Conclusion: Cill Donnain's prehistoric landscape

Mike Parker Pearson and Marek Zvelebil

The evolution of settlement on Cill Donnain's machair

Mike Parker Pearson

The formation of the machair plain by the mid-third millennium BC provided a *tabula rasa* for Beaker-period settlement occupying the western seaboard of the Western Isles. The previous ground surface was now buried many metres below this kilometre-wide layer of deep sand. Only at Northton in Harris (Simpson *et al.* 2006) is there any trace of the Neolithic settlement that may have occupied this coastal zone before it was inundated by calcareous sand. That earlier activity dates to around 3000 BC in the Middle Neolithic, half a millennium before the earliest settlements on top of the machair. Given the third-millennium date for machair formation, there is therefore no trace of occupation dating to the Late Neolithic in the machair areas. It seems likely that before the settlement of the machair in the Beaker period, this western coastal zone had long been abandoned to sand incursions; the paucity of Late Neolithic remains (*c.*3000–2400 BC) from the Western Isles more generally, particularly when contrasted with Orkney (Parker Pearson 2004), hints at a period of non-monumental activity only, if not stagnation.

Beaker-period settlements appear to have been numerous within the Western Isles (Armit 1996: 88–9; Sharples 2009; 2012a; Hamilton and Sharples 2012), with the known sites on South Uist's machair being relatively widely spaced, five miles or more apart, at Gortan on the south coast (Barber 2003), Cladh Hallan in the southwest (Parker Pearson *et al.* 2004: 50–1), Cill Donnain I (Hamilton and Sharples 2012) and Sligeanach (Sharples 2012a) in the middle of the island, and Machair Mheadhanach in the north (Parker Pearson 2012c).

It is impossible to know whether more such settlements of this period have been destroyed by coastal erosion but those settlements that are situated along the west coast of South Uist coincide closely with locations of Bronze Age settlement mounds that were generally built further inland. Since there are no Bronze Age settlement areas without Beaker sites in their vicinity, it is a reasonable assumption that no Beaker settlement mounds complexes have been lost to the sea.

Within the Cill Donnain settlement complex (Figure 17.1), settlement mounds 17, 18 and 176 at Sligeanach,[1] just 500m northwest of the Cill Donnain wheelhouse (Cill Donnain III, site 85), have been found to date to the Beaker period (Sharples 2012a). The same distance southwest of Cill Donnain III lies site 87 (Cill Donnain I), a settlement mound containing one or more stone-footed buildings and a probable stone cist (Hamilton and Sharples 2012).

Cill Donnain I was investigated by the first SEARCH teams at the same time as Cill Donnain III, and in 1988 Jean-Luc Schwenninger discovered a handful of worked flints, pottery sherds and a bone point here. These finds could not be located when Hamilton and Sharples (2012) analysed the Cill Donnain I assemblage of finds collected more recently; they have since been discovered incorporated into the Cill Donnain wheelhouse excavation archive. This finds group from the initial work in 1988 is therefore reported here.[2] These finds include a fine barbed-and-tanged flint arrowhead, three flint scrapers, the tip of a bone point and two sherds of pottery (Figure 17.2). One of these is a sherd of Beaker with incised decoration and the other is the rim of a chevron-decorated Early Bronze Age vessel of Food Vessel style.

Although Schwenninger recorded the stratigraphic position of Cill Donnain I (Figure 17.3), there was no full plan of it (Figure 17.4) until many years later when a

---

[1] Site numbers refer to the inventory of all machair sites published in Parker Pearson 2012c.

[2] Finds from Cill Donnain I site 87 found since 1988 are listed in Parker Pearson (2012c: 53) and Hamilton and Sharples (2012: 202–9).

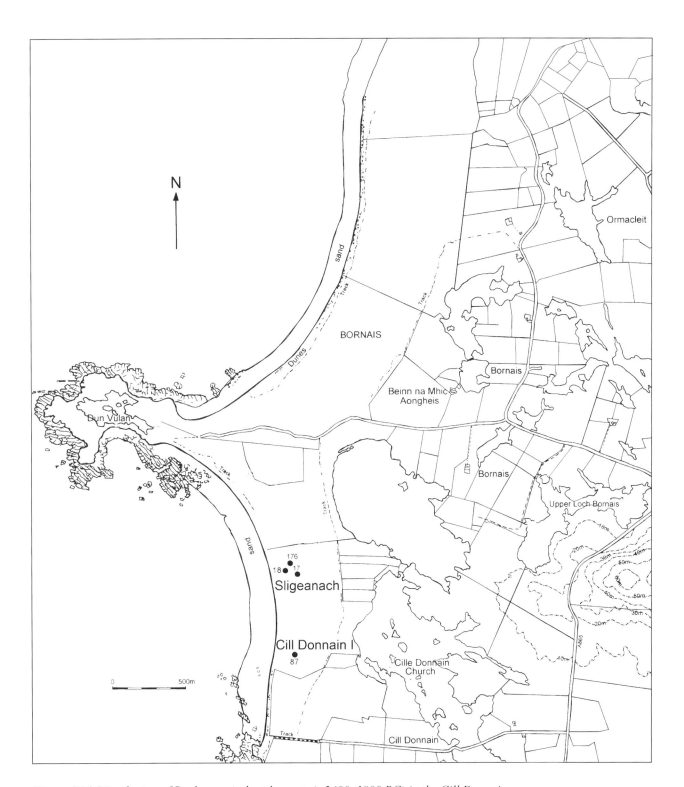

Figure 17.1 Distribution of Beaker-period settlements (c.2400–1800 BC) in the Cill Donnain area

Cardiff University team carried out geophysical surveys across the exposed mound's surface in 1996 (Hamilton and Sharples 2012). A small test-excavation was carried at Cill Donnain I in 1988 but no further intervention has taken place, even though house remains protrude from the surface of the mound. Dates of 2350–1890 cal BC (OxA-3353; 3710±80 BP) and 2140–1690 cal BC (OxA-3354; 3560±80 BP) from carbonized plant remains recovered during the 1988 excavation (Gilbertson *et al.* 1996) place Cill Donnain

I within the same chronological bracket for Beaker-period activity as the three Sligeanach sites half a mile to the north (Hamilton and Sharples 2012; Sharples 2012a).

At Sligeanach, mound 18 produced sherds of Food Vessel pottery (Figure 17.5), indicating that it continued to be occupied either during the Beaker period or after Beakers went out of use. A single sherd from Cill Donnain I could derive from a Food Vessel but it would have to be of a unique form (Hamilton and Sharples 2012:

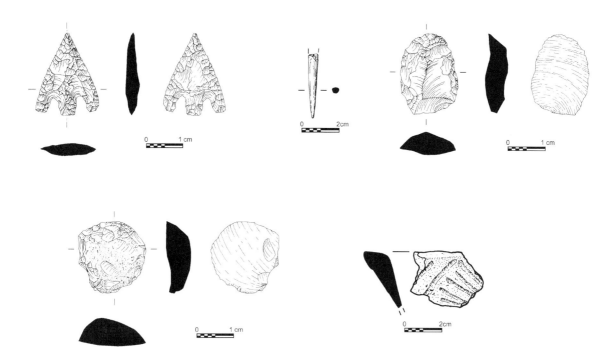

Figure 17.2 Barbed-and-tanged arrowhead, scrapers, bone point and pottery from Cill Donnain I (site 87), a Beaker-period and Early Bronze Age settlement

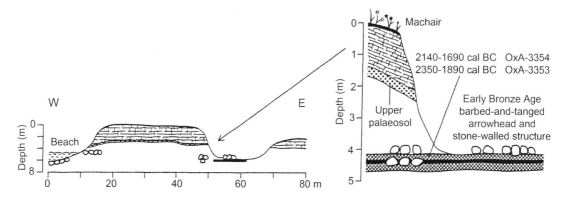

Figure 17.3 Schematic section drawing of the location of Cill Donnain I (site 87) within machair dunes

207–9). As mentioned above, the 1988 rim sherd from Cill Donnain I (Figure 17.2) is probably from a Food Vessel as well.

The assemblage from Cill Donnain I is remarkable. The barbed-and-tanged arrowhead and a leaf-shaped arrowhead, the four bone pins/points and a broken stone battle-axe (Hamilton and Sharples 2012: fig. 10.7) are not artefacts that are usually found as discarded refuse on settlements. In contrast, the material culture from Beaker period/Early Bronze Age mounds 17, 18 and 176 at Sligeanach is relatively prosaic.[3] The same may be said of the Early Bronze Age assemblages from Gortan (Barber 2003), Machair Mheadhanach (Hamilton and Sharples 2012) and Cladh Hallan (Parker Pearson *et al.* in prep.). This raises the possibility that Cill Donnain I (site 87) had a special status not shared by the other Early Bronze Age settlements of South Uist. Of course, very little of any of

these settlements has been examined by large-scale excavation (and Gortan was largely washed away prior to excavation of that small portion that remained) so this speculation must be tested through future excavations.

Further investigation of these sites has to be a high priority, given the rarity of Beaker-period and Early Bronze Age houses in Britain and Europe. These South Uist machair sites provide not only the opportunity to investigate possible differences in status but also to divine why three adjacent sites were using three or more different styles of ceramics (Beaker, Food Vessel/Vase Urn, and Cordoned Urn) within the same settlement complex. The Cill Donnain Cordoned Urn settlement described in Chapter 3 is currently unique within Britain although there are other excavated settlement sites with this ceramic style from Ireland (Pollock and Waterman 1964; Grogan and Roche 2009; 2010).

---

3   With the exception of a copper-alloy awl from mound 18 (Sharples 2012a: 236).

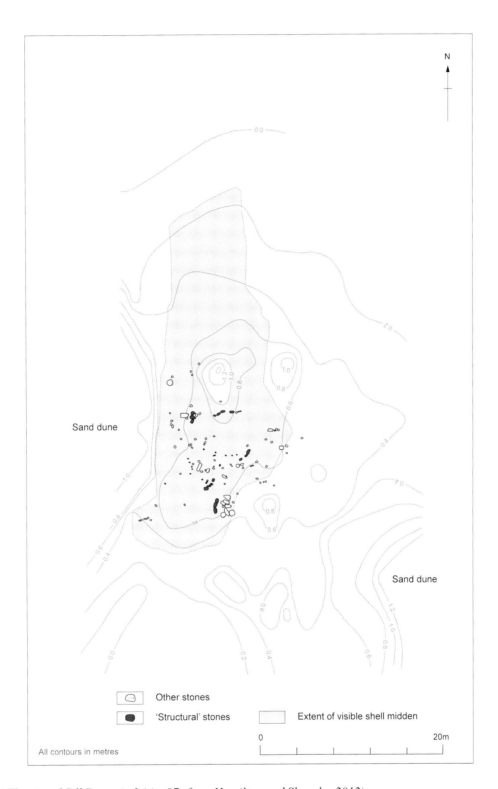

Figure 17.4 The site of Cill Donnain I (site 87; from Hamilton and Sharples 2012)

The lack of sufficient carbonized residue from any of the sherds of Cordoned Urn pottery from Cill Donnain III from which to obtain radiocarbon dates makes it difficult to place the Early–Middle Bronze Age activity on this site chronologically in relation to that at Sligeanach and Cill Donnain I (see Sharples 2012a: tab. 11.8 for the Sligeanach radiocarbon dates). That said, dates for Cordoned Urns normally fall within the period *c.*1900–1400/1300

BC (Sheridan 2003: 207), the later part of the Early Bronze Age and the Middle Bronze Age; for example, a Cordoned Urn, decorated with incisions and two cordons, from Benderloch, Argyll, contained carbonized material on its interior that returned a date of 1626–1408 cal BC at 95.4% probability (AA-26980; MacGregor 1998). An unincised Cordoned Urn from Findhorn is dated by short-lived pyre debris to 1880–1520 cal BC at

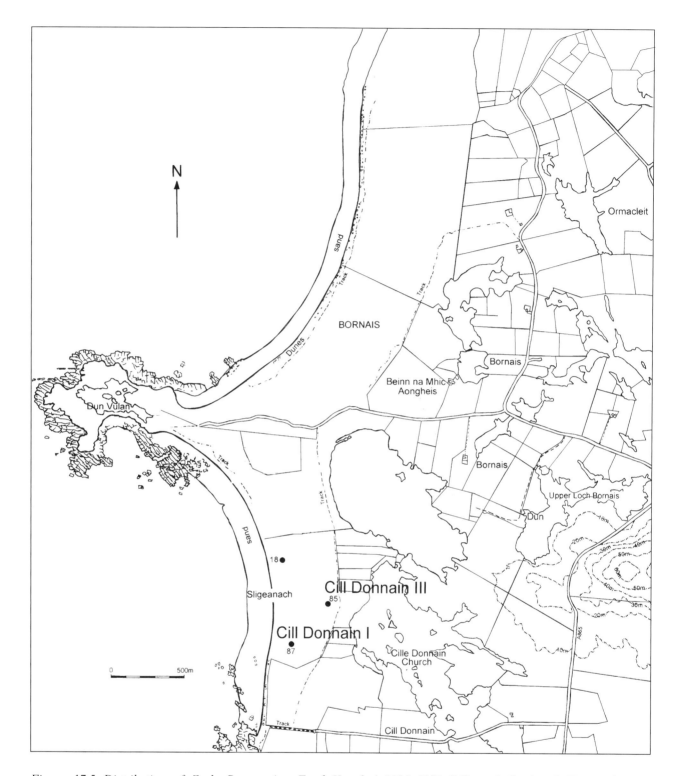

Figure 17.5 Distribution of Early Bronze Age Food Vessel (c.2200–1800 BC) and Cordoned Urn settlements (c.1900–1500 BC) in the Cill Donnain area

95.4% probability (OxA-7622; Shepherd and Shepherd 2001).

The simplest hypothesis by which to explain the inter-relationship of these Early Bronze Age settlements on Cill Donnain machair is that the inhabitants of sites 87 and 18 moved 500m inland to Cill Donnain III, at the same time adopting the new Cordoned Urn ceramic style. Yet the dimensions of the Cill Donnain III mound are

much smaller than these other two sites; either the population was shrinking or fissioning, or more Cordoned Urn settlements remain buried beneath the large settlement mound and dune immediately east of Cill Donnain III.

Cordoned Urn ceramics have also been found at Cladh Hallan (from a site largely destroyed by sand quarrying), and it is tempting to speculate that late Early Bronze Age and Middle Bronze Age settlements occupied the same

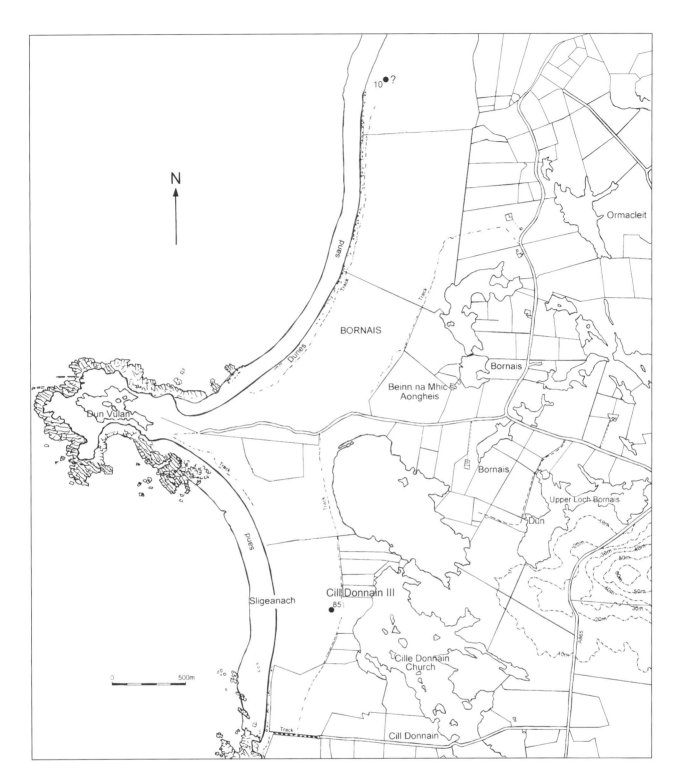

Figure 17.6 Distribution of Late Bronze Age settlements (c.1300–750 BC) in the Cill Donnain area

approximate locations as their earlier counterparts in South Uist. That said, no Cordoned Urn pottery has been recovered from Machair Mheadhanach, a major complex of prehistoric settlement mounds in the north of the island, though such deposits could very possibly be located towards the bases of any of these large mounds that have produced Late Bronze Age/Early Iron Age pottery on their surfaces.

Certainly by the Late Bronze Age, there is evidence for settlement at all three locations. The fact that swords and other implements were cast at Cill Donnain III (see Chapter 10) as well as at Cladh Hallan (Cowie in prep.) implies that bronze-working was more widespread in the Western Isles than previously thought, possibly associated with many or even most of the islands' Late Bronze Age settlements.

Within the vicinity of Cill Donnain, a small site on Ormacleit machair (mound 10; Figure 17.6), adjacent to a large Middle Iron Age settlement mound two miles to

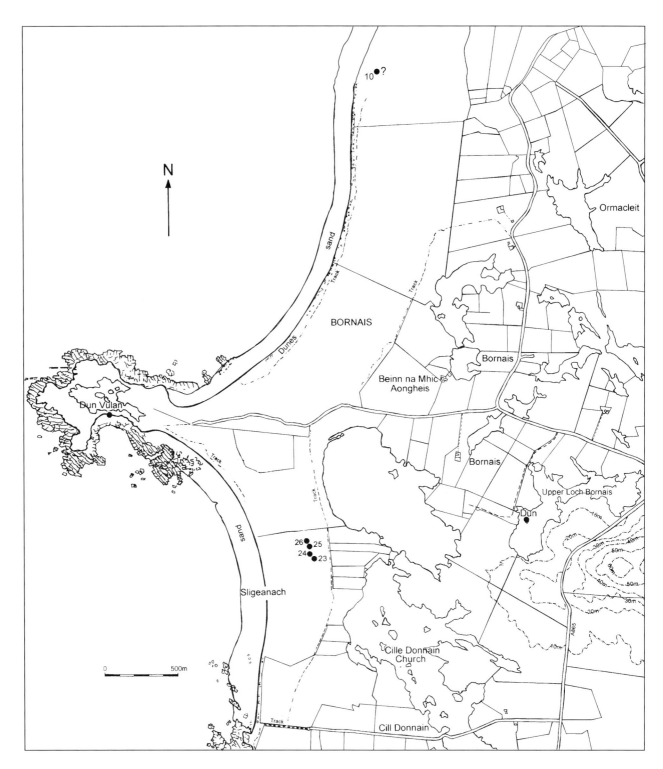

Figure 17.7 Distribution of Early Iron Age settlements (c.750–200 BC) in the Cill Donnain area

its north, has produced pottery that can be dated to either the Late Bronze Age (*c*.1300–750 BC) or the Early Iron Age (*c*.750–200 BC). If the former, then it is evidence that the Bronze Age settlement pattern was changing, with the formation of new sites beyond the three large complexes of Cladh Hallan, Cill Donnain and Machair Mheadhanach. If the latter, then its founding was part of a radical re-organization of the settled landscape in the Early Iron Age.

Thanks to the project's excavations of varying size within the townships of Cill Donnain and Bornais to its north, we now have a large number of settlements with radiocarbon dates that place them within the middle of the first millennium BC. Their Early Iron Age Plain Ware is generally undiagnostic and it is difficult to date small assemblages on typological grounds, a problem that hampered attempts to date these sites with absolute certainty during field survey (see Parker Pearson 2012c).

Now we can recognise Early Iron Age settlements at Sligeanach mounds 23–26 (Sharples 2012a), beneath the broch of Dun Vulan (Parker Pearson and Sharples 1999: 58), beneath a Middle Iron Age building on an islet within Upper Loch Bornais (Marshall and Parker Pearson 2012; marked as 'Dun' on Figure 17.7) and possibly on Ormacleit machair (site 10).

Coupled with a break in the settlement sequence at Cill Donnain III (where there is no Early Iron Age phase), this pattern of Early Iron Age settlement (Figure 17.7) demonstrates a radical break with the Bronze Age settlement distribution. It would seem that the inhabitants of Cill Donnain III moved 400m–500m northwest to establish new houses at Sligeanach (the inland mounds, sites 23–26; see Sharples 2012a). People also established new dwellings on partly or wholly artificial islets within freshwater lochs at Ardvule (later to be built into the broch of Dun Vulan) and Upper Loch Bornais.

This shift in settlement locations in the Early Iron Age could represent social and economic changes. In social terms, groups were becoming dispersed across the landscape, freeing themselves from traditional structures of authority within this new, decentralized pattern of settlement. In economic terms, the islet settlements were well placed to exploit the blacklands beyond the machair margins or at least the interfaces between machair and blacklands. Sharples (2012b) has suggested that such changes may have constituted the formation of the 'proto-township' pattern of landholding proposed by Parker Pearson (1996; 2012c) for the Middle Iron Age (*c*.200 BC–AD 300); it is certainly possible that the machair strip along the Uists' west coast was filled with archaeologically invisible Early Iron Age settlement mounds spaced approximately one or two kilometres apart, as the Middle Iron Age sites tend to be.

However, Sharples' results pertain only to Sligeanach which is better interpreted as a settlement shift from nearby Cill Donnain rather than an infilling of the machair by a rapidly growing population. It is more likely that the Middle Iron Age 'proto-township' filling-up of the landscape was preceded by an Early Iron Age transformation in which traditional centres were abandoned and new islet locations were taken up in addition to machair locations. This would accord well with evidence from Lewis where islets such as Dun Bharabhat (Harding and Dixon 2000; Church 2002) and An Dunan (Gilmore 2002: 59) and the promontory enclosure of Gob Eirer (Nesbitt *et al.* 2011) were occupied in this period. Specifically, the ceramics from Gob Eirer place its occupation in the sixth century BC, by comparison with the closely dated ceramic sequence from Cladh Hallan (Parker Pearson *et al.* in prep.). We might also add the site of Bagh nam Feadag on the island of Grimsay (North Uist), where a roundhouse associated with what appears to be Early Iron Age pottery lies beneath a Middle Iron Age wheelhouse (McKenzie 2005: 55–9, 140).

By the Middle Iron Age (*c*.200 BC–AD 300), the Cill Donnain landscape was densely settled (Figure 17.8). The Cill Donnain III wheelhouse is probably just the northern tip of a large settlement mound (site 85) buried beneath the dune to its immediate east. In addition, there is a probable wheelhouse just half a kilometre to the northwest at Sligeanach (site 27; Sharples 2012a), with Middle Iron Age pottery coming from a small mound (site 16) next to it. A further 500m to the northwest, a very tall settlement mound (site 15) has produced Middle Iron Age pottery (Parker Pearson 2012c). The islets of Dun Vulan and Upper Loch Bornais continued to be occupied in this period, the former as a broch whose foundations were constructed during 350 BC–AD 20 (Parker Pearson and Sharples 1999: 211). Mound 1 on Bornais machair was also inhabited in the Middle Iron Age (Sharples 2012b), as was a settlement mound a mile further north at Ormacleit (mound 9).

During the Late Iron Age (*c*.AD 300–800) occupation continued at Cill Donnain III, along with mound 1 at Bornais and within and outside the broch of Dun Vulan (Figure 17.9). At Bornais, occupation on mound 1 may have been replaced by dwellings at the base of the adjacent mound 2, using Late Iron Age Plain Ware dating to after AD 600 (Sharples pers. comm.). Further north, three small mounds on Ormacleit machair (sites 4, 5 and 7) have produced Late Iron Age pottery.

There are many settlement remains from the Norse period in the Cill Donnain area (Figure 17.10). Most of these sites have been recognised on the basis of their distinctive platter ware, a style of pizza-shaped ceramic baking tray that dates from the Norse period to the fourteenth century (Lane 2005: 194). Just south of Cill Donnain III, within the same sand blow-out, is site 83, belonging to the Norse period, where the remains of stone walls litter the ground surface. Another settlement (site 84) just over a hundred metres to the west of Cill Donnain III has also produced the distinctive platter ware of the Norse and early Medieval period.

Whilst the islet sites of Dun Vulan and Upper Loch Bornais were abandoned by this time, there are remains of seven Norse-period settlement mounds on the machair of Upper and Lower Bornais that lies between Ardvule and Upper Loch Bornais. The largest group (mounds 1–3 at Bornais; Sharples 2005; 2012b; Sharples and Parker Pearson 1999) constituted a major focus of settlement in South Uist, possibly as an island centre. It is also likely that the church site of Cille Donnain (on a promontory and islets within Loch Chill Donnain less than half a kilometre southeast of Cill Donnain III) was founded in the Late Norse period (Fleming and Woolf 1992; Fleming 2012; Parker Pearson 2012a). Settlement also continued at this time within the complex on Ormacleit machair further north.

The onset of the Norse period most certainly represented a major dislocation in the lives of the people of South Uist yet its settlement pattern was relatively similar to that of

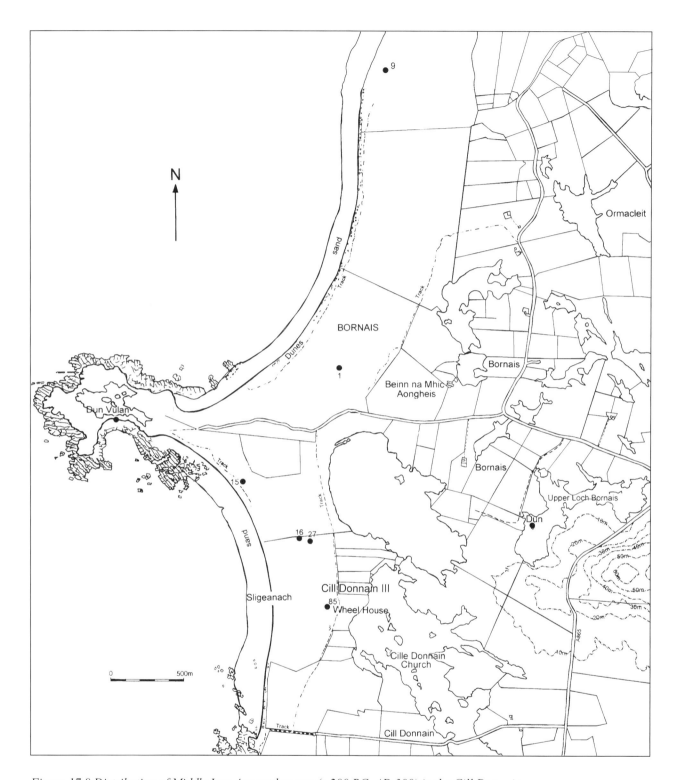

Figure 17.8 Distribution of Middle Iron Age settlements (c.200 BC–AD 300) in the Cill Donnain area

preceding periods in terms of utilization of the machair (Sharples and Parker Pearson 1999; Parker Pearson 2012c). A more dramatic break came during the later Medieval period, when the machair sites were largely abandoned and new settlements developed on the acidic soils of the black-lands further inland (Figure 17.11).

This is demonstrated most dramatically by the termin-ation of occupation at mounds 2–3 on Bornais machair and the establishment of a settlement at Beinn na Mhic Aongheis (Hill of the Son of Angus; Parker Pearson *et al.* 2012) just over half a kilometre to their southeast. It is likely that there was a similar shift from the Cill Donnain machair settlements (sites 83 and 84), which probably relocated to an unidentified site close to Cille Donnain church: excavations at the church site uncovered large quantities of Medieval occupation debris that appear to have come from an as-yet unlocated, nearby settlement (Parker Pearson 2012a).

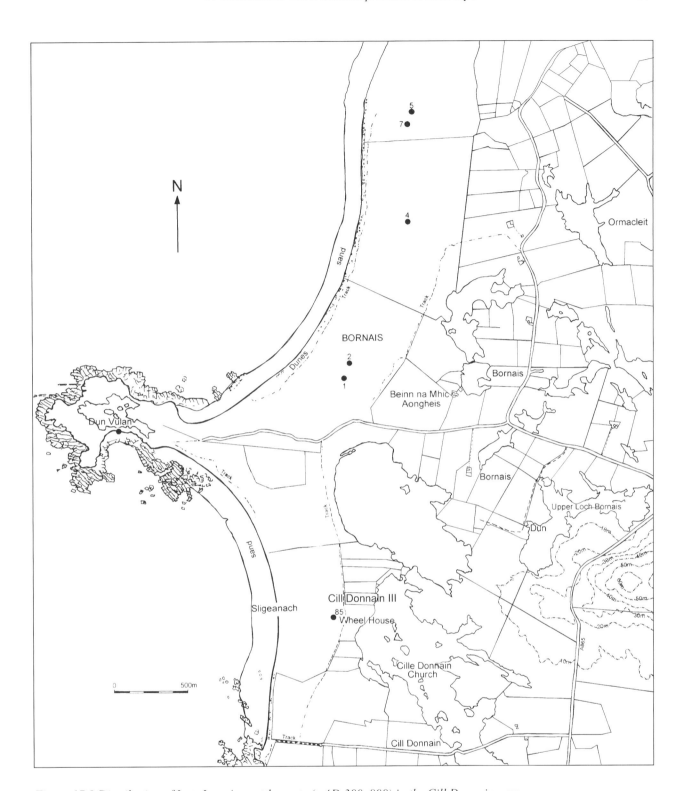

Figure 17.9 Distribution of Late Iron Age settlements (c.AD 300–800) in the Cill Donnain area

Occupation and activity at Cill Donnain in the Iron Age

Mike Parker Pearson with Marek Zvelebil

The excavations at Cill Donnain III uncovered the remains of a small, circular Iron Age house of a type known as an aisled wheelhouse. These are found only in the Outer Hebrides and Shetland (Crawford 2002). Although many have been excavated, their date range has remained a subject for argument, with Armit (2006) proposing their construction and use from a start possibly before 200 BC to an end before the second century AD, and Sharples dating them from the first century BC to the fifth to sixth centuries AD (2012b: 18–19, 314–15).

As Sharples has shown (*ibid.*), the dates for wheel-

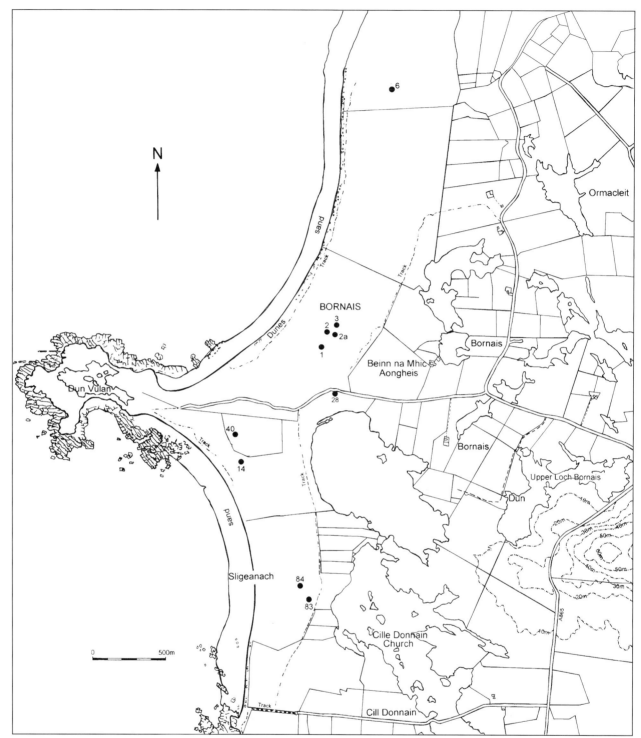

Figure 17.10 Distribution of Norse-period settlements (c.AD 800–1300) in the Cill Donnain area

house construction before the first century BC are problematic. This includes Cnip, where unusually early radiocarbon dates were obtained from foundational deposits of potentially curated animal and human remains (Armit 2006: 220; Armit and Shapland 2013), a situation also the case at Cill Donnain III. Here the human skull fragment from context 162 was potentially a curated item prior to deposition. Secondly the scenario in which layer 104 is part of the wheelhouse's wall core (rather than an earlier layer) raises the possibility that earlier midden material was introduced during construction of the wheelhouse, either fortuitously or deliberately.

The sequence at Cill Donnain III confirms Sharples's identification of a late end to wheelhouse construction and use, it being built probably after the second century AD (*cal AD 170–360 at 95% probability* and probably *cal AD 205–310 [at 68% probability]*). Furthermore, its use continued until the late fifth or early sixth centuries AD (*cal AD 495–540 at 68% probability*). It was thus one of the later wheelhouses to be built in the Western Isles.

Figure 17.11 Distribution of Later Medieval and Post-Medieval settlements (c.1300–1700) in the Cill Donnain area

The Cill Donnain III wheelhouse was associated with the remains of pottery, animal bones, carbonized grain and other domestic refuse; the house probably belonged to a simple farming family rather than to a social elite, since the surrounding debris reflects day-to-day activities of ordinary people in the Iron Age. The building was probably not constructed in isolation since cultural deposits extend eastwards from the excavated area underneath the large dune identified as site 85 (Parker Pearson 2012c). We may thus expect the wheelhouse to have been one component of a larger settlement. The locality was not deserted after the destruction or abandonment of the wheelhouse; it continued to be used for the dumping of domestic refuse, which gradually covered the remains of the structure.

In its shape and size, the Cill Donnain wheelhouse is closely comparable with Middle Iron Age wheelhouses of South Uist (Figure 17.12), Barra (Figure 17.13) and the remainder of the Western Isles (Figure 17.14). Its architecture, portable material culture and ceramics are

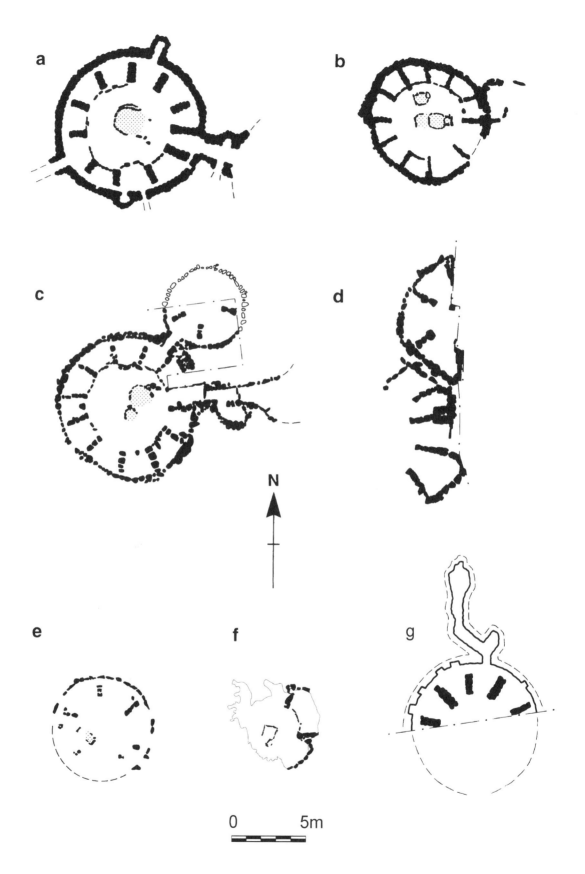

Figure 17.12 Excavated wheelhouses of South Uist: a) Kilpheder (after Lethbridge 1952), b) A' Cheardach Bheag (after Young and Richardson 1960), c) A' Cheardach Mhor (after Fairhurst 1971), d) Hornish Point (after Barber 2003), e) Cill Donnain III (this volume), f) Bornais mound 1 (after Sharples 2012b), g) Gleann Uisinis (after Thomas 1866–1868)

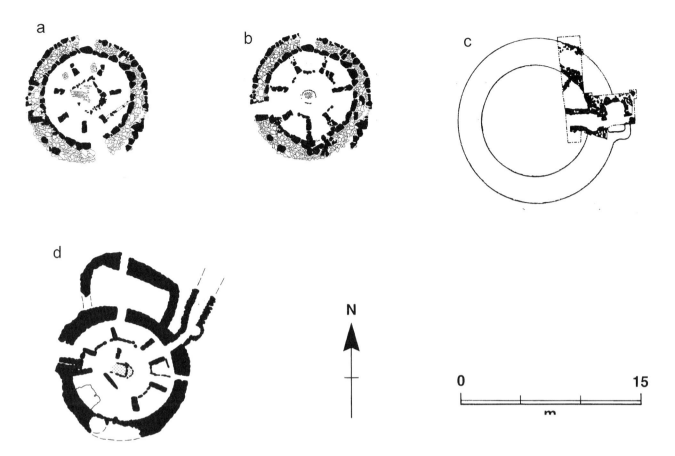

Figure 17.13 Excavated wheelhouses of Barra: a) Allt Chrisal (T17) first phase (after Foster and Pouncett 2000), b) Allt Chrisal (T17) second phase (after Foster and Pouncett 2000), c) Allasdale dunes (after Wessex Archaeology 2008), d) Allasdale (after Young 1953)

closely comparable with other excavated South Uist examples of wheelhouses at Kilpheder (Lethbridge 1952), A' Cheardach Bheag (Fairhurst 1971), A' Cheardach Mhor (Young and Richardson 1960), Hornish Point (Barber 2003) and Bornais mound 1 (Sharples 2012b). On the other hand, the dimensions of the Cill Donnain structure are far less massive than all the other South Uist examples, including partially excavated wheelhouses at Upper Loch Bornais (Marshall and Parker Pearson 2012), Cill Donnain Sligeanach (Sharples 2012a) and the unexcavated building at Uisinis (Thomas 1866–1868). Cill Donnain III seems altogether a far simpler structure in terms of its design and building techniques. Indeed, it is one of the smallest wheelhouses of 38 known and likely examples in the Western Isles.

The moorland wheelhouses of Barra are as small as and smaller than Cill Donnain III. With an internal diameter of 6.5m, a floor area of 33.4sq m and a probable roof height of 2m at the apex, Cill Donnain III is slightly larger than Allt Chrisal (T17), the smallest excavated wheelhouse on Barra, which has a diameter of 6.3m (Foster and Pouncett 2000). Further probable but unexcavated wheelhouses on the moorlands of Barra and South Uist (Figure 17.15; Branigan and Foster 1995; 2000; Raven 2012) have similarly small dimensions comparable to Cill Donnain and Allt Chrisal.

In contrast, the wheelhouse at Allasdale dunes on Barra's west-coast machair is much larger, estimated as being as much as 17.2m in diameter with an internal diameter of 12.1m (Wessex Archaeology 2008: 31). However, this estimate is based upon limited evaluation; a more conservative estimate, based on the wheelhouse's likely symmetry and the axis of the entrance passage towards the centre of the building, would give it dimensions of around 14m externally and 10m internally. Even so, this wheelhouse is much larger than other examples from Barra, and supports the general rule that wheelhouses on moorland tend to be smaller than those on machair.

It may be the case that, while the Cill Donnain III house was built to approximately the same design as the others, it formed a dwelling for people of a lower social rank, perhaps commoners. Alternatively, its small size could reflect the size of its household or even the nature of specialized activities that took place within it. Not much bigger than the ancillary roundhouse attached to the Kilpheder wheelhouse (Lethbridge 1952), the excavated Cill Donnain house could similarly have had a subsidiary position within a larger wheelhouse complex.

The Cill Donnain wheelhouse was built on top of a series of sand layers that appear to have derived from disturbed Late Bronze Age deposits as well as layers deposited during the Middle Iron Age. One of these was a

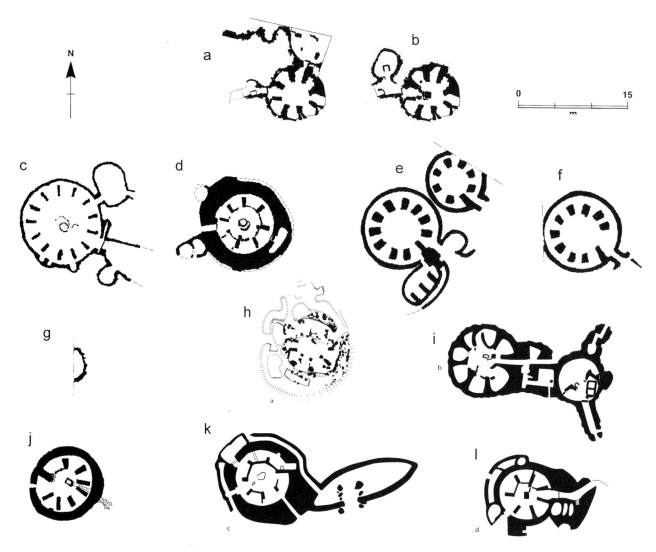

Figure 17.14 Excavated wheelhouses of North Uist and Lewis: a) Cnip phase 1, Lewis (after Armit 2006), b) Cnip phase 2, Lewis (after Armit 2006), c) Sollas, North Uist (after Campbell 1991), d) Clettraval, North Uist (after Scott 1948), e) the Udal, North Uist (after Crawford in Selkirk 1996), f) the Udal, North Uist (after Crawford in Selkirk 1996), g) Baile Sear, North Uist (after Barber 2003), h) Eilean Maleit, North Uist (after Armit 1998), i) Bac Mhic Connain, North Uist (after Beveridge 1911), j) Bagh nam Feadag, Grimsay (after McKenzie 2005), k) Gearraidh Iochdrach, North Uist (after Beveridge 1911), l) Cnoc a Comhdhalach, North Uist (after Beveridge 1911)

thin layer of organic sand (59), similar in nature to the floor layers (166=170) within the wheelhouse but pre-dating the house's construction and confined to the western half of the house. This may have been laid down as a building surface to enable the construction of the wheelhouse without churning up the soft sand layers below. A similar 'floor layer' was identified beneath a wheelhouse excavated in 2010 at Baile Sear in North Uist (Tom Dawson pers. comm.).

The thickest of these pre-construction layers was a largely sterile layer (131=162) of possibly windblown sand. In this layer, dated by OSL to AD 25–625 (1670±300 BP), and by the presence of Middle Iron Age pottery (*c*.200 BC – AD 300) in layers above it, was placed a fragment of a human skull. The skull, dated to 540–393 cal BC at 91.1% probability (SUERC-37629; 2385±30 BP), was probably that of a young woman with

a healed injury or infection on top of her head. Although there was no evidence for a pit in which this antique fragment had been placed, it was positioned about a metre south of where the wheelhouse's hearth would subsequently be built. The case for this skull fragment being a foundation deposit, rather than a casual loss, is a strong one given the circumstances of human bone deposition in so many Hebridean roundhouses dating from the Bronze Age to the Late Iron Age (Armit 2006: 244–8; Armit and Ginn 2007; Mulville *et al.* 2003; Parker Pearson *et al.* 2004: 74–9; SCAPE Trust 2008). For example, a very similar fragment of unusually ancient human skull, consisting of frontal bone and upper orbits, was found in a small pit beneath the floor of a wheelhouse at Cnip (McSweeney in Armit 2006: 134).

The Cill Donnain III wheelhouse was constructed in *cal AD 170–360 (95% probability)* and probably *cal AD*

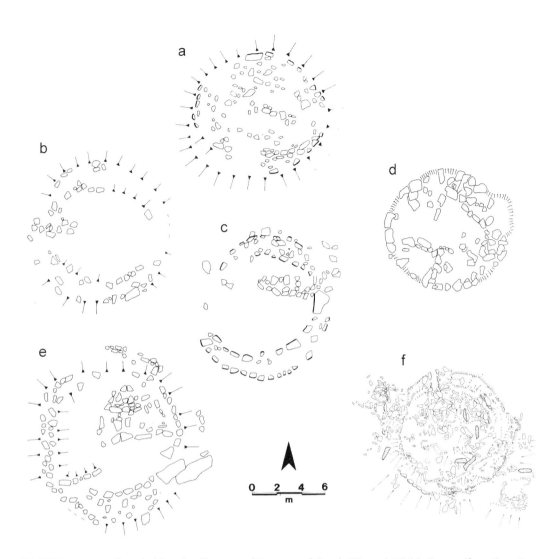

Figure 17.15 Unexcavated probable wheelhouses of Barra and South Uist: a) T166, Barra (from Branigan and Foster 1995: fig. 3.9), b) T132, Barra (from Branigan and Foster 1995: fig. 3.9), c) T160, Barra (from Branigan and Foster 1995: fig. 3.9), d) USS 013, South Uist (from Raven 2012: fig. 7.12), e) T164, Barra (from Branigan and Foster 1995: fig. 3.9), f) K34, Barra (from Branigan 2000: fig. 11.1)

205–310 (68% probability). It was built in an unusual manner. Instead of being dug into the underlying sand as a sunken-floored dwelling – as the vast majority of machair wheelhouses were – it was built free-standing from the ground surface, in a manner normally restricted to wheelhouse sites on the solid and rocky ground off the machair (Armit 2006: 206). As Armit has pointed out (*ibid.*), this free-standing design places greater constraints on a building's size, which may explain why this building was so small.

To build such a structure on top of the sand rather than within it created stresses and strains from the corbelling and timber roof that would have been more effectively controlled by revetting the building into the underlying sand. However, the evaluation of the large wheelhouse in the machair dunes at Allasdale in Barra reveals that this building was not only substantial (see above) but was also built as a free-standing structure (Wessex Archaeology 2008). Thus such constraints were presumably overcome in this case.

The Cill Donnain III wheelhouse's wall was constructed with a wall core of sand faced on the inside by a line of vertically-set gneiss slabs and on the outside by a poorly preserved circuit of small stones originally standing to two or more courses high (Figures 17.16–17.19). The vertical slabs of the inner wall face might have supported drystone masonry courses on top of them in the manner of Structures 4 and 5 at Cnip in Lewis (Armit 2006: 60–71), though the wheelhouse was so thoroughly robbed-out that any such courses had disappeared long before excavation.

The roof was supported on six or seven piers that were not bonded to the inside wall face but were free-standing to form an 'aisled wheelhouse' – so-called because the gap between the piers and the wall (in this case of about 0.4m) provided a potential 'aisle' around the interior's perimeter. As Armit has observed, there appears to be no functional reason why unbonded piers were chosen over bonded ones, and he therefore considers them a deliberate design choice rather than a necessary by-product of

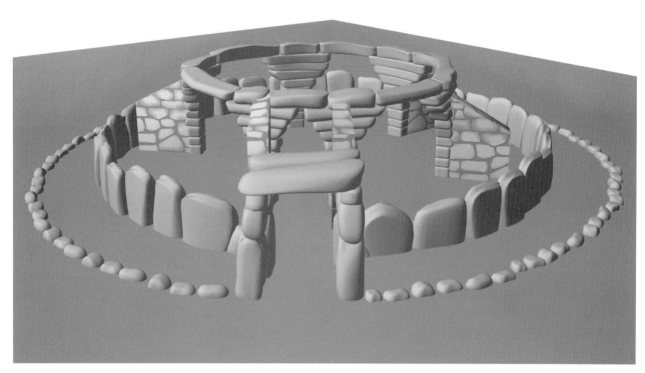

Figure 17.16 A reconstruction of the Cill Donnain III wheelhouse, showing the stone frame of the building

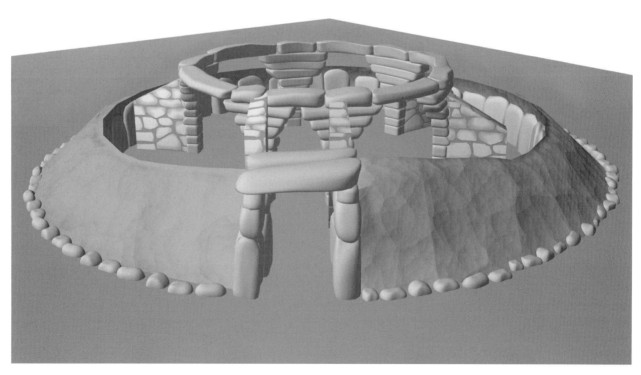

Figure 17.17 A reconstruction of the Cill Donnain III wheelhouse, showing the walls in place

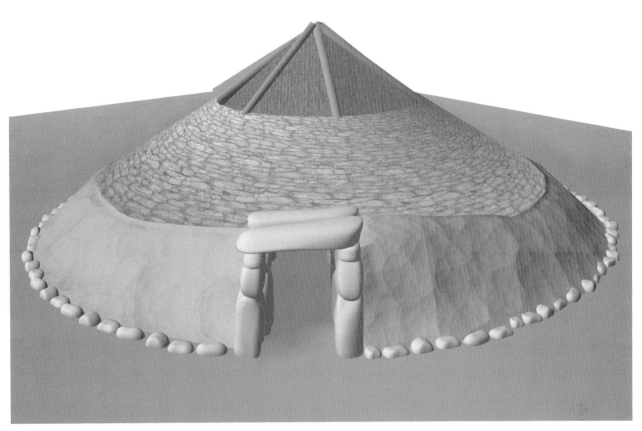

Figure 17.18 A reconstruction of the Cill Donnain III wheelhouse, showing the roof partly completed

Figure 17.19 A reconstruction of the completed Cill Donnain III wheelhouse

wheelhouse building (Armit 2006: 205). He also points to evidence for a chronological shift in wheelhouse construction from unbonded to bonded piers (*ibid.*) but this clearly does not apply to Cill Donnain, one of the latest known wheelhouses.

The hearth within the Cill Donnain III wheelhouse is unusual for two reasons.

- Firstly, it is not placed centrally within the building, being positioned a metre or so southwest of the centre and close to the remains of the southwest pier. Although hearths are not always placed centrally within wheelhouses, this hearth's position is somewhat extreme. This is probably because the hearth was originally constructed as a square setting 1.5m × 1.5m and was subsequently modified into its narrow form (see Chapter 6).
- Secondly, its long and thin rectangular plan as a modified setting is at odds with other examples. All of the hearths in wheelhouses from South Uist and Barra are circular or curvilinear except for those at Cill Donnain, in House 1 at nearby Bornais mound 1 (Sharples 2012b: 42–3), T17 (first phase) and the second phase at Allasdale (Figures 17.12–17.13). In North Uist and Lewis, the situation is reversed with curvilinear hearths known only from Sollas and Gearraidh Iochdrach in North Uist (Figure 17.14). This geographical distinction may also have had a chronological dimension since the Cill Donnain and Bornais wheelhouses are so late in the sequence.

Just why the Cill Donnain hearth was made narrower (1.52m long × 0.60m wide) is perplexing. The only Western Isles wheelhouse hearth to be narrower is the lower of two hearths (just a metre long and half a metre wide) within the wheelhouse of Bagh nam Feadag (Grimsay; Wood 1999; McKenzie 2005: 78). For the Cill Donnain hearth, its narrowness after alteration combined with its peripheral location to one side of the central area of the wheelhouse suggest that it was modified in order to maximize space for other activities within the core of the dwelling. It seems no longer to have acted as a focus around which the household would have clustered, given that anyone sitting on its west side would have had to contend with an awkwardly positioned stone pier and a low-roofed recess within the western cell. Instead, open space in the centre of the house was now maximized, possibly to compensate for the house's cramped dimensions.

The spread of peat ash and carbonized wood fragments leading northwards from the Cill Donnain hearth shows that the hearth was raked out and utilized from the north and northeast, a part of the floor layer that was carpeted with over 700 sherds of pottery, trampled and broken into small fragments. Most of these were distributed within the northwest quadrant of the central area and in the northeast corbelled cell. With an average sherd weight of 4.2g for pottery from the wheelhouse floor, it is curious that the pottery is so completely fragmented when we compare it to pottery assemblages from other wheelhouses such as Cnip (MacSween 2006).

On the basis of wear patterns within the floor layer, access into the Cill Donnain III house from the doorway to the southeast might have been redirected in later years, to lead people westwards on entering the house, towards the narrow gap between the southwest pier and the hearth, though this route would have run very close to the small pier base on the southwest side of the entrance; if this pier was still standing to full height, it seems unlikely that anyone could have passed so close to it along that route.

A second possible route northwestwards towards the centre of the house – obscured by later activity – cannot be ruled out. In common with other wheelhouses, there were few types of artefacts other than pottery from the house floor (Parker Pearson and Sharples 1999: 230). Notable exceptions are four pieces of worked antler, two from the northeast corner of the northwest cell.

With large areas of the floor layer presumed destroyed by later activity, it is difficult to gain any further understanding of the spatial arrangement of activities within the house. Very little pottery was deposited within its south side. There was no sign of any stone settings or furnishings that might indicate the positions of sleeping areas; any of the cells on the east, south or west sides would have suited. Even so, the available evidence for spatial organization does not support the sunwise model (Fitzpatrick 1997).

The food preparation area, on the basis of ceramic concentrations, is in the north and northwest (see Figure 6.25) rather than in the southeast, and the hearth is in the southwest and not in the centre. The northern cells are full of broken pottery and are thus unlikely to be sleeping areas as predicted by the model. Craft-working evidence is slim but the pieces of worked antler suggest a northerly location for it, rather than in the southwest according to the model. All in all, this house was apparently designed and used according to very different principles to those of the sunwise model.

The Cill Donnain III wheelhouse in the context of the Hebridean Iron Age

Mike Parker Pearson

The Cill Donnain wheelhouse thus throws up a series of anomalous features. Whether we can even be certain that it was a dwelling for a family or household group is problematic. Its cleared central area, with the hearth on its periphery, suggests that activities requiring a reasonable amount of space were carried out in this otherwise small and pokey building. Might it even have been a subsidiary building for a larger establishment – a cookhouse and/or servants' quarters perhaps?

The perfect symmetry of its interior wall face and the quality of the stones in the surviving bases of its northeast, north and northwest piers suggest that it was built with architectural flair and care. It provides a contrast with the very irregular form of the badly damaged fifth–sixth century wheelhouse within nearby mound 1 at Bornais (Sharples 2012b). Of course, servants' quarters need not be shoddily built, since they may be designed to reflect the quality of their masters' own dwelling. Unfortunately such speculation cannot be grounded in evidence without future investigation of the larger settlement mound on the northern and western periphery of which the wheelhouse sat.

The use of the Cill Donnain III wheelhouse seems to have lasted some two centuries. Having been built around AD 205–310, the last use of the repositioned hearth (layer 177) probably took place in the late fifth or early sixth centuries AD (*cal AD 495–540 at 68% probability*). Thereafter – or at the same time – the house underwent a couple of minor modifications.

The wheelhouse's interior was modified by the renovation of the narrow hearth into a smaller, more rectangular arrangement, and by the construction of a short stretch of walling to the north of the hearth, extending into the house's interior from the northwest pier. This served to block off the previous axis of use and movement from the hearth to the northern half of the wheelhouse's interior. It is hard to establish just why this might have been done. Perhaps the northern half of the wheelhouse was designated as separate space from the cooking and food production, perhaps as a sleeping area, though there is no evidence for this (in the form of any bowl-shaped depressions in the cells).

As with so many wheelhouses, the house's abandonment was by no means the end of its use. It was comprehensively robbed of stones from its outer wall face, its interior piers and its corbelled cell roofs, the latter leaving piles of rubble in the northwest, northeast and southern cells. Stones were also removed from the stones set on edge that formed the basal course of the inner wall face; most of those in the south and west were taken out, together with single stones from the east wall, to provide access across the eroded wall core into the wheelhouse's interior. The reason for this was that a small structure with pitched-slab walls was constructed within the northern half of the house. Its southeast-facing doorway could be accessed not only through the ruined doorway of the wheelhouse but also through two gaps in the east wall. A gap in the northwest wall, coupled with the wheelhouse's floor being eroded in this location, may be evidence of another access into the ruined interior from the west.

It seems perhaps strange that such thorough dismantling was not 100% complete. Why leave the pier bases and most of the inner wall face when these stones were of a good size and quality? In contrast to the severely robbed-out house within mound 1 at Bornais, there seems to have been some reluctance to complete the job. During excavation, many of us were very aware that the stones looked like a mini-monument, sufficiently recognizable as a stone-walled circular house for it to be worth re-erecting

the surviving stones in the grounds of Taigh-tasgaidh Chill Donnain, where the reconstructed wheelhouse can be seen today.

Some wheelhouses, such as Kilpheder (Lethbridge 1952) and Cnip (Armit 2006), were left almost untouched after their abandonment whilst others were largely dismantled. Perhaps the reasons for this differential treatment were entirely prosaic and practical, determined by the community's needs for easily accessible building materials. Alternatively, people's understanding of their past and their interest in preserving vestiges of where they or their ancestors once lived might have been a factor.

Ultimately the Cill Donnain wheelhouse's ruins were engulfed in windblown sand, leaving only the tops of the inner wall face's stones poking through. This part of the settlement mound was then covered in the Late Iron Age by a thick layer of domestic rubbish that extended at least 20m north–south and 15m east–west. The ceramic sherds found in these midden layers were as thoroughly fragmented as those left on the wheelhouse's floor, which suggests that this was refuse from the floors of one or more houses probably located somewhere to the east, within the heart of the settlement mound. Just why this material was spread here is hard to know. Ploughmarks indicate that the area of Late Iron Age midden was cultivated east–west at least once. The deposition of the midden material might also have served to stabilize open areas along the settlement mound's exposed western flank, thus protecting the settlement from wind erosion.

Social and economic status

Most of the non-ceramic material culture excavated at Cill Donnain III derives from this pre-Norse Late Iron Age midden material, although some of the finds are unstratified from the midden's surface. The artefacts include a wide array of copper-alloy and ferrous items, metalworking slag, worked and unworked pumice, coarse stone tools such as hammerstones, and artefacts of bone, antler and ivory.

The presence of ironworking (and copper-alloy working) residues is particularly interesting because of their near-complete or complete absence on the nearby sites of Dun Vulan, Sligeanach, Bornais and Upper Loch Bornais. The presence of slag from layers infilling the wheelhouse from its occupation onwards also points to long-term smithing at Cill Donnain III, probably somewhere to the east of the wheelhouse within the settlement complex beneath the dune.

Evidence for ironworking has been found at other wheelhouses such as A 'Cheardach Bheag (Fairhurst 1971: 90) and Cnip 2/3 (Armit and Dunwell 1992; McLaren and Heald in Armit 2006) but it is more unusual than the evidence for non-ferrous metallurgy, found on 18 sites of probable Iron Age date in the Western Isles (Heald and Hunter in Armit 2006: 160). However, Heald and

Hunter note that the metalworking debris from these sites may be much later than their primary occupation in the Middle Iron Age.

The quantities of finished metalwork at Cill Donnain III, in the form of discarded iron and copper-alloy artefacts, are much greater than the quantities from Middle–Late Iron Age layers at Dun Vulan (Parker Pearson and Sharples 1999: 228–30) and Bornais mound 1 (Sharples 2012b: tabs 62, 109), even though greater volumes of stratified deposits were excavated at these latter two sites. Most of these metal finds from Cill Donnain III were found in the mixed midden deposits (phase 9) at the end of the sequence and thus derive from contexts other than the wheelhouse.

Since the Cill Donnain wheelhouse is a small building on the edge of a much larger settlement mound (today mostly buried under a deep sand dune), it might have been a peripheral structure within a much larger and grander settlement. This settlement was almost certainly larger than the Iron Age settlement of Bornais mound 1 and quite probably Dun Vulan too. Thus its social and economic status is likely to have been relatively high in the Late Iron Age.

Further evidence for Cill Donnain III's high status is provided by four finds of ivory artefacts. Such material, presumably from marine mammal teeth, is extremely rare in the Atlantic Iron Age before the Norse period. Its use at Cill Donnain is not restricted to the Late Iron Age, with ivory items from Late Bronze Age occupation (phase 2) and wheelhouse construction (phase 4), as well as from the phase 9 midden. One of the finds from phase 4 is an ivory off-cut, suggesting that ivory artefacts might have been manufactured at Cill Donnain. Thus, Cill Donnain III provides evidence for the manufacturing of artefacts not found on neighbouring settlements.

Economic specialization

One intriguing possibility for the organization of ironworking in the Western Isles during the Middle Iron Age is that it was carried out at centres that had been working metal since the Bronze Age. Now that Late Bronze Age mould fragments have been recognized at Cill Donnain III as well as at Cladh Hallan (Cowie in prep.), there is evidence that two out of three, if not all of, South Uist's settlement complexes in that period (Cladh Hallan, Cill Donnain and Machair Mheadhanach) were casting bronze.

If there were continuity in metalworking centres or metalworking settlements, this could explain why there is evidence of Middle and Late Iron Age ironworking at Cill Donnain III and metalworking at Machair Mheadhanach on mounds 126 and 141 (Parker Pearson 2012c: 57, 59). In addition, there is metal slag from a Late Iron Age site at Ormacleit (site 7), and from three undated sites: Cladh Hallan site 196, Sligeanach site 22 (Cill Donnain), South Bornais site 11, and Ormacleit site 10 (Parker Pearson 2012c: 42–4, 64).

Given the possibility that Ormacleit site 10 – in close proximity to site 7 – could date to the Late Bronze Age, together with the proximity of sites 11 and 22 to Cill Donnain, this provides a future hypothesis to be explored. Late Bronze Age settlements have not been found around Cnip in Lewis (Armit 2006) or Eilean Olabhat in North Uist (Armit *et al.* 2008), two locations of Iron Age metalworking, but the presence of Early Bronze Age burials from both may indicate that these were centres of settlement during the Bronze Age.

A further aspect of differentiation between the contemporaneous and neighbouring sites of Cill Donnain III, Dun Vulan and Bornais mound 1 in the early Late Iron Age is visible in terms of crop-processing. The many fragments of rotary querns and bone quern spindles from Dun Vulan dating to this period (Parker Pearson and Sharples 1999: 217, 230–2) are far more numerous than from the two wheelhouses. It is possible that much of the grain from different farmsteads along this part of South Uist's coast was processed in the settlement in and around the ruinous remains of the broch.

Whilst there is good evidence for specialization in metalworking and milling among these Middle–Late Iron Age settlements, this is not the case for other crafts. This is partly because the residues of metalworking and corn-grinding are easily recoverable. When seeking evidence for weaving, we rely on rare artefacts of bone and antler such as needles, beaters and so-called weaving combs (long-handled combs, as found at Bornais mound 1 [Sharples 2012b: 275–8] and Cnip [Hunter 2006: 143]). Spinning is rather easier to document on most sites, with the frequent discovery of bone, stone and pottery spindle whorls: there are just two from Cill Donnain III.

Hide-working is also documented on many sites through the presence of bone awls and points, pumice (used to remove hair and fat) and polishing stones: again, Cill Donnain III's midden has produced worked pumice and bone points. Pottery-making is also likely to have been carried out by many different communities, and occasionally finds are made (such as bone spatulae) that could be potters' tools (Hallén 1994: 207); there is one such candidate from Cill Donnain. The relative lack of major differences in pottery fabrics across the Western Isles, resulting from the ubiquity of gneiss-derived clays, currently prevents any attempts at identifying regional exchange networks for ceramics.

Whilst most of the craft-working evidence suggests local and domestic modes of production, the agricultural evidence gives us a further dimension. Middle and Late Iron Age carbonized cereal assemblages from the Western Isles are unrelentingly dominated by hulled barley, and Cill Donnain III is no exception. A few sites have produced occasional charred grains of oats and possibly flax, wheat and rye, although these may be contaminants. With large-scale flotation programmes at Dun Vulan (Smith 1999) and Bornais (Colledge and Smith in Sharples 2012b), together with Cnip, Loch Bharabhat and Loch na

Beirgh in Lewis (Church 2000; 2002; Church and Cressey 2006), it is possible to consider the environments in which the crops were grown on the basis of the ecological niches of accompanying weeds of cultivation.

Smith (1999) concluded that the abundance of species favouring damp and acid ground at Dun Vulan as well as Baile Sear and Hornish Point (Jones 2003) suggests that use of blacklands for arable is as plausible as the use of machair. In contrast, Church and Cressey (2006: 193) conclude tentatively that the Lewis sites cultivated their crops on the machair. Similarly, Summers and Bond (in Sharples 2012b) conclude that there are no taxa from mound 1 at Bornais that strongly suggest cultivation of the blackland's more acidic soils.

The unsystematic, judgemental sampling strategy employed at Cill Donnain prevents any such comparison with assemblages of charred plant remains from these other sites, which is a shame given the close proximity of Dun Vulan and Bornais. All we can say is that the topographical position of Cill Donnain III might have affected access to the soils on which its crops were grown, since it is separated from areas of blackland by large expanses of water in the form of freshwater Lochs Bornais and Chill Donnain. Given that we have evidence of ploughing in the top of the midden, it would seem likely that most of Cill Donnain's crops were cultivated on the machair.

The possibility of trade in agricultural produce in prehistoric societies is rarely examined in situations lacking evident markets or central places, creating a tendency to envisage entirely self-sufficient communities within household-based societies; the settlements of the Atlantic Iron Age fall into this category. For Lewis, Church and Cressey (2006: 193) have argued that the greater diversity of plant remains at the broch of Loch na Beirgh compared to the Cnip wheelhouse and Loch Bharabhat islet is due to differences in sampling and contexts recovered. However, the differences between the broch of Dun Vulan and the Bornais wheelhouse in crop availability – above all, the presence of flax at Bornais mound 1 (Summers and Bond in Sharples 2012b: 230–2) – might owe something to the differential social and economic status of the two settlements.

As Mulville discovered in 1999, Dun Vulan might have been importing certain agricultural commodities in the form of pigs and specifically their front-leg joints (Mulville 1999: 272–4). It is not impossible that such exchanges, whether as tribute or as some other form of transaction, involved sacks of barley as well as animals and joints of meat. Archaeological evidence for trade is often limited to raw materials such as metal and manufactured items (such as the Continental Roman brooch from Cill Donnain III), but this small-scale agricultural society might have maintained its cohesion across the Western Isles through an elaborate network of commodity exchanges triggered at rites of passage and celebratory events in the lives of households.

Food consumption

The faunal remains from Cill Donnain III show a predominance of sheep and cattle over pigs. This can be interpreted as part of a wider distinction between the diet of those living in brochs and the diet of those living in wheelhouses, in which pigs mostly form 1%–12% of these three domesticates in wheelhouse assemblages and 12%–24% in broch assemblages within western Scotland (Mulville 1999: tab. 10.43). Specifically within the Dun Vulan environs, pigs formed a higher proportion of domesticated species at Dun Vulan than at Bornais mound 1 or Cill Donnain (Mulville in Sharples 2012b: tab. 111). Similarly, the number of imported exotic species found at Dun Vulan (pine marten, badger, hare, roe deer) suggests that Dun Vulan had a higher social status (Mulville 1999: 265, 273, tab. 10.30).

The economic and social status of venison consumption in the Iron Age has attracted discussion because of the occasional depictions of deer on material culture and because of the wide variation in the presence of deer bones within settlements (Mulville 1999: 273; Armit 2006: 237–9). For example, red deer were a major food source for the inhabitants of Cnip, Loch Bharabhat and Loch na Beirgh in Lewis but are almost absent in the food remains from Iron Age settlements in South Uist (Mulville in Sharples 2012b: tab. 111). With one possible interpretation under consideration being that red deer had died out in South Uist by the Iron Age, it was something of a surprise to discover that red deer were, in fact, an important resource for the Late Iron Age inhabitants of Bornais, who were systematically hunting juvenile and immature deer in the hills (Mulville in Sharples 2012b: 341–2). By contrast, Cill Donnain III and Dun Vulan (Mulville 1999: 258–64) have produced very few skeletal remains of red deer, indicating very different food preferences (or access to resources) among neighbouring, contemporaneous settlements.

The level of consumption of beef in relation to mutton at Cill Donnain appears to have varied through time. The post-Bronze Age faunal assemblage (phases 3–9) is dominated by cattle apart from phase 5, associated with the occupation of the wheelhouse, which is dominated by sheep/goat. By the Late Iron Age, the balance tipped back towards cattle; whatever unlocated activities the midden accumulated from (no doubt still buried under the dune), the creators of the midden consumed much more beef than mutton.

Across the Western Isles, relative abundances of cattle and sheep vary from site to site and context to context (Mulville 1999: tab. 10.43; Mulville in Sharples 2012b: tab. 111). At Sollas the midden contained higher proportions of cattle than did the wheelhouse remains of site A. Another site that stands out as unusual in this respect is Cnip wheelhouse where beef formed 68% of the carcass weight of all meat from mammals (McCormick 2006: 164–5). By comparison, venison formed 18%, mutton 3% and pork 7%.

If these proportions are a direct indication of the Cnip settlement's animal husbandry, then cattle played a more important role than could be expected from the site's severe environmental setting (Armit 2006: 236). However, we should remember that faunal remains derive directly from food selection and only indirectly from animal husbandry. There is no guarantee that the Cnip cattle were home-raised with no 'food miles' accumulated by bringing them from, for example, more distant pastures in the Uists.

When we examine the full context of food consumption at Cnip, it becomes clear that this particular wheelhouse consumed an unusually large quantity of pottery. As Armit notes, the 84kg of ceramics consists of 6,370 sherds from an estimated 2,882 vessels; from this, he calculates that fragments of 15 vessels entered archaeological contexts on average every year (Armit 2006: 243). He concludes that 'large numbers of pottery vessels were present within the wheelhouse throughout its use' (*ibid.*).

It is worth considering whether the status of Cnip was more than that of a self-sufficient dwelling: it was perhaps also a place for feasting. The discovery of a suspected tuning peg for a lyre, and a gaming piece (Hunter 2006: 147–9) intimates that music and gaming also took place there.

Cosmological aspects of architecture and inhabitation

The typological similarities of Hebridean wheelhouses often draw archaeologists to perceive these architecturally distinctive buildings as a unitary phenomenon, individual examples of self-contained farming lifestyles, with households reproducing themselves as independent units. An alternative view, proposed by Iain Crawford (2002: 126–8), is that the architectural form of the wheelhouses was motivated by religious rather than habitational concerns; he interprets their unique architecture of conspicuous and extravagant construction, together with their associated animal sacrifices, as evidence that they were built by a religious cult. In future, we need to explain their differences and diversity within the middle ground between these two extremes of emphasis on either economy or religion.

The extent to which the architecture of wheelhouses – and roundhouses more generally – was more than a response to the need for shelter and warmth has been a topic of discussion for many years now (*e.g.* Fitzpatrick 1994; 1997; Parker Pearson 1996). Oswald's observation (1997) that most roundhouses in southern Britain had entrances towards the east and especially the southeast has been borne out by other studies (Parker Pearson 1999; Parker Pearson and Richards 1994; Pope 2007). East in its broadest sense was also the direction towards which most Iron Age burials – as well as the entrances of most enclosures, hillforts and brochs – were oriented (Hill 1996; Parker Pearson *et al.* 1996).

Fitzpatrick's sunwise cosmological model (1994; 1997) sought to provide an explanatory framework not only for this consistency of direction in doorways but also for the circularity of roundhouses and the organization of activities within: houses and the activities performed in them were metaphorically linked to the passage of time in the diurnal movement of the sun and the passage from life to death. Thus from sunrise in the east, the day's activities proceeded clockwise around the house with cooking in the southeast, daytime craft-working in the southwest and sleeping in the north.

The model has been applied to Middle Iron Age wheelhouses and brochs (Parker Pearson and Sharples 1999: 16–21, 350–3) and has been supported by more recent research such as McKenzie's analysis of the use of space within the wheelhouse at Bagh nam Feadag, Grimsay (McKenzie 2005: 159–61). Yet, as noted above, it seems not to apply to the Cill Donnain wheelhouse, at least in terms of the spatial organization of activities within it. Whilst this wheelhouse has a conventional roundhouse orientation for its doorway (towards the southeast) and pathways of movement consistent with the sunwise model, the probable location of the food preparation and craft zone in the northwest quadrant is anomalous.

One of the interesting characteristics of the orientation of Scottish broch doorways and British hillfort entrances is that a substantial proportion of them have broadly west-facing entrances (Parker Pearson *et al.* 1996; Parker Pearson and Sharples 1999: 352; Hill 1996). The same is also turning out to be true for Hebridean wheelhouses, with west-facing doorways at the two machair sites at Cnip and at the moorland sites of Allt Chrisal and Allasdale (Barra), Bagh nam Feadag (Grimsay), Clettraval and Eilean Maleit (North Uist; Scott 1948; Armit 1998). An example of a west-facing Early Iron Age building is the small sub-rectangular structure at An Dunan (Lewis), dating to 400–100 cal BC and containing human bones on its large central hearth (Gilmore 2002: 59).

This wealth of examples of wheelhouses and roundhouses situated on exposed Hebridean hillsides with doorways facing into the teeth of the Atlantic westerlies exposes the inadequacy of theories that explain roundhouse orientation in terms of the avoidance of strong winds (*e.g.* Pope 2007). Similarly, the elaborate entrance passages and ante-rooms between the threshold and the outside world for many wheelhouses undermines any notion that facing east or southeast was aimed at maximizing light within the roundhouse: where such passages and ante-rooms are present, sunlight would never have effectively illuminated the interior of the house.

The evidence from wheelhouses allows us to successfully dispense with purely pragmatic concerns of prevailing wind directions and natural illumination of interiors as explanations of house orientation and internal spatial organization (Armit 1996: 250). Yet the sunwise theory, although it works well for roundhouses of the

Late Bronze Age and Early Iron Age at Cladh Hallan (Parker Pearson *et al.* in prep.), is not wholly sufficient for explaining the variability found in Middle Iron Age wheelhouses. Armit (2006: 250) points out that, although wheelhouse doorways predominantly face east or southeast (11 cases in his catalogue), four face north, northeast and southwest, while seven face west. There is sufficient variation, he suggests, to demonstrate that we have not established entirely what the principles were behind wheelhouse orientations.

One of the problems of the dataset is that the anomalous buildings that face neither east nor west are from old excavations by Beveridge (1911) in North Uist as well as Jack Scott's unpublished excavation at Bruthach a'Tuath in Benbecula (also known as Bruach Ban; the entrance here appears to have faced southeast; MacKie 2007: 1142–4; Sharples 2012b: 11, fig. 11). It is simply not possible to verify whether these were original entrances or gaps made in later re-occupation. More importantly, we can be sure of the west-facing entrances because these wheelhouses were mostly dug according to modern standards.

A previous idea that the west-facing wheelhouses were cosmological opposites of the conventional orientation to east or southeast put forward the notion that such buildings might have had special uses because of the special status of their inhabitants or the activities performed within. Metalworking associations (Parker Pearson and Sharples 1999: 17) were suggested, along with night-time use by ritual specialists and for feasting (Parker Pearson *et al.* 2004: 101). The tentative link with metallurgy can now be dispensed with but there may still be mileage in the latter hypothesis.

When we examine the path of movement into the west-facing Cnip wheelhouse, an upright slab within the doorway's north side constrains movement, imposing an anti-clockwise route into the house, by blocking entry to the northern half of the building (Armit 2006: 42). What is interesting is that this slab was needed to physically prevent people from moving in the sunwise direction that was presumably engrained in their daily routines and practices. The Cnip wheelhouse was organized so as to be the opposite of the everyday, perhaps related to its role in feasting, music and gaming.

But how do we explain the other west-facing wheelhouses? Clettraval is constructed on the back of a Neolithic chambered tomb, so perhaps its association with a previous monument was an important factor in orienting the doorway in opposition to the norm. The placing of stone flooring around the south side of the central space (Scott 1948: 47) indicates that, as with Cnip, movement into the interior at Clettraval was anticlockwise.

Little can be said about Eilean Maleit and Bagh nam Feadag because of their poor standard of excavations, though McKenzie (2005) has done an excellent job of salvaging information from the archive left by the excavator of Bagh nam Feadag. He shows that the majority of pottery from inside the wheelhouse probably came from the northwest quadrant, thereby suggesting that the spatial distribution of activities within Bagh nam Feadag was a rotation around 180° of the sunwise model, rather than a reversal of it, as in the case of Clettraval and Cnip. A similar case of rotation about 180° appears to account for the distribution of peat ash (and thus food preparation) within the Allasdale wheelhouse in Barra (Young 1953).

The Allt Chrisal wheelhouse (T17; Figure 17.13) in Barra is an interesting case because it was not only built on top of an earlier roundhouse but underwent modification from an aisled wheelhouse with unbonded piers and a south-southeast-facing doorway to a wheelhouse with bonded piers and a west-facing doorway (Foster and Pouncett 2000). It thus offers an opportunity to find out whether there was anything unusual about the house and its transformation that could explain why a west-facing orientation became necessary.

Even though bone did not survive within the soils at Allt Chrisal, its architecture, stratigraphic sequence and non-perishable material culture may provide insights into the significance of doorway orientation. Unlike Cnip, this wheelhouse produced only moderate amounts of pottery and no evidence for music or gaming, but the treatment of its interior was very unusual:

- At some point during its first phase of occupation, its residents gave up sweeping out the interior and allowed layers of ash to cover the entire floor. The central hearth became completely hidden under a growing mound of peat ash 0.50m deep that occupied the entire central area of the building and limited space for any activities within the house (Foster and Pouncett 2000: 156–7).

- Where pottery was recorded within the house floor, it seems that it was concentrated in the southeast cell (as predicted by the sunwise model but, because of the doorway's south-southeast orientation, on its right side).

- When the Allt Chrisal wheelhouse was renovated, probably between the first and third centuries AD, the new west-facing doorway was accompanied by the closing-off of the aisle around the periphery of the interior, by the construction of a formal stone kerb to separate the cells from the central area of the house, and by the construction of a much smaller, circular hearth just 0.80m in diameter (Foster and Pouncett 2000: 159–61).

- The house continued to be inhabited, and the range of ceramics and stone tools suggests that activities involving these items did not vary from before.

- Once again, ash from the hearth spread throughout the interior of the house to form a compact floor surface but the depth of ash within the hearth reached a depth of only 0.25m.

Ultimately there is little that we can point to for explaining the change in doorway orientation at Allt Chrisal. The central mound of ash on which the circular hearth was perched was so large that it is hard to imagine that this very small wheelhouse could have been lived in comfortably or effectively by a busy and active household. Was the failure to clean out the hearth the result of laziness, incapacity or ritual prohibition? There was clearly something very odd about the residents of Allt Chrisal but just what it was eludes us. It certainly cannot be classed as a 'normal' dwelling.

Returning to the machair of South Uist, the poorly-preserved Late Iron Age wheelhouse excavated within mound 1 at Bornais, within sight of Cill Donnain, had a west-facing doorway (Sharples 2012b). This certainly appears to have been the case in its first phase before it burned down; after the fire a new structure was constructed on top of the charred, collapsed roof timbers that lay on the floor of the wheelhouse. As discussed above, this building was in use in the fifth–sixth centuries AD around the same time as the Cill Donnain III wheelhouse.

Whilst there are many aspects of architecture and economy shared by the Bornais and Cill Donnain III wheelhouses, there are also intriguing differences, some of which may relate to their oppositional orientations. For example, the Bornais mound 1 wheelhouse has certain aspects in common with Cnip, such as the role of venison in its cuisine and the evidence for gaming; in fact, Bornais has produced the most impressive range of Late Iron Age gaming pieces from the region (in the form of dice, counters and decorated astragali; Sharples 2012b: 266–71). The pottery also includes a number of big cooking vessels capable of feeding large gatherings (Lane in Sharples 2012b: 257). Among the other finds, attractive weaving tools (weaving combs and square tablets) and a fragment of an ogham-inscribed animal bone (Sharples 2012b: 271–8) also hint at activities not found at Cill Donnain III. The first house within Bornais mound 1 appears to have been used only intermittently; although ending its days as a store and a dog kennel (*ibid.*: 323), there is enough evidence to suggest that it may have been used not as an ordinary dwelling but to host periodic gatherings.

The second house to be built at Bornais mound 1, on the ruins of the wheelhouse, also had some unusual features. The elaborate enclosing of its hearth with cattle metapodials is testament not only to the consumption of considerable quantities of beef – over 2,800kg (Sharples 2012b: 100) – but also the display and recording of such feasting events. The large quantities of sintered sand (fuel ash slag) from this hearth also point to the attainment of temperatures much higher than those normally reached in the central hearths of other roundhouses and wheelhouses on the machair, suggesting that the fires generated on this hearth did more than simply warm just a household group.

All in all, the contrasts between the contemporary, neighbouring wheelhouses of Bornais mound 1 and Cill Donnain III sharpen our understanding of how some of the west-facing houses played a special role in hospitality, feasting and entertainment. Such differentiation in activities may not necessarily coincide with our conventional notions of social status (as embodied in the distinction between brochs and wheelhouses); indeed, it might well have cut across architectural and social manifestations of class and status.

Conclusion

Mike Parker Pearson

In conclusion, the wheelhouse of Cill Donnain III provides a good deal of new material to contribute to the developing corpus of excavated Iron Age houses in the Western Isles. The archaeological layers beneath and subsequent to the Cill Donnain wheelhouse also provide glimpses of moments within a long sequence of occupation, such as the Early–Middle Bronze Age occupation layers associated with Cordoned Urn ceramics, the Late Bronze Age deposits with ceramic refractories for casting bronze swords, and the Late Iron Age midden at the end of the sequence, which covered the abandoned wheelhouse and contained redeposited material mixed from different periods.

Although the Cill Donnain III wheelhouse is one of the smallest examples of its type and contained little in the way of artefacts other than ceramics and some antler artefacts, it lay on the northern and western edge of a very substantial settlement mound that is mostly covered today by a high dune. Artefacts from layers above and below the wheelhouse indicate that, although the house itself was not a high-status building by any means, it probably formed part of a significant, large settlement where iron, copper alloy and ivory were worked at various times between the Late Bronze Age and the Late Iron Age. Before the establishment of the large Norse settlement at Bornais, Cill Donnain might have been the pre-eminent settlement in South Uist.

The roundhouses and wheelhouses of the Western Isles have to be among the most important examples of structures from the entire British Iron Age because of the degree of preservation of their standing architecture and stratigraphic sequences. With so much more to go on than eavesdrip gullies and postholes – the standard fare of Iron Age roundhouse archaeology in most of Britain – they are unmatched repositories of information on the intimate details of everyday life in the Iron Age.

For those sites on the machair, the excellent preservation of animal bones is a further boon to the archaeologist, allowing interesting contrasts to be identified in the foodways and animal husbandry of the inhabitants. In particular, comparison between the broadly contemporary neighbouring settlements of Dun Vulan, Bornais and Cill Donnain shows that it is unlikely that each was an independent unit and that all were linked within a complex network of social and economic interdependency. This is a fertile bed for developing new theories and hypotheses about social and economic life in the Iron Age and exploring the complex interaction between practicality, cosmology and ritual action.

Appendix Context list and phasing for the 1989, 1990 and 1991 excavations at Cill Donnain III

Cill Donnain III Phasing

1 = EBA Cordoned Urn layers
2 = LBA/EIA layers
3 = Late MIA pre-wheelhouse layers
4 = Late MIA wheelhouse construction
5 = Late MIA wheelhouse initial occupation
6 = Late MIA wheelhouse modification
7 = Early LIA wheelhouse abandonment
8 = Early LIA bothy-type structure
9 = LIA midden
10 = Modern or disturbed layers

Context no.	Year	Area of site	Phase	Context type
1	1989	West area	9	Midden (=005)
2	1989	West area	4, 9	Windblown sand
3	1989	West area	3, 4	Layers beneath wheelhouse (=059 *etc.*)
4	1989	West area	4, 5, 7	Wall core (=24), Fill outside house, Fill inside house (=25)
5	1989	West area	4, 7	Void left by robbed-out wheelhouse wall
6	1989	West area	6, 7	Wheelhouse wall core
7	1989	West area	5, 6, 7, 8, 9	Windblown sand lenses
8	1989	West area	5	Fill outside house
9	1989	West area	6	Wheelhouse wall core
10	1989	West area	4	Wheelhouse wall 169
11	1989	West area	5	Fill outside house
12	1989	West area	6, 7, 8, 9	Peat ash lenses
13	1989	West area	9	Midden layer (was 18)
14	1989	West area	6, 7	Sand fill (=025)
15	1989	West area	9	Midden layer
16	1989	Wheelhouse	6	Hearth layer
17	1989	West area	9	Windblown sand
1	1990	All areas	10	Topsoil
2	1990	Midden	9	Windblown sand
3	1990	All areas	9	Midden layer
4	1990	Midden	9	Windblown sand
5	1990	Midden	9	Midden layer
6	1990	Midden	9	Sand fill
7	1990	Midden	9	Midden layer
8	1990	Midden	9	Midden layer

Context no.	Year	Area of site	Phase	Context type
9	1990	Midden	9	Midden layer
10	1990	Midden	9	Pit
11	1990	Midden	9	Peat ash and shell
12	1990	Midden	9	Sand fill
13	1990	Midden	9	Peat ash
14	1990	Midden	9	Midden layer
15	1990	Midden	9	Midden layer
16	1990	Midden	9	Windblown sand
17	1990	Midden	9	Windblown sand
18	1990	Midden	9	Peat ash
19	1990	Midden	9	Windblown sand
20	1990	Midden	9	Peat ash
21	1990	All areas	9	Sand fill
22	1990	1991 extension	9	Organic layer
23	1990	Midden	9	Peat ash
24	1990	Wheelhouse	4	Wall core
25	1990	Wheelhouse	7	Sand fill (=176)
26	1990	Wheelhouse	7	Midden layer
27	1990	Outside wheelhouse	9	Midden layer
28	1990	Wheelhouse	8	Sand fill
29	1990	Wheelhouse	9	Midden layer
30	1990	All areas	3	Sand fill
31	1990	Wheelhouse	9	Midden layer
32	1990	Outside wheelhouse	3	Pre-midden layer
33	1990	Wheelhouse	9	Midden layer
34	1990	1991 extension	3	Sand fill
35	1990	1991 extension	3	Sand fill
36	1990	All areas	9	Sand fill
37	1990	Beneath wheelhouse	3	Peat ash
38–50	Void			
51	1990	Midden	9	Midden layer
52	1990	All areas	3	Sand fill
53	1990	Midden	9	Peat ash
54	1990	Midden	9	Midden layer
55	1990	Southwest area	10	Redeposited sand
56	1990	Southwest area	10	Redeposited sand
57	1990	Midden	10	Displaced boulder
58	1990	Midden	9	Midden layer
59	1990	Outside wheelhouse	3	Layers beneath wheelhouse (=3/1989 *etc.*)
60	1990	Outside wheelhouse	3	Organic layer
61	1990	Outside wheelhouse	3	Sand fill
62–99	Void			
100	1991	1991 extension	10	Topsoil
101	1991	1991 extension	9	Loose sand
102	1991	1991 extension	9	Sand
103	1991	1991 extension	9	Midden layer
104	1991	1991 extension	3	Organic layer
105	1991	Beneath wheelhouse	3	Sand fill
106	1991	1991 extension	3	Sand fill
107–129	Void			
130	1991	Beneath wheelhouse	3	Sand fill
131	1991	Northwest trench	3	Sand fill
132	1991	Northwest trench	3	Hearth
133	1991	Northwest trench	2	Sand fill
134	1991	Northwest trench	2	Sand fill

Context no.	Year	Area of site	Phase	Context type
135	1991	Northwest trench	2	Windblown sand
136	1991	Northwest trench	10	Modern disturbance
137	1991	Northwest trench	2	Organic layer
138	1991	Northwest trench	2	Organic layer
139	1991	Northwest trench	2	Organic layer
140	1991	Northwest trench	1	Organic layer
141	1991	Northwest trench	1	Windblown sand
142	1991	Northwest trench	2	Pit and pit fill
143	1991	Northwest trench	2	Sand fill
144	1991	Northwest trench	2	Organic layer
145	1991	Northwest trench	2	Windblown sand
146	1991	Northwest trench	1	Sand fill
147	1991	Northwest trench	1	Organic layer
148	1991	Northwest trench	1	Organic layer
149	1991	Northwest trench	1	Sand fill
150	1991	Northwest trench	1	Windblown sand
151	1991	Northwest trench	1	Sand fill
152	1991	Northwest trench	1	Shell sand fill
153	1991	Northwest trench	1	Floor layer
154	1991	Northwest trench	1	Windblown sand
155	1991	Northwest trench	1	Floor layer
156	1991	Northwest trench	1	Windblown sand
157	1991	Northwest trench	1	Peat ash
158–159	Void			
160	1991	All areas	3	Sand fill
161	1991	All areas	3	Sand fill
162	1991	All areas	3	Sand fill
163	1991	1991 extension	3	Organic layer
164	1991	1991 extension	3	Peat ash
165	1991	1991 extension	3	Sand fill
166	1991	Wheelhouse	5	Floor layer
167	1991	Wheelhouse	8	Circular stone building
168	1991	Wheelhouse	4	Stone pier
169	1991	Wheelhouse	4	Circular stone wall
170	1991	Wheelhouse	5	Floor layer
171	1991	Outside wheelhouse	3	Peat ash
172	1991	Wheelhouse	7	Sand fill
173	1991	Beneath wheelhouse	3	Shell sand fill
174	1991	Wheelhouse	6	Stone wall
175	1991	Wheelhouse	7	Stones
176	1991	Wheelhouse	7	Sand fill
177	1991	Wheelhouse	5	Hearth fill
178	1991	Wheelhouse	5	Hearth
179	1991	Wheelhouse	5	Hearth fill
180	1991	Wheelhouse	5	Stone lining of pit
181	1991	Beneath wheelhouse	3	Sand fill
182	1991	Wheelhouse	6	Gully and fill
183	1991	Wheelhouse	5	Pit fill
184	1991	Wheelhouse	5	Stone-lined pit
185	1991	Wheelhouse	4	Pit fill
186	1991	Wheelhouse	4	Pit
187	1991	Beneath wheelhouse	3	Sand fill
188	1991	Wheelhouse	4	Post pad/packing
189	1991	Beneath wheelhouse	3	Hearth
190	1991	1989/1990 area	3	Gully fill

Context no.	Year	Area of site	Phase	Context type
191	1991	1989/1990 area	3	Gully
192	1991	Wheelhouse	4	Stonehole and fill
193	1991	Wheelhouse	4	Stonehole and fill
194	1991	Wheelhouse	4	Stonehole and fill
195	1991	Wheelhouse	4	Stonehole and fill
196	1991	Wheelhouse	4	Stonehole and fill
197	1991	Wheelhouse	4	Stonehole and fill
198	1991	Wheelhouse	4	Stonehole and fill
199	1991	Wheelhouse	4	Stonehole and fill
200	1991	Wheelhouse	4	Stonehole and fill
201	1991	Wheelhouse	4	Stonehole and fill
202	1991	Wheelhouse	4	Pit and pit fill
203	1991	Wheelhouse	4	Pit and pit fill
204	1991	Wheelhouse	4	Posthole and fill
205	1991	Wheelhouse	4	Posthole and fill
206	1991	Wheelhouse	4	Pit and pit fill
207	1991	Wheelhouse	4	Pit and pit fill
208	1991	Wheelhouse	4	Pit and pit fill
209	1991	Wheelhouse	4	Stonehole and fill
210	1991	Wheelhouse	4	Stonehole and fill
211	1991	Wheelhouse	4	Stonehole and fill
212	1991	Wheelhouse	4	Posthole and fill
213	1991	Wheelhouse	4	Posthole and fill
214	1991	Wheelhouse	4	Slot
215	1991	Beneath wheelhouse	3	Gully and gully fill
216	1991	Beneath wheelhouse	3	Windblown sand
217	1991	Wheelhouse	4	Posthole and fill
218	1991	Wheelhouse	4	Pit and pit fill
219	1991	Wheelhouse	4	Posthole and fill
220	1991	Wheelhouse	4	Pit and pit fill
221	1991	Wheelhouse	5	Pit fill
222	1991	Beneath wheelhouse	3	Pit fill
223	1991	Beneath wheelhouse	3	Pit

Bibliography

Albarella, U. and Davis, S.J.M. 1994. *The Saxon and Medieval Animal Bones Excavated 1985–1989 from West Cotton, Northamptonshire.* Ancient Monuments Laboratory Report 17/94. London: English Heritage.

Albarella, U., Johnstone, C. and Vickers, K. 2008. The development of animal husbandry from the Late Iron Age to the end of the Roman period: a case study from south-east Britain. *Journal of Archaeological Science* 35: 1828–48.

Amorosi, T., Buckland, P.C., Edwards, K.J., Mainland, I., McGovern, T.H., Sadler, J.P. and Skidmore P. 1998. They did not live by grass alone: the politics and paleoecology of animal fodder in the North Atlantic region. *Environmental Archaeology* 1: 41–55.

Armit, I. 1990. Epilogue: the Atlantic Scottish Iron Age. In I. Armit (ed.) *Beyond the Brochs: changing perspectives on the later Iron Age in Atlantic Scotland.* Edinburgh: Edinburgh University Press. 194–210.

Armit, I. 1996. *The Archaeology of Skye and the Western Isles.* Edinburgh: Edinburgh University Press.

Armit, I. 1998. Re-excavation of the Iron Age wheelhouse and earlier structure at Eilean Maleit, North Uist. *Proceedings of the Society of Antiquaries of Scotland* 128: 255–71.

Armit, I. 2006. *Anatomy of an Iron Age Roundhouse: the Cnip wheelhouse excavations, Lewis.* Edinburgh: Society of Antiquaries of Scotland.

Armit, I. and Dunwell, A.J. 1992. Excavations at Cnip, sites 2 and 3, Lewis, 1989. *Proceedings of the Society of Antiquaries of Scotland* 122: 137–48.

Armit, I. and Ginn, V. 2007. Beyond the grave: human remains from domestic contexts in Atlantic Scotland. *Proceedings of the Prehistoric Society* 73: 113–34.

Armit, I. and Shapland, F. 2013. Death and display in the North Atlantic: the Bronze and Iron Age human remains from Cnip, Lewis, Outer Hebrides. *Journal of the North Atlantic* 6.

Armit, I., Campbell, E. and Dunwell, A. J. 2008. Excavation of an Iron Age, early historic and medieval settlement and metal-working site at Eilean Olabhat, North Uist. *Proceedings of the Society of Antiquaries of Scotland* 138: 27–104.

Ashmore, P. 1999. Radiocarbon dating: avoiding errors by avoiding mixed samples. *Antiquity* 73: 124–30.

Barber, J. 2003 *Bronze Age Farms and Iron Age Farm Mounds of the Outer Hebrides.* Edinburgh: Scottish Archaeological Internet Reports 3. http://www.sair.org.uk/sair3.

Bayliss, A., van der Plicht, J., Bronk Ramsey, C., McCormac, G., Healy, F. and Whittle, A. 2011. Towards generational time-scales: the quantitative interpretation of archaeological chronologies. In A. Whittle, F. Healy and A. Bayliss, *Gathering Time: dating the Early Neolithic enclosures of southern Britain and Ireland.* Oxford: Oxbow Books. 17–59.

Beedham, G.E. 1972. *Identification of the British Mollusca.* Amersham: Hulton Educational Publications Ltd.

Beijetinck, W. 1947. *Zadenatlas der Nederland Flora.* Wageningen: Veenman & Zonen.

Berggren, G. 1969. *Atlas of Seeds and Small Fruits of Northwest-European Plant Species. Part 2, Cyperaceae.* Stockholm: Swedish Museum of Natural History.

Berggren, G. 1981. *Atlas of Seeds and Small Fruits of Northwest-European Plant Species, with Morphological Descriptions. Part 3, Salicaceae – Cruciferae.* Stockholm: Swedish Museum of Natural History.

Beveridge, E. 1911. *North Uist: its archaeology and topography with notes upon the early history of the Outer Hebrides.* Edinburgh: William Brown.

Binford, L.R. 1978. *Nunamiut Ethnoarchaeology.* New York: Academic Press.

Boessneck, J. 1969. Osteological differences between sheep *(Ovis aries* Linne) and goats *(Capra hircus* Linne). In D. Brothwell and E.S. Higgs (eds) *Science in Archaeology.* (2nd edition). London: Thames & Hudson. 331–58.

Böhme, A. 1972. Die Fibeln der Kastelle Saalburg und Zugmantel. *Saalburg Jahrbuch* 29: 5–112.

Boyd, J.M. 1979. The natural environment of the Outer Hebrides. *Proceedings of the Royal Society of Edinburgh* 77B: 3–19.

Boyd, J.M. and Boyd, I.L. 1990. *The Hebrides: a natural history.* London: Collins.

Brain, C.K. 1981. *The Hunters or the Hunted?: an introduction to African cave taphonomy.* Chicago: Chicago University Press.

Branigan, K. 2005. *From Clan to Clearance: history and archaeology on the Isle of Barra c.850–1850 AD.* Oxford: Oxbow.

Branigan, K. and Foster, P. 1995. *Barra: archaeological research on Ben Tangaval.* Sheffield: Sheffield Academic Press.

Branigan, K. and Foster, P. 2000. *From Barra to Berneray: archaeological survey and excavation in the southern isles of the Outer Hebrides.* Sheffield: Sheffield Academic Press.

Branigan, K. and Foster, P. 2002. *Barra and the Bishop's Isles: living on the margin.* Stroud: Tempus.

Brodie, N. 1994. *The Neolithic–Bronze Age Transition in Britain: a critical review of some archaeological and craniological concepts.* Oxford: BAR (British Series) 238.

Bronk Ramsey, C. 1995. Radiocarbon calibration and analysis of stratigraphy: the OxCal program. *Radiocarbon* 37: 425–30.

Bronk Ramsey, C. 1998. Probability and dating. *Radiocarbon* 40: 461–74.

Bronk Ramsey, C. 2001. Development of the radiocarbon calibration program OxCal, *Radiocarbon* 43: 355–63.

Bronk Ramsey, C. 2009. Bayesian analysis of radiocarbon dates. *Radiocarbon* 51: 337–60.

Bronk Ramsey, C. and Hedges, R.E.M. 1989. Use of the CO2 source in radiocarbon dating by AMS. *Radiocarbon* 31: 298–304.

Brothwell D.R. 1981. *Digging Up Bones.* Ithaca: Cornell University Press.

Buck, C.E., Cavanagh, W.G. and Litton, C.D. 1996. *Bayesian Approach to Interpreting Archaeological Data.* Chichester: Wiley.

Buckland, P.C., Amorosi, T., Barlow, L.K., Dugmore, A.J., Mayewski, P.A., McGovern, T.H., Ogilvie, A.E.J., Sadler, J.P. and Skidmore, P. 1996. Bioarchaeological and climatological evidence for the fate of Norse farmers in medieval Greenland. *Antiquity* 70: 88–96.

Callander, J.G. and Grant, W.G. 1934. A long stalled chambered cairn or mausoleum (Rousay type) near Midhowe, Rousay, Orkney. *Proceedings of the Society of Antiquaries of Scotland* 68: 320–50.

Campbell, E. 1991. Excavations of a wheelhouse and other Iron Age structures at Sollas, North Uist, by R J C Atkinson in 1957. *Proceedings of the Society of Antiquaries of Scotland* 121: 117–73.

Campbell, E. 2002. The Western Isles pottery sequence. In B. Ballin-Smith and I. Banks (eds) *In the Shadow of the Brochs: the Iron Age in Scotland.* Stroud: Tempus. 139–44.

Campbell, E., Housley, R. and Taylor, M. 2004. Charred food residues from Hebridean Iron Age pottery: analysis and dating. In R. Housley and G. Coles (eds) *Atlantic Connections and Adaptations: economics, environments and subsistence in lands bordering the North Atlantic.* Oxford: Oxbow. 65–85.

Carmichael, A. 1884. *Grazing and agrestic customs of the Outer Hebrides.* Edinburgh: Great Britain Crofters Commission.

Cartledge, J. and Grimbley, C. 1999. The bird bone. In M. Parker Pearson and N. Sharples with J. Mulville and H. Smith, *Between Land and Sea: excavations at Dun Vulan, South Uist.* Sheffield: Sheffield Academic Press. 282–8.

Cerón-Carrasco, R. 2006. The sieved fish remains. In I. Armit, *Anatomy of an Iron Age Roundhouse: the Cnip wheelhouse excavations, Lewis.* Edinburgh: Society of Antiquaries of Scotland. 173–80.

Cerón-Carrasco, R. and Parker Pearson, M. 1999 The fish bones. In M. Parker Pearson and N. Sharples with J. Mulville and H. Smith, *Between Land and Sea: excavations at Dun Vulan, South Uist.* Sheffield: Sheffield Academic Press. 274–82.

Childe, V.G. 1931. *Skara Brae: a Pictish village in Orkney.* London: Kegan Paul.

Church, M.J. 2000. Carbonised plant macrofossils and charcoal. In D.W. Harding and T.N. Dixon, *Dun Bharabhat, Cnip: an Iron Age settlement in West Lewis.* Edinburgh: Edinburgh University Press (Calanais Research Series 2). 120–30.

Church, M.J. 2002. The archaeological and archaeobotanical implications of a destruction layer in Dun Bharabhat, Lewis. In B. Ballin Smith and I. Banks (eds) *In the Shadow of the Brochs: the Iron Age in Scotland.* Stroud: Tempus. 67–75.

Church, M.J. and Cressey, M. 2006. Carbonised plant macrofossils and charcoal. In I. Armit, *Anatomy of an Iron Age Roundhouse: The Cnip wheelhouse excavations, Lewis.* Edinburgh: Society of Antiquaries of Scotland. 182–94.

Clarke, A.D. 1962. Report on the animal remains. In A. Young and K.M. Richardson, A Cheardach Mhor, Drimore, South Uist. *Proceedings of the Society of Antiquaries of Scotland* 93: 135–73.

Clutton-Brock, J. 1981. *Domesticated Animals from Early Times.* London: Heinemann and British Museum (Natural History).

Collins, G.H. 1981. Petrological examination of pottery sherds. In J. Ritchie and A. Lane, Dun Cul Bhuirg, Iona, Argyll. *Proceedings of the Society of Antiquaries of Scotland* 110: 224.

Cowie, T. In prep. Ceramic material associated with metalworking. In M. Parker Pearson, J. Mulville, H.

Smith and P. Marshall, *Cladh Hallan: roundhouses, burial and mummification in later prehistory.* SEARCH monograph 8. Oxford: Oxbow.

Craig, O.E., Taylor, G., Mulville, J., Collins M.J. and Parker Pearson, M. 2005. The identification of prehistoric dairying activities in the Western Isles of Scotland: an integrated biomolecular approach. *Journal of Archaeological Science.* 32: 91–103.

Crawford, I. 2002. The wheelhouse. In B. Ballin Smith and I. Banks (eds) *In the Shadow of the Brochs: the Iron Age in Scotland.* Stroud: Tempus. 111–28.

Cumberpatch, C.G. 1992. The pottery from Cill Donnain, South Uist. Unpublished interim report.

Davies, G. and Slater, J. In prep. Bone and antler tools. In M. Parker Pearson, J. Mulville, H. Smith and P. Marshall, *Cladh Hallan: roundhouses, burial and mummification in later prehistory.* SEARCH monograph 8. Oxford: Oxbow.

Davis, S.J.M. 1992. *A Rapid Method for Recording Information about Mammal Bones from Archaeological Sites.* Ancient Monuments Laboratory Report 19/92. London: English Heritage.

DeNiro, M.J. 1985. Postmortem preservation and alteration of *in vivo* bone collagen ratios in relation to paleodietary reconstruction. *Nature* 317: 806–9.

Dickson, C. and Dickson, J.H. 2000. *Plants and People in Ancient Scotland.* Stroud: Tempus.

Dungworth, D. 1999. The industrial waste. In M. Parker Pearson and N. Sharples with J. Mulville and H. Smith, *Between Land and Sea: excavations at Dun Vulan, South Uist.* Sheffield: Sheffield Academic Press. 230.

Dungworth, D. forthcoming. Iron working debris. In M. Parker Pearson, H. Smith, J. Mulville and M. Brennand, *Cille Pheadair: a Norse-period farmstead in South Uist.* SEARCH monograph 7. Oxford: Oxbow.

Edmonds, M. and Martin, K. In prep. The worked stone assemblage. In M. Parker Pearson, J. Mulville, H. Smith and P. Marshall, *Cladh Hallan: roundhouses, burial and mummification in later prehistory.* SEARCH monograph 8. Oxford: Oxbow.

Edwards, K.J. and Ralston, I.B.M. (eds) 2003. *Scotland After the Ice Age: environment, archaeology and history, 8000 BC–AD 1000.* Edinburgh: Edinburgh University Press.

Edwards, K.J., Whittington, G. and Ritchie, W. 2005. The possible role of humans in the early stages of machair evolution: palaeoenvironmental investigations in the Outer Hebrides, Scotland. *Journal of Archaeological Science* 32: 435–49 http://journals.ohiolink.edu/ejc/article.cgi?issn=03054403&issue=v32i0003&article=435_tprohiiitohs

Fairhurst, H. 1971. The wheelhouse site A' Cheardach Bheag on Drimore machair, South Uist. *Glasgow Archaeological Journal* 2: 72–106.

Fenton, A. 1978. *The Island Blackhouse.* Edinburgh: HMSO.

Fenton, A. 1986. *The Shape of the Past 2. Essays in Scottish Ethnography.* Edinburgh: John Donald.

Finlay, J. 1991. The animal bone. In E. Campbell, Excavations of a wheelhouse and other Iron Age structures at Sollas, North Uist by R J C Atkinson in 1957. *Proceedings of the Society of Antiquaries of Scotland* 121: 117–73.

Fitzpatrick, A.P. 1994. Outside in: the structure of an Early Iron Age house at Dunston Park, Thatcham, Berkshire. In A. Fitzpatrick and E. Morris (eds) *The Iron Age in Wessex: recent work.* Salisbury: Trust for Wessex Archaeology & AFEAF. 68–72.

Fitzpatrick, A.P. 1997. Everyday life in Iron Age Wessex. In A. Gwilt and C. Haselgrove (eds) *Reconstructing Iron Age Societies: new approaches to the British Iron Age.* Oxford: Oxbow. 73–86.

Fleming, A. 2012. The blacklands survey: Cill Donnain and Gearraidh Bhailteas townships. In M. Parker Pearson (ed.) *From Machair to Mountains: archaeological survey and excavation in South Uist.* SEARCH monograph 4. Oxford: Oxbow. 74–82.

Fleming, A. and Woolf, A. 1992. Cille Donnain: a Late Norse church in South Uist. *Proceedings of the Society of Antiquaries of Scotland* 122: 329–50.

Foster, P. and Pouncett, J. 2000. The excavation of Iron Age and later structures at Alt Chrisal T17, Barra, 1996–1999. In K. Branigan and P. Foster, *From Barra to Berneray: archaeological survey and excavation in the Southern Isles of the Outer Hebrides.* SEARCH monograph 5. Sheffield: Sheffield Academic Press. 147–90.

Foster, S. 1990. Pins, combs and the chronology of later Atlantic Iron Age settlement. In I. Armit (ed.) *Beyond the Brochs: changing perspectives on the later Iron Age in Atlantic Scotland.* Edinburgh: Edinburgh University Press. 143–74.

Foxon, A. 1991. Bone, antler, tooth and horn technology and utilisation in prehistoric Scotland. Unpublished PhD thesis, University of Glasgow.

Freeman, S.P.H.T., Cook, G.T., Dougans, A.B., Naysmith, P., Wilcken, K.M. and Xu, S. 2010. Improved SSAMS performance. *Nuclear Instruments and Methods B* 268: 715–17.

Gilbertson, D., Kent, M. and Grattan, J. (eds) 1996. *The Outer Hebrides: the last 14,000 years.* Sheffield: Sheffield Academic Press.

Gilmour, S. 2002. Mid-first millennium BC settlement in the Atlantic west? In B. Ballin Smith and I. Banks (eds) *In the Shadow of the Brochs: the Iron Age in Scotland.* Stroud: Tempus. 55–66.

Glentworth, R. 1979. Observations on the soils of the Outer Hebrides. *Proceedings of the Royal Society of Edinburgh* 77B: 123–37.

Grant, A. 1982. The use of tooth wear as a guide to the age of domestic ungulates. In B. Wilson, C. Grigson and S. Payne (eds) *Ageing and Sexing Animal Bones from Archaeological Sites.* Oxford: BAR (International Series) 109. 91–108.

Grant, J.W. 1979. Cereals and grass production in Lewis and the Uists. *Proceedings of the Royal Society of Edinburgh* 77B: 527–33.

Grigson, C. 1982. Sex and age determination of some bones and teeth of domestic cattle: a review of the literature. In B. Wilson, C. Grigson and S. Payne (eds) *Ageing and Sexing Animal Bones from Archaeological Sites*. Oxford: BAR (International Series) 109. 7–23.

Grogan, E. and Roche, H. 2009. An assessment of middle Bronze Age domestic pottery in Ireland. In G. Cooney, K. Becker, J. Coles, M. Ryan and S. Sievers (eds) *Relics of Old Decency: archaeological studies in later prehistory. A Festschrift for Barry Raftery*. Bray: Wordwell and UCD School of Archaeology. 127–36.

Grogan, E. and Roche, H. 2010. Clay and fire: the development and distribution of pottery traditions in prehistoric Ireland. In M. Stanley, E. Danaher and J. Eogan (eds) *Creative Minds*. Archaeology and the National Roads Authority Monograph Series 7. Dublin: National Roads Authority. 27–45.

Hallén, Y. 1994. The use of bone and antler at Foshigarry and Bac Mhic Connain, two Iron Age sites on North Uist, Western Isles. *Proceedings of the Society of Antiquaries of Scotland* 124: 189–231.

Halstead, P. 1985. A study of mandibular teeth from Romano-British contexts at Maxey. In F. Pryor and C. French (eds) Archaeology and environment in the lower Welland valley. Vol. 1. *East Anglian Archaeology* 27: 219–24.

Halstead, P. 1998. Mortality models and milking: problems of uniformitarianism, optimality and equifinality reconsidered. *Anthropozoologica* 27: 3–20.

Halstead, P. 2003. Animal bones from Baleshare and Hornish Point. In J. Barber, *Bronze Age Farms and Iron Age Farm Mounds of the Outer Hebrides*. Edinburgh: Scottish Archaeological Internet Reports 3. http://www.sair.org.uk/sair3/sair3.pdf.%20142-8.

Halstead, P., Collins, P. and Isaakidou, V. 2002. Sorting the sheep from the goats: morphological distinctions between the mandibles and mandibular teeth of adult *Ovis* and *Capra*. *Journal of Archaeological Science* 29: 545–53.

Hamilton, M. and Sharples, N. 2012. Early Bronze Age settlements at Machair Mheadhanach and Cill Donnain. In M. Parker Pearson (ed.) *From Machair to Mountains: archaeological survey and excavation in South Uist*. SEARCH monograph 4. Oxford: Oxbow. 199–214.

Hamilton Dyer, S. 2006. Bird remains. In I. Armit, *Anatomy of an Iron Age Roundhouse: the Cnip wheelhouse excavations, Lewis*. Edinburgh, Society of Antiquaries of Scotland. 172.

Hamshaw-Thomas. J.R. 1991. Kildonan, South Uist: faunal analysis. Unpublished report, University of Sheffield.

Harding, D.W. and Armit, I. 1990. Survey and excavation in West Lewis. In I. Armit (ed.) *Beyond the Brochs: changing perspectives on the later Iron Age in Atlantic Scotland*. Edinburgh: Edinburgh University Press. 71–107.

Harding, D.W. and Dixon, T.N. 2000. *Dun Bharabhat, Cnip, an Iron Age Settlement in West Lewis. Volume 1, The Structures and Material Culture*. Calanais Research Monograph 2. Edinburgh: University of Edinburgh.

Hayward, P.J. and Ryland, J.S. (eds) 1990. *The Marine Fauna of the British Isles and North-West Europe. Volume 2: Molluscs to Chordates*. Oxford: Oxford Science Publications.

Hedges, R.E.M., Bronk Ramsey, C. and Housley, R.A. 1989. The Oxford accelerator mass spectrometry facility: technical developments in routine dating. *Archaeometry* 31: 99–113.

Hedges, R.E.M., Housley, R.A., Bronk Ramsey, C. and Van Klinken, G.J. 1992. Radiocarbon dates from the Oxford AMS system: *Archaeometry* datelist 15. *Archaeometry* 34: 337–57.

Henshall, A.S. 1964. A dagger-grave and other cist burials at Ashgrove, Methilhill, Fife. *Proceedings of the Society of Antiquaries of Scotland* 97: 166–79.

Hill, J.D. 1996. Hill-forts and the Iron Age of Wessex. In T.C. Champion and J.R. Collis (eds) *The Iron Age in Britain and Ireland: recent trends*. Sheffield: Sheffield Academic Press. 95–116.

Hillman, G.C. 1981. Reconstructing crop husbandry practices from charred remains. In R. Mercer (ed.) *Farming Practice in British Prehistory*. Edinburgh: Edinburgh University Press. 123–62.

Hillman, G.C. 1982. Evidence for spelting malt. In R. Leech (ed.) *Excavations at Catsgore 1970–1973: a Romano-British village*. Bristol: Western Archaeological Trust (Excavation Monograph 2). 137–41.

Hudson, G. 1991. The geomorphology and soils of the Outer Hebrides. In R.J. Pankhurst and J. Mullins (eds) *Flora of the Outer Hebrides*. London: Natural History Museum. 19–27.

Hunter, F. 2006. Bone and antler. In I. Armit, *Anatomy of an Iron Age Roundhouse: the Cnip wheelhouse excavations, Lewis*. Edinburgh: Society of Antiquaries of Scotland. 136–51.

Jobst, W. 1975. *Die Römischen Fibeln aus Lauriacum*. Linz: Wimmer.

Jones, G. 2003. The charred plant remains from Baleshare and Hornish Point. In J. Barber, *Bronze Age Farms and Iron Age Farm Mounds of the Outer Hebrides*. Edinburgh: Scottish Archaeological Internet Reports 3. www.sair.org.uk/sair3/sair3.pdf. 153–8.

Katzenberg, M.A. and Krouse, H.R. 1989. Application of stable isotopes in human tissues to problems in identification. *Canadian Society of Forensic Science Journal* 22: 7–19.

Kennedy Allen, L. 1988. The shifting sands of South Uist – a study of the machair palaeosols: man's presence and influence. Unpublished MA dissertation, University of Sheffield.

Lane, A. 1990. Hebridean pottery: problems of definition, chronology, presence and absence. In I. Armit (ed.) *Beyond the Brochs: changing perspectives on the later Iron Age in Atlantic Scotland.* Edinburgh: Edinburgh University Press. 108–30.

Lane, A. 2005. Pottery. In N. Sharples, *A Norse Farmstead in the Outer Hebrides: excavations at Mound 3, Bornais, South Uist.* Oxford: Oxbow. 194–5.

Lanting, J.N. and van der Plicht, J. 1998. Reservoir effects and apparent ^{14}C ages. *Journal of Irish Archaeology* 9: 151–65.

La Trobe-Bateman, E. 1999. The pottery. In M. Parker Pearson and N. Sharples, with J. Mulville and H. Smith, *Between Land and Sea: excavations at Dun Vulan, South Uist.* SEARCH monograph 3. Sheffield: Sheffield Academic Press. 211–17.

Legge, A.J. 1981. Aspects of cattle husbandry. In R.J. Mercer (ed.) *Farming Practice in British Prehistory.* Edinburgh: Edinburgh University Press. 169–81.

Lethbridge, T.C. 1952. Excavations at Kilpheder, South Uist, and the problem of the brochs and wheel-houses. *Proceedings of the Prehistoric Society* 18: 176–93.

Longin, R. 1971. New method of collagen extraction for radiocarbon dating. *Nature* 230: 241–2.

Lyman, R.L. 1994. *Vertebrate Taphonomy.* Cambridge: Cambridge University Press.

Manley, H. In prep. Pottery fabrics. In M. Parker Pearson, J. Mulville, H. Smith and P. Marshall, *Cladh Hallan: roundhouses, burial and mummification in later prehistory.* SEARCH monograph 8. Oxford: Oxbow.

Marshall, P. and Parker Pearson, M. 2012. Excavations of an Iron Age islet settlement in Upper Loch Bornish. In M. Parker Pearson (ed.) *From Machair to Mountains: archaeological survey and excavation in South Uist.* SEARCH monograph 4. Oxford: Oxbow. 259–70.

Martin, M. 1703 [1989]. *A Description of the Western Islands of Scotland.* Edinburgh: James Thin.

McCormick, F. 1992. Early faunal evidence for dairying. *Oxford Journal of Archaeology* 11: 201–9.

McCormick, F. 1998. Calf slaughter as a response to marginality. In C.M. Mills and G. Coles (eds) *Life on the Edge: human settlement and marginality.* Oxford: Oxbow. 49–53.

McCormick, F. 2006. Animal bone. In I. Armit, *Anatomy of an Iron Age roundhouse: the Cnip wheelhouse excavations, Lewis.* Edinburgh: Society of Antiquaries of Scotland. 161–71.

MacGregor, G. 1998. The excavation of a cordoned urn at Benderloch, Argyll. *Proceedings of the Society of Antiquaries of Scotland* 128: 143–59.

McKenzie, A.J. 2005. Analysis of a wheelhouse and other structures in Grimsay, Western Isles. Unpublished MPhil thesis, University of Glasgow.

MacKie, E.W. 1974. *Dun Mor Vaul: an Iron Age broch on Tiree.* Glasgow: University of Glasgow Press.

MacKie, E.W. 2007. *The Roundhouses, Brochs and Wheelhouses of Atlantic Scotland c.700 BC–AD 500: architecture and material culture. Part 2 (II), The Northern and Southern Mainland and the Western Islands.* Oxford: BAR (British Series) 444(II).

MacSween, A. 2006. Pottery. In I. Armit, *Anatomy of an Iron Age Roundhouse: the Cnip wheelhouse excavations, Lewis.* Edinburgh: Society of Antiquaries of Scotland. 88–131.

Mook, W.G. 1986. Business meeting: recommendations/resolutions adopted by the twelfth International Radiocarbon Conference. *Radiocarbon* 28: 799.

Morin, E. 2007. Fat composition and Nunamiut decision-making: a new look at the marrow and bone grease indices. *Journal of Archaeological Science* 34: 69–82.

Morris J. 2005. Red deer's role in social expression on the isles of Scotland. In A.G. Pluskowski (ed.) *Just Skin and Bones: new perspectives on human–animal relations in the historic past.* Oxford: BAR (International Series) 1410. 9–18.

Mulville, J. 1999. The mammal bone. In M. Parker Pearson and N. Sharples, with J. Mulville and H. Smith, *Between Land and Sea: excavations at Dun Vulan, South Uist.* SEARCH monograph 3. Sheffield: Sheffield Academic Press. 234–74.

Mulville, J. 2002. The role of cetacea in prehistoric and historic Atlantic Scotland. *International Journal of Osteoarchaeology.* 12: 34–48.

Mulville, J. and Powell, A. In prep. The animal bone. In M. Parker Pearson, J. Mulville, H. Smith and P. Marshall, *Cladh Hallan: roundhouses, burial and mummification in later prehistory.* SEARCH monograph 8. Oxford: Oxbow.

Mulville, J., Madgwick, R., Stevens, R., O'Connell, T., Craig, O., Powell, A., Sharples, N. and Parker Pearson, M. 2009. Isotopic analysis of faunal material from South Uist, Western Isles, Scotland. *Journal of the North Atlantic,* 2: 51–9.

Mulville, J., Parker Pearson, M., Sharples, N., Smith, H. and Chamberlain, A.T. 2003. Quarters, arcs and squares: human and animal remains in the Hebridean Late Iron Age. In J. Downes and A. Ritchie (eds) *Sea Change: Orkney and northern Europe in the later Iron Age.* Balgarvies: Pinkfoot Press. 20–34.

Nesbitt, C., Church, M.J. and Gilmour, S. 2011. Domestic, industrial, (en)closed? Survey and excavation of a Late Bronze Age/Early Iron Age promontory enclosure at Gob Eirer, Lewis, Western Isles. *Proceedings of the Society of Antiquaries of Scotland* 141: 31–74.

Newton A.J. and Dugmore A.J. 2003. Analysis of pumice from Baleshare. In J. Barber, *Bronze Age Farms and Iron Age Farm Mounds of the Outer Hebrides.* Edinburgh: Scottish Archaeological Internet Reports 3. www.sair.org.uk/sair3/sair3.pdf. 135–8.

O'Connor, T.P. 1989. Bones from Anglo-Scandinavian levels at 16–22 Coppergate. *The Archaeology of York* 15 (3). London: Council for British Archaeology. 137–207.

Oswald, A. 1997. A doorway on the past: practical and mystic concerns in the orientation of roundhouse doorways. In A. Gwilt and C. Haselgrove (eds) *Reconstructing Iron Age Societies: new approaches to the British Iron Age*. Oxford: Oxbow. 87–95.

Outram, A.K. 1999. A comparison of Palaeoeskimo and medieval Norse bone fat exploitation in western Greenland. *Arctic Anthropology* 36: 103–17.

Parker Pearson, M. 1996. Food, fertility and front doors in the first millennium BC. In T.C. Champion and J.R. Collis (eds) *The Iron Age in Britain and Ireland: recent trends*. Sheffield: J.R. Collis Publications. 117–32.

Parker Pearson, M. 1999. Food, sex and death: cosmologies in the British Iron Age with particular reference to East Yorkshire. *Cambridge Archaeological Journal* 9: 43–69.

Parker Pearson, M. 2003. Cill Donnain. *Discovery and Excavation in Scotland* 4.

Parker Pearson, M. 2004. Island prehistories: a view of Orkney from South Uist. In J. Cherry, C. Scarre and S. Shennan (eds) *Explaining Social Change: studies in honour of Colin Renfrew*. Cambridge: McDonald Institute. 127–40.

Parker Pearson, M. 2012a. Excavations at Cille Donnain church. In M. Parker Pearson (ed.) *From Machair to Mountains: archaeological survey and excavation in South Uist*. SEARCH monograph 4. Oxford: Oxbow. 284–93.

Parker Pearson, M. (ed.) 2012b. *From Machair to Mountains: archaeological survey and excavation in South Uist*. SEARCH monograph 4. Oxford: Oxbow.

Parker Pearson, M. 2012c. The machair survey. In M. Parker Pearson (ed.) *From Machair to Mountains: archaeological survey and excavation in South Uist*. SEARCH monograph 4. Oxford: Oxbow. 12–73.

Parker Pearson, M. 2012d. Settlement, agriculture and society in South Uist before the Clearances. In M. Parker Pearson (ed.) *From Machair to Mountains: archaeological survey and excavation in South Uist*. SEARCH monograph 4. Oxford: Oxbow. 401–25.

Parker Pearson, M. and Parsons, V. In prep. The pottery. In M. Parker Pearson, J. Mulville, H. Smith and P. Marshall, *Cladh Hallan: roundhouses, burial and mummification in later prehistory*. SEARCH monograph 8. Oxford: Oxbow.

Parker Pearson, M. and Richards, C. (eds) 1994. *Architecture and Order: approaches to social space*. London: Routledge.

Parker Pearson, M. and Seddon, K. 2004. Cill Donnain (Kildonan) (South Uist parish), earlier Bronze Age Cordoned Urn settlement. *Discovery and Excavation in Scotland* 5: 139.

Parker Pearson, M. and Sharples, N. with Mulville, J. and Smith, H. 1999. *Between Land and Sea: excavations at the broch of Dun Vulan, South Uist*. SEARCH monograph 3. Sheffield: Sheffield Academic Press.

Parker Pearson, M., Marshall, P. and Smith H. 2012. Excavations at A Beinn na Mhic Aongheis (the Hill of the Son of Angus), Bornais. In M. Parker Pearson (ed.) *From Machair to Mountains: archaeological survey and excavation in South Uist*. SEARCH monograph 4. Oxford: Oxbow. 308–30.

Parker Pearson, M., Mulville, J., Smith, H. and Marshall, P. In prep. *Cladh Hallan: roundhouses, burial and mummification in later prehistory*. SEARCH monograph 8. Oxford: Oxbow.

Parker Pearson, M., Sharples, N. and Mulville, J. 1996. Brochs and Iron Age society: a reappraisal. *Antiquity* 70: 57–67.

Parker Pearson, M., Sharples, N. and Symonds, J. with Mulville, J., Raven, J., Smith, H. and Woolf, A. 2004. *South Uist: archaeology and history of a Hebridean island*. Stroud: Tempus.

Parker Pearson, M., Smith, H., Mulville, J. and Brennand, M. Forthcoming. *Cille Pheadair: a Norse-period farmstead in South Uist*. SEARCH monograph 7. Oxford: Oxbow.

Payne. S. 1972. Partial recovery and sample bias. In E.S. Higgs (ed.) *Papers in Economic Prehistory*. Cambridge: Cambridge University Press. 49–64.

Payne, S. 1973. Kill-off patterns in sheep and goats: the mandibles from Asvan Kalé. *Anatolian Studies* 23: 281–303.

Payne, S. 1985. Morphological distinctions between mandibular teeth of young sheep, *Ovis*, and goats, *Capra*. *Journal of Archaeological Science* 12: 139–47.

Payne, S. and Bull, G. 1988. Components of variation in measurements of pig bones and teeth, and the use of measurements to distinguish wild from domestic pig remains. *Archaeozoologia* 2: 27–66.

Payne, S. and Munson, P.J. 1985. Ruby and how many squirrels? The destruction of bones by dogs. In N.R.J. Fieller, D.D. Gilbertson, and N.G.A. Ralph (eds) *Palaeobiological Investigations: research design, methods and data analysis*. Oxford: BAR (International Series) 266. 31–9.

Pollock, A.J. and Waterman, D. 1964. A Bronze Age habitation site at Downpatrick. *Ulster Journal of Archaeology* 27: 31–58.

Pope, R.E. 2007. Ritual and the roundhouse: a critique of recent ideas on domestic space in later British prehistory. In C.C. Haselgrove and R.E. Pope (eds) *The Earlier Iron Age in Britain and the near Continent*. Oxford: Oxbow. 204–28.

Prummel, W. and Frisch, H-J. 1986. A guide for the distinction of species, sex and body size in bones of sheep and goat. *Journal of Archaeological Science* 13: 567–77.

Raven, J. 2012. The shielings survey: central South Uist. In M. Parker Pearson (ed.) *From Machair to Mountains: archaeological survey and excavation in South Uist*. SEARCH monograph 4. Oxford: Oxbow. 160–79.

Reimer, P.J., Baillie, M.G.L., Bard, E., Bayliss, A., Beck, J.W., Blackwell, P.G., Bronk Ramsey, C., Buck, C.E., Burr, G.S., Edwards, R.L., Friedrich, M., Grootes, P.M., Guilderson, T.P., Hajdas, I., Heaton, T.J., Hogg, A.G., Hughen, K.A., Kaiser, K.F., Kromer, B., McCormac, G., Manning, S., Reimer, R.W., Remmele, S., Richards, D.A., Southon, J.R., Talamo, S., Taylor, F.W., Turney, C.S.M., van der Plicht, J. and Weyhenmeyer, C.E. 2009. INTCAL09 and MARINE09 radiocarbon age calibration curves, 0–50,000 years cal BP. *Radiocarbon* 51: 1111–50.

Richardson, R.M. 1960. A Roman brooch from the Outer Hebrides, with notes on others of its type. *Antiquaries Journal* 40: 200–13.

Ritchie, W. 1976. The meaning and definition of machair. *Transactions of the Botanical Society of Edinburgh* 42: 431–40.

Ritchie, W. 1979. Machair development and chronology of the Uists and adjacent islands. *Proceedings of the Royal Society of Edinburgh* 77B: 107–22.

Ritchie, W. 1985. Inter-tidal and sub-tidal organic deposits and sea level changes in the Uists, Outer Hebrides. *Scottish Journal of Geology* 21: 161–76.

Ritchie, W. and Whittington, G. 1994. Non-synchronous aeolian sand movements in the Uists: the evidence of the intertidal organic and sand deposits at Cladach Mór, North Uist. *Scottish Geographical Magazine* 110: 40–6.

Ritchie, W., Whittington, G. and Edwards, K.J. 2001. Holocene changes in the geomorphology and vegetational history of the Atlantic littoral of the Uists, Outer Hebrides, Scotland. *Proceedings of the Royal Society of Edinburgh* 92: 121–36.

Ritchie, J.N.G. and Lane, A. 1981. Dun Cul Bhuirg, Iona, Argyll. *Proceedings of the Society of Antiquaries of Scotland* 110: 209–29.

Ritchie, J.N.G. and Welfare, H. 1983. Excavations at Ardnave, Islay. *Proceedings of the Society of Antiquaries of Scotland* 113: 302–66.

Rixson, D. 1989. Butchery evidence on animal bones. *Circaea* 6: 49–62.

Robertson, A. 1970. Roman finds from non-Roman sites in Scotland. *Britannia* 1: 98–226.

Rozanski, K., Stichler, W., Gonfiantini, R., Scott, E.M., Beukens, R.P., Kromer, B. and van der Plicht, J. 1992. The IAEA ^{14}C intercomparison exercise 1990. *Radiocarbon* 34: 506–19.

Rye, O. 1981. *Pottery Technology*. Washington DC: Taraxacum Press.

SCAPE Trust (Scottish Coastal Archaeology and the Problem of Erosion) 2006. Eroding human remains dated. http://www.scapetrust.org/html/news2.html

SCAPE Trust (Scottish Coastal Archaeology and the Problem of Erosion) 2008. Baile Sear excavation 2008. http://www.scapetrust.org/html/news2.html

Schoeninger, M.J., and DeNiro M.J. 1984. Nitrogen and carbon isotopic composition of bone collagen from marine and terrestrial animals. *Geochimica et Cosmochimica Acta* 48: 625–39.

Schwenninger, J.-L. 1996. The evolution of coastal sand dunes in the southern isles of the Outer Hebrides of Scotland. Unpublished PhD thesis, University of London.

Scott, E.M. 2003. The third international radiocarbon intercomparison (TIRI) and the fourth international radiocarbon intercomparison (FIRI) 1990–2002: results, analyses, and conclusions. *Radiocarbon* 45: 135–408.

Scott, E.M., Cook G., and Naysmith, P. 2010. The fifth international radiocarbon intercomparison (VIRI): an assessment of laboratory performance in stage 3. *Radiocarbon* 53: 859–65.

Scott, W.L. 1948. Gallo-British colonies: the aisled round-house culture in the North. *Proceedings of the Prehistoric Society* 14: 46–125.

Selkirk, A. 1996. The Udal. *Current Archaeology* 13: 84–94.

Serjeantson, D. No date. Mammal, bird and fish remains from the Udal (North). N. Uist: interim report. Unpublished report.

Serjeantson, D. 1990. The introduction of mammals to the Outer Hebrides and the role of boats in stock management. *Anthropozoologica* 13: 7–18.

Serjeantson, D. 2003. Bird bones from Baleshare and Hornish Point. In J. Barber, *Bronze Age Farms and Iron Age Farm Mounds of the Outer Hebrides*. Scottish Archaeological Internet Reports 3. http://www.sair.org.uk/sair3.

Shackleton, J.C. 1988. *Excavations at Francthi Cave, Greece: marine molluscan remains from Francthi Cave*. Fascicule 4. Bloomington & Indianapolis: Indiana University Press.

Sharples, N.M. 1997. The Iron Age and Norse settlement at Bornish, South Uist: an interim report on the 1996 excavations. Cardiff: School of History and Archaeology. http://www.cf.ac.uk/uwcc/hisar/archaeology/reports/hebrides96/

Sharples, N.M. 2005. *A Norse Farmstead in the Outer Hebrides: excavations at mound 3, Bornais, South Uist*. Oxford: Oxbow.

Sharples, N. 2009. Beaker settlement in the Western Isles. In M.J. Allen, N. Sharples & T. O'Connor (eds) *Land and People: papers in memory of John G. Evans*. Oxford: Oxbow. 147–58.

Sharples, N.M. 2012a. The Beaker-period and Early Bronze Age settlement at Sligeanach, Cill Donnain. In M. Parker Pearson (ed.) *From Machair to Mountains: archaeological survey and excavation in South Uist*. SEARCH monograph 4. Oxford: Oxbow. 215–58.

Sharples, N.M. (ed.) 2012b. *A Late Iron Age Farmstead in the Outer Hebrides: excavations at mound 1, Bornais, South Uist*. Oxford: Oxbow.

Sharples, N. and Parker Pearson, M. 1999. Norse settlement in the Outer Hebrides. *Norwegian Archaeological Review* 32: 41–62.

Shepherd, I.A.G. and Shepherd, A.N. 2001. A Cordoned Urn burial with faience from 102 Findhorn, Moray. *Proceedings of the Society of Antiquaries of Scotland* 131: 101–28.

Shepherd, I.A.G. and Tuckwell, A.N. 1977. Traces of Beaker period cultivation at Rosinish, Benbecula. *Proceedings of the Society of Antiquaries of Scotland* 108: 108–13.

Sheridan, A. 2003. New dates for Scottish Bronze Age cinerary urns: results from the National Museums of Scotland Dating Cremated Bones project. In A. Gibson (ed.) *Prehistoric Pottery: people, pattern and purpose*. Oxford: BAR (International Series) 1156. 201–26.

Sherratt, A. 1981. Plough and pastoralism: aspects of the secondary products revolution. In N. Hammond, I. Hodder and G. Isaac (eds) *Pattern of the Past: studies in honour of David Clarke*. Cambridge: Cambridge University Press. 261–305

Silver, I. A. 1969. The ageing of domestic animals. In D. Brothwell and E.S. Higgs (eds) *Science in Archaeology.* 2nd edition. London: Thames & Hudson. 283–302.

Simpson, D.D.A., Murphy, E.M. and Gregory, R.A. 2006. *Excavations at Northton, Isle of Harris.* Oxford: BAR (British Series) 408.

Slota jr, P.J., Jull, A.J.T., Linick, T.W. and Toolin, L.J. 1987. Preparation of small samples for ^{14}C accelerator targets by catalytic reduction of CO. *Radiocarbon* 29: 303–6.

Smith, H. 1999. The plant remains. In M. Parker Pearson and N. Sharples, with J. Mulville and H. Smith, *Between Land and Sea: excavations at Dun Vulan, South Uist.* SEARCH monograph 3. Sheffield: Sheffield Academic Press. 297–336.

Smith, H. 2012. The ethnohistory of Hebridean agriculture. In M. Parker Pearson (ed.) *From Machair to Mountains: archaeological survey and excavation in South Uist.* SEARCH monograph 4. Oxford: Oxbow. 379–400.

Smith, H. In prep. The plant remains. In M. Parker Pearson, P. Marshall, J. Mulville and H. Smith, *Cladh Hallan: roundhouses, burial and mummification in later prehistory.* SEARCH monograph 8. Oxford: Oxbow Books.

Smith, H. and Mulville, J. 2004. Resource management in the Outer Hebrides: an assessment of the faunal and floral evidence from archaeological investigations. In R.A. Housley and G. Coles (eds) *Atlantic Connections and Adaptations: economies, environments and subsistence in lands bordering the North Atlantic.* Oxford: Oxbow. 48–64.

Stace, C. 1991. *New Flora of the British Isles.* 2nd edition. Cambridge: Cambridge University Press.

Stenhouse, M.J. and Baxter, M.S. 1983. ^{14}C dating reproducibility: evidence from routine dating of archaeological samples. *PACT* 8: 147–61.

Stuiver, M. and Kra, R.S. 1986. Editorial comment. *Radiocarbon* 28(2B): ii.

Stuiver, M. and Polach, H.A. 1977. Reporting of ^{14}C data. *Radiocarbon* 19: 355–63.

Stuiver, M. and Reimer, P.J. 1986. A computer program for radiocarbon age calculation. *Radiocarbon* 28: 1022–30.

Stuiver, M. and Reimer, P.J. 1993. Extended ^{14}C data base and revised CALIB 3.0 ^{14}C age calibration program. *Radiocarbon* 35: 215–30.

Swain, H. 1988. Pottery survival in the field. *Scottish Archaeological Review* 5: 87–9.

Tabraham, C. 1979. Excavations at Dun Carloway broch, Isle of Lewis. *Proceedings of the Society of Antiquaries of Scotland* 108: 156–67.

Thomas, F.L.W. 1866–68. On the primitive dwellings and hypogea of the Outer Hebrides. *Proceedings of the Society of Antiquaries of Scotland* 7: 153–95.

Topping, P. 1985. Later prehistoric pottery from Dun Cul Bhuirg, Iona, Argyll. *Proceedings of the Society of Antiquaries of Scotland* 115: 199–209.

Topping, P. 1986. Neutron activation analysis of later prehistoric pottery from the Western Isles of Scotland. *Proceedings of the Prehistoric Society* 52: 105–30.

Topping, P. 1987. Typology and chronology in the later prehistoric pottery assemblages of the Western Isles. *Proceedings of the Society of Antiquaries of Scotland* 117: 67–84.

Tuross, N., Fogel, M.L. and Hare, P.E. 1988. C^{14} variability in the preservation of the isotopic composition of collagen from fossil bone. *Geochimica et Cosmochimica Acta* 52: 929–35.

ul Haq, S. 1989. Remains of the mammalian fauna from Kildonan, South Uist. Unpublished Masters dissertation, University of Sheffield.

Vandeputte, K., Moens, L. and Dams, R. 1996. Improved sealed-tube combustion of organic samples to CO$_2$ for stable isotope analysis, radiocarbon dating and percent carbon determinations. *Analytical Letters* 29: 2761–73.

van der Veen, M. 1992. *Crop Husbandry Regimes: an archaeobotanical study of farming in northern England 1000 BC–AD 500.* Sheffield: J.R. Collis Publications.

von den Driesch, A. 1976. *A Guide to the Measurement of Animal Bones from Archaeological Sites.* Massachusetts: Peabody Museum Bulletin 1.

Waddell, J. 1995. The Cordoned Urn tradition. In I.A. Kinnes and G. Varndell (eds) *'Unbaked Urns of Rudely Shape': essays on British and Irish pottery for Ian Longworth.* Oxford: Oxbow. 113–22.

Ward, G.K. and Wilson, S.R. 1978. Procedures for comparing and combining radiocarbon age determinations: a critique. *Archaeometry* 20: 19–31.

Watson, J.P.N. 1979. The estimation of relative frequencies of mammalian species: Khirokitia 1972. *Journal of Archaeological Science* 6: 127–37.

Wessex Archaeology 2008. Allasdale Dunes, Barra, Western Isles, Scotland: archaeological evaluation and assessment of results. http://www.scribd.com/doc/11779971/Allasdale-Dunes-Barra-Western-Isles

Wood, J.S. 1999. *An Archaeological Field Survey of a Wheelhouse and Surrounding Area at Bagh nam Feadag, Grimsay, North Uist.* Glasgow: Glasgow University & Association of Certified Field Archaeologists. Occasional Paper 44.

Young, A. 1953. An aisled farmhouse at Allasdale, Isle of Barra. *Proceedings of the Society of Antiquaries of Scotland* 87: 80–105.

Young, A. 1956. Excavations at Dun Cuier, Isle of Barra, Outer Hebrides. *Proceedings of the Society of Antiquaries of Scotland* 89: 290–328.

Young, A. and Richardson, K.M. 1960. A Cheardach Mhor, Drimore, South Uist. *Proceedings of the Society of Antiquaries of Scotland* 93: 135–73.

Zvelebil, M. 1989. Cill Donnain. SEARCH interim report. Unpublished report, University of Sheffield.

Zvelebil, M. 1990. Cill Donnain. SEARCH interim report. Unpublished report, University of Sheffield.

Zvelebil, M. 1991. Cill Donnain. SEARCH interim report. Unpublished report, University of Sheffield.

Index

A'Cheardach Bheag, South Uist 8, 171, 203, 209, Figure 17.12
A'Cheardach Mhor, South Uist 8, 114, 203, Figure 17.12
abandonment and robbing 15, 18, 63–4, 69–70, 78–81, 118–19, 121, 189, 201, 209, Figures 6.2, 7.3, 7.10–7.11, 7.13; *see also* re-use
activity areas *see* space, use of
agricultural practices 88, 93–4, 109, 119, 176–7, 211; *see also* animal husbandry; barley; crop processing *etc.*
Aird a'Mhachair, South Uist 6
Allasdale, Barra 114, 203, 205, 208, 212–13, Figure 17.13
Allt Chrisal, Barra 143–4, 203, 212–14, Figure 17.13
An Dunan, Lewis 197, 212
animal (mammal; *see separate entries for* bird; fish; shell, marine; whale)
  age 156, 161–5, 171–3, Table 13.8
  bone distribution and density 37, 40, 45–7, 156–7, 172, Table 13.1
  bone fragmentation 156–7, Table 13.2
  bone identification and recording 155–7
  butchery, gnawing and burning 156–7, 161–2, 167, 171–3, Tables 13.3–13.4, 13.10–13.11
  comparative assemblages *see named sites* (*e.g.* Cladh Hallan, Dun Vulan, Sollas *etc.*)
  husbandry 156, 168, 171–3, 211–12, 215

isotopic analysis 172
measurements 167–8, Tables 13.12–13.13
meat yield *see* meat; skeletal elements
minimum numbers 157, Table 13.5
pathology 165, 167, Table 13.9
sex 165
size and weight *see* measurements
skeletal elements 161–2, 210, Tables 13.6i–13.6iii
species abundance 157, 161, 168–9, 171, 211
species present *see* cat; cattle; deer; dog; otter; pig; rabbit; seal; sheep; whale; wild animals
antler
  beads and toggles 154
  grooved 78, 150
  handles 78, 146, 150, 154, Table 12.2
  manufacturing waste and worked pieces 50-1, 64, 66, 68, 70, 81, 88, 93, 145–6, 148–50, 153–4, 162, 167, 173, 208, Tables 12.1–12.2, 13.7, 13.10
  pegs 49–50, 148, 154, Figure 12.3, Table 12.2
  rings 78, 145–6, 148, 150, 153, Figure 12.3, Table 12.2
Ardnave, Islay 39
Armit, I. 65, 119, 199, 205; *see also* Cnip, Lewis
arrowheads 7, 190, 192, Figure 17.2
ash 50, 66, 69, 77, 79, 81, 92–3, 95, 119

Bac Mhic Connain, North Uist 145, Figure 17.14
Bagh nam Feadag, Grimsay 47, 197, 208, 212–13, Figure 17.14
Baile Sear, North Uist 143–4, 171–3, 176, 204, 211, Figure 17.14,
barley
  cultivation 176–7
  distribution and density *see* plant remains
  processing 176–7
  radiocarbon dates *see* radiocarbon dating
  species 176–7
  for figure and table numbers see plant remains
Barra 1, 3, Figures 1.1, 17.15; *see also named sites*
battle-axes 7, 192
beads and toggles *see* antler; bone; whale bone
Beaker period 3, 6–7, 29, 39, 190–2, Figures 17.1–17.4
Beinn na Mhic Aongheis, South Uist 198, Figures 1.1, 17.10
Beirgh, Lewis *see* Loch na Beirgh
Benbecula 1, 3, Figures 1.1–1.2
bird bone 161–2, 171
blacklands 3, 9, 197–8, 210
bone
  artefacts by phase Tables 12.1–12.2
  beads and toggles 88, 146, 150, 152, Figure 12.1, Table 12.2
  combs *see* combs
  cut/chop/saw-marked *see* animal butchery
  dice *see* dice

discs and spindle whorls 78, 146, 150, 153, 210, Figure 12.2, Table 12.2
drill-bits 146, Table 12.2
drilled 167
handles 146, 152–3, Table 12.2
modelling tools 146, 149–50, Figure 12.1, Table 12.2
needles 88, 146, 150, 152, 210, Table 12.2
pegs 146, 148, 150, 153, Figure 12.2, Table 12.2
pins and points 88, 94, 147–8, 150, 152–3, 190, 192, 210, Figures 12.1, 17.2, Table 12.2
points *see* pins and points
spatulae 93, 146, 152–3, 210, Figure 12.2, Table 12.2
spindle whorls *see* discs and spindle whorls
weaving beaters 146, 153, Figure 12.1, Table 12.2
see also antler; whale bone
Bornais, South Uist, 8, 24, 88, Figures 1.1, 1.4, 17.8–17.12
Mound 1 (Iron Age) 8, 64, 66, 106, 110, 113–14, 117–19, 129, 132, 135, 139, 143, 145–7, 150, 156, 162, 171–3, 177, 184–5, 203, 208–11, 214–15
Norse period 8, 106, 177, 184, 197–8, 214
brochs and duns *see named sites* (*e.g.* Dun Vulan; Dun Mor Vaul *etc.*)
bronze artefacts *see* copper-alloy
bronze-casting *see* metalworking; moulds
brooches 18, 119, 129–30, 210, Figure 10.1
Bruthach a'Tuath, Benbecula 213

cat 157, 161–2, Table 13.5–13.6
cattle
age 156, 161–3, 171–3, Table 13.8
bone distribution and density *see* animal bone
bone identification and recording 155–6
butchery, gnawing and burning 156–7, 161, 167, 171–3, Tables 13.3–13.4, 13.10–13.11
husbandry 171–3
isotopic analysis 172
measurements 167–8, Tables 13.12–13.13

meat yield *see* meat; skeletal elements
minimum numbers Table 13.5
pathology 165, 167, Table 13.9
relative abundance 157, 168–9, 211
sex 165
size and weight *see* measurements
skeletal elements 161, Tables 13.6i–13.6iii
cells *see* piers and cells; roof and roofing materials
ceramic
crucibles *see* crucibles
discs 51, 106, 128, 146, 210, Figure 9.15
moulds *see* moulds, ceramic
cetacean *see* whale
chambered tombs *see* Neolithic period
chronology of wheelhouse *see* radiocarbon dating, Cill Donnain III wheelhouse
Cill Donnain I (Early Bronze Age, site 87), South Uist 6–7, 39, 141–2, 190–3, Figures 17.1–17.5
Cill Donnain II (site 86), South Uist 6
Cille Donnain church, South Uist 8–9, 197–8, Figures 1.1, 17.10
Cille Pheadair (Norse settlement), South Uist 24, 184, Figure 1.1; *see also* Kilpheder wheelhouse
Cille Pheadair (Pictish cairn), South Uist 6, Figure 1.1
Cladh Hallan, South Uist 8, 24, 33, 37, 39, 43, 46–7, 57, 64, 88, 114–15, 120, 133–4, 142–5, 147, 171–2, 190, 192, 194, 196–7, 210, Figure 1.1
clay *see* ceramic discs; crucibles; moulds; pottery clay sources
Clettraval, North Uist 47, 113, 212, Figure 17.14
climate 1
Cnip, Lewis 46, 65, 81, 106, 114–15, 117, 119, 150, 152, 156, 168–9, 171, 176, 200, 204, 208–14, Figure 17.14
Cnoc a Comhdhalach, North Uist Figure 17.14
cobble tools *see* hammerstones; stone tools
combs 146, 150, 210, Figure 12.1, Table 12.2

copper-alloy
belt-fittings 88, 130–1, Figure 10.1
brooches 18, 88, 119, 129–30, 210, Figure 10.1
casting waste 131
distribution 90, 129, 210
pins 6, 13, 129, 131, Figure 10.1
rings 80, 129, 131, Figure 10.1
rods and bars 90, 131, Figure 10.1
strips and sheets 50, 129, 131, Figure 10.1
swords 133–4, 147, 195, 214
Cordoned Urns 7, 18, 27, 31, 33, 35, 39, 43, 106, 110, 114, 117, 119–20, 186, 192–5, 214, Figure 3.16
counters *see* gaming pieces
crop processing and storage 176–7, 210 (*for crop cultivation see* agricultural practices; *for crop species see* barley; oat; flax *etc.*)
crucibles 134–5
cup-marked stones 88, 139, Table 11.1

dairying *see* cattle husbandry
deer, red 157, 161–2, 165, 171, 173, 211, Tables 13.3–13.8; *see also* antler
dice 145, 214
diet 167, 171–3, 184–5, 211–12, 214–15; *see also* meat
dimensions of wheelhouses 63–6
dog 157, 161–2, 165, 171, 214, Table 13.5–13.6
domestic activities 212–14; *see also* crop processing; space, use of; weaving *etc.*
doorways *see* entrances
Downpatrick, Ireland 114
drains *see* gullies
dress *see* beads and toggles; combs *etc.*
Dun Bharabhat, Lewis 176, 197, 210–11
Dun Carloway, Lewis 114
Dun Cuier, Barra 114, 145
Dun Cuier ware 117, 121
Dun Cul Bhuirg, Iona 114
Dun Vulan, South Uist xiv, 7–8, 46–7, 64, 88, 106, 114–15, 118–19, 129, 132, 139, 143–7, 150, 152, 154, 156, 162, 171–3, 177, 197, 209–11, 215, Figures 1.1, 1.4, 17.7–17.9

Eilean Maleit, North Uist 212–13, Figure 17.14

Eilean Olabhat, North Uist 210

entrances
    Cill Donnain III wheelhouse 18, 57, 64–5, 68–70, 80–1, 208, Figures 2.8, 5.10, 6.1–6.2, 6.8 *etc.*
    roundhouses, wheelhouses and brochs 212–14
    secondary structure within wheelhouse 80, 209, Figures 7.11, 7.14

erosion 10, 102, 209

farming *see* agricultural practices; animal husbandry; crop processing *etc.*

faunal remains *see* animal bone; bird bone; fish bone; shell, marine; whale bone

feasting 212–14

fish bone 156

fishing 156

flax 177, 210–11

flint artefacts 7, 18, 67, 70, 139, 141–3, 190, 192, Figures 11.2, 17.1, Table 11.2; *see also* stone tools

floors 18, 21, 23, 37, 39, 50, 68–70, 80–1, 145, 177, 208, 213, Figures 6.21–6.24, Table 12.1

fodder *see* animal husbandry

food and cooking *see* diet; meat

foundation deposits 46, 54, 200, 204,

fuel 162, 176

fuel ash slag 135, 214, Tables 10.7–10.8

gaming pieces 147, 212, 214; *see also* dice

Gearraidh Iochdrach, North Uist 208, Figure 17.14

geology and topography 1, 3–4, 10, Figures 1.1–1.3

geophysical survey 191

gneiss 1, 106–7, 210

Gob Eirer, Lewis 197

Gortan, South Uist 190, 192

gullies 46–7, 68, 77, 80, 90, 177, 189, Figures 5.4–5.5, 6.2–6.3, 6.5, 8.5

hammerstones 35, 64, 67–8, 88, 90, 93, 139–42, Figures 8.13, 11.1, Table 11.1

handles *see* antler handles; bone handles

Harris 1, Figure 1.1; *see also named sites*

hearths 15, 18, 47–8, 57, 65–7, 77, 81, 177, 189, 208–9, 212–14, Figures 5.7, 6.1–6.2, 6.17, 6.19–6.21, 7.2, 7.4–7.10

hides and skins 146, 171, 210

Historic Scotland xiv, 24

historical sources 9, 172

Hornish Point, South Uist 171, 173, 176, 203, 211, Figure 17.12

houses
    Beaker period 190, 192
    Early Bronze Age/Middle Bronze Age 7, 37, 39, 192
    Iron Age *see* wheelhouses

human remains 6, 45–6, 51, 54, 186, 200, 204, 212, Figures 5.3, 5.15, 16.1, Table 16.1

hunting 161–2, 165, 171, 173, 211

imports 8, 129–30, 211, Figure 10.1; *see also* brooches; trade and exchange

Ireland 33, 39, 114, 120, 192

iron
    artefact analysis 132
    bars and rods 49, 133, Figure 10.2
    distribution in excavations 88, 132, 210
    knives 132–3
    nails 88, 132
    rings 88, 132–3, Figure 10.2
    sheets, strips and plates 132–3

ironworking *see* metalworking; slag

isotopic analysis *see* stable isotopes; cattle isotopic analysis *etc.*

ivory 40, 64, 88, 145, 147–8, 153, 210, 214, Figure 12.1, Table 12.1

Kilellan, Islay 169

Kilpheder wheelhouse, South Uist 66, 171, 203, 209, Figure 17.12; *for Norse site see* Cille Pheadair

knives and knifemarks *see* animal butchery; iron knives

Lane, A. 106–7, 110, 112–14

lead artefacts 131

leather-working *see* bone needles; hides and skins; pumice

Lewis 1, Figure 1.1; *see also named sites*

lipid residues *see* pottery residue analysis

Loch Bharabhat, Lewis *see under* Dun Bharabhat

Loch na Beirgh, Lewis 210–11

machair 3–4, 6–9, 33, 88, 190, 198, 210; Figures 1.2–1.3

Machair Mheadhanach, South Uist 7, 190, 192, 195–6, 210

marine resources *see* fish; seaweed; shell *etc.*

marshes 4

meat 161–2, 171–3, 210–11; *see also* animal butchery; diet

medieval period 6, 8–9, 198

Mesolithic period 3

metalworking 133–5, 195, 209–10, 213–14, Tables 10.2–10.8; *see also* copper-alloy; crucibles; iron; moulds; slag

middens 8, 10, 15, 18, 49, 78, 83, 88–90, 92–5, 117–19, 121, 129, 145, 177, 178, 180, 183–4, 189, 201, 209, 211, 214, Figures 2.5, 2.16–2.18, 5.11, 6.9, 8.1–8.3, 8.5–8.22, Table 15.5

Midhowe, Orkney 146–7

milk *see* cattle husbandry; pottery residue analysis; sheep husbandry

Mine Howe, Orkney 147

modification *see* re-use

molluscs *see* shell, marine

moulds, ceramic 18, 37, 40, 43, 45–6, 54, 93, 118, 120, 133–4, 210, 214, Figure 10.4, Table 10.1

Neolithic period 3, 171, 176, 190, 213

North Uist 1, 3, Figures 1.1–1.2; *see also named sites*

Northton, Harris 39, 171, 190

Norse period 5–6, 8, 24, 106, 147, 177, 184, 197–8, 210, 214

oats 176–7, 210

optically stimulated luminescence dating 33, 45, 204, Figure 3.15, Table 3.1

orientation 212–14

Orkney 190; *see also named sites*

Ormacleit, South Uist 195–7, 210, Figures 1.1, 17.6–17.10

otter 157, 161–2, 171, 173, Table 13.5

peat *see* ash; fuel

peat soils *see* blacklands

personal ornaments and dress fittings *see* beads and toggles; brooches; combs; pins; rings

piers and cells 1, 3, 18, 57, 64–7, 80, 205, 208–9, Figure 2.7–2.8, 6.1–6.2, 6.13–6.15, 17.16–17.17

pig
  age 164–5, 173, Table 13.8
  bone distribution and density *see* animal bone
  butchery, gnawing and burning 156–7, 162, 167, 173, Tables 13.3–13.4, 13.10
  husbandry 173
  measurements 167–8, Tables 13.12–13.13
  meat yield *see* meat; skeletal elements
  minimum numbers Table 13.5
  pathology 165, Table 13.9
  relative abundance 157, 161, 169, 171, 211
  sex 165
  skeletal elements 162, 210, Tables 13.6i–13.6iii

pins and points
  antler and bone 7, 37, 50, 64, 88, 94, 145–8, 150, 190, 192, 210, Figures 12.1, 12.3, 17.2, Table 12.2
  copper-alloy 6, 13, 129, 131, Figure 10.1
  ivory 40, 43, 145, 148, Figure 12.1

pits and postholes 31, 40, 43, 47, 57, 59, 63, 66–8, 177, 189, Figures 3.10, 4.5–4.7, 5.4–5.5, 5.8, 6.2–6.3, 6.5, 6.18–6.19

plant remains *see also* barley; flax; oats; rye; wheat
  distribution and densities 175–7, Tables14.1–14.3
  identification and recording 174
  weed species present 175–6, Tables 14.1–14.3

ploughmarks 18, 32, 40, 88, 93–4, 209, Figures 4.2–4.3, 8.4, 8.20–8.21

points, bone and antler *see* pins and points

post-medieval and early historic period and artefacts 6, 9, 172, 198, Figure 17.11

pottery
  in chronological order:
  Beaker 7, 39, 190, 192, Figure 17.2
  Early Bronze Age 7, 190
  Cordoned Urn *see* EBA/MBA
  Early Bronze Age/Middle Bronze Age 7, 18, 27, 31, 33, 35, 39, 43, 106, 110, 114, 117, 119–20, 186, 192–5, 214, Figure 3.16
  Late Bronze Age 7–8, 18, 41,110, Figure 9.5
  Late Bronze Age/Early Iron Age 40–1, 43, 45, 51, 54, 68, 114–15, 117–121, 195
  Early Iron Age 7, 196
  Middle Iron Age 33, 35, 41, 45, 54, 64, 79, 88, 94, 106–27 *passim*, Figures 9.6–9.7, 9.10–9.12
  Late Iron Age 80, 88, 94, 106–27 *passim*, 197, Figures 9.8–9.11, 9.13–9.14
  Norse 197
  Late Medieval 8, 107

pottery analysis
  chronology 6, 18, 33, 39, 54, 106, 113–15, 117–19
  clay sources 106
  decoration and finishing 54, 109–10, 112–13, 117–21, Figures 9.1–9.2, Tables 9.1, 9.3–9.6
  distribution and densities 39–41, 45–7, 70, 119, 208–9, 211, 213, Figures 3.16, 6.24, Tables 9.1–9.3
  fabric 106–7, 109–10, 117–18, 210, Table 9.2
  fragmentation 43, 106, 109, 119, 208–9, Figure 9.3, Table 9.1
  grass–marked 110
  manufacture 106–7, 109–13, 210
  morphology 54, 109, 114, 117–18, 214, Tables 9.3, 9.7
  residue analysis 172, 186
  rim form *see* morphology
  sooting 113

pumice 88, 139, 143–4, 210, Figure 11.3, Table 11.3

quartz and quartzite 1, 110, 113, 142

querns and quern handles 139, 146, 150, 210

rabbits 45, 157, 161, Table 13.5–13.6

radiocarbon dating
  Aird a'Mhachair 6
  Cill Donnain area 6
  Cill Donnain I 7, 191, Figures 17.3
  Cill Donnain III wheelhouse 18–19, 43, 45, 49–50, 57, 66, 77 [footnote], 88, 90, 94, 117–18, 121, 186–9, 200, 204–5, 209, Figures 16.1–16.2, Tables 16.1–16.2
  Cille Pheadair 6
  Cnip 200
  Cordoned Urns 33, 39, 193–4
  Dun Vulan 8

reconstruction of Cill Donnain III wheelhouse xiv, 19, 209, Figure 2.13

refractories, clay *see* moulds, ceramic

religion and ritual 212–14; *see also* foundation deposits; orientation

research design and excavation/sampling strategy 10–24, 171, 177, 185, 210

residues *see* pottery residue analysis

re-use of wheelhouse 18, 69–70, 72, 77–83, 118–19, 209, 213, Figures 7.1–7.14

rings
  antler 145–6, 148, 150, 153, Figure 12.3, Table 12.2
  copper-alloy 80, 129, 131, Figure 10.1
  iron 88, 132–3, Figure 10.2

ritual deposition *see* foundation deposits; religion and ritual

Rocket Range excavations *see* A'Cheardach Bheag; A'Cheardach Mhor

Roman period artefacts *see* brooches

roof and roofing materials 63–6, 78–9, 81, 83, 205, 209, 214, Figure 17.18

Rosinish, Benbecula 39

rye 176–7, 210

sampling *see* research design

sea level 3

seal 157, 161–2, 171, 173, Table 13.5–13.6

SEARCH project xiv, 1, 4–5, 10, 23, Figure 1.1

seaweed 172

secondary structure within the wheelhouse 77, 80–1, 83, 209, Figures 7.11–7.14

settlement distribution 190, 194–8, Figures 1.4, 17.1, 17.5–17.11

settlements
in chronological order:
Neolithic 3, 6, 190
Beaker 3, 6–7, 9, 29, 39, 190–2, Figures 17.1, 17.3–17.4
Early Bronze Age/Middle Bronze Age 1, 6–7, 9, 18–19, 21, 27–39 *passim*, 120, 191–5, 214, Figures 17.3–17.5
Late Bronze Age 6–8, 195–6, 210, Figure 17.6
Late Bronze Age/Early Iron Age 37, 195–6; *see also named sites* (Cladh Hallan *etc.*)
Early Iron Age 7–8, 195–7, Figure 17.7
Middle Iron Age 8, 195–197, 210, Figure 17.8; *see also* wheelhouses
Late Iron Age 8–9, 197, 210, Figure 17.9; *see also named sites* (Bornais, Dun Vulan *etc.*)
Norse 5, 8, 197–8, 214, Figure 17.10; *see also named sites* (Bornais; Cille Pheadair *etc.*)
medieval 8–9, 198, Figure 17.11
post-medieval and early historic 9, 198, Figure 17.11

Sharples, N. xiv, 7, 199–200; *see also* Bornais; Sligeanach

sheep
age 156, 163–4, 172–3, Table 13.8
bone distribution and density *see* animal bone
bone identification and recording 155–6
butchery, gnawing and burning 156–7, 161–2, 167, 173, Tables 13.3–13.4, 13.10
husbandry 172–3
measurements 167–8, Tables 13.12–13.13
meat yield *see* meat; skeletal elements

minimum numbers Table 13.5
pathology 165, Table 13.9
relative abundance 157, 161, 168–9, 211
sex 165
skeletal elements 161–2, Tables 13.6i–13.6iii

shell, marine 10, 178–85, Figures 15.1–15.8, Tables 15.1–15.7
Shetland 1, 199
Skara Brae, Orkney 147
Skye 147
slag 68, 70, 80, 88, 93, 135, 209–10, Tables 10.2–10.8
slate 67, 139, 144
Sligeanach, South Uist 7, 37, 39, 141–2, 177, 184–5, 190–1, 193, 197, 203, 210, Figures 1.1, 1.4, 17.1, 17.5, 17.7–17.8
soils *see* blacklands; geology; machair
Sollas, North Uist 106, 112–15, 117, 169, 173, 208, 211, Figure 17.14
space, use of 69–70, 80–1, 208–9, 212–14, Figures 3.16, 6.24
spindle whorls *see* bone discs; ceramic discs
stable isotopes, analysis of 172, 186–7
standing stones 6, 39
stone, decorated 77, Figures 7.6–7.8; *see also* cup-marked stones
stone tools 7, 35, 68, 139, 210, 213, Table 11.1; *see also* battle-axes; flint artefacts; hammer-stones
students xiv, 15, 24, 26, Figures 2.6, 2.9, 2.11
swords 133–4, 147, 195, 214

trade and exchange 210–11, 215; *see also* imports

Udal, North Uist 110, 117, Figure 17.14
Upper Loch Bornais, South Uist

7–8, 197, 203, 209, Figures 1.1, 1.4, 17.7–17.8
Uisinis, South Uist 203, Figures 1.1, 17.12

walls
Cill Donnain III wheelhouse 13–14, 18, 21, 23, 49, 57, 63–4, 72, 80–1, 92, 205, 208–9, Figures 2.7–2.8, 2.16–2.18, 6.1–6.3, 6.6–6.7, 6.9–6.12, 8.19, 17.16–17.19
in southern trench 72, 74, 101, Figures 6.25–6.27, 8.23
Late Bronze Age/Early Iron Age 40, Figure 4.4
of later modification of wheelhouse 18, 77–83, 209, Figures 7.1–7.2, 7.4–7.5, 7.8, 7.10–7.14
roundhouses and wheelhouses 57
weaving and weaving artefacts 146, 150, 153, 210, Figure 12.1, Table 12.2
whale
and other cetacean bone 92–3, 146, 157, 161–2, 171, Figure 8.6, Table 13.7
bone artefacts and worked pieces 78, 81, 88, 94, 148, 150, 153, Figure 12.2, Tables 12.1–12.2
wheat 176–7, 210
wheelhouses 1, 65, 199–215, Figures 17.12–17.13; *see also* Cnip; Bornais; Kilpheder; Sollas *etc.*
whetstones 139
wild animals 171, 173, 211; *see also* deer; otter; seal *etc.*
wild plants *see* plant remains
wool 172–3

Zvelebil, M. xiv, 5–6, 19, 21, 24, 26, Figures [preface], 2.5, 2.11